Fear and Loathing
in Fitzrovia

In memory of
Ruth Willetts (1931-2000),
who had happy memories of Soho.

Fear and Loathing in Fitzrovia

Paul Willetts

DEWI LEWIS

PUBLISHING

First published in the UK in 2003 by
Dewi Lewis Publishing
8 Broomfield Road
Heaton Moor
Stockport SK4 4ND
+44 (0)161 442 9450

www.dewilewispublishing.com

ISBN: 1-899235-69-8

Design & artwork production: Dewi Lewis Publishing
Printed and bound in Great Britain by
Biddles Ltd, Guildford and King's Lynn

3   5   7   9   8   6   4   2

First Edition

Contents

Whom the Gods wish to destroy
they first call promising.

Cyril Connolly

Introduction

Nearly four decades after his death, Julian Maclaren-Ross is now remembered as much for the bohemian excesses of his life as for the enduring wit and panache of his writing. Alongside other flamboyant, hard-drinking Soho luminaries like Francis Bacon and Jeffrey Bernard, he has entered the burgeoning mythology of that most self-mythologising of districts.

No memoir of metropolitan literary life in the Forties and Fifties would be complete without a vivid supporting part for him, invariably one where he wreaks inadvertent havoc on the author's hitherto orderly existence. No earnest study of London's artistic demi-monde would be complete without quotations from *Memoirs of the Forties*, his classic paean to the vanished world of the blackout, "buzz bombs", and boozy nights with Dylan Thomas. And no misty-eyed portrait of mid-century Soho would be complete without an appearance by him. Tall and aloof, he's more often than not seen standing at the bar of the Wheatsheaf pub or in some shadowy dive. Resplendent in his trademark camel-hair coat, worn over an immaculate suit, a fresh carnation in his buttonhole, a malacca cane propped beside him, a cigarette-holder clenched between his teeth, mirror-sunglasses lending him a gangsterish demeanour at odds with his otherwise dandified costume, he cuts an incongruous figure. Around him, a gaggle of fawning cronies provide an attentive audience for a relentless, well-rehearsed monologue, declaimed in a distinctively deadpan drawl.

For Maclaren-Ross, the pubs and clubs offered an atmospherically lit film-set on which he could perform. Immersing himself as thoroughly as any Method actor in the role he'd chosen, he projected an unforgettable persona, part Oscar Wilde, part Hollywood heavy. Long before he succumbed to the rigours of an existence that would have rapidly finished off anyone with a less robust constitution, he'd become the embodiment of raffish bohemianism.

Such is the allure of the role he assumed, a blend of maverick talent, saturnine good looks, theatrical aplomb, and spectacular self-destructiveness imbuing him with the beguiling glamour, the lurid fascination of James Dean, Jackson Pollock or any of the other icons of wayward and troubled artistry, he has spawned upwards of half-a-dozen fictional characters. Easily the best known and most memorable of these is the bibulous novelist X. Trapnel, whose tragi-comic antics so enliven *Books Do Furnish A Room*, the tenth volume of *A Dance To The Music of Time*, Anthony Powell's celebrated sequence of novels.

Besides replicating many of Maclaren-Ross's abundant sartorial and conversational idiosyncrasies, not to mention his taste for anachronistic accoutrements and unremitting self-dramatisation, Trapnel shares his inherent contradictions. Despite possessing a potent sense of his own identity, his personality was riven by ostensibly incompatible traits and aspirations. On one hand, he was a brazen exhibitionist. On the other, he was someone who betrayed an almost pathological hatred of being photographed. He was notorious for his abrasive and imperious manner, yet he distinguished himself as a sensitive and open-minded critic. He was utterly self-absorbed, yet prone to literary hero-worship. He led a life of domestic turbulence, yet unconsciously hankered after the comforts of conventional family life. He adopted the garb of a homosexual dandy, yet remained consistently and energetically heterosexual. He wrote in a compulsively self-revelatory vein, yet harboured a concurrent yearning to be mysterious and enigmatic. He affected a mask of aristocratic disdain, yet he was instinctively drawn towards life's victims. He craved literary and material success, yet romanticised the threadbare trappings of failure. How apt, then, that he should become so fixated by the tale of *Dr Jekyll and Mr Hyde*, his fixation culminating in the conviction that his personality had been taken over by the demonic Mr Hyde.

As so many of the people who knew him have pointed out, he was his own worst enemy. Like F. Scott Fitzgerald before him, he was a mediocre caretaker of his own immense talent. While his rampant egotism may have equipped him with an invaluable determination to fulfil his literary ambitions, it also saddled him with a win or bust approach to life, with an often ruinous refusal to compromise. The unshakable belief that, as a man of letters, he was entitled to a luxurious and profligate existence, exerted a comparably corrosive effect. His dogged determination to live in a style befitting a successful author, even when that success proved elusive, sucked him into a vortex of debt, the angle of descent sharpened by alcoholism, drug-dependency, sexual obsession, and mental illness.

Chaotic though much of his life was, circumstances making it hard for him to pursue his vocation, he maintained a gargantuan and omnivorous appetite for writing. Behind his assiduously cultivated façade of fin-de-siècle indolence, he was both versatile and industrious, sustained drinking sessions often prefacing protracted spells of work, fatigue warded off by hefty doses of amphetamines. Thanks to his mastery of an impressive breadth of tone and idiom, extending from the laconic to the lyrical, the comic to the tragic, he was adept at producing memoirs, novels, short stories, criticism, parodies, translations, essays, radio scripts, and screenplays. But it was as the author of a series of informal, irreverent, wryly humorous short stories that he achieved literary lionisation during the mid-Forties. With these deservedly acclaimed, deceptively artless despatches from the lower echelons of the army and the seedy world of West End pubs and drinking clubs, he annexed new, barely explored territory for English fiction. By embracing the slang, the swearing, the solecisms, the repetitions, and the rhythms of everyday speech, he not only challenged the prevailing censorship, but also created a counterpart to the supple, demotic style pioneered by American writers like Ring Lardner, Damon Runyon, William Saroyan and James M. Cain. In that sense, he's the unacknowledged precursor of all the vernacular fiction, all the chatty reportage that's so ubiquitous these days. What's more, his army stories anticipated the output of the so-called New Journalists of the Sixties who, in books such as Hunter S. Thompson's *Hell's Angels*, conveyed an impression of immediacy and drama by applying the techniques of fiction-writing to reportage.

My own interest in his work dates back to the early Eighties. Quite by chance (just the type of happy accident it's tempting to attribute to the machinations of Fate), I came across one of his stories while I was leafing through a battered edition of *The Saturday Book*, a long since defunct miscellany of fiction, journalism, and photos. I found it in the back room of a decrepit secondhand bookshop, run by a wheezing ex-teddy boy, the smell of whose chain-smoked cigarettes had impregnated the stock.

When I first got the book home, I read Maclaren-Ross's story, set in the Soho world he immortalised. And when I reached the end, I read it again. I'd never read anything like it. At least nothing from that era. I felt as if I'd been buttonholed in a wartime pub by a deft raconteur, itching to tell me about his inexplicably failed romance with a captivating but capricious girl, his obvious distress camouflaged by a stoical manner.

I suppose I was also attracted by its setting, an interest in Soho having been planted by my mother who, when I was a child, had regaled me with tales of her own bohemian high-jinks there. Curiosity whetted, I began hunting for books by Maclaren-Ross, along with other magazines and anthologies in which his stories originally appeared. Since most of his work, irrespective of whether it purports to be fiction or autobiography, is about himself, I soon became familiar with the strange, circuitous path his life took: from Edwardian England to the Twenties Riviera, from plush hotels to sleeping rough, from fame to neglect. Intrigued by the jagged trajectory of his career, by his exemplary defeat at the hands of what Cyril Connolly branded "the enemies of promise", I started scouring the memoirs of his contemporaries. Before long, I was toying with the idea of writing a biography of him. There followed a few months of sporadic research. These ended with me consigning my notes to the bottom drawer, deterred by the apparently insurmountable difficulties implicit in tracing such an itinerant existence, lived for the most part in hotels, boarding houses, bedsits, and squalid flats. There were just too many inconsistencies, too many events that couldn't be corroborated, too many fleeting relationships, too many gaps in the chronology. As Russell Gwinnett, the fictional, disconcertingly kinky American biographer of X. Trapnel, put it, his life was "a field where accuracy was hard to come by."[1] So I wasn't surprised when, several years later, I heard that he'd already vanquished another prospective biographer: the film-maker and novelist Christopher Petit, whose failure yielded a persuasive essay on the Maclaren-Ross mystique.

A further twelve or thirteen years slipped by before I was ready to renew the hunt for my evasive quarry. Only this time there was a sense of urgency. Whenever I looked at the obituary columns, another link with him seemed to have been severed. If I left it much longer, all the people who had known him would be dead, an irreplaceable treasure trove of memories disappearing with them.

At the second attempt, my earlier curiosity braced by newfound determination, I made swift progress. The breakthrough occurred when I tracked down C.K. "Mac" Jaeger, his longest-standing and closest friend, a skittish octogenarian whose animated and evocative recollections of their shared past invested the project with both exhilarating immediacy and fresh impetus. All of a sudden, it didn't seem so daunting.

Like a back-packer setting off on a round-the-world trip, I had a head full of preconceptions about my destination, about what I'd encounter along the way. The most salient of these was that old cliché about biography: the one that says the more you find out about someone, the less you like them, sympathy being supplanted by antipathy. Then there was the notion that his transient way of life would make it impossible to unearth the material I needed to produce anything even approximating a comprehensive biography, his every movement triangulated with unerring precision. On top of all this, I was sceptical about the factual content of his writing. Everything I'd read about him portrayed him as someone who preferred the iridescent sheen of fantasy to the lustreless patina of reality. "To any professional novelist embarking on an autobiography," he conceded in a moment of candour, "the temptation to rearrange the actual events 'so as to make a good story' is almost irresistible."[2] Even by the standards of a genre typified by embellishment, exaggeration, and self-aggrandisement, he had a reputation as an exceptionally unreliable narrator of his own life.

In the course of a long and arduous yet absorbing journey, enlivened by several scrapes that Maclaren-Ross would surely have appreciated, not least my near-arrest while loitering outside one of his former addresses, these preconceptions have, to varying degrees, been contradicted. Far from feeling distaste for my subject, I've come to feel more sympathetic towards him, that sympathy — it has to be said — tempered at times by exasperation. I've even lost my initial, pervasive scepticism about the factual content of his autobiographical writing. Admittedly, he *did* have a penchant for garnishing his reminiscences with parenthetical suggestions of intriguing possibilities, for distorting the truth in an effort to lend facts the shapeliness and resonance of fiction. But I've found him to be a far less slippery chronicler of events than I'd been led to believe, independent sources often verifying seemingly improbable recollections.

Another big surprise concerned the amount of information available about him. I had, at the outset, assumed this would be extremely scarce, its scarcity dictating the nature of the book I'd produce. On the basis of that assumption, I envisaged writing as much about my detective-work as about Maclaren-Ross's life, A.J.A. Symonds's *The Quest for Corvo* offering the obvious template. Against expectations, my files quickly swelled, enabling me to step back into the wings and leave the stage to the true star of the show. Of course this was only possible due to the help of numerous libraries and archives, a few of which had the foresight to acquire Maclaren-Ross's letters, manuscripts, and miscellaneous papers, anything from rent books to court summonses. Additional assistance has come from his family, together with his surviving friends and acquaintances, among whom there's been such a disturbingly high mortality rate that I began to feel like a literary Grim Reaper, a notebook and dictaphone substituting for a scythe. At risk of sounding embarrassingly over-familiar, they — and everyone else for that matter — feature under the names by which he knew them. Hence the inconsistent juxtaposition of nicknames, surnames, and Christian names.

Though I've amassed a vast quantity of information about Maclaren-Ross, there remain periods where the density of it decreases, occasionally to the point where his version of events, coloured by all the usual mixed motives, is the only version available. And there remain one or two aspects of his life which, short of some unknown stash of papers being miraculously unearthed or some previously untraceable witness stepping forward, appear impervious to enquiry. Still, I hope that I have, for the most part, disentangled fact from fiction, myth from reality. In doing so, there was always the danger of replacing the mythical with the mundane. As things turned out, the facts of his life were even more bizarre than the vibrant stories he wove around them.

A Wandering Disposition

Unlike so many other literary dandies, the effervescence of their personalities often concealing humdrum origins, Julian Maclaren-Ross hailed from a colourful, cosmopolitan family. Despite his disharmonious relationship with his parents, he grew up to be proud of his antecedents, yet unaware of some of the more remarkable aspects of his genealogy.

Born in Toronto in 1859, Maclaren-Ross's father was one of seven children, four boys and three girls, whose parents were both from affluent families with wide-ranging connections. He was christened John Lambden Ross, his unusual middle-name, by which he came to be known, commemorating his mother Carolina's membership of the wealthy Lambdin dynasty. As well as owning a plantation in Cuba, they had an estate on the east coast of America, not far from the pukka Baltimore Academy of the Visitation where the devoutly Roman Catholic Carolina was educated. Prosperity and financial acumen were not, however, confined to the maternal side of Lambden's family. His father William Ross was a Scottish businessman who owned the Thistle Line, a Liverpool-based shipping company.

Lambden's early years were spent in Havana. Courtesy of Carolina, whose mother was a Spanish-speaking South American, he received a bilingual upbringing. As a child, he was taken to live in England. For all his father's dislike of Popery, Lambden ended up being sent to a Catholic boarding school in France, his linguistic repertoire soon expanding to encompass French. Having rounded off his secondary education at an English public school, "a sort of minor hell, referred to [...] as the happiest days of his life",[1] he went on to study law at Heidelberg University. But he didn't stay long enough to graduate, preferring instead to drift back to England by way of Berlin. Now resident in London, where his parents had a house, he established himself as a rakish young man-about-town, his broad shoulders, blue eyes, handsome features, heavy build, lofty stature, and wavy auburn hair rendering him conspicuous. Moving in circles that overlapped with those of Oscar Wilde, his friends included Oscar's brother Willie Wilde, and Alex Ross, brother of Oscar's openly homosexual lover, Robbie Ross, himself a regular guest of Lambden's mother. In keeping with the new man-about-town persona, Lambden joined a gentlemen's club. He also swapped his impressive, roomy family home at 1 Lexham Gardens in South Kensington for chambers in Mayfair, where he acquired a mistress and a voguish addiction to horse-racing. This mired him in such debt that he had to appeal for assistance from his father, who feared that Lambden was destined for the bankruptcy courts. All too aware of his manifest financial ineptitude, Lambden's father only agreed to bail him out on condition he accepted an ultimatum. Given the choice between joining the family firm, or going to Canada and working for the Bank of Quebec, the Presidency of which was held by a relative, he opted for the latter.

Before taking up his post there, he visited relations in America and Cuba. No more able to settle in snowbound Canada than anywhere else, he gravitated back to England, where a dull job in the shipping office awaited him. Not surprisingly, Lambden found it impossible to fit into the dreary and repetitive routine of interminable board meetings and stuffy dinners with local businessmen. Exasperated by this latest evidence of his shiftlessness, his father packed him off on a round-the-world tour.

Far from quenching the wanderlust he'd developed, his travels merely imbued him with a taste for further adventure. On his return to drab old Blighty, he seems to have resumed his career in the family business. Seeking to spice up his life, in May 1883 he obtained a commission as a Captain in the Second Battalion of the Lancashire Engineer Volunteers, a territorial army unit based in the industrial town of St Helen's, just outside Liverpool. Between then and the following summer, he left the army, probably invalided out after the onset of rheumatoid arthritis, which gave him a pronounced limp that necessitated a walking-stick.

Because he no longer took as much exercise as before, he began to put on weight over the next few years. To control his ballooning torso, he headed for a spa resort in Alsace. While he was staying at a boarding-house there, he became romantically involved with a much younger fellow guest, who shared his rootless background. His paramour was Gertrude Pollok, a tiny, timid, wasp-waisted, black-haired eighteen-year-old whose dark skin proclaimed her Anglo-Indian ancestry. From his family's perspective, her suitability as a potential bride was reduced by her Protestant background and the taint of scandal attached to her name, due to her father's recently declared bankruptcy. Yet Lambden went ahead and married Gertrude in December 1891.

Impecunious though his new wife was, she could lay claim to an illustrious lineage, the peripheral components of which appear to have been unknown to her. Through her father, she was distantly related to the Cossart family, proprietors of Cossart Gordon & Co, the thriving

Madeiran wine exporters; to Sir George Scovell, whose code-breaking exploits had enabled Wellington to defeat Napoleon in the Peninsular War; to the owners of a remote Scottish castle; and to members of the Portuguese aristocracy. Her direct family-line also boasted a high proportion of other prominent people.

Over the previous three generations, the Polloks had enjoyed a distinguished history of military service in colonial India. It was a career first chosen by Gertrude's great-grandfather Thomas Pollok, who enlisted as a cadet with the East India Company. His ensuing ascent through the hierarchy was halted when he took part in the so-called "White Mutiny" of 1809-10. Staged as a protest against new government regulations, which the mutineers feared might loosen Britain's grasp on the country, it ended in anti-climax, the rebel troops aborting their southward march. Its failure resulted in Thomas Pollok being forced to resign his commission. On account of the mitigating circumstances, he was eventually permitted to re-enter the army. By the time he retired in 1837, he had redeemed his tarnished reputation, having risen to the rank of Major-General. In acknowledgement of his achievements on the battlefield, Queen Victoria installed him as a Companion of the Bath, his high-standing within society consolidated by a knighthood. He had, in the meantime, fathered two sons and a daughter. Following his example, both sons signed on as cadets with the East India Company. Within only five years William, the younger of the two, had been installed as a Colonel.

At that relatively early stage in the British occupation, inter-racial liaisons carried no stigma. Like many of his fellow officers, William got into a relationship with "a native woman".[2] Her name was Jumal Bee. Four months before she was due to give birth to their child, William died of heat-stroke. Their son, his mixed race parentage imperceptible in the pallor of his skin, appears to have suffered the double blow of losing his mother in childbirth.

The orphaned boy was seven-years-old when he was belatedly baptised Fitzwilliam Pollok. He was then shunted off to London to live with his paternal grandmother. When she too died, he was placed under the guardianship of Lieutenant-General Sir James Lushington, one of her husband's fellow mutineers. On the recommendation of his guardian, who held the chairmanship of the Court of Directors of the East India Company, he was inducted into the Madras Infantry. Aged sixteen, the seeds already sown for what he came to regard as his "wandering disposition",[3] Fitzwilliam travelled by steamship from Southampton to India.

While he and the other recruits were being trained, a fellow cadet introduced him to the joys of hunting, a pastime that would dominate his life. Once their training was over, the young Fitzwilliam was deployed to the regional headquarters at Bangalore. For most of his nine months there, he pursued his new hobby with bloodthirsty vigour, cataloguing the carnage in a vivid, if repetitive diary. Extracts from this were later published in the Calcutta-based *Oriental Sporting Journal* under the waggish pen-name of "Poonghee", a form of Burmese Buddhist priest.

From Bangalore, Fitzwilliam was transferred to a regiment garrisoned on the Deccan Plateau, where he spent the next two years decimating the indigenous wildlife. In the early months of 1853, he was assigned for duty with the Royal Engineers, who were on a road-building mission in Burma. En route there by boat, he survived an outbreak of cholera and helped to quell a mutiny.

His road-building assignment completed, he found himself redeployed to the Public Tasks Department. In between supervising other engineering projects and enjoying his all-consuming hobby, he bagged himself a wife, who bore three children in quick succession. But she died while they were still in their infancy. A little over two years later, during a foray to London to purchase improved weaponry, he met Emilie Leslie, then in her early twenties. That September, she became his second wife, accompanying him back to the subcontinent. By 1872, she'd given birth to four children, Gertrude being the youngest of them.

Incapable of supporting his expanding family on his army salary, even though it was supplemented by a legacy, he took a couple of years' leave. He spent it trying to make a living as a tea-planter in Assam. The expected profits never materialised, so he reluctantly resumed his military career. His next posting was to Table Island, off the coast of Africa, where he was placed in sole charge of a party of twenty-four murderous convicts, detailed to construct a lighthouse. Leaving him to carry out his unenviable duties, his wife and family made their way back to England via a slow and circuitous route, stopping off for lengthy spells in Portugal, Spain, and France, their peripatetic existence contributing towards Gertrude's fluency in French, not to mention apparent command of Portuguese, Hindustani, and Arabic.

During the autumn of 1878, Fitzwilliam retired from the army with the rank of Colonel. He then rejoined his family, who had settled in the Channel Islands. The following year he published the two-volume *Sport in British Burmah, Assam and the Cassyiah and Jyntiah Hills*, drawn from his voluminous hunting diaries. Part travel book, part memoir, part how-to manual, it recorded his adventures and celebrated his grisly passion for slaughtering everything from snipe and wild boar to elephants and tigers. The book's novel setting, conveyed in succinct and unadorned prose, allied to his gift for dynamic storytelling, made it popular enough to justify a prompt reprinting.

Through the commercial success of his literary debut, his financial problems must have temporarily abated, only to be rekindled by the birth of two more children, Henry and Herbert. Evading his creditors, he seems to have decamped to the Continent. In the summer of 1891, he was declared bankrupt. Perhaps motivated by a Walter Scott-like determination to use his writing as a means of extricating himself from his humiliating predicament, he churned out a flurry of other weighty, cross-generic hunting tomes, sufficiently eclectic to include culinary tips and recipes for the likes of plantain pudding and the un-prepossessingly titled fowl curry. Between 1894 and 1900, he published *Incidents of Foreign Sport and Travel, Wild Sports of Burma and Assam*, and *Fifty Years' Reminiscences of India* which featured a falsified account of his early years. Omitting any mention of his mixed race parentage, clearly a source of shame, he conjured up an idyllic childhood, dominated by the doting father who, in reality, he never knew.

Meanwhile, his daughter Gertrude had, together with her new husband, started her own family. Their first child was a son, whom they named William, commonly referred to as "Willie". A few years after that, she gave birth to their second child, Caroline, known as "Carol". Gertrude's father had, however, died before the arrival of the next addition to their family, whose exceptional talent, memorable personality, and flair for getting himself into difficult situations would earn him a niche in literary history.

The exoticism of Julian Maclaren-Ross's forebears contrasts sharply with the galling anonymity of his birthplace in the fast-growing London suburbs. Though he tried to infuse it with rousing portents by claiming that he was born at midnight in the middle of a thunderstorm, even his singular talent for dramatising his past was thwarted by the unremarkable circumstances in which his life began.

He was born on Sunday 7 July 1912 in the front bedroom of 18 Whitworth Road, otherwise known as "St Fagan's", a plain redbrick detached house in a staunchly middle-class district of South Norwood. Positioned well away from the junction with the thriving High Street, it was so quiet you could have forgotten you were in Britain's biggest city, the prevailing hush breached by little more than the sporadic clatter of carts, carriages, and the odd car, interspersed by the whistling and rumbling of trains passing through the local station. The house, its broad façade separated from the pavement by only a sliver of flowerbed, was owned by the widowed Mrs Lilian McLaren, from whom Lambden and Gertrude Ross were renting two furnished rooms. These consisted of a downstairs living-room and the upstairs bedroom where Mrs Ross — who took after her enduringly fertile mother — gave birth. Because she was approaching her fortieth birthday, the risks associated with her age exacerbated by an irregular heartbeat, it must have been an awkward labour. Out of gratitude to Mrs McLaren, who helped her through it, when she visited the local Register Office in Croydon just over a month later, she named her newborn son James McLaren Ross. At her husband's insistence, the child was subsequently baptised a Roman Catholic.

A fourteen year age-gap separated "Jimmy", as his parents nicknamed him, from his sister Carol, who was away at boarding school. Being almost twenty years Jimmy's senior, his brother Willie had digs elsewhere in London. Their father, whose shoulders were now stooped and whose once handsome features were hidden beneath a pointed beard, evidently found it hard to readjust to having a child around the house again. He was just too old and set in his ways, constant physical discomfort leaving him impatient and irascible. To compound the problems caused by his arthritis, he had to wear a tight truss to counteract the effects of a hernia. Added to which, he was prone to vertigo and bouts of migraine, as well as rashes and hayfever every summer.

Glad of an excuse to escape from their landlady, whom he disliked because she was so talkative, he moved his family out of their cramped south London lodgings soon after Jimmy's birth. They swapped these for a rented house in Ramsgate, where they were joined by Carol, who had just been expelled from the latest of a series of convent schools, the fees for which were covered by Carolina, her widowed grandmother.

In their new home, they settled into a conventionally cosy upper-middle-class Edwardian existence, funded by income from the £46,942 estate left by Lambden's father, whose complex will incorporated numerous safeguards against Lambden's profligacy. Held in trust, the money — worth about £3.2 million today — was invested in either Russian or British Empire-based companies. The income from these investments, forwarded to Lambden in quarterly instalments, was boosted by his earnings from government translation work. When he was not immersed in this, he made endless notes for a cherished but never-to-be-written biography of Napoleon Bonaparte, his inability to bring it to fruition setting a dangerous precedent for Jimmy.

The German invasion of the Low Countries and the outbreak of the First World War brought with it a rapid influx of refugees. In their own small way, the Ross family contributed towards solving the crisis by engaging a displaced Belgian woman as a nanny for their infant son.

Jimmy didn't have to wait long before the war made its next intrusion into his life. One night towards the end of May 1915, his awestruck father, who had spotted a Zeppelin hovering over Ramsgate, snatched him from his cot and carried him out onto the lawn to look at it. Previous appearances by Zeppelins earlier that month had made their mark on the town, but this time there were to be no explosions.

Within a matter of months, the war would make a more tangible impact. Perhaps seeking a respite from what were now regular, highly destructive night-time Zeppelin attacks, Jimmy and family went on holiday. In their absence, a bomb — most likely dropped during the aeroplane raids that took place between mid-September 1915 and mid-February 1916 — wrecked their home.

Lambden took this narrow escape as the cue for them to leave Ramsgate and settle on the south coast, probably in Teignmouth, where they rented another house. Even so, they couldn't get away from the war raging across the Channel, an unavoidable reminder of it offered by the Belgian refugees who thronged the town's cobbled streets.

Despite moving house, the family retained the services of Jimmy's nanny, though her fondness for anti-German atrocity stories led to her eventual dismissal. Unlike most of his less cosmopolitan countrymen, Lambden held a deep-seated revulsion for "anything likely to promote hatred between nations",[4] this even extending to his refusal "to countenance the use of the word 'Boche'."[5]

The unlamented nanny was replaced by a housemaid who suffered a similar fate. In an attempt to keep Jimmy's wilful seventeen-year-old sister busy, his parents passed on the responsibility to her. Dutifully fulfilling her new role, Carol took Jimmy for frequent walks round the town, where her defiantly flamboyant clothes, which were a source of altercations with their father, attracted admiring attention from the young soldiers on leave. But her teenage melancholy and growing sense of being stymied by her parents made her a dull companion for her little brother.

Their mother did her best to keep him happy by telling him tall stories culled from both her own much-travelled childhood and the adventurous life of her father. As a special treat, she would read to him from *Wild Sports of Burma and Assam*, the section recounting her father's stint on Table Island making a particular impression. More significantly, she instilled in Jimmy a lasting respect for his grandfather and a sense that storytelling was part of the family tradition.

The frontispiece to *Wild Sports* features a formal studio photograph of Fitzwilliam Pollok, taken many years before publication. Attired in evening-dress, he is pictured gazing moodily off-camera, his pose indicative of urbanity and self-confidence, his face swathed in dark whiskers, his dense black hair brushed away from his high forehead. Jimmy's mother was fond of pointing out the pronounced resemblance between him and Jimmy, who had inherited the same colouring, the same dark eyes, the same upright posture. She may also have sensed that these were not the only characteristics which her father had bequeathed him.

Jimmy's elder brother — who had, in accordance with his socialist principles, enlisted in the army as a Private — was fortunate enough not to have been sent to the Western Front. Instead, he had become a junior officer serving in the headquarters in Cairo, from where he was due to be posted back to Bournemouth, now something of a garrison town. Lured by the prospect of Willie's imminent transfer, his father suggested they find alternative accommodation closer to there. And so, sometime between the tail-end of 1916 and the opening months of 1917, they rented a furnished house at 80 Paisley Road in Southbourne, a suburb of Bournemouth. Their new home was a large, greybrick gable-fronted family house, divided from its neighbours by two narrow alleys. At the front there was only a tiny garden. As if to compensate for this, it had a more generous walled one at the back, abutted by a small conservatory.

To get to the nearest shops, they had to take no more than a brisk walk up the long but shallow incline that led into the commercial spine of Southbourne. Only a few years earlier, the town had been an independent seaside resort. But it had since merged with neighbouring Boscombe which had, in turn, been subsumed by Bournemouth. It nonetheless maintained its distinctive identity. Besides boasting a separate shopping area, it had its own pier and pleasure gardens, all unscathed by the war.

During the early days of their tenancy, Jimmy saw little of either of his parents. His mother devoted most of her time to overseeing the work of the cook and the maid she'd recruited, as well as playing the piano in the drawing-room at the back of the house. His austere and remote father, the severity of whose appearance was accentuated by sombre three-piece suits, their sole embellishment provided by the glistening gold chain of his fob-watch, meanwhile shut himself away in one of the downstairs rooms, commandeered for use as a study. In a custom-made easy-chair, its robust construction designed to withstand his eighteen-stone bulk, he sat incessantly sucking liquorice pastilles as a substitute for the cigarettes he'd once smoked. Through a magnifying-glass, he pored over the paperwork on his desk. This comprised passages for translation from French into English, sent to him by Whitehall; the notes he'd made for his planned biography; and the racing form, almost the only habit left from his days as a young man-about-town. Next to his desk stood a brightly hued globe which had survived the bombing of their house in Ramsgate. Jimmy wasn't allowed to touch it. Nor was he permitted to enter the study. He was, likewise, banned from venturing into the kitchen by the stern new cook. His territory primarily consisted of a small upstairs playroom. Under the supervision of the maid, her place briefly taken by a despised woman referred to as "Nurse", he spent most of his time there. Deprived of even the diverting presence of Carol, who had finally persuaded their father to let her enlist in the Women's Auxiliary Ambulance Corps, Jimmy was left to his own devices. "A creature of crazes",[6] he kept himself busy with the box of watercolours his mother had bought him, using these to fill in the colouring books he'd also been given.

No more than a few weeks before Jimmy's sixth birthday, the war made another of its periodic intrusions into his otherwise tranquil life. From an upstairs window or, perhaps, from the garden, he caught sight of a rapidly descending two-seater aircraft which he assumed was a stricken German raider. In fact, it was a Royal Flying Corps plane from the training unit that had lately been established at the nearby Ensbury Park aerodrome. The pilot was hoping to land it on a field not far from where Jimmy and his family lived. Before the pilot could set the aircraft down, however, the engine suddenly recovered and started to climb. But the motor soon cut out again, sending the plane crashing into a clump of trees only a few hundred yards away. Neither of the people on board were injured, yet in Jimmy's gruesome imagination the incident was transformed into a fatal crash in which the German aviator was incinerated.

As the summer faded, there was still no sign of Willie, whose posting back to England had been so confidently predicted. That Christmas, though, his uniformed, nineteen-year-old sister came home on leave from the depot in Woolwich, where she was stationed. While she'd been away, Carol had taken to wearing lipstick and perfume. Her outraged parents were given even greater grounds for disapproval when she told them about her engagement to a French-Canadian soldier. Her father, in particular, was furious. Throughout her stay, arguments frequently flared up between Carol and her parents, who must have been pleased when she received a telegram informing her that her fiancé had been despatched to the other end of the country. In her grief, she announced that she wanted to be known not as Carol but as "May", short for Mary, the middle name she shared with her mother.

So far, Jimmy had received no formal education, though his mother had taught him to read and write, spelling being his forte. To demonstrate his prowess, he would run "around asking everyone for the longest words they knew. [...Carol] when on leave, suffered most from this mania, not being herself a resoundingly good speller."[7]

Now that Jimmy was getting older, his father began to display more interest in him. Every morning, "except on days of torrential rain, when he sallied forth alone, sheltered by the ivory-handled umbrella that was a companion-piece to his stick",[8] Lambden would go for a brisk walk, dragging Jimmy behind him. From January 1918 onwards, Lambden — whom Jimmy addressed as "Father" — also got into the routine of taking him on trips to the cinema each afternoon. On the first of these jaunts, they went to the Picture House, just across the road from the Hippodrome Theatre in Boscombe. It had tea-rooms and a plush auditorium, as well as its own orchestra which accompanied the matinee of *Civilisation*, Thomas H. Ince's pacifist tract, misleadingly billed in the local paper as "a thrilling war picture".[9] But Jimmy was so terrified by it, his father had misgivings about taking him again.

The next time they went to the cinema together, Lambden was careful to choose something more appropriate: a cowboy film, supported by an adventure serial, the villain's role "played with suave ferocity by Warner Oland."[10] So began his childhood obsession with adventure serials, their defenceless heroines stalked by sinister and mysterious figures, some hooded, masked or cloaked, others clad in diving suits or in the bandages of an Egyptian mummy. His enthusiasm fuelled by the fan magazines his parents bought him, Jimmy and his father became regulars at the Picture House and the more spartan Boscombe Cinema. There the juvenile audience, seated on benches, annoyed his father and sometimes drowned out the elephantine piano accompaniment with warning shouts to the hero, yelling, stamping, and wolf-whistling.

Inspired by the music he heard there, Jimmy sneaked into the drawing-room at home and used his mother's piano to recreate it. Since the room was at the end of a passage that could be sealed off by a second door, his parents allowed him to hammer away at the keyboard, the exception being when his father was having his accustomed late afternoon siesta. Little by little, Jimmy took over the room. When he wasn't playing the piano, he'd be contentedly painting or drawing.

Combining his two longest established pastimes, he started designing meticulously lettered posters for the imaginary cinema he ran. These he drew in multi-coloured chalks on large slates, hung in frames round the room, each film's screening times listed at the bottom. Soon he was also drawing crude story-boards for his own make-believe films.

In about the middle of 1918, his father contemplated hiring a private tutor for him. Finding that suitable young men were in short supply, most of them having been pressed into military service, Lambden made up his mind to take charge of his son's education himself. Each morning, Jimmy reported to the study, where he was given lessons not just in the three "R"s but in other subjects like geography and history, something Jimmy so disliked he always did his best to distract his father by steering him onto his pet subject — the Tichbourne claimant, whose trial Lambden had supposedly attended. Similar digressions studded the geography lessons, Jimmy listening entranced as his father talked about all the distant countries he'd visited, about blizzards in Canada, storms off the Cape of Good Hope, and a trip down the Mississippi on a showboat. Yet Lambden was reluctant to discuss his experiences in South Africa where, it seems, he told Jimmy that he had fought in the Boer War, his limp passed off as a war wound. It appears that he also lied to Jimmy about spending a brief period in the Royal Canadian Mounted Police, a tale that must have been concocted in a bid to impress his son.

A matter of months into their new regime, life at Paisley Road was thrown into disarray by the arrival of one of Jimmy's paternal aunts — either Ida or Caroline. An intolerant, exacting, former suffragette who spoke American-accented English, she was attended by her French maid. Her fierce presence led to Jimmy being banished to the kitchen during meal-times. Enmeshed in a family feud over their inheritance, she was anxious to enlist the support of her brother, with whom she negotiated in conspiratorial Spanish. But her persistent sniping at other family members, specifically their sister Mary, proved a strain on Lambden, the consequent quarrel precipitating her sudden departure.

Elsewhere that year, other negotiations of wider significance reached a more successful outcome. On the morning of Sunday 10 November rumours of an impending armistice between the warring nations had been circulating in the Bournemouth area. Union Jacks were draped from the windows of neighbouring houses and the streets hung with bunting. From late in the afternoon, a dense crowd gathered in the centre of Boscombe, where they sang, cheered, and waved football-rattles and flags. That evening they were joined by Jimmy and his father who had, in a grudging concession to jingoism, bought him a small flag to wave.

But it wasn't until about 10.30am the following day that the rumours of an armistice were confirmed when *The Bournemouth Daily Echo* received a brief message from their London office. "Wind of it had reached the crowd," the newspaper reported later that day, "and excitement was at fever-heat, when the communication was read from the steps of the office".[11]

With the war at an end, the Ross family eagerly awaited the return of their daughter and elder son, who was still stationed in the Middle East. While Jimmy must have barely been able to remember Willie, his fond memories of his sister made him impatient for her demobilisation. Since he'd last seen May, her fiancé had broken off their engagement, having been posted overseas. Away from home, her subversive streak had grown even more flagrant. Now she not only smoked after meals and listened to ragtime records, but also had her hair styled in a modish, dyed-blonde bob.

On her return to Paisley Road, she inherited two of her father's principal duties. In the mornings she took Jimmy for his walk, her preferred destination being Boscombe, where she stopped off at various lending-libraries. Jimmy's relish for reading was, in the process, revived. And he became a fan of the Sherlock Holmes stories, plus the recently inaugurated series of Tarzan books.

Most afternoons his sister took him to the cinema, followed by tea at Bobby's, the big department store in Bournemouth. It was on one of these trips into the town centre that May became aware of a bespectacled, pipe-smoking, prematurely greying man almost two decades older than her, who cropped up with intriguing regularity. When she eventually got into conversation with the stiff, unromantically named Ted Miller, it turned out that he lived with his bewhiskered, white-haired father, a former accountant, on a street parallel to Paisley Road. She and "Rudolf", as she dubbed her suitor, started going ice-skating together and attending tea dances at the Winter Garden. Yet she must have known the relationship wouldn't earn her parents' approval, because Ted had never settled down to what might have been regarded as a proper career. After a spell in Canada, where he'd worked as a driver for the Hudson Bay Company, he had drifted into another poorly paid post, on this occasion as a part-time doctor's assistant.

The early days of their romance coincided with the sudden reappearance of the charming, elegantly uniformed Willie, who had taken to affecting a monocle and a short amber cigarette-holder. He wasted no time in revealing his engagement to a Voluntary Aid

Detachment nurse he'd met while he was in the army. He also set about befriending Jimmy by helping him with his imaginary cinema and teaching him to draw the exuberantly plumed cockerel logo of the Pathé company.

In defiance of their father, who had forbidden May from seeing Ted on account of his age and inauspicious prospects, she continued her relationship with him. Moreover, she stayed out later and later, even requesting a latch-key, which the indignant Lambden refused. And one night, in mid-September 1920, she didn't come home at all, resulting in a fierce row. To "defend herself from the accusation of having behaved, at the least, like a hussy [... she] came out with her bombshell."[12] Her revelation was that she and Ted had been married secretly at Christchurch Register Office over a week earlier.

So scandalised was Lambden by her behaviour, he ordered her to leave the house. As a parting shot, she announced that she and her husband were planning to emigrate to Canada. In common with the rest of the household, Lambden probably assumed she'd attempt a reconciliation before she left. But she was too obstinate for that. Jimmy did, however, see her once more when his mother took him to say goodbye to her outside Ted's ordinary bay-fronted Victorian home at 14 Herberton Road, where the newlyweds had been living.

Hearing of his elder son's plans to set up a school in partnership with his wife-to-be, who had previously been a teacher, Lambden — alert for any opportunity to shirk his paternal responsibilities — cajoled Willie into gaining some teaching experience by becoming Jimmy's tutor. Lessons were, as before, held in the study. Jimmy found his brother "tirelessly patient in his method of teaching"[13] and, like their father, prone to entertaining digressions.

But his brother's stint as a tutor was soon interrupted by a summons for a medical examination at a nearby hospital. The doctors there discovered that he'd contracted tuberculosis. It was only in its early stages, so they prescribed a course of treatment at the Sanitary Hospital in Bournemouth. On resuming his teaching duties the morning after this upsetting discovery, hung-over from all the drink he'd knocked back in an effort to deaden his anxiety, the normally mild and tolerant Willie lost his temper with Jimmy. Possibly provoked by his younger brother's inattention, he shouted at him and slapped him across the cheek, in that moment dispelling all his trust and admiration. Willie later apologised, the apology accompanied by the gift of a toy pistol, yet Jimmy continued to harbour resentment towards him. From that day onwards, he was "never quite at ease with him [...] always watching warily for another outbreak, once slapped, twice shy."[14]

Around the middle of 1921, his brother, whose poor health had earned him a pension from the army, was admitted to the Sanitary Hospital for the conventional "rest-cure". Since May was living in Canada and Willie was poised to marry his fiancée once his treatment was completed, Lambden concluded that there was no sense in maintaining such a spacious house. Nor was there any reason for them to stay in Southbourne. When the lease came up for renewal, he decided to transplant his family to Marseilles, where his sister Mary had settled with her husband. Another major incentive for moving there must have been financial. Coupled with the healthy exchange rate, the British tax laws made expatriate life an alluring proposition for anyone with independent means, all income tax deductions from dividends and interest payments being subject to a refund. Under these conditions, the Ross family, like thousands of their compatriots endowed with modest private incomes, could aspire to a far higher standard of living.

Fitzwilliam Pollok, c.1875

Carol (a.k.a. May) Ross, c.1925 (© The Estate of Carol Ross)

Ted Miller, c.1925 (© The Estate of Carol Ross)

Julian Maclaren-Ross's birthplace, 2000 (© Paul Willetts)

The Bizarre Life Of Julian Maclaren-Ross

The Boy Most
Likely To Exceed

In the autumn of 1921, Jimmy and his parents set off for the south of France. After a six-and-a-half-hour crossing on the steamer that plied the route between Southampton and Le Havre, they completed their passage to Marseilles with an even longer train journey. Slow as the transition between vaporous England and the crisply lit Mediterranean was, it could do little to prepare eight-year-old Jimmy for the jarring contrast. To a child accustomed to the orderliness and gentility of British seaside resorts, the seething street-life of Marseilles, with which they were immediately confronted, was bound to present an alarming if intriguing spectacle. Vendors of cheap novelties hawked their wares; beggars, many of them hideously mutilated, accosted passers-by; and the pavements were crowded with people of numerous races, united in the characteristically demonstrative Provençal mannerisms, their conversation paralleled by flurries of energetic semaphore.

Jimmy's parents, having taken up residence in a hotel, introduced him to his childless Aunt Mary and her husband, Gustave Schatz, who shared an upstairs apartment on a fashionable boulevard. "Uncle Gustave", a bald, stocky, former French army officer with "a black moustache [...] curling fiercely upwards and waxed at the ends,"[1] held a partnership in an ailing hair-dye business. Though his command of the English language didn't extend beyond a few stock phrases, he doted on his wife's nephew. Aunt Mary was a tall, histrionic woman with a dress sense to match, favouring "crêpe-de-chine coats and cloaks [that] trailed out behind her."[2] What's more, "she was hung with jewelled chains and each of her large white pianist's hands, much given to emphatic and dramatic gestures, was decorated on every finger with heavy rings, disparagingly referred to by [Jimmy's] father as knuckle-dusters."[3] At every opportunity, she showered her nephew with gifts of pocket money, expensive exercise books, chocolates, marrons glacés, and jars of quince jelly "for which [Jimmy] at that time had a not easily satisfied passion."[4]

Once he'd recovered from a severe attack of diarrhoea that coincided with his arrival, Jimmy seems to have adapted swiftly to his new surroundings. He and his parents would start the day by breakfasting on brioches and croissants dunked in coffee: black coffee in his case because, even as a child, he disliked milk. The rest of the morning would be spent in cafés, supping syrupy soft drinks flavoured with grenadine or orgeat. Around midday, his father would slope off to a bar, before rejoining them for their daily walk. Jimmy and his mother, braving the beggars who lined the Rue Paradis, would comb the bookshops in search of titles from the Sexton Blake Library, his allegiances having shifted from Sherlock Holmes to the almost plagiaristically similar Sexton Blake. Issued at the rate of four cheap paperback novelettes each month, in which Blake vied with a cast of master-criminals, these were emblazoned with dramatic covers, a typical jacket depicting the intrepid hero apprehending a cowering grave robber.

His mother also kept him entertained by taking him on trips to the cinema, where he depended on her to translate the inter-titles for him. He was disconcerted to find that all the familiar American movie stars were known by French nicknames, Harold Lloyd being abbreviated to "Lui", and Charlie Chaplin to "Charlot".

When his mother had to nurse Lambden through a brief illness, Jimmy was allowed to go to the cinema by himself. Released from parental supervision, he explored the notorious Old Port, straying off the main streets into the labyrinth of twisting, aromatic alleyways. But his freedom was only temporary. As soon as his father had recovered, his mother joined Jimmy on his afternoon wanderings. It was on one of these that they came across Monsieur Félix's puppet theatre, positioned in a wind-swept square, every performance watched by a clamorous but fascinated audience of children. For several months Jimmy became so obsessed by these traditional shows, starring the big-nosed, stick-wielding Guignol, that his mother bought him his own set of puppets.

Early in November this idyllic, untroubled interlude was truncated by a telegram from England. Written by his brother's fiancée, it informed them that Willie had died of tuberculosis. The news came as a terrible blow to his parents, whose distress wasn't shared by Jimmy, his lingering resentment towards Willie inuring him against the grief that left their mother too frail to travel to the funeral.

As a possible by-product of the bereavement, Lambden started exchanging regular letters with his estranged daughter. In the year or so since her sudden departure, she and Ted had settled in Toronto. Bearing out all Lambden's fears, the couple's shaky financial position had forced her to take a job as a clerk. Yet he and May at last reached a rapprochement, perhaps hastened by the birth of her first child, Logan, and the revelation that she too had contracted tuberculosis, its diagnosis forcing her to register at a sanatorium in Manitoba. Unlike her brother who had, presumably, been responsible for infecting her, she made a slow recovery. Impatient with the regime of protracted rest, she had, however, discharged herself before she was given the official all-clear.

Back in France, it wasn't long before another family relationship fell foul of Lambden's fractious temperament. Unwilling to accept the validity of anyone else's viewpoint, he got into a row with Aunt Mary about the way she was handling the business affairs of her husband, who had gone into enforced retirement after suffering a mental breakdown.

Now that Lambden was no longer on speaking terms with Aunt Mary, it seemed pointless for them to remain in Marseilles. So he shifted his family to Paris and sublet an apartment — near the Boulevard Raspail in Montparnasse — from its long-term tenants, who were poised to go away for the summer. While Jimmy and his parents were living there, the noise from the sawmill below making it hard for them to stay at home during the day, they regularly took him to watch puppet-shows in the Champs Elysées and the Luxembourg Gardens.

Their brief tenancy at an end, Lambden booked their passage back to England. Had it not been for the painful associations with the Bournemouth area, they would have returned there. As it was, they chose Bognor Regis instead, renting a furnished bungalow a couple of miles down the coast from the town centre, somewhere in Elmer Sands. Their new home, amid a cluster of old railway carriages that had been converted into makeshift houses, was set back only a short distance from the beach.

For about the next six months, Jimmy — who had celebrated his tenth birthday in Paris — played contentedly with the daughter of a neighbour, went with his father on Saturday afternoon trips to watch Bognor United play football, and immersed himself in the boys' comics that had taken over from puppetry as his latest craze. Of the many such weeklies available, his favourites were *Pluck: The Great Sport and Adventure Story-Paper*, launched in October 1922, and its sister-paper *The Rocket*, launched the following February. Both specialised in rousing, casually xenophobic yarns — with titles like *The Fangs of the Unknown* and *The Black Claw* — about scheming Chinamen and evil witch-doctors being foiled by intrepid schoolboys. And both interspersed these multiple-part tales with puzzles, competitions, and sports serials. Imitating the ghoulish adventure stories he read in their cheaply printed pages, Jimmy made his first stabs at fiction-writing.

His father, meanwhile, pondered the question of where Jimmy should be educated. The preferred option was a prep school, providing him with a slipway into the public school system, the thought of which terrified Jimmy. Remembering all too well his father's recollections of his own hellish stint of fagging and ritual humiliation, it came as a great relief when these plans were quietly abandoned.

Having made peace with the mournful Aunt Mary, whose husband had since been committed to an asylum, Lambden agreed to her suggestion that they rent a villa together on the outskirts of Marseilles. In the summer of 1923, Jimmy and his parents travelled to London, from where they'd booked tickets on the twice-daily boat-train. To break the journey, his mother, who had kept in touch with Mrs McLaren, arranged for them to stay the night with their former landlady. Lambden — apparently growing short of cash, his quarterly allowance possibly reduced by the loss of his family's Russian investments after the revolution — only countenanced this because it saved him the cost of a hotel.

Since their departure from South Norwood, Mrs McLaren had moved four doors up Whitworth Road, though she still supplemented her income by letting a couple of rooms. The evening Jimmy and his parents arrived, she introduced them to her current tenant, the vicar of a local church.

Next day they caught the boat-train down to Folkestone. From there, they made the short but rough crossing to Boulogne, in whose bustling harbour — dominated by two hills, one capped by a church, the other by the ramparts of the old town — ferries, ocean liners, and trawlers docked, the wind laced with the smell of fish, brine, and seaweed.

Their destination was a villa in Endoûme, on the south-western fringe of Marseilles, where they settled into a reassuringly familiar routine. Under his father's tutelage, Jimmy continued to spend part of each day learning a smattering of arithmetic and geography, an appreciation of literature, and a knowledge of most of the key dates in history, all from a British standpoint. Every few weeks, the routine was enlivened by trips with his mother into the city, reached via the busy circular tramway that ran in both directions from the Cours St Louis.

Like so many of Lambden's domestic arrangements, the shared villa provided only stopgap accommodation. No sooner had his family grown accustomed to life there than he uprooted them yet again. Driven to distraction by the prickly midsummer heat and the clatter of his sister's typewriter, which he compared to the noise of a horse kicking its box to pieces, he transplanted them down the coast to Nice. There they moved into one of the moderately-priced hotels catering for the annual influx of tourists who came to taste the stylish life of the Riviera, where American film stars mingled with aristocrats and royalty from all over the world. Many of these hotels housed other British families living on pensions and dividends. Indeed, the city was famous for its English community, so large it could sustain its own golf, tennis, and social clubs, its own churches, pharmacy, weekly out-of-season newspaper, and tea-rooms, where homesick expats could eat scones and sip stewed Darjeeling. In certain areas, especially the smart, aptly named Promenade des Anglais, English was even the dominant language. Yet it probably wasn't this, nor the city's raucous, bohemian nightlife, nor the plethora of chic cafés and restaurants, nor the handsome nineteenth-century streets and pink-stuccoed squares that attracted Jimmy's father. More likely, it was a mixture of the reputedly congenial climate, as well as the entertaining presence of Herbert, better known as "Bertie", his affable if roguish young brother-in-law, who lived there with the doddering Emilie Pollok.

Because they were now within easy reach of the local cinemas, Lambden got back into the habit of taking Jimmy to matinee screenings of the latest serials. Ignoring the eleven-year-old Jimmy's preference for adventure stories, his father insisted on them seeing downbeat, socially-concerned dramas about working-class life.

When Jimmy was not being taken to the pictures or sitting through lessons, he was permitted to play with the local French boys, who hung round the old cannons in the Jardin Albert Premier. Located between the sea-front and the famous, fussily decorated Casino Municipal, this was a large, elegant park, planted with tall, withered-looking palm trees. As he possessed only a rudimentary command of formal French, Jimmy was often picked on by the other boys, who spoke the Italianate, proletarian Niçois dialect. Despite joining them in relay races, games of marbles, and cops and robbers, his sense of himself as an outsider in a hostile environment persisted. His French did, however, improve. And his vocabulary was bolstered by a battery of insulting colloquial phrases. These, combined with his rapidly increasing height, left him less vulnerable to bullying.

Tiring of Jimmy's boisterous and demanding presence, his father was, by the following year, making plans to send him away to school. The headmaster of the English school in Nice tried to recruit him as a pupil, but Lambden resisted, ostensibly because "there was no point in living in France if you were going to go to an English school".[5] For Jimmy's father, who was determined to "get him out of the way",[6] it had the added disadvantage of being a day-school.

During the early autumn of 1924 — by which time his sister and her family, now expanded to include a second son,[7] had emigrated to the milder climes of New Zealand — his father inspected a boarding school in Grasse, midway between Nice and Cannes. In the end, though, he decided to send Jimmy to Le Châlet, a tiny Catholic boys' crammer not far from the ancient fortified town of Antibes. Set in extensive grounds, crisscrossed by gravel paths, flanked by trees and tufts of bamboo, it consisted of a linoleum-floored dormitory and a single, large classroom with two picture-windows, looking out across the Baie des Anges. It was run by a priest, known as Monsieur L'Abbé. Aside from his wide-ranging teaching duties, he was responsible for saying Mass in the school chapel and preparing his charges for their first Holy Communion. Assistance in practical matters was supplied by Philomène who, with the help of her decorous daughter, acted as matron, cook, and housekeeper.

To avoid any risk of Jimmy's mother disgracing him by blubbing in front of the other boys, she didn't accompany him and his father on his dreaded one-way trip to his new school. He arrived there in October 1924, ready for the start of the new term. Watching Lambden walk away from him "with as buoyant a stride as his limp would allow, a load lifted from his mind",[8] Jimmy felt disconsolate and bitter. It was to prove a turning point in their relationship, irreparably damaging whatever intimacy had existed between them.

On his arrival at Le Châlet, dressed in the uniform of black overalls and sturdy boots, there were only two other pupils, neither of whom spoke any English. He was, in any event, prohibited from speaking his native tongue. Monsieur L'Abbé — a powerfully-built, energetic disciplinarian "with a stern, plump, clerical face, shining slightly blue about the jowls"[9] — introduced him to his classmates as "Jacques", the nearest Gallic equivalent to James. But he soon fell out with them.

Until then, Jimmy's childhood had been solitary, pampered, and easy-going, so it was hard for him to cope with the school's harsh and inflexible regime, his misery intensified by dental problems, perhaps connected with the pronounced overbite that lent his jawline a determined, slightly pugnacious cast. These necessitated recurrent, excruciating sessions with the nearby dentist, "an elderly man with a grey walrus moustache",[10] who gave him a mouth full of deep fillings.

Each day at school commenced with gulped bowls of soup and coffee, followed by a dash for the classroom, where Monsieur L'Abbé taught French grammar, composition, and history, along with Latin, arithmetic, drawing, and penmanship. Rather than incur his teacher's scorn, Jimmy was temporarily forced to ditch the tiny, ultra-legible handwriting he'd evolved, its cramped and painstaking lettering intended to mimic the typography of a book. In its place, he had to adopt the approved cursive style. He also had to drop the Niçois accent and the slang he'd picked up from his friends in the park.

Breaches of discipline were penalised by either lines in Latin or corporal punishment — something to which Lambden, despite his bad temper, had never resorted. Monsieur L'Abbé's preferred form of corporal punishment was to make the culprit stand to attention, the back of his hand extended, the fingertips squeezed together. Onto the victim's knuckles, the sadistic cleric "struck with the sharp edge of a ruler on the tender inside joints of the victim's fingers. If the victim so much as flinched, he was given an extra couple of strokes."[11] As Jimmy later recalled, "stoicism was the order of the day, tears absolutely out of the question."[12]

The school day ended with an hour of evening prep, conducted "in absolute silence broken only by the crackle of wood catching alight in the big stove and the industrious scratching of [...] pens."[13] Were any incentive needed, it was made clear to the pupils that a monthly tally of their marks would be posted to their parents.

Jimmy's only relief from homesickness and the scholastic slog came in the form of letters from his father, written at Monsieur L'Abbé's insistence in French, and expeditions into Antibes, where he sought refuge in the English Lending Library. Tucked away in a badly lit, musty room, behind a bright modern bookshop in the Place Macé, the library mainly comprised damp-spotted Victorian volumes. Among these, he discovered the writings of Edgar Alan Poe and Wilkie Collins, whose work stimulated a lasting predilection for the horror and crime genres.

In the ensuing months he was joined at Le Châlet by five more pupils. The newcomers included a Scottish boy who spoke very little French, but whose thick brogue Jimmy found impenetrable. Throughout that first term away from home, he must have pined for the Christmas holiday when he could rejoin his parents who had, in the meantime, moved out of their hotel. Probably in pursuit of more tranquil surroundings, they'd taken a villa in St André, a village just beyond the city's northern rim.

By the spring of 1925, Jimmy had settled into the school's strict regime. And Monsieur L'Abbé had put him forward for his first confession, which took place in the local church. Ultimately, however, it was literature and not the confession booth that provided his chosen arena for self-revelation.

*

At the end of the academic year, by which stage his father had decided he was ready to start secondary school, Jimmy left Le Châlet for good. Living in the villa next-door to his parents, there was an English family who had a fifteen-year-old daughter and two sons of a similar age to him. That summer, he teamed up with the two brothers. From the bustling Old Town in Nice, where darkened shops edged the narrow streets and miniature squares, long lines of washing suspended overhead, the three of them bought themselves toy pistols that fired small packets of gunpowder instead of bullets. These could also be hurled like hand-grenades. Irritated by the racket they made, Lambden promptly banned them. In search of a pastime that wouldn't annoy his father, Jimmy and his friends taught themselves to play chess. Yet his sudden passion for the game was treated with contempt by Lambden, who regarded it as just another fad.

For his thirteenth birthday, Aunt Mary, who was more indulgent of his childhood crazes, gave Jimmy the ivory chess set he craved. Equipped with that, the three boys became bewitched by the game, playing nothing else all day. They even took chess books out of the library and puzzled over chess problems. And when the friendly headmaster of the English school in Nice heard about Jimmy's current enthusiasm, he enrolled him in a chess club.

But his devotion to the game was curtailed by the beginning of the new school year. The genteel impoverishment of his parents notwithstanding, he was, in the autumn of 1925, sent to the Collège Roustan, an austere Catholic boarding school in Antibes. Compared to Le Châlet, it must have seemed dauntingly large, its unfamiliar old buildings emanating menace. Because he was not just a new boy but also a foreigner, he was an obvious target for bullies. His head clamped between his assailant's knees, they gave him what was known as the "savon", rubbing their knuckles across his skull "in a fierce dry shampoo."[14] Such was his precocity, he was placed in a class consisting of boys two years older than him. Inadvertently stoking his unpopularity, the teachers sometimes singled him out as a fine example to the others. His fellow pupils exacted retribution by teasing him incessantly about his shabby, long since outgrown overcoat, which he wore because his parents couldn't afford a replacement. It seems to have taken a while before he was properly integrated into the school, a mutual affinity for the adventure stories of José Moselli assisting his gradual assimilation.

When he was sixteen, Jimmy left the Collège Roustan, from where he was despatched to Paris to round off his schooling, the intention being that he'd go on to university. Like his sister before him, though, his education was destined to come to a premature and unsatisfactory conclusion. In early 1929, he betrayed the headstrong, rebellious streak that ran through both sides of his family. By getting into a furious row with a teacher, he was expelled from school.

He then moved back in with his parents, who were still living in the environs of Nice, most likely in their villa in St André. Freed from the shackles of school, he spent a lot of time at the cinema, where he developed a passion for the doom-laden films of Erich von Stroheim. And he sampled the notoriously flashy and uninhibited café society that flourished in Nice, climaxing in the annual carnival every March. Celebrated in opulent venues such as the Casino Municipal and the Opèra, the carnival was made up of a frenzied round of parties, dances, and masked balls, plus elaborate torchlit, flower-strewn processions and firework displays, the trees along the Avenue de la Victoire festooned with plump, softly glowing lanterns. On account of his painful shyness, the mere prospect of meeting strangers invariably inducing a nervous tremor, Jimmy could, in a setting like this, only be a passive and peripheral figure despite his imposing height — a fraction under six feet tall.

As someone who had been locally educated and spoke fluent French, unsullied by any trace of a foreign accent, his circle of friends wasn't confined to the insular and often chauvinistic English community, the behaviour of the younger members of which attracted so much censure. It extended far beyond this constricted circuit of tennis tournaments, charitable events, and insipid home cuisine. For the most part, his friends were drawn from the sizeable and impecunious Russian emigré population, whose members included grand dukes, princes, barons, and generals, many of them reduced to working as waiters in swish hotels, or driving taxis along the Promenade des Anglais. Together with his newfound friends, "the flotsam of Nice, cast up, for one reason or another, on this brittle shore of chancy pleasure",[15] Jimmy lived on the cusp between high and low life. He listened to jazz in dance-halls, sauntered along La Croisette in Cannes, and idled away the hours over glasses of pernod or vieux marc not only in cafés but also in the newly constructed Palais de la Méditerranée in Nice, where he became a regular. Hailed as "the most luxurious palace of amusement in the world",[16] its capacious premises hosted film shows, operas, beauty contests, chess tournaments, photographic exhibitions, and a programme of up to five different plays each week, mostly performed in French by touring professional companies.

A few months after his return to Nice, Jimmy read *The Picture of Dorian Gray* which made such an impression on him that he developed "a passionate interest in everything pertaining to its author."[17] Because he'd already heard that Oscar Wilde had been an acquaintance of his father's, he pestered him for stories about his hero. Lambden obliged with recollections of Wilde, whom he remembered as having "great charm when he chose to use it."[18] Yet, in Lambden's opinion, Wilde seemed "to take a deliberate pride in antagonising everybody."[19]

To Jimmy's delight, his father went on to tell him a self-serving anecdote about his first encounter with Wilde. The meeting took place in the dining room of the club where Lambden was entertaining a mutual friend, a visiting French comedian who performed under the name of "Marius". Recognising him, Wilde — clad in a damson velvet dinner-jacket — sidled over to their table, sat down and, oblivious to Lambden's presence, started speaking French to Marius, who "made several embarrassed attempts to interrupt the flow and introduce his host."[20] But Wilde sidestepped these and ploughed on. "At last, as the savoury was served, Wilde turned to [Lambden] with a start of apology, and addressing him in English [said]: 'I do hope you'll forgive me, sir, and you too, my dear Marius — the pleasure of seeing you again must be my excuse — it is really unpardonable to intrude at your table and to speak a language perhaps unfamiliar to your friend' "[21] Stung by his condescension, Lambden replied in French, eventually reverting to English and adding, "If I may be allowed to say so, sir, you speak French very well — for an Irishman."[22]

By his own admission Jimmy's father only succeeded in delivering such a scathing put-down because he had caught Wilde off-guard. Still, he said that Wilde "took it very well — very sportingly indeed — and whenever [they] met after that he was always extremely civil."[23]

Under the influence of what had grown into a fixation with Wilde, Jimmy became fastidious about his appearance, the seeds of this sartorial self-awareness having been sown by the earlier hurtful teasing he had endured. In his determination to stand out, he drew attention to the resemblance he bore to the young Oscar, with whom he shared the same dark, wavy hair, and pale, well-padded but handsome face. Taking the verbal and sartorial sheen of *The Picture of Dorian Gray's* protagonist, Lord Henry Wotton, and its equally dandified author as his template, the teenage Jimmy — unaware of his own blue-blooded connections — donned a self-consciously anachronistic costume. Usually sporting an orchid or carnation in his buttonhole, he swanned around in a white mess-jacket, worn in combination with a matching crêpe-de-chine shirt, linen trousers and, if he was feeling really extravagant, two-tone shoes and a crimson sash in lieu of a belt. His debonair outfit was embellished by a cane and a silver snuff-box, as well as a long cigarette-holder, through which he smoked pack after pack of gold-tipped Turkish cigarettes. But he was too vain to acquire the more functional accoutrement he needed: namely the glasses necessary to correct his imperfect eyesight, his myopia contributing towards his self-absorption and his tendency to embroider his descriptions of events, imagination filling in the details his purblind eyes failed to register.

Besides altering his appearance, Jimmy cultivated a languid, and haughty manner, honing a facility for sharp-tongued repartee, and addressing his friends either by their surnames or as "My dear boy." Behind this convenient, ready-made pose, with its aura of ambiguous sexuality, unspecified corruption, and unshockable cynicism, he shielded his innate vulnerability, inexperience, and introversion. It was an act of self-invention that echoed his maternal grandfather's earlier denial of his potentially awkward mixed-race origins.

Rounding off the transformation from Jimmy Ross, an unobtrusive, bookish schoolboy, into "a dangerous dandy [...] an army of one, with a regimental tradition that went back to Beau Brummel",[24] he followed the precedent set by his sister and changed his name. Like an actor devising a stage-name, he was careful to choose one more appropriate to the persona he wished to convey. He now insisted on being called "Julian", though his parents annoyed him by continuing to call him "Jimmy", a nickname he'd grown to detest, its continued use reinforcing his mounting animosity towards them. In pursuit of the distinctive monicker he felt he deserved, he also started using his middle name, its unambiguously tartan origins emphasising what he liked to call his "Scotch" roots, plain old "Ross" being displaced by the unique, vaguely aristocratic "McLaren Ross".

This was to be the earliest of many roles he was to adopt in the course of his struggle to sculpt reality into a more palatable form. For him, as for his fin-de-siècle forerunners, life and art became indistinguishable. By looking and behaving as he imagined an artist should, he took his first step towards realising his new conception of himself.

At that juncture, his creative impulses were primarily directed towards painting, yet he nurtured vague dreams of becoming a writer, too. These were largely uncontaminated by the mundane practicalities of writing. Not that his lack of productivity prevented him from indulging in what would turn into an enduring vice. Even then, he loved to talk somewhat boastfully about the books he planned to write, books such as *Paradox*, his mooted novel about Oscar Wilde, books destined never to make the strenuous transition from his imagination into manuscript form.

Neither of his parents, whose investment-income must have been hit by the recent stockmarket crash, approved of his artistic aspirations or the way of life he'd so wholeheartedly embraced. While his father, lapsing into his favourite posture as a grouchy old colonel, was prepared to openly criticise him and suggest that he pursue a commission in the army instead, Julian's diminutive mother, whom he intimidated by virtue of his height, lordly bearing, and fierce temper, dared not voice her objections. Like innumerable parents before and since, they hoped he was going through no more than a passing phase. But their manifest disapproval only served to alienate him still further.

Aware of his fixation with Oscar Wilde, during June 1930 or thereabouts, an older friend of Julian's arranged to introduce him to Frank Harris, his idol's biographer and steadfast ally. Elderly though Harris was, an air of disgrace hovered round him, the residue of successive financial scandals, not to mention the publication of his allegedly pornographic autobiography, *My Life and Loves*, over which a generation of smut-seeking schoolboys, Julian included, had furtively pored. Harris also had a reputation as a formidable, often forbidding person. It was with understandable trepidation and agonising self-consciousness that Julian, his nervousness increased because he'd never met a published writer, approached his lunch date with the septuagenarian Harris.

His host and young wife, Nelly O'Hara, lived in an apartment in the Villa Edouard Sept in Cimiez, a suburb of Nice, perched on a hill overlooking the city, where extensive Roman ruins coexisted with pricey villas and large, elegant hotels like the vast Hotel Majestic. So attuned were Julian's senses to links — no matter how tenuous — with historical or contemporary celebrities, it's hard to imagine he wouldn't, as the butler ushered him and his friend through the front door, have experienced a frisson of pleasure at seeing the memorabilia proudly displayed on the walls. Advancing down the long hallway, he would have passed parallel ranks of etchings by Whistler, and photographs of Shaw, Tolstoy, and Maeterlinck, side by side with framed letters from Wilde, Pater, Carlyle, and Emerson.

The rheumy-eyed Harris defied Julian's preconception of him as a tall, deep-voiced man with a bone-crushing handshake, yet he lived up to his reputation in other respects. Just as his guest had feared, he proved hospitable but tetchy and embarrassingly direct, Julian's foppish clothing eliciting a matter-of-fact enquiry about whether he was "a bugger".[25] Even the eagerly awaited chance to quiz him about Wilde didn't go as Julian had hoped, his host declaring that he had nothing to add to what he'd already written in his biography. The exception was a "brief and pungent comment on the character of Lord Alfred Douglas, which was certainly not in his book, and which Mrs Harris was called upon to confirm from the head of the table."[26]

About six months later, Julian glimpsed Harris hunched over an aperitif at a table outside the Casino Municipal. Still smarting from what had happened, Julian made no effort to speak to him. At one of the round of parties Julian had taken to attending, he did, however, get into conversation with another ageing author, the altogether more gregarious E. Phillips Oppenheim, whose stream of best-selling thrillers, many of them set on the Riviera, had earned him a reputation as "The Prince of Storytellers".

In between socialising and making regular trips to the cinema, the early sound films of the svelte John Barrymore exerting predictable magnetism, Julian was lounging round at home, where he passed the days playing his large record collection. This encompassed everything from a prized stash of Bix Biederbecke recordings to more commonplace discs by the exuberant New York band-leader Ted Lewis, who occupied a side-altar in his personal pantheon. And when he wasn't listening to records or playing the piano, he was reading some of the fashionable writers of the day, among them Jean Cocteau, Michael Arlen, William Gerhardi, Carl Van Vechten, and Ethel Mannin. With their emphasis on the darker side of life, they appealed to his standard-issue teenage morbidity.

As if Julian wasn't giving his parents sufficient cause for concern, news must have filtered through to them that their daughter, who seems to have reverted to calling herself Carol, had left her husband. Unencumbered by any children, her three surviving offspring having all, for mysterious reasons, been fostered out with other New Zealand families, in October 1930 she moved to Auckland with Leon Cheavin, the man who would become her second husband.

Sometime during the following summer, Julian — his antics paling in comparison — was lucky enough to pick up an American edition of Dashiell Hammett's *The Glass Key*. Its bleak settings, resilient characters and terse, wisecracking dialogue gave him an entrée into the laconic, vernacular vein of American writing which would leave such an indelible mark on both his life and literary output. In tandem with the early short stories of Ernest Hemingway, Hammett offered a seductive new personal and professional model. Without relinquishing his earlier foppish incarnation, Julian began to affect the mannerisms of the doomed, hard-drinking heroes he'd come to admire, their melancholy and romanticism, like his own, disguised by a tough, sardonic façade.

His imagination fired by a similarly incongruous mixture of the so-called hardboiled school of writing and the Sexton Blake books, for which he maintained an abiding loyalty, he also penned several detective stories. In the hope of impressing a beautiful young Russian girl who spent most of her time knitting a sweater for her absent fiancé, he lent these to her. Much as she liked them, they didn't persuade her to ditch her boyfriend. While they were in her possession, another of her admirers sneaked a look at one of the stories, which he dismissed as "strained and artificial."[27]

The other admirer was an acquaintance of Julian's by the name of Peter Brooke (not to be confused with the theatre director of the same name). Julian had come across him that summer at a dance held in the Salle Mercier, tucked behind the Boulevard Tsarewitch in the Russian quarter of Nice. At that age Brooke remembered Julian as being "extremely indrawn".[28] Fresh from cycling through France and Spain, his southbound progress impeded by the civil war, the tall, good-looking, widely travelled Brooke was working as a swimming instructor at the Yacht Club in Juan-des-Pins, not far down the coast from Antibes.

Several months passed before Julian's next sighting of him. Through a friend who, writing under the playful byline of "Chamois", contributed to the English-language weekly, *The Monte Carlo and Menton News*, Julian talked himself into his first — no doubt unpaid — journalistic assignment. His job was to review a production of *The Importance of Being Earnest* for the paper's *News From Nice* section. Being such a staunch Wildean, it was a task he would have relished. The play was due to be staged by the Anglo-American Repertory Company. Despite their grand title, they were no more than an amateur dramatic group, hastily recruited from the English community by Ruth Putnam Mason, a vivacious American girl with artistic pretensions. For a single day in mid-December, she hired the Palais de la Méditerranée's ornately decorated theatre: the same theatre where Julian had, only the previous month, seen the black cabaret star Josephine Baker go through her raunchy act. Of the two scheduled performances of the play, Julian attended the matinee. The role of Algy was taken by a lounge-suited, high-cheekboned Peter Brooke, whose ambition was to become a professional actor. "He put up a rousing show," according to Julian. "Great panache and aplomb, and his voice carried easily to every corner of the theatre, while the actor playing Ernest was barely audible over the footlights."[29]

Julian's brief, unsigned review appeared in the next edition of *The Monte Carlo and Menton News*. "The performance was a great success," he wrote with unforeseen generosity, reminiscent less of a critic than a publicist. "There will be more plays by this excellent company, which later on intends to proceed to America."[30] The publication of his review marked the tentative launch of his career as a writer, his much-criticised aspirations inevitably fortified by the sight of his first piece in print.

Marseilles street-scene,
c.1920

Promenade des Anglais,
Nice, c.1930

Studio portrait of Nina Hamnett,
presented by her to Judah Kleinfeld,
1931 (© Sally Fiber)

Immodest Proposals

By the age of nineteen Julian was a fixture on the Riviera social scene. So much so that *The Monte Carlo and Menton News* listed him among "the large and distinguished audience"[1] in attendance at a high society event held one afternoon during the second week of March 1932. The venue for this was the picturesque Hotel Gallia in Nice, just above the public gardens on the Avenue de Sospel. Together with guests who included the British Consul, a French viscountess, and an exiled Russian princess, Julian took his seat in the drawing-room, its walls adorned with murals of rosy-cheeked children, and fluttering cherubs. There the young, predominantly aristocratic pupils of a local theatrical school presented a short play, a sequence of songs and dances, and a ballet, the diminutive participants in which were clad in costumes designed to represent the four seasons.

But Julian's father, then in his early seventies, remained scornful of his sybaritic, gadabout way of life and much-advertised artistic leanings. In the sanctimonious "rich deep port-wine voice"[2] that Julian enjoyed mimicking, his father would lecture him, counselling him with smug hypocrisy to find a job. Obstinately ignoring his advice, Julian was still living at home, still swanning round the Riviera when he celebrated his twenty-first birthday. To commemorate the occasion, he began to receive a share of the income from his paternal grandfather's estate. And his father presented him with a gold fob-watch, complete with an inscription inside. Yet their relationship continued to deteriorate, reaching it nadir towards the end of 1933. In a row that must have seemed like a repeat performance of the confrontation with Carol over a decade earlier, Julian was thrown out of the family home.

If he was ever going to achieve his ambitions, he felt that he had to return to England. "Armed with all the accoutrements of self-confidence and the flowing bowl of optimism,"[3] plus the ample £20-a-month allowance from the family trust-fund, paid to him via the Royal Bank of Canada, he left Nice and made the cross-Channel journey he'd last undertaken ten years previously. Alone in what had, for him, become a foreign country, he headed for the comforting familiarity of Bognor. Following the example set by his parents, he became a resident in a small hotel.

His escape from his nagging father and fretful mother, coupled with his arrival in a town shot through with pleasant childhood memories, didn't, however, bring instant contentment. For one thing, he had trouble getting used to the rigours of the British climate. Away from the social life he'd established in Nice, he was also afflicted by loneliness, his Gallic background cutting him off from his peers, his overtures at friendship repeatedly rebuffed.

A reprieve from this dispiriting sense of isolation was provided by a trip to France during late 1934. There he spent time with Varuna, an exotically bejewelled, cheroot-smoking member of the Asian side of his mother's family. Formerly a vocalist in a dance-band, her singing-voice reminiscent of Dinah Shore's, Varuna was now living in Paris, where she performed intermittently at the Cabaret Mars in bohemian Montparnasse. Thanks to her upbringing in Pondicherry, capital of what had been French-controlled India, she spoke fluent English and French, her utterances sprinkled with slang, which she pronounced with jocular emphasis. Since she was a regular on the densely seated terrace of the Café du Dôme, close to where she worked, Julian joined her there, amid customers including the Australian artist Horace Brodzky and Nancy Cunard, the tearaway beauty and personification of Twenties excess. Together with Varuna, Julian socialised with the self-consciously rebellious forty-four-year-old painter Nina Hamnett, someone he may well have first come across as a character in Ethel Mannin's 1931 novel, *Ragged Banners*. Nina — whose autobiography, *Laughing Torso*, had recently been the subject of a scandalous court case instigated by the satanist Aleister Crowley — introduced him to her friends as "James", but he was careful to correct her, announcing that he considered "Julian" better suited to his personality. Out-talking even the talkative Nina, he recounted his life-story and revealed his intention to forge a literary career.

After the glamour of Paris, it can't have been easy to resume his circumscribed existence in Bognor. Compensation came in the form of a chaste but intense relationship with an awestruck adolescent girl, who was holidaying with her parents in the same hotel as him. Because she shared his broad taste in jazz, embracing performers as disparate as Fats Waller and Nat Gonella, he experienced none of the inhibitions he felt in talking to most girls. When they weren't discussing jazz or listening to records, they'd play tennis together, go swimming, sit in deckchairs, and take evening walks along the promenade. Late at night, after the other guests had gone to bed, they'd dance in the hotel lounge. Before she and her parents went home, Julian made an informal proposal to her, suggesting they should get married when she was old enough.

He would look back on their time together with fondness, though it proved only the prelude to what he described as "his first, real, agonising"[4] love affair. This time it was with a girl his own age, whose identity, like that of her predecessor, remains a mystery. He met her through the social club, run by the hotel where they were both residents, and where she had a reputation as "a chaser [... of] anything in trousers".[5] Their courtship culminated in another engagement. But their romance ended unhappily when she met and suddenly married someone else. In the wake of her defection, Julian moved to London, motivated by the ambition to become a contributor to *Punch* and, perhaps, to dodge any further embarrassing encounters with her, unavoidable in a town the size of Bognor.

On arriving in the capital during mid-1935 or thereabouts, he settled in the north London suburb of Highbury. Blessed with both the free time and money to haunt the Charing Cross Road bookshops and buy new novels as soon as they came out, he was able to gratify his insatiable appetite for contemporary fiction in most of its many guises. He still had a particular affinity for sparely written hardboiled thrillers, yet his tastes were catholic enough to accommodate the ostensibly incompatible, Jean Cocteau and Gertrude Stein competing for shelf-space with Dashiell Hammett and Patrick Hamilton. He even stayed loyal to *Detective Weekly*, a pulp journal featuring the Sexton Blake serials, which had offered such a reassuring line of continuity throughout his disrupted childhood and adolescence.

Bookshops were not the only West End amenity which Julian used. He also tried out the sumptuous Café Royal on Regent Street, a building replete with fin-de-siècle artistic associations certain to captivate him. Oscar Wilde, Aubrey Beardsley, Max Beerbohm, and Ronald Firbank were just a few of the talented customers who had once graced its maze of private rooms, restaurants, and bars.

Seeking an altogether different ambience from the Café Royal, he made his first forays into an area with a long-running reputation for bohemianism, for being London's answer to Greenwich Village or Montparnasse. The area was, of course, Soho. Its diverse population, its cafés and restaurants, its patisseries and delicatessens, the competing aromas of freshly ground coffee and cured meat wafting across the streets, must have offered a nostalgic reminder of Paris and the Riviera.

Soho was not then, as it now is, bounded by Oxford Street. Instead, it extended northwards, forming an enclave between there and Goodge Street. The pre-eminent meeting place in that area, sometimes called North Soho, was the Fitzroy Tavern on the corner of Windmill and

Charlotte Streets. In tribute to its freshly retired landlord, Judah Kleinfeld, who had passed on the tenancy to his rotund daughter Annie and her equally corpulent East End Jewish husband Charlie Allchild, it was still referred to as "Kleinfeld's" or "Klein's". It consisted of the relatively smart, L-shaped Saloon Bar, and the smaller Public Bar, the bare floorboards of which were strewn with sawdust. Both bars, their atmosphere of raucous fraternity enhanced by music from an electric pianola and by an array of potent drinks like the peppery concoction sold as "Jerusalem Brandy", were decorated with an impressive collection of First World War cap badges, helmets, flags, and patriotic recruiting posters. Beneath ceilings frothing with what, from a distance, resembled mould, but on closer inspection proved to be paper money skewered by darts (the proceeds from which were periodically harvested and used to fund "Pennies From Heaven" children's parties), bell-bottomed sailors on shore-leave mixed with the Fitzroy's famously bohemian clientele. Julian's friend Nina Hamnett, for whom art had begun to take second place to alcohol, was among the latter. So too was the lecherous, grey-bearded painter Augustus John, who once bragged that the Fitzroy was like Clapham Junction because everyone passed through there sooner or later. Its clientele featured numerous local characters, none more extrovert than the self-styled "Zulu Prince Monolulu" or the "Tiger Woman". Playing up to her feline nickname as well as the notoriety she'd earned through appearing as the star witness in the libel action brought by Aleister Crowley, the outrageous and seductive Betty May was prone to crouch on all fours and lap up saucers of brandy. With his garishly coloured satin jackets, one of them patterned with four-leaf clovers, horseshoes, and winning-posts, the black tipster Zulu Prince Monolulu was a similarly striking figure.

An exhibitionist among exhibitionists, Julian — malacca cane in his right hand, bunched white gloves in the other — would stand at the bar, showing off and proclaiming his artistic ambitions. Yet, maybe because he wasn't much of a drinker, Soho failed to exert its potentially addictive charms.

Drawing on his tentative romance with the young girl he'd met in Bognor the previous year, Julian wrote his first adult short story. In *Five Finger Exercises*, its title a brazen double entendre, he recast himself in the role of a worldly thirty-year-old painter who seduces a sexually inexperienced teenager, staying in the same seaside hotel as him. By the demure standards of "those pre-*Lolita* days",[6] it was such a daring choice of subject that all the editors to whom Julian sent it promptly returned the manuscript. And "several literary agents refused point-blank to handle it".[7]

Undiscouraged by this setback, he embarked on a novel, also with romance at its core. Like many a novice writer whose first love and first novel are indivisible, he found inspiration in his relationship with his former fiancée. By the autumn of 1935, he'd completed a novel based on it. Entitled *House of Cards*, the book was written in an elliptical, sharply edited style, indebted to the cinema, to Ernest Hemingway, and to Anthony Powell, whose *From A View To A Death* ranked among his favourite novels. Only a couple of pages of an early draft, together with a more substantial section of a revised version, a detailed chapter-plan, and some notes, seem to have survived. If these provide any indication of the original, it sought to allay the pain of rejection by imposing a happy ending on the story of "Gerald St John" and "Miss Lorraine Archer", as he and his erstwhile fiancée had become.

He submitted *House of Cards*, the typescript bound ostentatiously, to the publishers, Victor Gollancz. In October 1935 he was invited to discuss it with Norman Collins, the heavy-browed novelist and Deputy-Chairman of the company, the offices of which were in Covent Garden. But Collins rejected it, the bad news softened by a comment about it showing promise.

Around that time, Julian got to know a young actress by the name of Elizabeth Gott, the high point of whose career had been a couple of fleeting, largely unnoticed West End appearances a few years earlier.[8] Attracted by her dark-haired good looks, abundant charm, kindly disposition, and severe, clean-cut style, he began a romance with her, though he first had to overcome his self-consciousness about being eight years her junior. Not that his embarrassment was warranted, the age-gap being more apparent in his mind than in reality.

Keen to impress, he took Elizabeth to the Café Royal, wooing her with cocktails on the balcony of its plush and spacious Brasserie, where affluent society figures mingled with successful writers, composers, and painters like J.B. Priestley, Constant Lambert, and Christopher Nevinson. With his handsome features, private income, conviction that he was destined for artistic stardom, and air of sophistication, augmented by the Riviera playboy outfit he invariably wore, one of several subtly different cream suits and brightly patterned silk ties combined with a white shirt and brown Oxford shoes, he must have seemed quite a catch.

The thirty-two-year-old Elizabeth was probably the first woman he had slept with, her undeniable allure multiplied by sexual novelty.

Beyond their mutual physical attraction, though, they had very little in common. All the same, when he proposed marriage to her, she accepted. The wedding was scheduled for Saturday 31 October 1936. In all likelihood, Elizabeth chose the venue for it. The church was, after all, no more than about half-a-mile from the cramped flat at the Regent's Park end of Gloucester Place, which she shared with a friend. It was a grand Catholic church with strong theatrical connections. When the wedding invitations were sent out, Julian made a point of not inviting his estranged parents, who had returned from France and taken a house on Glamis Street, right in the middle of Bognor.

Julian himself was, by then, living in Fortis Green, wedged between the respectable north London districts of Muswell Hill, Highgate, and East Finchley. There he rented a room in his landlady Mrs Wightman's small two-storey, bay-windowed Edwardian terraced villa. This was at 41 Collingwood Avenue, midway down a gently inclined street of identical houses, each with a dinky front garden, traversed by a neat tiled path.

In the run-up to the wedding, his by now frail and senile father was admitted to the Royal West Sussex Hospital in Chichester, suffering from broncho-pneumonia, complicated by a gangrenous toe. On Monday 7 September, Lambden died, aged seventy-eight, the funeral bringing about a partial reconciliation between Julian and his mother. She subsequently gave him a couple of his father's possessions. These comprised a malacca cane with a cheap pinchbeck top, and a gold-nibbed, black-barrelled Parker fountain-pen, which Julian dubbed "the Hooded Terror".[9] Fraught though his relationship with his father had been, Julian cherished them.

If he and Elizabeth were looking for propitious omens for their marriage, these were provided by the unseasonally mild weather which greeted their wedding day. While the bride's family were well represented that morning, the pews set aside for Julian's friends and family were sparsely populated. Under a high, vaulted ceiling, he and Granville James, his best-man, whom he appears to have got to know while he was living in Bognor, awaited the bride. Escorted by her civil engineer father, Elizabeth made her way down the long aisle and took her seat facing the ornately carved marble and alabaster altar. No more than an hour later, the priest had pronounced them man and wife.

Neither the priest's presence nor the sanctified surroundings deterred Julian from entering false details on the marriage certificate. Succumbing to the urge to reshape the truth, he metamorphosed from twenty-four-year-old James McLaren Ross into thirty-one-year-old

James Julian Maclaren-Ross, the extra letter and hyphen adding just the required touch of distinction. In the process, he took another step towards reinventing himself in the guise of the urbane figure he yearned to become.

His new wife was reluctant to leave London, but Julian, who must have felt duty-bound to be near his freshly widowed mother, talked Elizabeth into moving to Bognor immediately after their marriage. In November that year, they used his allowance to rent a furnished flat on Limmer Lane, just behind the sea-front at Felpham, a suburb connecting the town with Middleton-on-Sea.

Seldom bothering to change out of his silk pyjamas, he spent his days in a paisley dressing-gown, chain-smoking through his long black cigarette-holder while he read novels, studied art books, and got on with his painting. Most of his pictures were oil portraits of either himself or Elizabeth. But none of them matched the high standards he set for himself.

As well as painting, he devoted a lot of time to writing short stories. Their rejection by a succession of magazine editors led him to turn his attention to the embryonic medium of live radio drama, the intrinsic potential of which wasn't, he believed, being fully exploited. In defiance of the clumsy conventions of the day, notably the use of a plummy-voiced announcer to outline the scene and read any stage directions, he set about the pioneering task of conveying everything through sound-effects and "completely naturalistic dialogue".[10] Yet he was no more satisfied with his melodramatic scripts than he was with his paintings. His willingness to subject them to "the searching criticism... [he would] apply to the work of others"[11] rendered him reluctant to submit any of them to the BBC.

In the meantime he expected Elizabeth to do the cooking and washing, and to carry out all the other chores. He even left her to perform strenuous, traditionally male duties such as bringing in buckets of coal and laying the fires they needed to keep the place warm.

For Elizabeth, the transition from central London, where she'd been surrounded by friends and acquaintances, to a wintry seaside resort, where she knew nobody, must have been especially hard. Despite her husband's long-running, if intermittent connection with the area, he had no friends there either. Deprived of social contact and thrown into an almost constant proximity they'd never before experienced, he and Elizabeth began to get on each other's nerves, the initial excitement of their courtship wearing off. This growing sense of disillusionment can't have been helped by the pervading pessimism of the period, by the fear of imminent war which, even then, gripped the town.

Belatedly conscious of the need to meet people and escape from their claustrophobic flat, Julian made up his mind to join the local Operatic and Dramatic Society, whose next get-together had been widely advertised. The Society's meetings were held at Leslie's Café in the High Street. When he got there, he found he was far too early. Apart from a tall, athletic, beaky-nosed, twinkly-eyed man with very little of his wispy blonde hair remaining, nobody else had turned up yet. Julian wasted no time in introducing himself over a cup of black coffee and a succession of cigarettes. The other man was impressed by Julian's immaculate, rather exotic appearance. His name was C.K. Jaeger, known to his friends as "Mac" in acknowledgement of his Scottish ancestry. Already a practised monologuist, Julian did most of the talking, regaling Mac with amusing anecdotes about his adventures with the White Russian emigrés in Nice.

Mac could tell that Julian had an acerbic side to his personality, yet the two of them struck up an instant rapport. Besides being almost exact contemporaries, they had a similar sense of humour, a similar relish for life's absurdities. They'd also both lived abroad. And they both had a taste for flamboyant and idiosyncratic clothing, Mac's preferred accessories being a kilt and sporran. And they both loved weaving stories from the raw material of their lives, Mac's peppered with nonchalant references to the famous people he'd encountered. And they both harboured literary aspirations, though Mac was way ahead on that score, having already published a couple of stories in *The London Evening Standard* and worked as a scriptwriter for the film studio founded by Alexander Korda.

Before the two men parted, they swapped addresses. Within a matter of weeks, Julian and Elizabeth had become regular visitors to Rose Cottage, the tiny thatched house at Hunt's Corner in Middleton-on-Sea, where Mac lived with his wife and baby daughter, Karel, who Julian always fussed over. Mac's wife, Lydia, was a trim, glamorous, and artistically well-connected woman. Her father, Thomas Nicholls, was a successful academic sculptor; one of her cousins was the actor Herbert Marshall; and she was close to the brilliant up-and-coming comedian Alastair Sim.

The two couples quickly became firm friends, Lydia and Elizabeth drawn together as much by circumstance as a mutual interest in the theatre. Like Julian's wife, Lydia had previously been on stage in the early Thirties. The more she and her husband got to know Julian, the more they marvelled at the level-headed Elizabeth's capacity to indulge him and tolerate his often risible antics. On the first of only a few occasions when Lydia visited Elizabeth at the flat on Limmer Lane, she caught sight of Julian through the bedroom window as she approached the front door. Desperate as always to strike just the right debonair pose, he dashed into the adjoining room the moment he spotted her. By the time his wife ushered Lydia into the sitting-room, he was sitting at the piano that came with the flat, expertly fingering a wistful chord.

Through the Jaegers, Julian met Martin Jordan, another, even younger, aspirant writer and painter. Trapped in a dull clerical job, Martin was delighted to discover someone whose artistic and literary ambitions mirrored his own. Julian's general demeanour, together with his appearance, his fanciful talk of having met Graham Greene, and his formidable productivity as a writer, earned Martin's respect. No doubt glad to have someone else to visit, Julian soon got into the habit of dropping round to the estate agency in Middleton-on-Sea where Martin worked. In front of an astonished and enthralled audience of clerks and typists, he would treat him to loud renditions of scenes from his favourite movies.

Both Julian and his wife, intent on expanding their tight social circle, had, by December 1936, become active participants in the Operatic and Dramatic Society. That month they auditioned for roles in a big production of *The Maid of the Mountains*, Franz Lehar's schmaltzy, tragi-comic operetta, set in the mountain stronghold of a band of brigands. Elizabeth's stage experience, attractive countenance, and pleasant singing voice earned her the prominent supporting role of Angela, "a proud but hard beauty."[12] Her husband, in stark contrast, had to be content with a mere walk-on part as a gun-toting bandit. Along with a sizeable orchestra and a cast of over thirty people, among them Mac and Lydia's friend Francis Allison, they attended the frequent rehearsals necessary to prepare the show for its premiere in the New Year. Despite the distractions these provided, the fissures in their marriage continued to widen, recurrent bickering in public presenting the most visible manifestation of this.

On the evening of Wednesday 3 February 1937, the first of four nightly performances of the production was presented at the Bognor Regis Theatre Royal. For all his off-stage theatricality, his role-playing tendencies, and his love of props and costumes, Julian's contribution was farcical. Unable to find one of the black wellington boots that formed part of his rudimentary costume, he hopped onto the stage alongside his fellow bandits. Asked by a furtive Francis Allison why he was only wearing one boot, he replied, in a loud whisper, "Because some sod pinched the other one..."[13]

Even so, the production was rapturously received by the large audience, many of whom had been bused in from neighbouring villages and suburbs. In the review that appeared the following week, *The Bognor Regis Observer* headlined it BOGNOR REGIS AMATEURS' GREATEST SUCCESS. "No local Society," the reviewer observed, "has been given a greater ovation than they received on the night of their final performance on Saturday."[14] Elizabeth must have been particularly gratified by the praise lavished on her for her "fine portrayal of Angela."[15]

With *The Maid of the Mountains* out of the way, Julian — who was a devotee of Graham Greene's early novels — concentrated on scripting an unauthorised radio dramatisation of the recently published *A Gun For Sale*. Having put the finishing touches to it by April, he invited Martin Jordan to join he and Elizabeth for a trial reading of the script at their flat. By that stage their marital problems were so salient, Martin assumed divorce must be looming. To make matters worse, the reading didn't go well, prompting Julian to shelve the script.

At some point in either late April or early May, after only about six months of marriage, the inevitable occurred. Abruptly severing all her contacts with Bognor, the long-suffering Elizabeth left him and went back to London. Instead of blaming himself, Julian — whose self-awareness never kept pace with his self-absorption — attributed their marital failure to a lack of money.

Now Elizabeth was no longer around to pamper him, the flat on Limmer Lane felt bleak and inhospitable. Within hours of her departure, he too had moved out, pausing only to bundle his few possessions into an old biscuit tin and a brown paper parcel, tied together with string. Luckily for him, Mac and Lydia were at home when he turned up at Rose Cottage. Forlorn and sorry for himself, he begged them to let him use their spare room. They had no hesitation in agreeing to his request, though they assumed it would only be a short-term arrangement.

Had the three of them not been such good friends, it might have developed into a nightmarish scenario, the house being barely big enough for three, let alone four people. Then again, Mac wasn't there all the time. Most days he commuted to London, where he had converted his father-in-law's former studio in Lambeth into a box-making factory, set up to provide work for unemployed ex-servicemen.

During the day, Julian went back to his normal routine. At about 11.00am each morning, he'd emerge sleepy-eyed from his bedroom.

For at least the next hour he'd hog the bathroom. His black hair meticulously styled, his hard-jawed face now shaven, he would go back to his room, where he would carefully knot his tie and put on a suit. He was then ready for the day's creative endeavours. Encouraged by Mac, who was impressed by the quality of his writing and, above all, by his exceptional ear for dialogue, Julian's literary output began to take precedence over his painting. In conscious imitation of the graphic, unembellished prose style of the writers he respected, their ranks swelling to include Samuel Beckett whose *More Pricks Than Kicks* he'd recently purchased, he resumed work on what he envisaged as a collection of short stories, all of them heavily autobiographical.

Not long after his arrival at Rose Cottage, Julian had got to know a young, garrulous, former expat, who lodged with Mac and Lydia's friend, Miss Dyson, the attractive blonde owner of a women's clothes shop in Middleton-on-Sea. Always alert for promising material for his writing, he'd sometimes invite his new friend round in the afternoons and milk him for anecdotes about life in colonial India. One of his favourites was a story about an abortive night on the tiles in riot-torn Madras during the Twenties. His prodigious memory, verging on total-recall, and his ear for the rhythms, elisions and cadences of other people's speech enabled him to faithfully reproduce it in written form, capturing his friend's Blimpish tone of voice, as well as conveying a powerful sense of spontaneity. He called it *A Drink at Harrison's.*

Another visitor to Rose Cottage, in the early days of his sojourn, was his worried mother, who was now living modestly in nearby Felpham. News of his marital break-up having percolated through to her, she popped round a few times. Because he still resented her perceived shortcomings as a parent, Julian never looked forward to these visits. The moment she arrived, the old tensions between them resurfaced, her perverse insistence on calling him "Jimmy" provoking instantaneous exasperation. He usually ended up seeking refuge in his room or simply going out, leaving the Jaegers to entertain his diffident, crestfallen mother. On her final visit she confessed to them "that she and Julian had never really got on, that he'd never shown any warmth towards her."[16]

In the evenings — by which time Mac had changed into a black velvet smoking jacket and matching cap, a meerschaum pipe clamped between his teeth — Julian would often join his hosts in marathon, after-dinner games of *Monopoly*. Bets laid on the outcome lent these a fiercely competitive edge. No money changed hands, but the ownership of most of the books in the house was in a state of perpetual flux. And on one fateful evening Mac made the mistake of wagering what he fondly referred to as his "teddy-bear coat".[17] By accumulating a lucrative cluster of chunky wooden hotels, straddling the Mayfair and Park Lane spaces, Julian won the coat: a long, voluminous, fluffy camel-hair garment which rapidly became as synonymous with him as his father's cane. On those rare evenings when things didn't go his way, Julian was liable to throw a tantrum. Cursing loudly, he'd "tip over the board, scattering playing pieces and *Monopoly* money across the floor, then stomp off to his room, vowing never to play again."[18]

Other evenings he accompanied either Mac or Lydia on trips to the Theatre Royal, which presented a mixture of touring professional productions and amateur shows. Of these, he most enjoyed melodramatic thrillers like Emlyn Williams's *Night Must Fall* and Edgar Wallace's *The Man Who Changed His Name*. No matter how ineptly they were performed, he "always emerged from the auditorium in high spirits."[19]

As frequently as twice-a-week, Julian would break his routine by catching the train to London for the day, where he'd sometimes meet up with Granville James. After work, Mac would partner him for an evening in Soho. On one such occasion, he took Mac on a preliminary detour to a bank near Trafalgar Square. Shown into the manager's office, he was greeted warmly and handed a slip of paper. He presented this to the cashier on his way out. At which the cashier laboriously counted out the enormous sum of £600, most likely wired to him by the trustees of his paternal grandfather's estate.

The frequency of his visits to Soho meant that he soon built up a wide circle of acquaintances, such as the intellectual, fast-talking Indian novelist Mulk Raj Anand. Usually Julian and Mac headed not for the still fashionable Fitzroy Tavern but for the Wheatsheaf, situated just beyond where Charlotte Street shimmies into Rathbone Place. Among the more compact pubs in the vicinity, the Wheatsheaf was built in the voguish inter-war mock-Tudor style, its leaded, stained-glass windows patterned with armorial devices, the broad passageway running through the building evocative of an old coaching inn. Next to its grimy competitors, its two small bars were models of polished comfort. These were both warm, brightly lit and normally crowded, the cloying smell of perspiration — an inescapable component of the pre-deodorant era — suffusing the air. At the front, there was the so-called Public Bar, dominated by a bow-window with a large china swan positioned on the sill. What little sunlight penetrated the room was tinted by the stained-glass, creating a distinctive subaqua quality. Beyond the Public Bar, there was the narrow, equally cramped Saloon Bar. The floor was laid with scuffed red lino. Distributed round it were a few circular tables and some chairs, upholstered in tatty emerald green rexine. Because the pub was owned by William Younger, the Scottish brewing firm, its wood-panelled walls were studded with squares of different tartans.

Part of the reason for the Wheatsheaf's growing popularity was that it served Younger's Scotch Ale, a much stronger brew than equivalent English beers. At that time Julian was far from being a heavy drinker, yet it isn't hard to see why he found pubby, unconventional Soho such a welcome contrast to Bognor. Its camaraderie, its profusion of colourful material for his anecdotes and stories, its contiguity with the louche world of spivs and criminals, its pervasive cult of failure, its sense of possibility, its echoes of the Continent, its reverence for unorthodox behaviour might all have been calculated to beguile him.

Before taking the train back to the south coast, Julian and Mac liked to go for a meal at Bertorelli's, a well-known, moderately-priced Italian restaurant just up the road from the Wheatsheaf. Julian always rounded off the day with a portion of what was then something of a culinary novelty — spaghetti bolognese.

While he was staying with the Jaegers, Mac — whom he had taken to addressing in a hammy Scottish accent as "Mac the Laird" — made an effort to introduce him to their wide circle of local friends, including the successful lawyer, A.G. Flavell. When they could afford it, he and Mac would meet Flavell in the bar of the Theatre Royal, where they'd chat and play protracted, uproarious, booze-fuelled games of Spoof. This entailed each player being dealt three matchsticks. Without letting the other Spoofers see, you placed between none and three of these in your right fist. Each player then took his turn at guessing the total number of matches held in "clenched fists raised like a party salute".[20] If you guessed the correct number, you dropped out of the game. The last person remaining was obliged to buy the next round of drinks. Believing it was unlucky if you didn't always use the same matchsticks, Julian carried round his own set, "grey with age, the sticks worn thin from constant clutching in a sweaty palm."[21]

Together with Mac and Martin Jordan, Julian also attended the newly formed writing group that convened at Rose Cottage every few weeks. Several meetings into its existence, the membership was swelled by the addition of Eugene Horsfall-Ertz, who was introduced to the group by Martin. A notable local eccentric, the gentle, bowler-hatted, poetry-writing Horsfall-Ertz would enter each evening with the same bizarre greeting: "I grind my spiritual boulder in the dust. How are you, brothers?"[22]

Occasional approving comments about Sir Oswald Mosley, leader of the Fascist and National Socialist Party, and Count Potocki of Montalk, the notorious publisher of *The Right Review*, gradually exposed Horsfall-Ertz's unpleasant political allegiances. Living in a town awash with blackshirts and Nazi sympathisers, in an era where a sly undercurrent of anti-semitism was deemed acceptable, the group found nothing shocking about what he said. Absurd and abhorrent though Julian considered the tenets of fascism, he adopted a stance of youthful disdain for politics. In any case, he and the others liked Horsfall-Ertz enough either to ignore his political opinions or dismiss them as merely an attempt to be provocative.

Gathered in the cosy sitting-room at Rose Cottage, the group would take turns to read their work aloud and then discuss it. Here, Julian displayed an endearing facet of his personality, his gift for incisive criticism balanced by a determination to be diplomatic and encouraging. When Martin read from his work-in-progress, *Mr Mint Meets Murder*, a whodunit featuring Mr Mint, "a sort of secular Father Brown"[23] who "lived at the seaside, wore a panama hat and had such a marvellous mind that messages and pleas for help came pouring into his neat bungalow from every secret service and police force in the world",[24] Julian drew up a helpful list of possible titles for future Mr Mint novels, such as *Mint Sauce* and *Mint in Aspic*. And when the group was joined one evening by Jordan's ageing father, who recited an embarrassingly lush, pseudo Victorian poem which began "Come, spring, thou herald of summer's / dawn / Thou omega of winter's lingering breath,"[25] Julian treated him with tact and kindness, instantly proposing they elect him an honorary member, "a gesture which pleased the old man no end."[26]

Julian's own contributions included *Happy As The Day Is Long*, a story he'd written about a Chelsea antique dealer and his seedy entourage, and *A Drink at Harrison's* which, to those of the group who were unaware of its origins, must have sounded like a miraculous act of ventriloquism. The demotic zest of his writing tended to earn him unanimous and sincere praise. A rare exception, though, was *Five Finger Exercises*. None of the other members of the group liked it. Yet, because it memorialised an episode in his life about which he felt nostalgic and because he thought of it as marking the beginning of his career as a writer, he retained "a sentimental attachment to it"[27] that outweighed its literary merits.

Mac and Lydia had assumed Julian would start looking for alternative accommodation once he'd got over the initial trauma of Elizabeth's departure. By the end of the summer of 1937, he had, on the surface at least, recovered, but he gave no indication that he had any plans to leave Rose Cottage. Neither Mac nor Lydia broached the subject, since they enjoyed having him around, especially now he'd regained the facetious attitude to life that had so endeared him to them in the first place. Wherever he looked, he seemed to find material for the witty anecdotes and short stories with which he entertained them. Even the dull job he and Mac found for a few days that summer, harvesting peas on a local farm, provided plenty to amuse him. As did his regular trips to the local barber, who claimed to be a conduit for messages from the spirit world.

Life with Julian nevertheless had its drawbacks. The most conspicuous of these was the grating lack of privacy. Lydia also came to resent his failure to help them out with their household expenses, though he continued to receive his allowance, the majority of it going on copious supplies of novels and unfiltered cigarettes. These lent him a rasping voice and an early morning smoker's cough, audible throughout the house. His extreme reluctance to take baths was another source of friction. He claimed this was because they were bad for him, but the real reason was that he disliked having to stand in the kitchen and blow down the pipes: a ritual necessary to coax the plumbing system into even a semblance of activity.

Prompted by both Julian's continued presence and their daughter Kavel's transition from baby to chubby-cheeked toddler, the Jaegers decided to put Rose Cottage on the market and rent a larger house. They had no difficulty selling the place, but the exorbitant rents prevalent in Bognor meant they had trouble finding anywhere else within their budget. Hearing of their plight, a sympathetic friend offered them the use of the upstairs rooms in his tiny Victorian cottage until they found somewhere else.

"Uncle Julian", as Kavel referred to him, had, however, no alternative accommodation lined up. Heedless of the offence and anxiety he might cause, about a month before they were due to leave, he packed up his things and surreptitiously vacated his room. The only sign of his presence was a thick ridge of cigarette-ash which Lydia discovered down the side of his bed. To assuage their fears and find out where Julian had gone, they quizzed everyone who knew him. But he'd let nobody into his confidence.

For fear of losing face, of betraying the melancholy beneath his mask of insouciance, he had kept his destination secret. From Rose Cottage, he had gone straight to London, where he'd tracked down

Elizabeth and attempted to rescue their marriage. When his mission ended in undignified failure, he retreated back to the south coast, their separation still not formalised by divorce proceedings.

Too ashamed to rejoin the Jaegers, he found himself a comfortable room at the St Helen's boarding house on Stocker Road in the West End of Bognor. Even after he'd re-established relations with Mac and Lydia, he remained reticent about where he had been, partly because it was a genuinely painful subject, and partly because he enjoyed nurturing an aura of mystery about himself.

Don't Forget To Smile

The following year began badly, the prospect of war looming ever larger. But first Julian had to contend with a more immediate crisis, brought about by the unexpected cancellation of his allowance, presumably precipitated by the demise of the family trust-fund. Now he was confronted by the irksome and unfamiliar necessity of earning a living. In search of a job that would not only support him but also furnish him with interesting material, he took to scanning the Situations Vacant columns of both local papers. Since it was outside the holiday season, there weren't many jobs advertised. Of the few listed, the majority were unsuitable ones — for domestic servants or errand boys.

Julian's creative impulses could so easily have been dissipated by the stress of the situation, yet he persevered with his writing. Cloistered in his room at St Helen's, he planned another radio thriller for submission to the BBC. Again, he came up with the idea of adapting a novel by an author he admired. The author in question was the pseudonymous Anthony Skene, whose output spanned hardback novels, paperback novelettes commissioned by the Sexton Blake Library, and stories written for pulp magazines like *The Thriller* and *Detective Weekly*.

Gallows Alley, the novel Julian decided to adapt, traces the rise and fall of a beautiful but manipulative shopkeeper's daughter, who becomes an acclaimed actress, only to be forced by drug addiction into a tragic liaison with a crooked doctor. So convinced was Julian of its viability as a 60-minute radio play, he sought the author's written permission before settling down to the task of dramatising it. Skene was happy to sanction his proposal, provided the play was produced by the end of the year.

His imagination fired by fond memories of bleakly realistic proto-film noir movies like *Winterset* and *Dead End*, Julian set to work on the script. Even his parlous financial position failed to erode his confident mood. When Mac dreamt up the idea of writing a series of spoof letters to *The Bognor Regis Observer* to publicise the new Drama Club Lydia had founded, the ebullient Julian offered vociferous encouragement. In the second week of January 1938, Mac got the campaign underway with a mischievous letter "on behalf of Bognor's budding authors",[1] supposedly penned by "Ivan Ivanovitch."[2] With Julian egging him on, he initiated a lively correspondence. A couple of weeks later, he discarded Ivan Ivanovitch in favour of a far superior satirical creation

— the reactionary Lieutenant-Colonel (retired) I. Wonder, whose escapades over the ensuing weeks anticipated those of Joe Orton and Kenneth Halliwell's "Edna Welthorpe (Mrs)" during the Fifties and Sixties. Mac must have had himself and Julian in mind when he wrote: "What those scrubly [sic] author-cum-playwright fellows want is someone with backbone to put (and keep) them in their places.

"It's a sine qua non, Sir (or whatever it's called) that authors, artists, poets, musicians and like gentry absolutely thrive in poverty and neglect. Why, Sir, look at history: there's that Beethoven feller: lived and died in poverty, and look at him now... world famous! And that Dutch portrait painting chap (VAN-Something-or-other); why, he lived in poverty and actually died a bankrupt, and look at him now... world famous!

"And so with the rest of 'em.

"Now where would they be, Sir, I'd like to know, if their contemporaries had been foolish enough to read their plays, hear their music or study their portraits [...]

"And gad, Sir! That correspondent of yours with a name like a machine-gun (IVAN FITZ-something), why, he's spreading Red ruin with his ridiculous modern ideas of pampering these author fellows. Gad, Sir! If only I had him on my parade ground, I'd have him facing a firing squad in less than half a pig's whisper [...]"[3]

A matter of days after *The Bognor Regis Observer* fell for this latest diatribe, Julian spotted an intriguing job advert at the back of its rival publication, *The Bognor Regis Post*. "Salesmen with or without previous experience required for Bognor district," it read. "Advantages:- (1) Salary of £2 per week and commission. (2) No canvassing. (3) Training and assistance on techniques. (4) Executive position waiting when qualified [...]"[4]

He showed the advert to Mac, who was also looking for a job by then, the box-making factory having gone out of business. They both decided to write off to the Electrolux company, the address of which was quoted at the bottom of the advert. In reply, they were surprised to receive letters offering them each a job and explaining that they had to complete a five-day training programme before they could start work.

On the morning the course was due to begin, Julian and Mac took the train down the coast to Hove. The company's Sales School was based at 12 Portland Road, the same premises that housed their showroom and Regional Head Office. To get to the Sales School, they had to walk through the smart, brightly lit shop, beyond which there was a large, gloomy room, traversed by rows of chairs. Most of these were already occupied by shabbily dressed men in their fifties and sixties, a high proportion of whom turned out to be veterans from the last war. Julian and Mac found a couple of seats at the back. Displayed on the walls around them, there were posters exhorting them to " 'SAIL IN AND SELL', 'DIG MORE DIRT' and 'DON'T FORGET TO SMILE'."[5] Next to these, there were other posters advertising Electrolux vacuum-cleaners. Facing the would-be salesmen, there was a low dais with an ultra-modern, long-trunked cleaner positioned in the centre. Above it hung a sign that said: "Every man is my superior in some branch of knowledge and in that shall I learn from him."[6]

At length, a diminutive, jaunty tutor in a pinstripe suit, his dapper music-hall comedian's posture accentuated by a pencil-moustache, slicked back hair, and a pipe, jigged onto the dais and said, "Good morning, gentlemen. Today we are going to sing 'I feel so happy, so happy...' "[7] His energetic rendition of the song provoked only a desultory response. Julian turned to Mac and whispered, "How can he bear to sing that rubbish to these penniless old people?"[8]

The preliminary sing-song at an end, the man on the dais launched into the opening instalment of the sales course, stressing the opportunities they were being offered. "We have men working with us now," he informed them, "who run their own cars — ambitious men like yourselves who have got to the top [...]"[9] He then went on to impress upon his audience the innate superiority of the product they'd be selling: "the world's finest and most up-to-date vacuum-cleaner. The greatest boon the housewife has come across yet."[10] Sprinkling his speech with sales slogans, obscene variations on which Julian would later devise, he outlined the tantalising rewards available to successful salesmen. For every vacuum-cleaner sold, they'd get a handsome commission of £3-8/-. As if that was not enough of an incentive, the leading salesman in the company's Southern Area would be awarded a £100 prize, plus a new Ford car.

Each day for the remainder of that week, Julian and Mac travelled to Hove to hear him expound the standard sales techniques. These were reinforced by a battery of helpful psychological ploys, ranging from always referring to the customer by name to identifying yourself with their troubles. Should the conventional techniques fail, salesmen were taught to work their way through all twenty-eight steps of the "Show More Dirt Demonstration".[11] By cleaning the prospective customer's curtains, picture-rails, upholstery, couches, chairs, and settees, then emptying the dirt into a pile on the carpet, it emphasised how filthy the house was, the implication being that the householder was in dire need of a vacuum-cleaner.

On completion of the course, the new recruits were issued with company credentials, a stack of advertising flyers which they were expected to distribute, and what was referred to as their "dem' kit".[12] This consisted of a heavy suitcase containing a vacuum-cleaner and its numerous attachments, used for demonstration purposes. Last of all, the recruits were each allocated a sales area. Making a stabbing motion with the stem of his pipe, the instructor pointed towards the centre of the map, pinned to the wall, and said to Mac: "Right, I'm giving you Brighton..."

"That's very kind of you," Mac replied.

"And you can have Worthing," the man told Julian.

Full of mock outrage, Julian waited until the instructor had moved on before saying, "How come *you've* got Brighton and I've only got Worthing...?"[13]

First thing on Monday morning, he and Mac travelled to Littlehampton Station, where they and the other salesmen, most of them clad in the unofficial uniform of raincoats and pork-pie hats, were gathered to meet their supervisor. While they were hanging round outside the station, Julian and Mac fell in with another well-read, down-on-his-luck recruit. Their new acquaintance combined a deep-seated resentment of the company's exploitation of its employees with a determination to win the Southern Area Sales Prize.

When their likable, if slothful Mediterranean supervisor, known simply as "the Greek", showed up, he led them to the nearby post office, where he enacted his daily rite. Removing his tie-pin, billed as "the Lucky Dem' Pin",[14] he handed it to each of the new recruits in turn, and made them shut their eyes and jab it into the open pages of the appropriate phone directory. The embarkation-point of each salesman's door-to-door session was determined by where the pin landed. Just before parting, Julian and Mac agreed to meet for a drink later on, so they could swap notes on how things had gone.

A cold February day, spent lugging his dem' kit round the residential part of Worthing, eroded Julian's previous optimism. It rapidly became apparent that the job was a lot harder than it had been portrayed. The so-called Lucky Dem' Pin failed to live up to its name, presenting him with entire streets where nobody could afford a vacuum-cleaner. Repeatedly, he went through his sales patter, all to no avail, several potential customers — dubbed "prospects" — slamming doors in his face.

As agreed, he met Mac in the pub after work, an arrangement they were to reprise most days, though neither of them were hardened drinkers. Over a pint, Julian entertained his friend with stories about his first day on the job, the dispiriting failure to earn any commission offset by the exciting literary possibilities it opened up. Julian wasn't the only one to notice these. When Mac announced that he planned to write something about door-to-door salesmen, his friend was indignant. "Me too," Julian said. "And *I'm* going to do it first…"[15]

True to his word, he soon shaped his experiences into fictional form, his eye for social nuances, his ability to swiftly appraise people honed by the demands of door-to-door work. But he was unable to find a publisher for the resultant short memoir[16] because it contained a number of libellous portraits of people he'd met through the job.

Before that, however, he completed his adaptation of *Gallows Alley*. Unlike any previous script he'd written, he felt it was worth sending to the BBC, its submission prompted by an article he'd read in *The Daily Telegraph and Morning Post* a couple of months previously, complaining about the dearth of new radio playwrights. Within only a few days of posting his manuscript, he received a standard acknowledgement from the BBC. Their speedy response led him to expect an equally punctual decision on whether to broadcast his play.

From mid-February into mid-March, he and Mac spent their days trudging round in their quest for what proved elusive sales, "feeling the wet pavement through the soles of shoes worn thin".[17] To lighten the burden of his dem' kit, Julian — who, "much as he needed the job, persisted in treating it as a joke"[18] — had acquired an old pram, in which he stowed the by now battered-looking suitcase.

The already long odds on them earning a commission were lengthened by the presence of salesmen from another firm. Every Sunday he and Mac posted a weekly report to the Hove office, invariably reading "No Sales".[19] Yet their meagre salary kept them just about solvent.

Between his footsore route-marches round Worthing, Julian parcelled up some of his manuscripts and sent them to the editor of *New Writing*, the fashionable hardback anthology that had done so much to propel Christopher Isherwood towards literary stardom. The parcel contained *Dance Marathon*, a "jazz poem"[20] he'd composed, along with nine of the short stories from his mooted collection, including *Five Finger Exercises* and *A Drink at Harrison's*.

One morning during the anxious period when he was awaiting a decision from both *New Writing* and the BBC, he and Mac arrived, as usual, at Littlehampton Station. There they encountered the other new recruit they'd met on their first day, his face beaming with triumph. They were astonished to hear he'd won the Area Sales Prize. When they asked him how he'd managed it, he wouldn't tell them. A few days later, he drove up to the station in the new car he'd won. Still reluctant to offer an explanation, he distributed the £100 prize among his fellow salesmen before the Greek appeared. Over the coming days, as customer after customer returned the vacuum-cleaners he claimed to have sold them, it became clear he'd perpetrated an ingenious but well-intentioned swindle. By paying the 10/- deposit on behalf of his customers, he was able to create the illusion of clinching a sale, each time earning a commission which outweighed the cost of the deposit.

Near the end of March, not long after his disappearance, both Julian and Mac received letters informing them that Electrolux, who only had to give them a single day's notice, were dispensing with their services. Julian retaliated by selling his dem' kit to a local pawn shop.

In the hope of landing a job with Hoover, Electrolux's main rival, he wrote to their head office in London. He tried to persuade Mac to follow suit, but Mac was sick of door-to-door work. Responding to Julian's application, which stated that he was an experienced salesman, Hoover offered him a £2-10/- advance. As an added inducement, they volunteered to cover the cost of his train fare to London, where he was invited to attend a sales course at one of their two Regent Street offices in the week beginning Monday 11 April.

A welcome distraction from his anxiety about the job situation was provided by the new Drama Club's inaugural production. In a supportive gesture to Lydia, who took the role of Elizabeth Moulton-Barrett in *The Barretts of Wimpole Street*, Julian accompanied her proud husband to its closing performance at the Theatre Royal. Together with Mac and Horsfall-Ertz, he joined the club's members for a post-production party, held in the stage-set Martin Jordan had designed.

The Saturday before his training was due to begin, Julian travelled up to London, where he found temporary digs in St George's Square, Pimlico. During the next week he attended his second course in the art of salesmanship. While he was in London, he went round to see Moray McLaren, the Assistant Director of Features and Drama at the BBC. Irritated by the delay, almost two months having elapsed since he sent them his script, he'd attempted to speed up the process by making an appointment to discuss his submission, as well as his ideas about radio drama. On his visit to McLaren's "monastic cell"[21] in the Art Deco edifice of Broadcasting House, he created such a favourable impression that McLaren — a stockily built man with grey hair flowing "from his brow into a mane at the back"[22] — raised the possibility of him being given a job with the BBC as soon as an appropriate post, possibly as a trainee producer, became vacant.

Julian also arranged to see the eponymous publisher Jonathan Cape, to whom he'd recently submitted *Five Finger Exercises*, his short story collection. After the sales course had finished for the day, he took a taxi over to Cape's offices. These were located in the lower half of an elegantly appointed eighteenth-century mansion at 30 Bedford Square, right in the heart of Bloomsbury. But the elderly, white-haired Jonathan Cape, his innate caution and conservatism expressed by his sober black suit, tactfully rejected the collection.

Once he'd finished the training course, Julian went back to Bognor and resumed his duties as a salesman, only this time he was allocated Littlehampton instead of Worthing. And now he was wise to all the tricks of the struggling salesman's trade. A favourite scam involved picking names at random from the phone-directory which he tacked onto his list of people requesting demonstrations. Another consisted of helping his supervisor run an illicit sideline in secondhand vacuum-cleaners.

Despite Jonathan Cape's rejection of his collection and the ominous lack of any word from *New Writing*, he continued to submit its constituent stories to magazines, among them the paperback miscellany *Penguin Parade*, which had been launched the previous year. He was overjoyed to hear that *Happy As The Day Is Long* had been accepted by its editor, Denys Kilham Roberts. The proposed payment was four guineas. But his jubilation was short-lived. When he wrote back to Kilham Roberts, requesting a cheque for the amount mentioned, he was informed that payment was not made on acceptance. An enquiry into when he *could* expect payment merely resulted in the return of his manuscript, arousing an understandable suspicion of publishers.

Concerned at how disheartened Julian was becoming, Mac attempted to help him break into print by introducing him to Morton Swinburne, editor of *The Bognor Regis Post*, for whom Mac wrote regular articles under a variety of pen-names. While Mac paced up and down outside the Post's offices at 100 London Road, Julian showed his portfolio of stories to Swinburne. He reappeared about ten minutes later, upset and annoyed because Swinburne had no more than skimmed through them and said, "It's not Shakespeare, is it...?"[23]

A couple of weeks after his visit to Broadcasting House, he received the hoped for letter from the BBC informing him that they'd like to broadcast *Gallows Alley*. His delight was, however, tempered by his experience with *Penguin Parade*. He wrote back to let McLaren know that he was working on a revised version of the play in between "hawking Hoovers".[24] And he invited McLaren to a reading of the script which he was planning to hold one weekend in May, just to see how it sounded.

With typical self-assurance, he persuaded Mrs Francis, the owner of the boarding house where he was living, to let him stage the event in her dining-room. Emboldened by his earlier amateur dramatic involvement, he recruited a small cast from his acquaintances. In front of an audience that included Mac and Lydia, plus Anthony Skene, they read through his script, Julian casting himself in the role of a ruthless gunman. It was just as well McLaren couldn't attend, because even Julian's hammy gusto failed to compensate for the leaden performances of the rest of the cast.

Short of money and uncertain how much longer he could hold on to his job, Julian wrote to McLaren later that month, requesting payment for his play. But McLaren explained that he wanted Val Gielgud, the Director of Features and Drama, to read it first. Early in June, Julian received the disappointing news that Gielgud considered *Gallows Alley* too bleak for broadcasting. Yet Gielgud was "very interested in [Julian's] way of writing"[25] and wanted to meet him, because he, like McLaren, regarded him as a talented writer worth nurturing.

His inability to get his work into print, reiterated by the belated rejection of the manuscripts he'd submitted to *New Writing*, led him to concentrate on his radio scripts. Late on the afternoon of Wednesday 14 June, he paid his second visit to Broadcasting House. There he met both McLaren and Gielgud, whose bald, bulbous-nosed appearance made it obvious he was the brother of the fêted young actor, John Gielgud. McLaren offered to give Julian "some preliminary help over plot outline",[26] the facet of his writing which, they felt, let him down.

Undeterred by the BBC's reservations about *Gallows Alley*, he found the time to draw up synopses of possible plays for their autumn schedule. Paying careful consideration to Gielgud's criticism of his previous script, he sent him the outline of a play written "in a much lighter vein".[27] Based on *Predicted Murder*, another Anthony Skene story, *The Stars Foretell Murder* was about an astrologer who conspires with a shady businessman to persuade a rich client that the planetary influences are favourable for an investment in one of the businessman's fraudulent schemes.

Julian also revived the idea of dramatising *A Gun For Sale*. To that end, he contacted Paramount Pictures, who owned the theatrical rights to the book. Permission was granted on condition that his adaptation was performed only once, and that the script could be freely used in their forthcoming feature film.[28]

Promising though these projects were, none of them brought in any extra income. And that was what Julian most needed. His worsening financial position left him unable to afford the rent at St Helen's. In the final days of June, he was forced to move to cheaper lodgings in a small, newish house on Kingsmead, a quiet suburban cul-de-sac branching off the main road through Felpham. But even these proved too costly for him, forcing him to decamp to Eastergate, a straggling village on the Chichester-Littlehampton road, where he found still cheaper lodgings.

During the second week of July, Julian took some time off work and went up to London to see Graham Greene, who had invited him to lunch to discuss his proposed dramatisation of *A Gun For Sale*. Since the mid-Thirties, Greene and his wife, Vivien, had been renting a tall, opulently furnished Queen Anne house at 14 North Side, looking out across Clapham Common. Clutching an advance copy of *Brighton Rock*, sent to him by Greene, Julian emerged from the tube. Because he'd mislaid the letter that had accompanied it, giving precise directions, he had trouble finding the house. When he eventually got there, an inhospitable old housekeeper let him into the stone-floored hall, which had a spectacular staircase leading off it. She told him to wait in the upstairs drawing-room. Its pale grey panelling, delicate papier mâché tables, and elegant chairs and sofa emphasised the disparity between himself and Greene, only eight years his senior but already an established man of letters. Julian hadn't been there long before his host appeared in the open doorway, "wearing a brown suit and large horn-rimmed spectacles, which he at once snatched off".[29] Putting Julian at his ease with "a spontaneous pleasant smile",[30] he suggested they go for a drink and fetch a couple of jugs of beer to have with their lunch. They went to a pub on the other side of the Common, where they chatted about their plans. Graham was amazed to hear what Julian did for a living, memories of it probably inspiring him to make the hero of *Our Man in Havana* a vacuum-cleaner salesman.

From the pub, they carried the jugs of cold beer back to Graham's house, where they lunched with his handsome wife, Vivien, "placid and sedate like a young Spanish matron".[31] Shortly before they got up from the table, she murmured something to her husband who, in an apologetic tone, said to Julian, "It's an awful nuisance but 'they' are asking to see you I'm afraid. I wonder if you'd mind."[32]

"They" turned out to be Graham's "two small, extremely pretty blonde children",[33] four-year-old Lucy and two-year-old Francis, who were coralled in the nursery. Julian, his voice acquiring the hearty timbre his father used to adopt when he'd "survived a social ordeal",[34] dutifully complimented Graham on how charming they were. He and Graham then retreated to the drawing-room. Restarting their conversation over a brandy, some coffee, and the remains of the beer, they soon discovered their shared infatuation with crime novels, gangster movies, the criminal underworld, and contemporary American short story writers. By the time Graham walked him to a bus-stop in the High Street, the alcohol and the mid-summer heat leaving Julian muzzy-headed, they'd laid the foundations for a firm friendship.

The sense of exhilaration, aroused by hobnobbing with one of his literary idols, didn't last long. When he got back to Bognor, he learnt that he was about to lose his job, Hoover's Branch Manager having discovered he'd sold a secondhand cleaner to a woman in Littlehampton. Though he was merely acting on behalf of his unscrupulous supervisor, he got the blame for it, and the company terminated his contract.

He was tempted to apply for another of the door-to-door jobs advertised in the local papers. On reflection he decided against it, preferring to concentrate on his scripts of *A Gun For Sale* and *The Stars Foretell Murder* while he followed up the possibility of employment with the BBC. On Monday 8 August, he wrote to them, pleading for "any sort of job".[35] Moray McLaren responded by return of post, saying there were no suitable ones available, but they'd let him know if anything turned up.

In desperation, he joined forces with Mac, who had circulated flyers round the Bognor area offering a garden maintenance service for £10-a-year. Not that either of them had any horticultural experience. Yet plenty of locals, among them Mac's friend, Sir Alan Cobham, the stunt pilot and leader of the Flying Circus, hired them to tend his garden in Middleton-on-Sea. Because he had no more appropriate clothes, Julian had to wear a suit. So reluctant was he to get dirty, he spent their opening session simply loitering beside the crouching Mac, his self-appointed role being to hand Mac the gardening tools. Chivvied into activity by his friend, on this and subsequent days, he took what he must have regarded as the easy option of mowing the lawn.

As word spread round each district in which they were working, large crowds would gather to watch him pushing a lawnmower, defiantly dapper, heroic in defeat, cigarette-holder angled away from the ground. But his suits rapidly lost their pristine pallor. And when that disappeared, so too did his audience.

Within only a few weeks, things started to go wrong. First, Mac inadvertently mistook Sir Alan's prize seedlings for weeds. Then he and Julian found they couldn't fulfil all the work they'd taken on, apparently inducing Julian to concoct the tall story of how he and Mac had ended up in the County Court, victims of a disgruntled customer.

After the gardening venture collapsed, Mac spent the latter half of the holiday season working on the Butlin's Funfair at Bognor, halfway along the eastern esplanade. Fascinated by its brash allure and by the people who frequented it, Julian started going there most afternoons. To see what the rest of the day held in store for him, he'd drop a penny into the fortune-telling machine and pull the lever. "Your Financial Position Will Improve"[36] was the message he always hoped for, instead of which he tended to get predictions like "Your Next Will Be A Boy".[37]

Through his visits to the funfair, Julian got to know the tough, resourceful, and roguish Micky Hopper, then in his late teens. When he first came across him, Micky was working on the hoop-la stall. Drawn, as ever, towards "the unprivileged shadows, the stoker's hold of life",[38] Julian wasted no time in cultivating a friendship with Micky, who must have seemed like an English equivalent of the characters in the hardboiled crime novels he so admired. Originally from Glasgow, Micky had left home at an early age, lorry-hopping, sleeping in doss-houses, and earning a living as best he could, somewhere along the line acquiring a Cockney accent and a wide repertoire of rhyming slang.

In the evenings Julian worked on both his script of *The Stars Foretell Murder* and his scrupulously faithful adaptation of *A Gun For Sale*, which was "progressing pretty well".[39] Immediately he'd finished it, he sent copies to the BBC and to Graham Greene for approval.

Probably because he couldn't keep up with the rent on his lodgings in Eastergate, Julian had, by late September, found himself a frugal, 10/-a-week ground-floor bedsit in Bognor. It was at the rear of a house at 15 Kimbell Terrace on Belmont Street, sandwiched between the promenade and the main shopping thoroughfare. But his new lodgings were extremely cold. To make matters worse, there were no meals provided, just a morning cup of tea. Nor were there any cooking facilities. And Mrs Morris, his perpetually carpet-slippered landlady, who lived there with her husband, seemed to cook nothing but kippers, the heavy odour of these pervading his room. At least in the early days of his tenancy, all these disadvantages were mitigated by the plentiful material Mr and Mrs Morris — who said they were descended from the High Kings of Ireland — gave him for the anecdotes with which he was, once more, regaling Mac and Lydia.

Now that his scripts were safely out of the way, Julian enquired about getting a job on the funfair where Mac was still working. By putting in a good word for Julian, his friend wangled him a job on the loo-pit, where the punters tried to toss ping-pong balls into jam-jars. No easy task. If they succeeded, their prize was a canary, selected from the cage at the back of the stall. While Mac dealt with the customers, it was Julian's responsibility to dish out the prizes. There weren't many holidaymakers around, so it was about half-an-hour before he had to catch his first canary. Afterwards he forgot to close the door of a cage, enabling the rest of the birds to escape. When the irate stallholder saw what had happened, the grey concrete esplanade flecked with the bright yellow and green of fugitive canaries, he sacked Julian on the spot.

Julian Maclaren-Ross (left) and
C.K. Jaeger (right), whose daughter
Karel is on his lap, sitting in the
garden of Greenleaves, 1940
(© C.K. Jaeger)

Hoover advertisement, 1938
(© Hoover plc)

Lydia Jaeger in costume
for her starring role in
The Barretts of Wimpole Street, 1938
(© C.K. Jaeger)

The Bizarre Life Of Julian Maclaren-Ross

The Man in the Teddy-Bear Coat

Julian had little choice but to register at the local Labour Exchange. This was housed in a small, grimy building on Merchant Street, a bleak dead-end road near the middle of Bognor. On his first trip there, he made a point of polishing his shoes and donning a fresh white shirt, all in an effort to maintain his dignity. Speaking in an unequivocally posh accent, his smart clothes topped by his teddy-bear coat, he courted derision from the men milling round in the street.

Inside the Labour Exchange, it "smelt of sweat and dirt".[1] When Julian was seen by one of the clerks, he was told his application would be vetted by the Unemployment Assistance Board. He duly received a visit from an inspector responsible for carrying out means tests. The inspector looked round his room, asked him how much the rent was and whether he had any other income, then made him sign a form. But Julian heard nothing more for about three weeks, in the course of which he fell into arrears with his landlady, whom he'd grown to detest. Each morning, when the post arrived, Mrs Morris would hover in the hallway while he opened his letters, just in case they contained a cheque. To tide himself over this tricky period, he was reduced to pawning the gold fob-watch his late, unlamented father had given him.

As September came to an end, the situation improved, albeit marginally. War was averted or at least postponed by the Munich agreement. And the long-delayed letter from the Unemployment Assistance Board finally arrived. The letter, notifying him that his application had been approved, instructed him to be at the Labour Exchange on Friday 6 October 1938 at 11.00am.

Due to the severe job shortage afflicting the town, a long, rowdy queue extended right down the street when he got there. His arrival, smart as ever, was greeted by cat-calls and whistles. With nothing to do but eavesdrop on the conversations around him, he waited until he and the others were allowed into the building. Behind the counter sat Mr Youseman, the pompous Supervisor, who paid Julian at the Unmarried Mens' Rate of 17/6d. Mr Youseman dispensed the cash with such palpable contempt that Julian took an instant dislike to him, afterwards making him the butt of many jokes, among them a parody of an

71

advertising slogan, "If you can't use wood, use man."[2]

On subsequent trips to the Labour Exchange, which was often late opening, Julian established himself as a dole queue hero by marching up to the locked door, hammering on it and calling out, "Open in the name of the people!"[3] As he rounded the corner of Merchant Street, the men queuing outside would greet him with a loud cheer, their applause acknowledged by a regal wave of his cane.

Uncongenial as these visits were, like so many of his other experiences they were swiftly recycled in his literary output. Now the temperature had started to dip, his room was too cold to work in, so he did most of his writing in the relative warmth of the Public Library, situated in the former Congressional Sunday School on London Road. The by-product of his mornings at the Labour Exchange was a short story called *Peace in Our Time* — later retitled *Civvy Street* — which he sent without success to a number of magazines, his wavering faith in his artistic vocation bolstered by reading Cyril Connolly's *Enemies of Promise*. He also transcribed another of his friend's anecdotes about India. To this memorable story of the far-reaching ramifications of a hit-and-run accident, he gave the snappy title, *A Bit of a Smash in Madras*.

In the penultimate week of October, his debt to Mrs Morris mounting steadily, he was turfed out of his lodgings. But he found other, even more centrally located accommodation in a tiny Victorian terraced house at 3 Argyll Street. Fearing that his tenancy there might be just as short-lived, his "financial position [...being] worse than ever",[4] the noticeably leaner-looking Julian wrote to the BBC demanding they come to a decision on both his scripts within the next seven days.

His letter provoked a response from Moray McLaren, saying they'd decided to accept his adaptation of *A Gun For Sale*, though McLaren wanted him to liaise with Graham Greene, who had requested several changes. Anxious to share the good news with Mac and Lydia, Julian headed over to the house on Mead Lane where they'd been living ever since they vacated Rose Cottage. The three of them toasted the successful outcome with a bottle of Mac's homemade wine.

By mid-November, there was even more to celebrate. The Jaegers had found somewhere they liked: a colonial-style bungalow. But the rent was higher than Mac could afford on the wage he was earning as a navvy, the funfair having closed for the winter. For him, the solution was simple. Mac planned to ask Julian to move in with them on condition he contributed to the rent and household costs. Left wary by Julian's previous stint as a lodger, Lydia was reluctant to sanction the arrangement. Her better judgement was, however, swayed by the prospect of escaping from their present cramped quarters.

Since Julian had only just received the initial half of his 30 guinea fee from the BBC, more than likely the first money he'd ever earned from writing, he had no hesitation in accepting Mac's offer. With his enthusiastic endorsement, the Jaegers went ahead and signed the lease.

Over the remainder of his tenancy at Argyle Road, Julian embarked on a flurry of activity. In accordance with Graham Greene's instructions, he revised his dramatisation of *A Gun For Sale*. He polished off another script, based on a play that Horsfall-Ertz had read to the writing group. And he made up his mind to adapt a novel Mac had lent him: the cult author G.S. Marlowe's *I Am Your Brother*, an horrific fable about an old woman who keeps her monstrous, reptilian offspring imprisoned in a darkened attic. First, he approached Marlowe and requested permission to adapt his book. He was rewarded with a swift and cordial response, inviting him to London to discuss the idea. In the second week of December, he took the train there, squeezing visits to Broadcasting House and Marlowe's flat into a single day.

When he arrived at the flat, in a peaceful residential district of Kensington, Julian was greeted by a glamorous girl, whom Marlowe introduced as his secretary. Far from being the short, sardonic Englishman Julian had inferred from his writing and genteel pen-name, he turned out to be a huge, amiable blonde Jew, whose clipped speech bore a heavy, possibly Viennese accent. Yet the true origins of Gabriel S. Marlowe, like so much else about him, remained appealingly nebulous.

The visit went even better than Julian had hoped. Not only did he secure permission to go ahead with adapting both *I Am Your Brother* and *Caracas*, one of Marlowe's short stories, but he also hit it off with his host, who suggested they meet again.

That month Julian rejoined Mac and Lydia, with whom he'd enjoyed such a happy spell at Rose Cottage. Their new home was in the unlikely surroundings of Aldwick, a fast-expanding, up-market suburb about a mile from the heart of Bognor, mainly comprising big stucco-clad mock-Tudor confections. Approached via an unmade road, pools of water accumulating in the potholes that punctuated it, their house was at 4 Robin's Drive, part of a short cul-de-sac of steep-roofed little bungalows, each of them fitted with a narrow verandah and a single, disproportionately large dormer-window, providing light for the attic. The house was distinguished by its fresh green paintwork, which inspired them to christen it "Greenleaves".

Julian was allocated the rear bedroom, overlooking the small, well-tended back garden. For this and the cost of the meals Lydia prepared, he handed over the majority of his dole money. The remaining shilling went on cigarettes, his usual Turkish brand abandoned in favour of a much cheaper, more pedestrian one. Even so, he could only sustain a fraction of his previous 50-a-day consumption.

Stretched out on his bed, Julian got on with his adaptation of Marlowe's novel. Occasionally venturing out of his room, he'd shuffle up to Mac, slobbering and contorting his features as he re-enacted the book's key scene, lowering his voice to a sinister, rasping tone as he slowly uttered the words, "I... am... your... brother..."[5]

In the run-up to Christmas, he also collaborated with Martin Jordan on a dramatisation of Harrison Ainsworth's romanticised 1839 account of the burglar Jack Sheppard's criminal career. Because it was a subject Mac had already earmarked, neither Julian nor Martin mentioned it to him.

Still jobless, though anything but idle, Julian and his landlord were so broke they were reduced to cadging money from friends, once teaming up for a raid on a Chichester solicitor whom the Jaegers knew. When they emerged from his house, a few shillings better off, the gloating Julian said, "That'll teach him to be at home on a Saturday morning..."[6]

But they quickly ran out of people willing to give them money. Faced by a desolate Christmas, devoid of any of the seasonal luxuries, Julian devised a cunning solution to their seemingly intractable problem. Only days before all the shops closed for the holiday, he led a sceptical Mac over to the nearest phone-box. From there, he used his last twopenny-bit to ring the butcher's shop across the road. Through the front window of the shop, he and Mac, who was wedged into the phone-box with him, watched the butcher answer the call. Putting on an even more hoity-toity accent than normal, Julian told the butcher that he'd just got back from London and had damn-all in the larder, so would he be a jolly good chap and send round a nice big turkey a.s.a.p.? "And, for goodness sake, don't forget to send me the bill",[7] he added with such apparent sincerity the butcher fell for his act. As if to reward his audacity, Julian's twopenny-bit was regurgitated when he replaced the receiver in its cradle, allowing him to pull the same trick on another credulous shopkeeper.

Against expectations, he and the Jaegers enjoyed a snowbound, traditionally self-indulgent Christmas, their turkey accompanied by plum pudding and fruit cake, washed down by bottles of wine. But they soon felt the repercussions of Julian's ruse. After the snow had thawed and the water had drained away sufficiently for the postman to reach their front door, two hefty bills arrived. These remained unpaid well into the New Year. Several reminders followed, along with warnings of legal action, all addressed to the Jaegers. Unable to settle their debts, Mac had to seek assistance from his affluent brother, who came to the rescue.

At the earliest opportunity, Julian made amends for the trouble his pre-Christmas ploy had caused. Knowing how much Mac admired the author of *I Am Your Brother*, he contacted Marlowe and suggested they get together to discuss his script. To Mac's delight, he obtained a dinner invitation for both of them to Marlowe's plush new flat in a modern block, not far from the Duke of York's Barracks in Chelsea. When they turned up there at the prearranged time, they rang the doorbell insistently, but nobody answered. On the verge of walking away, they gave the bell one final ring. At last Marlowe opened up and showed them in to the lounge, where he poured them both a drink. With no explanation, he left the room. A good thirty minutes went by, his guests beginning to feel increasingly awkward, before he reappeared and proposed they adjourn to the dining-room. Awaiting them on the long, highly polished dining table, there were "three place settings, a neatly wrapped parcel of fish and chips on each plate."[8]

About a month later, Julian submitted his script of *I Am Your Brother* to the BBC who had, by then, contrived to mislay the only copy of his adaptation of *The Stars Foretell Murder*. The next week Gielgud responded to this latest submission with a rejection letter on the grounds that "the majority of [their] listeners would find the theme too gruesome."[9] Julian's consequent gloom was lifted by the news that the BBC had accepted *The Stars Foretell Murder*, the script of which had now resurfaced. Soon afterwards he received the first instalment of his 20 guinea fee. For a while it seemed as if a relatively lucrative career as a radio playwright might be beckoning, a prospect that propelled Julian into a state of euphoria. Coming out of Sainsbury's one day that week, clutching a celebratory bag of chipolatas, he spotted Mac on the other side of the busy street. He caught his friend's attention by waving the bag above his head. In as sonorous and oracular a voice as he could muster, he called out: "The stars foretell... sausages."[10] When he and Mac got home, they cooked the entire pack.

His mood was further buoyed by the acquisition of his first girlfriend since Elizabeth departed. He had more in common with Eileen Cooke than he'd ever had with his wife, not least a shared passion for contemporary fiction. He probably met her in the Lantern Café, the small tearoom she ran on nearby Aldwick Road, just down the street from the house where she lived with her father, her brother and his wife. The older Mr Cooke so disapproved of her new admirer's black humour and cynicism that Eileen had to discourage Julian from visiting her at home. Instead, he'd go to see her every morning at the café. And he'd often join her when she took her dog, Patch, for long walks. During these, he talked about his favourite books, Hemingway's *A Farewell To Arms* offering a recurrent focus for his effusions. One or two evenings a week, he and Eileen would also go out together, dancing and drinking. Much to the disapproval of the Jaegers, who felt he was exploiting her, the good-natured Eileen, like her predecessor, started mothering him, bringing him food parcels, as well as doing his washing and ironing.

Now settled at Greenleaves, most nights he and Mac, who had annexed the cluttered attic for use as a study, would entertain themselves and Lydia by reading aloud extracts from their work. Julian would sometimes act out the latest draft of one of his radio scripts. Alternatively, he'd treat them to the umpteenth rendition of *A Bit of a Smash in Madras*, or another of the stories from his extensive back-catalogue, each re-reading of which led him to make minor, almost imperceptible revisions.

Mac would reciprocate with extracts from *Are Ye There, Lord?*, his bizarre Biblical comedy, written in Scots dialect. These would usually send Julian into hysterical laughter, "rich laughter [...] now bass, now tenor."[11] For weeks after he heard the scene where Moses's wife says, "If I'm no' back in time, dinna forget to take the washing in",[12] he'd repeat the line whenever he went off to meet Eileen.

Early in 1939, Mac showed him the prologue and opening chapters of *Angels on Horseback*, the novel he'd just started. Supportive as ever, Julian found plenty in it to praise, though its vein of whimsical fantasy was far removed from the laconic, downbeat writing he most admired. Set in a town bearing more than a passing resemblance to Bognor, it was decked with in-jokes certain to appeal to Julian, among them the transformation of Morton Swinburne into "Mr Swineburne". It also appealed to him by virtue of its playful, instantly recognisable portraits of he and the other members of their writing group. He was cast as the narcissistic "Count Facto the Magnificent", wielding a sword and dressed in a "uniform of blue and gold",[13] a self-portrait entitled St Facto and the Dragon hanging proudly on his wall. Martin Jordan, on the other hand, featured in the less memorable guise of "Mr Daniel Squib". And Eugene Horsfall-Ertz took the central role of "Professor Limbo", an allusion to "Limbo's Corner", the weekly column he wrote for *The Bognor Regis Observer*.

Delighted by Julian's positive comments, Mac asked him to read each successive chapter as soon as it was written. Once the manuscript had been completed, Julian even offered to type it, ready for it to be submitted to a publisher, though Mac insisted on paying him for his trouble. Not with cash but with cheap cigarettes — one for every page. Julian chain-smoked these while he worked his way through the stack of exercise-books in which the novel was written, a dense cloud filling his bedroom as he tapped away on the portable typewriter he'd bought on an instalment-plan he could ill-afford.

So far, two of Julian's plays had been accepted by the BBC, yet neither of them had been scheduled for broadcast. Denied the second half of his much-needed fee, payable on production, he become digruntled with the Corporation's ponderous workings.

During the second week of March, his mind was taken off his problems by a front-page story in *The Daily Express*, which Mac bought most days. It reported a lurid French murder trial that soon came to fascinate him. Already a knowledgable student of criminological literature, he read each new report with morbid zeal. The accused was the German-born Eugen Weidmann, a debonair, softly spoken poetry-lover who, along with four accomplices, had robbed and murdered half-a-dozen people in Paris, where he'd been plotting a series of kidnappings. Weidmann's ability to disguise himself, enhanced by his fluency in English, French, and German, made him a real-life counterpart to the elusive master-criminals who inhabited the adventure stories with which Julian had grown up. For Julian, Weidmann possessed the same spurious glamour, the same villainous artistry he discerned in the crimes of other serial killers like "Brides-in-the-Bath" Smith, Sydney Fox, and Neill Cream, whom he considered the "criminological equivalent of [...] Hardy, Conrad or Henry James."[14] Transfixed by the case, he talked about one day writing a novel based on Weidmann's crimes.

Just over a week into the 17-day trial, culminating in the defendant's execution, Julian received a letter from the BBC, enclosing "a revised and slightly abbreviated version of [the script of] *A Gun For Sale*",[15] drafted with Graham Greene's approval by a junior member of the department. In reaction to this latest twist in the saga, Julian wrote them a hurried, tetchy note. Besides enquiring whether *A Gun For Sale* and *The Stars Foretell Murder* were timetabled for production, he asked when he could expect the 20 guineas he was owed. To back up his case, he cited a recent piece by Jonah Barrington, *The Daily Express* radio critic, referring to the BBC as having a policy of payment on acceptance.

Julian's note yielded a propitiatory reply from McLaren, letting him know that *A Gun For Sale* had been included in their July – September 1939 schedule, though there was still no exact date for the production. Nor was there any mention of payment. Hoping that Jonah Barrington might somehow influence the BBC to pay up, Julian penned a lengthy letter to him. This corrected what Julian regarded as the misleading impression the piece had given, quoting his own predicament in considerable detail.

By involving Barrington, he only magnified his difficulties. When *The Sunday Express's* resident astrologer, R.H. Naylor, whose column was called *What the Stars Foretell*, heard about Julian's similarly titled play, he complained to the BBC, accusing them of breech of copyright. Alarmed by the problems Julian was causing, McLaren arranged to see him again to discuss the matter. At their meeting, McLaren reassured him that Naylor's accusation had no legal basis. He also told him that the BBC intended to produce *A Gun For Sale* at the earliest possible juncture.

Sure enough, in mid-May Julian was informed that the play had been scheduled for broadcast around the beginning of September. But there was still no news about *The Stars Foretell Murder*. The only consolation was that, according to the contract he'd signed six months previously, he was now eligible for the second half of his fee, regardless of whether the piece went into production.

Spurred on by the impending broadcast of at least one of his plays, he devoted that summer to scripting two more G.S. Marlowe adaptations, both based on short stories, one of them about a pawn-broker's disastrous obsession with a nightclub singer, the other a comedy about a madman who hypnotises a Harley Street specialist and transfers his insanity to the doctor. Julian submitted these to the BBC, but he'd already so antagonised McLaren and Gielgud with his hectoring letters that they were reluctant to even consider any more scripts by him.

On the first Friday of August, McLaren wrote to Julian updating him on the latest development regarding his ill-fated dramatisation of *A Gun For Sale*. Its production had been postponed by the Programme Committee, who felt that "any play, however fantastic, dealing with the possibility of a general war or with such controversial subjects as an armaments racket is certain of a hostile reception."[16] Under normal circumstances, Julian would have protested vehemently. Not this time, though, because he was too distracted by the ubiquitous preparations for war.

The long-anticipated hostilities were declared the very week *A Gun For Sale* was due to be transmitted. A combination of the disrupted radio schedules, the BBC's decision to stop broadcasting thrillers, and the threat of sudden conscription persuaded Julian to conclude there was no point in either continuing to write drama, or keeping up the payments on the typewriter he'd bought.

With the outbreak of war, there were none of the expected air raids. Yet the conflict quickly became impossible to ignore, even in a backwater like Bognor. Trips into town were liable to be disrupted by poison gas exercises, requiring everyone in the locality to wear the gas-masks with which they'd been issued. The main post office was gradually concealed behind a protective wall of sandbags; the beaches were declared a prohibited area, patrolled by the police; the esplanade was disfigured by concrete tank-traps, pill-boxes, and miles of barbed-wire; and the Butlin's Funfair closed down, its closure leaving Julian's friend, Micky Hopper, out of work. To Lydia's annoyance, Julian invited Micky to pop round to Greenleaves whenever he wanted. Under the influence of Micky, who sometimes brought his freebooting Cockney pals round with him, rhyming slang and terms like "charva"[17] and "scarper"[18] and "palone"[19] were incorporated into the household language. Even Lydia found herself referring to the "Cain and Abel"[20] instead of the table. And Mac joked about how, on account of all their dubious visitors, they ought to alter the bungalow's name from Greenleaves to "Tealeaves".[21]

Sitting beside the fire while Julian and Mac got on with their writing, Micky would find something to read from among the piles of books that dotted every available surface. His preference was for slangy, straightforwardly written pictures of working-class life, for books such as *They Drive By Night*, *Brighton Rock*, and *Down and Out In London and Paris*. These led him to announce that he was going to try his hand at a short story. Nobody paid much attention, but when he showed them his pencil-written manuscript they were pleasantly surprised. Composed entirely in believable dialogue, it portrayed life in a doss house. So enthusiastic was the response from Julian and Mac, he dashed off a series of other stories. He also started an autobiography called *Dog End*, portions of which Julian considered "outrageously obscene".[22] As a favour to Micky, Julian selected three of the best stories, corrected the spelling, and typed them up, so they could be submitted for publication. Meanwhile, inspired by one of Julian's library books, featuring reproductions of paintings by Salvador Dali and Tristram Hillier, Micky planned some surrealist pictures of his own. He transferred two of his designs onto canvas and, supervised by Julian, rendered them in oils. In true surrealist style, he titled them *The Birth of a Nation* and *The Parson Preached a Sermon on Palm Sunday*, the titles bearing no relation to their subjects.

Julian knew it was only a matter of time before he and the others were conscripted for military service, yet he wouldn't allow that to scupper his literary ambitions. Encouraged by the friendship he'd forged with Graham Greene, with whom he'd taken to exchanging regular phone-calls and letters, he made another stab at turning his experiences as a vacuum-cleaner salesman into a novel, as well as trying to sell some of his short stories. In mid-November, he spotted a half-page advert in the *The New Statesman and Nation*, promoting a soon-to-be-launched monthly magazine, intended to showcase the work of established writers alongside unknowns. The magazine was called *Horizon* and the editor was Cyril Connolly, already familiar to Julian both as an essayist and as the author of *Enemies of Promise*. Julian sent him a folder containing the handwritten manuscripts of four stories. These consisted of *A Bit of a Smash in Madras*, *Happy As The Day Is Long*, *Five Finger Exercises*, and *The Snows of Yesterday*, a poignant, skilfully fictionalised account of his childhood visit to his parents' former landlady in South Norwood. While he awaited a decision, an old friend of Micky's — a pimp who had once served a prison sentence — suddenly showed up and talked Micky into leaving town with him. Watching them drive off together in an ostentatious red sportscar, Julian was convinced that was the last he'd ever see of Micky.

For a month or so after Micky left, the two surrealist canvases remained propped in the corner of the sitting-room. Bored with dusting them and worried about the risk of her infant daughter scraping off some of the lead-based paint and eating it, Lydia eventually consigned them to the attic.

By December that year, neither Julian nor Mac had received their call-up papers. To add to the frustrating sense of stasis, the BBC had decided there was no prospect of broadcasting *A Gun For Sale*, so they paid Julian the rest of his fee. More disturbingly, there had been no news from *Horizon*, aside from a printed acknowledgement-slip. Annoyed at the delay, Julian sent Connolly a postcard asking for his stories back. Connolly replied promptly, explaining that the folder had been misfiled and the stories inside were now being read.

Not expecting anything to come of it, Julian carried on as before, his routine livened up by an invitation to join the Jaegers for a reading of *Julius Caesar* at the house in Littlehampton where Martin Jordan lived with his parents. Just before Christmas, Julian received a long, friendly letter from Connolly, who agreed to publish *A Bit of a Smash in Madras* and expressed his intention to feature the other stories at some future date. Payment would be at the rate of two guineas per thousand words.

To mark his forthcoming debut as a published fiction writer, Julian bought a bottle of cheap wine which he shared with Mac and Lydia. He also treated himself to a trip to the Pier Cinema, where the newly released Fred Astaire movie, *The Story of Vernon and Irene Castle*, was being screened. Seated in the massive cinema cinema, the music blotting out the swish of the sea below, he felt a sense of "elation and tremendous triumph".[23]

On Monday 1 January 1940, a month later than planned, the magazine in which his story would be appearing was launched. Its 3,500 print-run rapidly sold out, necessitating a second edition that sold out too. But his elation began to recede when both Cyril Connolly and Stephen Spender, *Horizon's* uncredited co-editor, revealed their reservations about his story. The most disconcerting of these had its origins in a letter Julian had sent Connolly, who had expressed astonishment that he'd produced *A Bit of a Smash in Madras* without ever having been to India. In his letter, Julian confessed that the story was based on a real-life incident, told to him by a friend. Eager to avert the possibility, however remote, of getting caught up in a libel suit, Connolly and Spender insisted on the story being relocated from Madras to the imaginary province of Chandrapore, the setting for E.M. Forster's *A Passage to India*. In doing so, it would obviously have to be retitled. The situation was aggravated by the news that the magazine's printers were likely to refuse to print it unless the expletive-studded text was censored.

Besides changing the opening sentence from "Absolute fact, I knew fuck-all about it"[24] to "Absolute fact I knew Sweet F.A. about it", Spender suggested a succession of substitute phrases that could be deployed throughout the rest of the story. He listed these "in the form of a short poem:
'Pissed-up.'
'By Christ.'
'Balls.'
'Bugger.'[25]

Equipped with Spender's unwittingly amusing list, Julian — whose story had "created a feeling of struggles and rows"[26] at *Horizon* — decided to confront Connolly, so he made an appointment to see him. This was fixed for sometime in March. On his uppers as usual, Julian seized the opportunity of a lift with Eileen and her chic friend Miss Dyson, known as "Dy". Eileen's friend owned a soft-topped Riley in which they were driving up to London to do some shopping. They dropped him in High Holborn. From there, he walked over to 6 Selwyn House, Lansdowne Terrace in Bloomsbury, where the magazine was based. As the original advert had made plain, the elegance of the address belied the rough-and-ready nature of its premises. These comprised not some well-appointed suite of offices, but the back-room of Spender's two-room flat, on the ground-floor of a narrow Georgian building, looking out across a playground.

The thirty-six-year-old Connolly, dressed in a tweed suit and silk tie, met Julian at the door. He was small and plump with doughy features to match, his eyes concealed beneath hooded lids, his rotund face crowned by dark, slightly receding hair, combed away from his forehead. He struck Julian as "a formidable person."[27] His indolent yet authoritative and vaguely military bearing led Julian to dub him "Colonel Connolly".[28]

It was on this first visit to Lansdowne Terrace that Julian also encountered Sonia Brownell, the most striking of the troop of talented and attractive girls who provided largely unpaid administrative assistance to *Horizon*. In a previous guise, Sonia had been an artists' model, posing for so many members of the Euston Road School of painters (among them William Coldstream, with whom she'd had an affair) she was nicknamed "the Euston Road Venus". Her dark, seductive eyes, her immaculately made-up face, her shoulder-length mid-blonde hair, her sceptically arched eyebrows, her forceful personality, her rapid and excitable way of talking, her tendency to litter her speech with perfectly pronounced French phrases, together with her influential role not just with Connolly but with that other important editor, John Lehmann,[29] all contributed to her considerable allure. Relishing the sexual power she wielded over men, she was, in the majority of cases, happy to flirt with them, tease them, and lead them on, only to lose interest as soon as they tried to start anything more serious. Most men who came into contact with her at this period seem to have ended up besotted by her. Despite his avowed predilection for brunettes, Julian was no exception, egged on by her friendliness and "extreme deference"[30] towards him. He joined a roster of devotees as diverse as Colonel Connolly himself; the writer George Stonier, better-known as "Fanfarlo"; and the future politician, Woodrow Wyatt, whose literary aspirations had sucked him into the Colonel's orbit. So conspicuous was Julian's amorous interest in her, which she purported to find embarrassing, the Colonel abruptly truncated their meeting, whisked him out of the office, and proposed they continue their discussion over lunch the following day.

On his way out, Julian — in a welcome breech of the established etiquette of payment on publication — was presented with a cheque for nine guineas. The Colonel then introduced him to the tall, bearded Bill Makins, the magazine's Business Manager, who was prepared to arrange overnight accommodation if he needed it. Accepting the Colonel's suggestion, Julian spent the rest of the day drinking beer and scotch with Makins, initially in a cellar bar in Russell Square, afterwards moving on to Makins's bedsit in neighbouring Guilford Street. Before the evening was over, he'd agreed to appoint the persuasive and dynamic Makins as his literary agent. It was through him that Julian found out that the Colonel had decided against publishing his three other stories, because he felt they weren't up to the standard of *A Bit of a Smash in Madras*. These were subsequently passed on by Stephen Spender to John Lehmann at *New Writing and Daylight*, for which Spender gave editorial support. But Lehmann chose not to accept them either.

As arranged, next day Julian went to the Café Royal, treated by Connolly as an annexe to his office. Positioned in a secluded spot on the gallery that ran round the back restaurant, the walls of it decked out with mirrors, not to mention paintings of mermaids and bunches of grapes, he was often to be found secreted at one of the tables in between the potted palms, its marble-top covered by books, manuscripts, and proofs. According to Julian, they chatted about *The Face on the Cutting-Room Floor*, "a pseudonymous near pastiche of the tough American crime-story"[31] that he suspected the Colonel had written. And he claimed that the Colonel had gone on to tell him an unflattering story about Somerset Maugham before settling down to discuss the changes to *A Bit of a Smash in Madras*, changes regarded by the Colonel as lamentable but essential. Afraid that a refusal to compromise might bring about a sequel to the *Penguin Parade* fiasco, Julian capitulated to all the Colonel's demands.

When they parted at around 2.00pm, he popped over to see Marlowe in his Chelsea pad. It was only then that his friend's financial plight became evident. In his desperation to evade his creditors, Marlowe turned out to be planning to flee to Norway. Not, with the benefit of hindsight, the most sensible of destinations for a Jewish intellectual. That year the Nazis invaded, and Julian never heard from Marlowe again, his apparent disappearance earning him an honorary place in Julian's pantheon of mystery men, like the Rumanian swindler who twice faked his own death.

*

It was now over a year since the BBC had accepted *The Stars Foretell Murder*. In spite of their abandonment of the policy of not broadcasting thrillers, Moray McLaren wrote to Julian on Wednesday 3 April to inform him that there was no possibility of them producing his play. Determined to salvage something from this latest debacle, Julian fired off a swift reply, asking the BBC to honour their contract by forwarding him the second half of his fee. Of course he could have done with the money himself, but he'd already promised to pay it to Anthony Skene as a commission.

Several more weeks went by without the cheque arriving. In addition, he had to face the discouraging news that "two sets of printers [had] flatly refused to print"[32] *A Bit of A Smash*, as his story had now been renamed. Yet Colonel Connolly wrote to assure him that he'd "publish the story if he had to get printers from Madras to do it."[33]

At the beginning of May, Julian contacted the BBC again, announcing that he was "not prepared to wait indefinitely".[34] His accompanying threat of court proceedings chivvied them into sending Anthony Skene the overdue cheque.

This frustrating end to his once promising ambitions to become a radio playwright was counterbalanced by his imminent breakthrough as a short story writer. Not only was he due to make his debut in *Horizon*, but the Colonel had also told him that they'd be interested in publishing the much longer story he was writing about his experiences in the South of France. Ironically entitled *The Simple Life*, it traced the fluctuating, complex relationships between a shady, drug-taking landlord and his expatriate tenants, sharing a remote chalet in the mountains beyond Nice during the summer of 1930. Makins led him to believe that the Colonel was prepared to devote an entire edition of the magazine to it.

The publication of the sixth issue of *Horizon* on Thursday 6 June at last launched Julian's literary career. Just as Makins had promised, the title of his contribution was featured on the John Piper-designed cover in bold, inky type, afforded extra prominence by being positioned right in the centre of a list that included George Orwell and J.B. Priestley. But Julian's satisfaction was diminished when he saw they'd misspelt his surname, crediting him as "J. Maclaryn-Ross".

His star-billing, combined with the magazine's growing reputation, ensured that his story attracted a significant readership. Its wry humour, crisp dialogue, and comic vivacity marked him out as one of the rising talents of English fiction. Moreover, its convincing sense of place must have prompted most of its readers to arrive at the same misconception as V.S. Pritchett. Like Colonel Connolly before him, Pritchett assumed its hitherto unknown author was an "Anglo-Indian writer who had roughed up his Kipling and had learnt something from Hemingway."[35]

Immediately after the publication of *A Bit of a Smash*, Julian was approached by Rupert Hart-Davis, the youngest of the triumvirate of directors in charge of the Jonathan Cape imprint. Hart-Davis, who had already proved himself an astute judge of both literary worth and commercial potential, offered to meet him to discuss the possibility of a book deal. In late June or early July, Julian went to see him in his small first-floor office in Bedford Square. Every inch the traditional gentleman publisher, Hart-Davis favoured tweedy clothes and a thick, neatly trimmed moustache which concealed his comparative youth. In characteristically straightforward style, he told Julian that he was positive Cape would publish a collection of his stories, provided he could write twenty more as good as the one *Horizon* had just published. So as to consolidate the positive impression made by *A Bit of a Smash*, Julian sent him some more manuscripts, among them what he envisaged as the title story, *A Drink At Harrison's*, now retitled *The Hell of a Time*.

Delighted and flattered though Julian was by the idea of joining Jonathan Cape's stable of authors, the target Hart-Davis had set him remained tantalisingly out of reach, because his call-up papers were bound to arrive before he had a chance to fulfil his brief. For Julian, the war seemed to have broken out at precisely the wrong time, its outbreak guaranteed to impede his nascent literary career. To him, it was a source not so much of terror but of inconvenience. Unlike Mac, whose understandable apprehension about military service rose with every passing day, he regarded the prospect with equanimity, borne out of an unswerving confidence in his ability to handle any situation in which he found himself. Within weeks of his meeting with Hart-Davis, that ostensibly boundless self-assurance would be put to the test.

Soldier of Misfortune

As a memento of their remaining weeks together, Mac talked the camera-shy Julian into letting Lydia take a snapshot of them seated in front of the verandah at Greenleaves. While Mac struck a casual pose, his infant daughter Karel perched on his knee, Julian appeared stiff and self-conscious. Squinting in the bright summer sunshine, eyes averted from the lens, he held a book over his cream-jacketed ribcage, like a shield or, maybe, an emblem of his chosen profession.

Not long after the picture was taken, he and Mac were summoned separately to London for the compulsory medical examination that served as the undignified prelude to conscription into the armed forces. His poor eyesight and flimsy nine-stone physique notwithstanding, Julian was, along with Mac, graded "A-1". The doctors, in other words, deemed them fit for front-line military service.

A few weeks afterwards, the first set of call-up papers arrived at Greenleaves. Addressed to Julian, these ordered him to report to the 302 ITC (Infantry Training Centre) at Blandford Camp in Dorset no later than noon on Thursday 18 July 1940. Before heading there, he sent the first half of the manuscript of *The Simple Life* to Bill Makins, who had promised to show it to Colonel Connolly. He also rounded up a selection of books that might be of interest to his ailing Aunt Mary, then posted them to her north London lodgings. Certain he'd be returning to Bognor when the war was over, he stored the rest of his books at Eileen's house, together with his manuscripts, letters, clothes, and typewriter, the hefty arrears on which had already led to threats of prosecution.

His parting from both Eileen and the Jaegers, who had become his surrogate family, was painful, yet he approached the ordeal with the dry-eyed stoicism of the fictional heroes he so admired. Weighed down by two attaché cases, containing his writing things, the only typescript of his play about Jack Sheppard, plus the unfinished manuscript of the concluding half of *The Simple Life*, he made his way to Bognor station, his teddy-bear coat insulating him against the heavy rain. When he boarded the train, the elderly porter — a veteran of several campaigns himself — gave him a few words of warning: "They can do anything in the army bar give you a baby. But keep you trap shut and your bowels open and you can't come to no harm."[1]

Like all wartime trains, the one he took down the coast would have been crowded with uniformed men. Hoping for some invaluable last minute tips on the tough guy act he'd been honing for so long, he spent the journey reading a Peter Cheyney thriller. Due to the late-running trains, he was still travelling when the noon deadline expired. Hardly the best way to start his army career. His predicament was, however, shared by plenty of other men.

Sometime towards the end of the afternoon, he joined the gaggle of conscripts who were waiting at Bournemouth station. From there, they were bused to their destination, 14 miles to the north-west of the city, the continued downpour veiling the nearby town of Blandford Forum.

The ITC consisted not of the dismal huddle of tents Julian had envisaged, but a series of wooden huts, distributed round a large parade-ground. On disembarking from the bus, he was stripped of his fancy hyphenated surname and enlisted in the Essex Regiment as No. 6027033 Private Ross, J. of the 7th Platoon of A Company, involuntarily maintaining his family tradition of military service. Though it was early evening by that time, his tardiness went unpunished.

Conspicuous in their civilian clothes, he and the others were "conducted to a clamorous cookhouse where meat-loaf, tinned marmalade and orange tea"[2] awaited them. He was then assigned to a big barrack-hut, known as "a spider" because of the way its rooms radiated out from the middle like a web. Altogether it housed twenty-five men. Each of them had an iron-framed bed with an accompanying wall-mounted locker, and electric reading-light. There was even central heating and an interconnected, graffiti-covered washroom with a plentiful supply of hot water. All a far cry from the rudimentary conditions he'd anticipated. It nonetheless brought back unpleasant memories of the dormitory at Le Châlet and the trauma of being a new boy in a strange environment.

Seeing his teddy-bear coat draped across his bed, a group of recruits from the previous intake huddled round it, telling their "mates to take a butcher's"[3] and speculating on "what kind of pansy would have the neck to go round in such a get-up."[4]

Throughout that evening, a stream of men clattered "up and down the wooden corridors, calling out at the entrance of each hut: 'Anybody here from Birmingham?' (Or Bradford or Tooting Bec, as the case may be.) Asked the name of [his] home town, [Julian] replied, 'Bognor Regis', since that [...] seemed a more suitable answer than Nice".[5] There was nobody else from Bognor, "but two blokes from Pompey, as [his] nearest neighbours, took fraternal charge of [him]"[6] and showed him round the camp, pointing out the chalky bomb-craters caused by a recent air-raid.

Next morning, he and his fellow conscripts were woken at six o'clock sharp. Being a habitually late riser, Julian had trouble springing punctually out of bed. He and the others were given an hour in which to wash, shave, and dress, ready for breakfast at seven, and the early parade at eight. It was hard for him to reacclimatise to the type of coercive "don't do as I do, do as I tell"[7] regime he'd last come across at school. But his education had at least prepared him for the travails of communal living, for the ribald humour, the farting, the incessant swearing, the monotonous scraping rhythm of boot-brushes, the whispering after lights-out, the squeaking bedsprings, and the murmur of people talking in their sleep.

On his first full day in the army, he was introduced by the Sergeant-Instructor to "the idiotic routine of square-bashing".[8] Since A Company hadn't yet been issued with rifles, these being in short supply, they used broomsticks instead. His myopia made it hard for him to synchronise his movements with everyone else's. And he had difficulty coping with the physical demands of drilling on account of the sedentary existence he'd been leading lately, a thirty-a-day nicotine habit eroding what little stamina he possessed. Yet he was far from unhappy, the rigours of training offset by the barrack-room camaraderie and the comedy he discerned in most situations. Shortly after his arrival at the ITC, he wrote Mac such a witty account of his initial impressions of the army that Mac passed it on to Martin Jordan, who was left "completely doubled up [...,] tears stream[ing] down his face."[9]

Soon Julian had struck up friendships with the Catholic chaplain, Father Rumfitt, who lent him books; with George Walsh, a driver from the Military Transport section, who was so interested in his writing that he borrowed a sheaf of manuscripts; and with "the boys"[10] in his hut, most of them known by their nicknames — "Lofty", "Taff", "Mick", "Jock", "Irish Pete", "Dusty" Miller, and "Spud" Murphy, to name but a few. Among them, there were two illiterates. One of these was an ex-miner who came to rely on Julian to compose love letters for him to his wife. Because she couldn't write either, his wife had to beg the same favour from the local parson, whose surprisingly spicy replies were "read aloud to the husband in the presence of the whole barrack-room."[11]

Julian's earlier optimism about his ability to cope with military life had, to date, been vindicated. The only causes for complaint were provided by their stingy rations, by the failure of his mother (who had settled in Southend) to reply to the conciliatory letter he'd written, and by the prospect of the impending compulsory course of innoculations, previewed with sadistic glee by the more experienced recruits.

From time to time, RAF fighter aircraft would roar overhead to jocular shouts of "Here comes Hitler!",[12] juxtaposed by whistling noises mimicking the sound of falling bombs. But there was no sign of the Luftwaffe, aside from the craters Julian had seen. His first experience of enemy attack came when he and the boys were lolling in the barrack-hut around tea-time. A series of distant explosions, unheralded by any air-raid sirens, sent a Lance-Corporal charging into their hut. He ordered them to shelter in the trenches, where they remained until the danger had passed.

About a fortnight into the training programme, Julian and the rest of the platoon — who had now been equipped with helmets and rifles — were marching across the baked-earth parade-ground one afternoon when his left knee inexplicably seized up. The resultant limp made it impossible for him to keep in step. He was told to fall out and report to the MO (Medical Officer) the following morning. Having examined Julian's knee, the MO referred him to a specialist at a local hospital, probably in Dorchester. There he was prescribed two sessions of electrical massage every week before being returned by ambulance to the ITC.

Much to his relief, the MO at Blandford Camp reassigned him to what were termed "light duties", these comprising clerical work in the Company Office. Not that he had much to do there, boredom rapidly setting in.

To keep himself entertained during the evenings, he became the pianist in the unit dance-band. Together they rehearsed the accompaniment to a stage show, featuring his pal, George Walsh, who performed an act in which he pretended to be an officer. Julian also devoted some of his spare-time to trying to set up a library at the camp. In between all that, he carried on writing *The Simple Life*. Such was the pleasure he derived from it, the nostalgic setting enabling him to escape from the ascetic present into the hedonistic past, it expanded way beyond the 10,000-word target specified by Colonel Connolly.

When Eileen, who had been given a lift in Dy's car, visited him on Saturday 10 August, bringing with his typewriter on which he planned to type up the second half of his novella, she found him in high spirits. That weekend she stayed in Blandford Forum, but army regulations prevented Julian from leaving the ITC for more than a few "lovely hours".[13] Reunited, the two of them wandered round the network of pretty Georgian streets, their chattering interrupted by passionate kisses that left Eileen's lips sore.

Hearing how inadequate his rations were, on her return to Bognor she posted Julian the first of what became a regular supply of cakes from her café. It reached him, battered by its journey through the postal system, about the same time as an encouraging letter from the Colonel, who announced that he'd read and enjoyed the first half of *The Simple Life*. He was now anxious to get hold of the rest of it. Well though Julian's writing had been going, he found the Colonel's impatience to read the finished manuscript so offputting it spawned a bout of self-doubt severe enough to make him wonder whether the success of *A Bit of a Smash* had been merely "a splash in the pan".[14]

His depression was intensified by what was known as "needle drill":[15] the painful course of innoculations he and the boys underwent during the third week of August. Its nauseating side-effects necessitated an obligatory 48 hours off duty, spent confined to camp. So worried was Eileen by the gloomy tenor of his latest letter, she wrote him an unusually prolix reply, urging him not to give in because she knew he was destined to achieve the literary fame he sought. Even though the Lantern Café was in danger of going out of business, she enclosed yet another food-parcel for him to share with the boys. Despite all her encouragement, he temporarily gave up writing prose fiction and went back to his half-finished radio drama about Jack Sheppard, which he dreamed of selling as a screenplay.

A dramatic diversion from his troubles came in the form of an official-looking envelope, handed to him by the Orderly Corporal while he was working in the Company Office on Friday 23 August. He didn't recognise the handwriting, but he could see it had been forwarded from Bognor by Lydia Jaeger. It contained a letter from Major R.C. Baker, who announced that he was defending Fusilier M. Hopper at a court-martial. The letter requested Julian's presence as a defence witness. To enable him to be there, the court-martial had been adjourned until the Saturday after next. As part of the defence case, Julian was asked to bring with him the manuscripts of the short stories Micky had left behind at Greenleaves.

The whole thing seemed so improbable that Julian wondered whether it might be an elaborate hoax. But his suspicions were allayed when another of the recruits in his unit showed him the inside front-page of that Sunday's *News of the World*. Under the headline "SOLDIERS' NOTEBOOK: 'DIRECT USE TO ENEMY' ALLEGATION",[16] it described how the court, meeting in private, had heard charges against Fusilier Michael Hopper for breaching the Defence Regulations. "It was alleged that Hopper had in his possession a notebook containing two sketches of an RAF station and information as to factories and bomber objectives in Great Britain," the article explained. "It was added that he also had a German dictionary."[17]

Further down that column, there was a summary of Micky's defence. "When asked how he had collected the information," the story went on, "Hopper was alleged to have replied that when living at Bognor Regis a novelist, Julien Maclaren Ross [sic] became interested in him as he had a flair for writing short stories. Hopper had decided to collect material for a book about the war after it was over."[18]

Positive that his friend was the victim of a mix-up, the minor inaccuracies in the article feeding his instinctive scepticism, Julian contacted Eileen and asked her to fish out Micky's manuscripts from among the stack of papers he'd left with her. He told her to post these to Major Baker when she found them.

On Monday morning he was sent to see his Company Commander, who had already been notified about the court-martial. In recognition of his pivotal role in it, Julian ended up being granted a week's leave to attend the hearing. Along with the accompanying documentation, he was given details of train times, as well as a return ticket to London, where the court-martial was being held. Unhappy about his scruffy appearance, his Company Commander ordered him to get his hair cut. To his chagrin, he was also ordered to draw a full set of equipment from the stores, which he'd have to lug across town.

As instructed, he reported to the Company Office next morning, carrying a bulging backpack, his hair cut to an acceptable length, his uniform adorned with carefully polished brass buckles. A ride in the back of an army truck had been organised for him from the ITC to Blandford Forum station.

London had changed considerably since his last visit. Its skyline was dotted with portly barrage balloons, their silver skins reflecting the light; an appreciable number of its buildings had been ravaged by bombing; and its streets were now flooded with the uniforms of numerous nationalities. In sapping heat that emphasised the unaccustomed weight of his backpack, still limping despite all the medical treatment he'd received, he made his way from Waterloo Station to the Royal Fusiliers' ITC at Hounslow Barracks in south-west London. When he got there, he was led down a cool passageway to the prison cell where Micky was being held. His friend looked much the same as ever. Though Micky had been in detention for almost two months, he was in a characteristically chirpy mood. He and Julian were allowed a brief chat before Julian was shown through to an unfinished outbuilding, as yet minus electricity, glass in the windows, or even a door. Inside there were several camp-beds. He was allocated one of these, then taken to see the acting CSM (Company Sergeant-Major), who told him that the officer defending Micky wanted to interview him at 0900 hours the following day. In the meantime Julian was permitted to leave the barracks on condition he returned by midnight. Taking advantage of this unexpected freedom, he went to the cinema that night. The sirens were wailing in another part of the city as he emerged from the darkened auditorium into the even darker street. Somewhere in the distance he could hear the angry hammering of anti-aircraft fire.

After an uncomfortable night's sleep, he went to see Major Baker, who discussed Micky's case with him and showed him the confiscated notebooks. The combination of German phrases copied from a dictionary and Micky's liberal use of contractions gave their contents the appearance of code. In explaining how he'd got to know Micky and had assisted him with his writing, Julian mentioned that Micky's artistic interests extended to painting too. Major Baker said it'd be helpful if examples of his pictures could be procured, so Julian suggested that Mac, who was still awaiting his call-up papers, should be summoned as a witness and asked to fetch the two paintings stowed in their attic. Exploiting the situation in order to give Eileen a free holiday in London, Julian recommended her as another potential defence witness.

Every morning for the rest of that week, Julian assisted Major Baker's painstaking preparation of the defence case by examining Micky's manuscripts and making sure every element of their story tallied. In the afternoons and evenings, he was free to go to the cinema and eat out, excursions that gave him "a pleasant rest from the routine of army life".[19]

When the day of the court-martial came round, he and Micky were shepherded into the back of a camouflaged civilian car that took them across London to the Duke of York's Barracks, where the hearing was due to be held in private. Micky, who was confident he'd get off the charges, talked about how he wanted to "go abroad"[20] and "see some action"[21] because "parades and bullshit got on his wick".[22] The moment they arrived at the barracks, Micky was escorted away while Julian hung round in an ante-room until he was called as the opening defence witness.

At length, a pair of Military Policemen marched him into the court-room, "looking a complete mess"[23] despite all the regalia he was wearing. Owing to the sensitive nature of the charges, the press were excluded. Once Julian had saluted the white-haired President of the Court and taken the oath, he was ushered over to the witness-stand, from where he gave his well-rehearsed testimony. Then Captain Nield, the Prosecuting Officer, grilled him about Micky's alleged literary aspirations, which the Captain treated with condescending disbelief. The cross-examination over, Julian was shepherded out of the court-room. On his way to the exit, he passed Mac, both Micky's surrealist canvases clamped under his arm.

Proceedings were finished by around lunchtime, leaving the President of the Court to decide on the verdict. Yet Major Baker was in no doubt Micky's acquittal was now a formality. Julian and Mac shook hands with Micky and wished him luck. Eileen, who had done her bit by supplying the Major with a written statement, was waiting for them outside. Over a slap-up lunch at the Café Royal, they celebrated the successful conclusion to Micky's trial and the forthcoming publication of *Angels on Horseback*, which was co-dedicated to Julian "for his encouragement".[24]

Since he still had a day-and-a-half's leave remaining, he and Eileen spent the rest of the weekend together in London, their nerves tested by regular sirens. His enjoyable sabbatical from army life ended on the evening of Sunday 1 September when he rejoined his regiment, many of whom would have read the sketchy reports of the trial printed in the national papers.

Numerous hospital visits had made no discernable difference to his troublesome knee, so the MO decided there wasn't any point in persisting with the treatment. Instead, he recommended Julian should appear before an army Medical Board, which would examine and re-grade him for a more appropriate role elsewhere. Having been officially declared sick, Julian was barred by the Company Commander from leaving his barrack-hut, where he spent his time writing letters to Eileen and lying in bed reading. Not just novels and literary magazines, but the army regulations, his effortless knack of parroting whole sections of them causing tension between him and the officers. His comrades, who regarded these apparently "cushy"[25] conditions with envy, "couldn't understand why... [he] wasnt [sic] contented."[26] He was, however, frustrated by the enforced inactivity. This gave him time to fret about the possibility of being invalided out of the army and prevented from making a direct contribution to the war-effort.

The tedium of the next seven or eight days was alleviated only by the arrival of a chocolate cake from Eileen, followed by a letter from her. Pessimistic about her chances of surviving the nightly air-raids, she revealed that she'd made her will, "leaving him enough to live on for a few months while [he wrote] a book."[27] Should her fears come true, she told him to "put the book, when it is published, on [her] grave."[28]

He was desperate for her to visit him, but a combination of a lack of money and the disrupted train services prevented her from getting to Dorset. His already low spirits were lowered even further by two irritating developments. To start with, he lent his typewriter to someone, who broke it. And, in the second week of September, he was transferred to the 1st Platoon, the change of unit requiring a change of barrack-hut, the move cutting him off from most of the friends he had made.

Within only a few days of shifting his accumulated belongings into a new hut, behind the A Company parade-ground, he received a summons to appear before the Medical Board. That same day he was driven ten miles by ambulance from Blandford Camp to Shaftesbury Military Hospital. He expected to be examined straightaway, then taken back to his unit. But the anticipated Medical Board hadn't yet been scheduled. While he was waiting for it, the Senior Medical Officer allocated him a bed in Ward 9, where he was issued with what were known as "Hospital Blues": the Sick Soldiers' Uniform of red tie, white flannelette shirt and blue serge jacket, as well as a matching waistcoat and trousers.

If he'd known he was going to be detained there, he wouldn't have left behind his possessions — everything from clean laundry and manuscripts to cash and cigarettes. Concerned that they might be stolen, he wrote to Father Rumfitt, explaining the situation and asking him to arrange for them to be forwarded to the hospital. He also asked the Chaplain to retrieve the manuscripts he'd lent to George Walsh.

Because he didn't have the cash to buy the Fifth Avenue brand of cigarettes which he had taken to smoking, he sent a telegram to Eileen requesting money. She obliged by wiring him 10/-. All she could spare. But it went astray, so he sought help from Aunt Mary, who gave him the cash he needed.

Besides returning the stories Julian had lent him, George Walsh loaded the rest of Julian's belongings onto one of the ambulances that made the daily run from the ITC to the hospital, where Julian was still waiting for his Medical Board. The understanding MO in charge of Ward 9, meanwhile, prescribed conventional massage and physiotherapy for his defective knee.

To help pass the time, Julian was allowed to take up a congenial job in the hospital library. Though he tried to persuade Eileen to visit him again, business at her café was still so slack she couldn't afford the train-fare to Shaftesbury. In any case, there was always the worry that she might arrive, only to discover he'd been posted elsewhere. It was far more sensible, she argued, to wait until he received his imminent three-monthly entitlement to seven days' leave. Unhindered by hospital visiting hours, they could then be together in Middleton-on-Sea, where she'd arranged for Dy to let them both stay. For the moment, however, Julian had to make do with a stream of entertaining, gossipy letters from her, usually signed "Fondest love dearest"[29] and including "an extra wag of [the] tail"[30] from her dog.

The Medical Board didn't meet until the first week of October. Once they had examined Julian, they reclassified him as "B-2": suitable only for garrison duties at home and abroad. Yet it transpired they'd inadvertently contravened the correct procedure, which required a prior examination by a surgical specialist. An appointment with just such a person was booked soon afterwards. The specialist discovered that Julian had irreparably damaged the tendon in his left knee. Julian was convinced this was the legacy of an incident when, as a twelve-year-old, he'd been knocked down by a bicycle. Whatever the cause, it made no difference to the diagnosis. The specialist ruled that Julian was unfit for the infantry. It was a verdict which must have pleased him, because he'd set his heart on more office work.

At that point, though, the MO responsible for regrading him went on leave. The deputising MO, who disagreed with the diagnosis, then ordered Julian to return to his unit to resume his training.

Back at the ITC in Dorset, he reported to an Orderly Sergeant he'd never seen before. The man informed him that his company had been evacuated. That night he joined a group of equally disorientated recruits who had taken refuge in an unlocked barrack-hut. On the morning of Tuesday 8 October they were driven by truck through the autumnal countryside to Blandford Forum or, perhaps, Bournemouth. There they got on a packed train, bound for an unknown destination. The journey was so long and circuitous Julian assumed they must have been in Scotland, instead of which they found themselves in East Anglia.

It was dark when they got there, the sky criss-crossed by searchlights. They were lined up outside the station before being ferried to their new ITC at Gibraltar Barracks, a castellated redbrick Victorian toy fort of a building on the outskirts of the market town of Bury St Edmunds, where Julian was inducted into 4 Platoon, Z Company of the Suffolk Regiment.

Their new barracks were much less comfortable than those they'd left behind. In place of proper beds, they slept on stacks of three thin brown matresses, laid on the floor. They had no sheets either.

Just coarse blankets that had recently been fumigated.

On resumption of training, it became apparent that Julian's knee-problem rendered him unable to perform even a correct about-turn, so he was sent for an interview with the resident MO, who gave him the impression that he regarded him as a malingerer. But Julian had the good fortune to be under the command of an understanding set of NCOs (Non-Commissioned Officers) and "an extraordinarily decent"[31] platoon Sergeant. Instead of adopting the stereotypically brutal approach, "they spent endless time and trouble on... [him], and other members of the awkward squad."[32] Grateful as he was for their forbearance, he hated being condemned to the ranks of the military inadequates, his obvious debility leading to further trips to see the MO.

In between these daily doses of humiliation, his sleep was broken by the sirens that sounded most nights. Each time this happened, the barracks were emptied. With only the searchlights, the distant flashes of anti-aircraft fire, and the odd incendiary bomb for illumination, Julian and his room-mates would stumble across to the adjacent trenches. Damp and shivering despite the long johns, battle dress, great coats, balaclavas, and woollen gloves they wore, they'd have to stay there until the All Clear sounded, giving them the chance to snatch a little more shut-eye before reveille.

Under the strain of tiredness, inedible food, military discipline, renewed training, and regular guard duty, exacerbated by a lack of money, by his mother's continued refusal to contact him, by Eileen's inability to visit, and by the repeated postponement of his leave, Julian became gaunt and dejected. Yet he strove to conceal his low spirits, especially in the letters he wrote Mac, who was now in the army too. Beneath his meticulously constructed façade of hardboiled resilience, Mac could tell he was finding it tougher than he was willing to admit, his morbid streak becoming ever more prominent.

To brace his flagging morale, Mac took to sending him facetious replies that harked back to their pre-war days together. Recurrent letters from Eileen, who had plenty of her own troubles, her business having folded, also arrived for him, enclosing bundles of homemade cigarettes. Less predictably, his mother finally contacted him and made an effort to resolve their differences.

As winter set in, Julian had to contend with the intense cold, plus all the other discomforts. These made it hard for him to carry on writing. Nevertheless, he persevered through November and the early part of December, doing most of his work on Sunday afternoons when he grabbed a seat in the smoke-filled Recreation Room. Setting aside his radio script, he completed the second half of *The Simple Life*, which he despatched to Colonel Connolly who, despite his earlier interest, rejected it. Julian then started working on what he envisaged as a sequence of thriller stories under the pseudonym "John Chapter". But his plans came to nothing, leading him to abandon writing for the time-being. He concentrated, instead, on trying to get his back-catalogue of short stories published in literary magazines and, ultimately, in book form.

On his instructions, Eileen appears to have plucked several of the stories from the pile of manuscripts he had left at her house. A wad of these were relayed to Bill Makins, who offered them to John Lehmann, the editor of *New Writing's* very popular and prestigious successor, *Penguin New Writing*. Another batch of them, comprising *The Hell of a Time* and the three stories both Lehmann and the Colonel had rejected, were passed back to Julian. He submitted these to *English Story*, a soon-to-be-launched hardback anthology, conceived as a twice-yearly forum for adventurous young writers. Unknown to him, its editor, Woodrow Wyatt, who ran the magazine with his wife Susan, was not only in the same regiment as him, but also stationed in the same training camp. Impressed by Julian's contributions, Wyatt tracked down their author and introduced himself.

He was a short, slim, round-cheeked former barrister with thick, pouting lips, dark neatly parted hair, and round horn-rimmed glasses. Though he was six years younger than Julian, he'd already risen to the rank of Second-Lieutenant. Like Julian, he had a contemptuous attitude towards rules and regulations. In deliberate violation of military procedure, which discouraged fraternisation between officers and Privates, he invited Julian back to his quarters, the blissful warmth from his small stove helping his guest to recover from a day spent shovelling snow. Sitting side by side on Wyatt's bunk, they smoked cigars and talked about "other things than training and what [they] were down for on tomorrow's detail".[33] The conviviality of the occasion was enhanced by Wyatt's announcement that he planned to feature *The Hell of a Time* in the second issue of *English Story*. He also said he was keen to print another piece at a later date. This spurred Julian on to submitting some more stories to *Penguin New Writing*.

Over the next few weeks Wyatt frequently repeated the invitation back to his quarters. Their evenings together, spent drinking and talking, offered Julian an invigorating release from service life. Being an admirer of his stories, Wyatt coaxed him into starting to write again. Possibly prompted by the time he caught Julian swanning round the barracks acting as if he was an officer, Wyatt urged the reluctant Julian to seek a commission. As an incentive, he stressed the benefits of rank: the improved living conditions and the chance to help his fellow soldiers. Obstinate as always, Julian made no immediate effort to follow his advice, though he did, at Wyatt's instigation, resume writing. Ordinarily, he would have mined his daily life for raw material, but he'd already made a decision not to write anything about the army, because he felt he wouldn't be able to "see it in proper perspective until afterwards."[34] For that reason he preferred to concentrate on achieving, through his writing, "a summing-up of the past."[35]

Present-day difficulties nonetheless remained inescapable. So frustrated was he by the army's failure to grant him the leave to which he was entitled, in mid-December he lodged a complaint about it. This led to him being branded "a bolshie".[36] Exasperated by his current powerlessness, he took Wyatt's advice and wrote to his Company Commander, asking whether he could apply for a commission. Because of his ineptitude on the parade-ground, the Company Commander was reluctant to nominate him as a potential officer. But these doubts seem to have been outweighed by the revelation that Julian's grandfather had been an Indian army Colonel.

Before he could be added to the roster of applicants for the OCTU (Officer Candidate Training Unit), he had to appear in front of a board of officers. They then referred him to the CO (Commanding Officer), who postponed making a decision until Julian's damaged knee had been assessed by a Medical Board. On their recommendation he was, a fortnight later, officially regraded "B-2".

By that stage he'd been transferred to another company, "where the Platoon Sergeant could not by any stretch of the imagination be described as a decent chap."[37] On the grounds that he was an aspiring officer, Julian was victimised by the Sergeant. Besides being made to lay barbed-wire with his bare hands, he was regularly ordered to stand on the edge of the parade-ground while the rest of his unit practised saluting him.

Now that the Medical Board had met, he was — sometime in January 1941 — re-interviewed by the CO, who informed him that there were no vacancies for officers. Next day, however, the Adjutant sent for him to discuss another more constructive use of his talents. There was a "hush-hush"[38] job available in the tropics, for which they needed intelligent volunteers, the Adjutant explained. If Julian put his name forward for the job, he'd gain promotion, maybe a commission, once he arrived there. Any alternative to the current regime appeared desirable, so Julian instantly accepted the offer.

But he hadn't heard anything more about this mysterious posting when he was, at last, allocated the much-delayed leave, which he'd arranged to spend with Eileen. Returning to Bognor for the first time since the previous summer, its streets rendered unfamiliar by the bomb-damaged buildings and the presence of Canadian soldiers, Julian seems to have taken up Dy's invitation to stay at her house. There he could enjoy the novelty of sleeping in a bed with proper sheets, undisturbed by the usual barrack-room cacophony. He was probably joined by Eileen, who was now running a small café on the barbed-wire-wreathed promenade.

For "seven days of heaven",[39] he felt like "a man again, not just [a] name and number."[40] His freshly reclaimed civilian clothes exempting him from the obligation to salute passing officers, he strolled round the town, periodically bumping into people he knew. That said, there weren't many of the old crowd left. Lydia and Karel Jaeger had moved to a safer part of the country, Martin Jordan had been called up, and Eugene Horsfall-Ertz had, as a suspected Nazi spy, been interned on the Isle of Man.

Making the most of their time together, Julian went with Eileen to the cinema, took a bus into the country for a picnic with her, and accompanied her to a party and on a trip to a nightclub in Chichester. At the end of his leave, with all the queasy dread of a child going back to school for the start of a new term, he rejoined his regiment, now denuded of the presence of Woodrow Wyatt, who had provided him with such material and emotional solace.

Unable "to sink [his] personality entirely in the army life or to forego what ambitions... [he had] as a writer because... [he happened] to have been enlisted",[41] he returned to Bury St Edmunds with renewed determination "to carry on and do what writing... [he could] in whatever conditions"[42] he faced. Utilising "almost every spare moment",[43] he alternated between writing two novels, the subjects of which could scarcely have been more different. While one of these was about Russian exiles, in all likelihood set on the Riviera, the other focused on his experiences as a vacuum-cleaner salesman. Despite the jarring contrast, both novels were progressing "tolerably well."[44] At some future date, he also — as he announced to his would-be publisher, Rupert Hart-Davis — contemplated writing an unashamedly autobiographical book about his experiences in army training camps.

By his own admission, Julian was "such a rotten correspondent"[45] he didn't get many letters. Of those that found their way to Gibraltar Barracks, there was one from John Lehmann, rejecting the stories he'd submitted because they didn't conform to the type of work published in *Penguin New Writing*. Disappointing though that must have been, Lehmann offered some consolation by expressing interest in seeing any new pieces he wrote. But most of Julian's energy was being absorbed by the army's inflexible routine, each day commencing with a compulsory pre-breakfast drill, rifles at the ready.

One morning near the start of May, overcome by a surge of pain and nausea, he committed the unpardonable sin of breaking ranks. The CSM, supervising the parade, was furious when he saw Julian walking towards him. Julian was marched back to the barrack-hut, where he was told to lie down. On examining him, the MO sent him to the Sick Bay.

It turned out he was suffering from pleurisy, complicated by pneumonia, the symptoms leaving him so feverish that he lost his appetite for both food and cigarettes. His fever took almost a week to clear. He was then moved to the civilian West Suffolk General Hospital in Bury St Edmunds, which had an annexe set aside for military personnel. In an elongated ward with french windows at the far end, opening onto an expanse of lawn, he slowly recuperated, the speed of his recovery inhibited by such frugal meals that he was always hungry. It wasn't until mid-May that the doctors permitted him to stagger out of bed and sit by the stove. To conclude his rehabilitation, he was transferred to a convalescent-home. He spent the next three weeks there. His prescribed recovery period completed, he was discharged in June and sent back to the ITC.

When he enquired about the post in the tropics for which he'd volunteered, he learnt that it had, in his absence, been re-allocated to someone else. But he was offered a job as a clerk in the Orderly Room at the Territorial Army Headquarters in Ipswich. He agreed to start there right away, even though it meant delaying his next already overdue leave.

Still weak from his recent illness, he took up his latest assignment. He was now based in the Drill Hall on the corner of Friarsbridge and Portman Roads, next to a parade-ground overlooking Ipswich Town Football Club's low-roofed stadium. Two other clerks were working in the Orderly Room, busily typing up orders on waxed stencil-paper. This stiflingly hot room, which had only a tiny window, was "so small that both the others had to stand up if the third one wished to go out."[46] If Julian or either of his colleagues made a typing error, the security-conscious CO would insist on them destroying the stencil and beginning again.

Around a month after he'd started his new job, he received a telegram revealing that his mother was seriously ill. When he approached his CO, he was given seven days' compassionate leave, so he could visit her. She'd been diagnosed as suffering from breast cancer. The prognosis must have been bleak. Even so, he seems to have been relatively unaffected by her deteriorating health, his already tenuous filial ties eroded by his lingering resentment towards her.

As soon as he got back from his leave, he found out that he was being transferred to an undisclosed destination. On Monday 11 August, together with a group of NCOs, he caught a train bound for the seaside town of Felixstowe, where he was absorbed into the HQ Company of the recently formed 70th Battalion of the Suffolk Regiment.

Instead of living in a barracks, he was billeted in a draughty old three-storey building, one of a row of requisitioned hotels along the promenade. Though he had the luxury of a top-floor room to himself, equipped with its own washbasin, initially he didn't have a bedstead, only a straw-filled mattress laid across the grubby floorboards.

Directly below were the headquarters of his battalion, a Young Soldiers' training unit so notoriously indisciplined that the regimental magazine speculated on whether the gaol was large enough to accommodate them all. Indeed, teenage members of the unit, many of them petty-criminals in civilian life, often went absent-without-leave.

During the day, Julian worked in the Company Office, where he'd been appointed Despatch Clerk to the Second-in-Command. Though he was the only Private in an office staffed by NCOs, he had to supervise a squad of seven runners, who were reluctant to take orders from someone of equal rank.

His sense of isolation increased by the unavailability of serious contemporary fiction in the local shops and libraries, he quickly established a lonely and unvarying schedule. Each morning got underway with reveille, followed by breakfast. Work began at 9.00am. His duties, which he considered so inconsequential anybody could have done them, mainly consisted of typing despatches, medical reports, letters, kit inventories, dental records, details of physical training exercises, and programmes for sports tournaments. Sometimes he was even expected to draw posters advertising these tournaments. He was also responsible for sending off letters and maintaining a tally of HQ Company's postal expenses, his efforts hindered by the pack of pet dogs that overran the place, chewing "pens and other office equipment".[47]

He and the rest of the clerical staff were permitted no mid-morning tea-break, yet Julian — who was known by his colleagues as "Rossy" — always managed to wangle one. Halfway through the morning, he'd go off to post the Company's letters. On his way to the main post office in the town centre, reached via the promenade, separated from the heavily mined sea by rusting coils of barbed wire, he'd stop off at Millar's Café and Restaurant, a low, broad-fronted building on Undercliff Road West, just across the street from the pier. It was a civilian establishment, notable for its Edwardian decor. But the majority of its customers, distributed round its three-hundred tightly packed seats, were in uniform, male servicemen mingling with a smattering of personnel from the Wrens (Women's Royal Naval Service) and the WAAF (Women's Auxiliary Air Force). Excluded from the half-basement, which was reserved for officers, who were the focus of most of the girls' attention, Julian would cross the foyer and ascend the short flight of steps leading up to the next floor, where a radio played in the background. While he drank black coffee, he'd seize the chance to get some writing done.

After he'd posted his consignment of letters, he would go back to the office and carry on with his work until lunchtime, its advent signalled by the clomping of heavy boots on the wooden staircase. He would then join Z Company on parade, the harbinger of their daily march down the sea-front to the improvised cookhouse. Their hands as well as their army-issue cutlery having been inspected by the Duty Officer, they'd file into the basement of another large requisitioned hotel, where they were served a main course and a stodgy pudding.

Except for one afternoon-a-week when he had to attend a cursory session of rifle practice, Julian would spend the rest of the afternoon wading through more paperwork. If he ran out of things to do, he'd peruse the copies of *Horizon* he kept there for just such idle moments.

When the working day finished, he'd once again trudge up the steep gradient of Convalescent Hill, connecting the promenade with the town centre. At his favourite café he'd order the same meal every evening: bacon, chips, and peas, plus two cheese sandwiches and yet another black coffee. In the event there was nothing he wanted to see at any of the local cinemas, he would go to the Public Library or one of the two canteens, where he'd do some more writing. By timing his return to the Company Office so he got there well before lights out, he was able to use the office typewriter to transcribe whatever he'd written.

Irksome as he continued to find the army, it offered just the boost his fledgling literary career needed. It gave him time in which to work. It simplified his life. It freed him from employment worries. It forced him to concentrate on fulfilling his ambitions. And, above all, it presented him with a plethora of "excellent material for satire".[48]

103

The opening page of the manuscript of *Accused Soldier*, an unpublished short story that formed the basis for *The Swag, the Spy and the Soldier* (© The Estate of Julian Maclaren-Ross)

Sonia Orwell, taken on her last day at *Horizon*, 1949 (© University College London Library)

The unchanging interior of Millar's Café and Restaurant, 1911 (© Neil Wylie/ John Smith)

Military Manouevres

Fed up with trying to get the runners under his command to obey orders, Julian applied for promotion to Lance-Corporal. But he was warned that his ineptitude on the parade-ground would preclude him from becoming an NCO. On hearing about Julian's doomed aspirations, one of the Subalterns suggested he seek a commission instead. His sense that the army wasn't making proper use of him offered just the motivation he needed to follow this advice. Within three days of submitting the appropriate form, his application was rejected, only adding to his mounting disenchantment with the military.

In about early November 1941, he received an unforeseen summons from his CO which, he believed, had been instigated by Woodrow Wyatt. The CO informed him that his name was being put forward to the War Office Selection Board, who were responsible for identifying suitable candidates for training as officers. He then found himself on the list of those nominated for the three-day programme of tests, a solitary Private among the Lance-Corporals and Sergeants. Word soon spread through the camp. Whenever he went into the canteen, his colleagues would rib him about it. In his eagerness to escape from the drudgery of life in the ranks, he prepared thoroughly for the test, polishing his brasses, blancoing his gaiters, ironing his best battle-dress, and even practising salutes in front of the mirror.

The selection procedure took place at another army base. It began with a series of written tests. These included an all too tempting opportunity for Julian and the other prospective officers, all wearing numbered yellow armbands over their sleeves, to write an honest account of what effect the army had had on them and what they thought of it. There was also a psychological evaluation. Part of this entailed a succession of photographs being flashed on a projector-screen, in the wake of which Julian and the others were expected to write a brief essay about what they'd seen. Had it not been for the myopia which made it hard for Julian to decipher them, the exercise would have been a doddle.

Next he was interviewed by the President of the Selection Board, who questioned him about what sort of commission he wanted. To which Julian replied that he hoped to make use of his bilingual background.

Where he really botched his application was on the last day, devoted to practical exercises probing their leadership capacities. For the final test, they were led down to a shallow but broad gulley, representing a deep ravine. The Major in charge sketched a scenario whereby they had to pretend they were fleeing from the advancing Germans, who would capture them unless they crossed the trench within twenty minutes. The others used some logs and a length of rope to improvise a narrow bridge across the make-believe ravine. But Julian's bad knee meant he was unable to negotiate it.

Left facing imminent capture by the enemy, he tried to redeem the situation by committing an act of selfless heroism. Tugging the logs free from the opposite bank, he imitated the noise of an explosion as he blew up the bridge. Far from being dazzled by his resourcefulness, the War Office Selection Board reported that he hadn't taken the test seriously enough to justify a place at the OCTU. His hopes scotched, a sense of grievance fostered by the apparent shortcomings of the successful candidates, he went back to the clerical grind, "resigned to a pipless and stripe-less uniform for the duration."[1]

And so, his Woodrow Wyatt-inspired bid to become an officer ended in abject failure. His friend's influence on his literary career was, however, more fruitful. With the backing of a five-strong advisory panel, encompassing the critic John Davenport and the writer H.E. Bates, Wyatt published *The Hell of a Time* in the second issue of *English Story*. Released in December, it provided an encouraging prelude to the New Year.

1942, in many respects, marked the zenith of the thriving short story market, wartime strictures creating a demand for concision. In this unusual context, even a specialist literary anthology like *English Story* could sell 10,000 copies-an-issue. Altogether there were well over a dozen magazines and miscellanies that featured short stories. Of these, many of them adopting a convenient pocket-sized format, *Lilliput* was by far the most popular and readily available. Its eclectic combination of short stories, non-fiction, chaste topless pin-ups, cartoons by the likes of Ronald Searle, plus photographs by people of the stature of Bill Brandt enabled it to achieve a staggering circulation of 300,000-a-month.

The pages of *Lilliput* may well have been where Julian first encountered the irreverent short stories of the Ukranian writer, Mikhail Zoshchenko. Among Julian's comrades, these deeply satirical, often inconclusive and uneventful but all too resonant sketches of government bungling and red tape were widely enjoyed. It was probably under Zoshchenko's influence that he abandoned his earlier conviction that he shouldn't write about the army, whose petty bureaucracy presented an ideal target for his rebellious instincts.

One off-duty afternoon during the early part of January, Julian began writing a story about a fellow Private who, badgered by his girlfriend, applies for a promotion. Juxtaposing the wryly humorous flavour of Zoshchenko's work with the lean, hardboiled style he'd long admired, he wrapped up the story, which he titled *The Tape*, in a single, frictionless sitting. Its completion marked the end of a long stretch when he'd had difficulty either knowing what to write about, or finishing anything. All of a sudden, the material he "must have been subconsciously accumulating fell into place",[2] and he was "swamped under with subjects".[3] Now he had trouble finding the free time to channel the torrent of ideas into prose. Because he found that his mood could be "so quickly altered by circumstances when in the army",[4] he felt obliged to bring his ideas to fruition "at top speed",[5] ideally putting the final touches to a story before he screwed the cap back on his pen. If the story didn't go according to plan, he wouldn't simply cross out the section he disliked. Instead, he'd go back to the opening line, carefully print a decorative capital, and start again.

By the second week of January 1942, he had polished off *I Had To Go Sick*, his second army story, "a completely autobiographical and absolutely true"[6] account of his frustrating wait for a Medical Board. Together with its predecessor, which he'd sent to *Horizon*, it promised to grow into a cycle of stories evoking previously undocumented aspects of current military life.

His rediscovered optimism must have been fortified by the letter he received a few days later. It was from Douglas Newton, one of the editors of a forthcoming anthology. The letter said they'd read his work in *Horizon* and *English Story*, and would like to fit one of his pieces into their collection. They were unable to offer him a fee, but he decided it was still worth submitting something. So he gave them the cherished yet hitherto unpublished *Five Finger Exercises*.

Meanwhile, Bill Makins — who had not yet been conscripted — was still trying to find a buyer for *The Simple Life*. Though both Chatto & Windus and Allen & Unwin were interested in it, they ended up rejecting it on the grounds of what they regarded as its uncommercial brevity. Refusing to be put off by either this or the disheartening discovery that Makins considered it inferior to his previous work, Julian went back to the problematic task of transmuting his experiences as a vacuum-cleaner salesman into a novel. He seems to have begun by drawing up a detailed plot outline. In a facetious nod to James M. Cain, author of *The Postman Always Rings Twice*, he envisaged calling it *The Salesman Only Rings Once*. When Makins showed Allen & Unwin a long extract from it, possibly culled from a previous draft, they expressed interest in publishing it. Makins duly fixed up a meeting between Julian and Philip Unwin, synchronised with Julian's next appearance in London on leave.

Sometime towards the end of January, he passed through the capital on his way to spend nine days with Eileen in Bognor. Before going to meet Unwin, whose firm was based near the British Museum, he popped round to *Horizon*'s office to see Makins. Despite the heavy bombing eighteen months earlier, which had so disfigured the streets and squares of Bloomsbury, Lansdowne Terrace was almost undamaged. At his subsequent late afternoon appointment with the cautious, soberly dressed Philip Unwin, Julian was offered what he considered an unacceptably low advance for his novel-in-progress. Afterwards, he went over to the comfortable, ornately panelled Museum Tavern, where he briefed his agent on the disappointing outcome of his meeting.

On Saturday 10 April, Julian's seventy-year-old mother succumbed to the cancer that had been diagnosed the previous summer. Even though he loathed anything that forced him to contemplate the inevitability of death, he made the effort to obtain leave and attend the funeral.

The resultant gloom, not helped by the icy wind blowing off the North Sea, appears to have been lifted by a new friendship that began about three weeks later. Entering the hotel where he lived and worked, he was told that an unnamed Welsh officer was looking for him. The officer had left a message, asking him to call in at the headquarters of the South Wales Border Regiment, just down the sea-front. There he met another client of Bill Makins: the shy, softly spoken young Welsh poet and short story writer Alun Lewis, who had been alerted to his presence in Felixstowe not by Makins, but by the army chaplain.

Disregarding regulations, Lewis invited him into the Officers' Mess. Coincidentally, Lewis's work had featured in the same edition of *English Story* as *The Hell of a Time*, perhaps explaining why Lewis had read it. On the assumption that Julian had lived in India, where the story was set, Lewis, who was convinced that his regiment were heading there, quizzed him about what to expect.

Lewis turned out to be billeted in the hotel next-door to him. Mutual isolation levering them into a friendship which, Julian acknowledged, would never have developed in civilian life, they started meeting in Millar's Café and Restaurant. Julian showed him *The*

Salesman Only Rings Once, Five Finger Exercises, and the army stories he'd been writing. Lewis reciprocated by lending him the typescripts of some of his own recent stories which, Julian believed, "got very near [...telling] the truth about the army".[7] Their dissimilar treatment of comparable material caused Julian to question the virtues of his own efforts. His confidence was further undermined by Lewis's unenthusiastic, prudish reaction to the work he'd been shown. With wounding candour, Lewis told him that "he found the subject [of *Five Finger Exercises*] distasteful."[8]

Their friendship nonetheless continued to develop, arousing the scorn of their senior officers. Like an adulterous couple, they took to arranging furtive meetings in backstreet pubs. Before they could incite any disciplinary measures, though, Lewis was posted to Dorset. He departed in the first week of June, promising to send a letter, but none ever arrived.

That month the *Fortune Anthology*, the volume to which Julian had submitted *Five Finger Exercises*, was published by the inappropriately named Fortune Press. His story featured in a line-up that included an article by Henry Miller, as well as poems by Lawrence Durrell and Wallace Stevens. When Bill Makins heard that Julian hadn't been paid for his contribution, he quipped that the *Fortune Anthology* should henceforth be known only by its initials. Julian's generosity was repaid by an anonymous notice in *The TLS* (*The Times Literary Supplement*) that made a scathing reference to *Five Finger Exercises*.

Peeved but undiscouraged, Julian seems to have pressed ahead with *The Salesman Only Rings Once*, which he'd come to regard "as a moral tale for those who think life before the war was a paradise."[9] The novel would now culminate with the outbreak of hostilities. To emphasise the juxtaposition between life before and during the war, there would be an epilogue set in May 1942, entitled *A Happy Ending For Those Who Like Them*, depicting the protagonist as an OCTU candidate. With half of the novel completed, he lent the manuscript to Woodrow Wyatt. Through his friend, Julian secured what he regarded as an attractive offer of a £100 advance from Collins & Co, payable on delivery of the finished novel.

At the same time he was expanding his stock of army stories, mostly very terse and comic in tone, a dozen of which had been completed by early July. Of these, he'd submitted four to various magazines and anthologies. All of them were accepted for publication. In addition to selling *I Had To Go Sick* to *Horizon*, he succeeded in placing *Death of a Comrade* — a subversive little sketch about a pointless fatality, unlikely to endear him to his superior officers — with *Tribune*, the low-paying but influential Labour Party weekly. He also placed a story with *Selected Writing*. And he sold the light-hearted *They Put Me In Charge of a Squad* to the paperback miscellany, *Modern Reading*. Its editor, Reginald Moore, also secured a promise from Julian to deliver a 40,000-word novel, earmarked for publication in a cheap paperback format.

As a writer, he was now doing better than he had ever done in peacetime, yet he "was dissatisfied and unhappy"[10] because he still felt stymied in his desire to make a worthwhile contribution to the war-effort. Ideas for further stories, in the meantime, occurred to him with gratifying regularity. Travelling down to Bognor on Friday 10 July to spend his leave with Eileen, three more subjects presented themselves. Seated at a table in the Beach Café, his girlfriend's new tea-room, he spent part of the following day writing these up, the effortless way they flowed from his pen feeding his ballooning self-belief, his newfound pride in his literary fecundity, his sense that his present output represented only a rehearsal for weightier work ahead.

From Eileen's café, he wrote a chatty letter to John Lehmann, breathlessly updating him on the fresh direction his writing had taken. The hope was, of course, that Lehmann might be more interested in his latest stories than he had been in any of their precursors. With its bias towards documentary writing, through which Lehmann hoped to reveal aspects of wartime life ignored by the propagandistic journalism of the day, *Penguin New Writing* was an obvious forum for Julian's new work.

After a few weeks' delay, during which Julian busied himself correcting the proofs of *I Had To Go Sick* and sending off pieces to *Lilliput* as well as the less populist *Life and Letters*, Lehmann wrote back, saying he'd like to read one of Julian's army stories. Julian responded by sending him the typescript of *Y-List*, an account of his hospitalisation a little over a year ago, which he planned to assimilate into a memoir of his army experiences, to be called *They Can't Give You A Baby*. Without the aid of notes or a diary, he'd taken only a single day to write it. In a self-effacing covering letter, he described it as being "not too bad [...] at any rate true to hospital life in the army."[11]

Besides submitting *Y-List* for possible inclusion in *Penguin New Writing*, he tried to persuade Lehmann to commission an article about working in a Company Office for the magazine's *Report To-day* section. But, as he explained to Lehmann, he needed a rapid decision, because he'd just heard that he was being transferred during the latter half of August to a clerical job in the Orderly Room in Southend, where he'd have "rather less leisure for writing."[12]

*

His career, so long becalmed by the war, made a significant advance with the publication of *I Had To Go Sick* in the August issue of *Horizon*. It provoked a slew of requests from editors for contributions, and a letter from Rupert Hart-Davis, who said he'd like to publish a collection of his army stories. It also earned him a letter of congratulation from Evelyn Waugh, who "thought that it showed genuine literary promise and accomplishment of a rare kind."[13]

This wasn't the only bit of good fortune Julian enjoyed that summer. While he was setting up a target in the rifle-butts one afternoon, his helmet was hit by a bullet which, miraculously, failed to pierce it. True to both army tradition and his propensity for dramatic gestures, he retrieved the bullet, a "twisted shard of metal, shaped like the business end of a scorpion",[14] and thereafter carried it round as a lucky charm. For now at least, it certainly seemed to be working its magic. On Wednesday 5 August Julian received Lehmann's reply, his relatively speedy response comparing favourably with the unpunctuality of his opposite numbers at *Lilliput* and *Life and Letters*. The reply could scarcely have been better. Though Lehmann had reservations about the way *Y-List* ended (reservations that Julian shared), he accepted it for publication, because he felt it displayed "wit, a story-telling flair, and a kind of dry pathos of characterisation that marked it out as the work of a highly original writer."[15] Naturally, Julian was delighted at the prospect of having his story published in a magazine he so admired. His success prompted him to send Lehmann *When I Last Got My Leave*, another army story, which he'd only just written.

Struck by Julian's "great verve, sardonic humour and masterly sense of timing and cutting",[16] Lehmann encouraged him to go ahead with the proposed piece about the Company Office. In his determination "to make sure [it was] good",[17] Julian devoted several days to it, straining for accuracy in his portrayal of "the constant boring routine".[18] Despite his impending transfer from Felixstowe, he had no desire to offend the people portrayed in the article which, with heavy irony, he'd entitled *Are You Happy In Your Work*. To safeguard against any possible complaints, he showed the relevant sections to each of them. They were all "very pleased especially the sergeant known in the text as Smiler."[19]

Midway through August, he sent off the completed article, accompanied by a story he'd finished only hours before. But the days slipped past without any word from Lehmann. Julian still hadn't heard anything by Saturday 22 August when he was scheduled to leave Felixstowe.

The rest of the staff in the office where he'd been working were also poised to be posted elsewhere. In order to save their successors the trouble of producing an inventory of the box of unused government-issue notebooks being left behind, they decided to throw it away. Not wanting to see so much good stationery go to waste, Julian asked if he could have it. Encumbered by a stack of narrow-feint notebooks, their stiff manila covers stamped with the royal insignia, he set off for No. 3 Infantry Depot at Southend, where he was due to be stationed for the duration of the war.

Prior to taking up his new posting, he was given 48 hours' leave, which he spent in London. Like innumerable other artistically-inclined servicemen who felt stifled and lonely amid the discipline, uniformity, and bureaucracy of the army, Julian found that heterodox Soho offered a perfect antidote. Its flourishing pub scene had been reinvigorated by the war, ever-present danger dissolving people's inhibitions and creating a frenetic live-for-the-moment ethos, a deceptive impression of community whose addictive allure was every bit as perilous as the more obvious wartime dangers. The pubs were places where, depending on your proclivities, you might pick up arty men or women, where you might find the comfort of a welcoming bed for the night, where you might bump into long-lost friends, where you might make important contacts, where rank counted for nothing. Not that the people who thronged the Soho pubs night after night wanted to talk about art or anything intellectual, most conversations eschewing shop-talk and tending towards the frivolous, towards interminable pub-games and tipsy hilarity, true drunkenness being difficult to attain due to the relative shortage of alcohol.

That weekend Julian headed for the Wheatsheaf which, since his joyous pre-war outings with Mac, had supplanted the Fitzroy as the epicentre of bohemian life in North Soho, sometimes referred to as "Fitzrovia" in honour of the Fitzroy's former pre-eminence. It was there that he probably encountered the supercilious, energetically self-promoting surrealist painter and theorist Toni del Renzio, sporting a hooped matelot shirt that emphasised his Italian good looks.

More significantly, the Wheatsheaf may also have been where Julian got into conversation with a girl named Scylla Yates, his infatuation with her overshadowing his deeper feelings for Eileen. Like him, Scylla was in the services. In her case, she was part of the WAAF, stationed not far from Norwich. Strictly speaking, Julian was still married, neither he nor Elizabeth having ever bothered to apply for a divorce, yet the mesmeric intensity of his attraction to Scylla led him to ask her to marry him. She accepted his proposal. They then started making plans for a wedding immediately his divorce came through.

His romantic interlude over, he took the train to Southend, where he commenced his posting at the Infantry Depot, which proved every bit as drab as it sounded, comprising row after row of small barrack-huts, inhabited by "the dregs and chuck-outs of the army."[20] The town wasn't any improvement on Felixstowe either, the unavailability of most of the latest books causing him to "feel out of touch."[21] And his job as a clerk in the Orderly Room of HQ Company was no more stimulating than his previous one, long stints at the typewriter inculcating in him a lasting hatred of typing. With palpable bitterness, he observed that he "seemed to be the only writer of [his] particular kind who was not either an officer entrusted with something he could do without despising [himself], or else out of the army and doing work of national importance."[22] Still, his transfer to Southend did have a single salient advantage. Namely that it was nearer to London and therefore nearer his fiancée.

A little under a week after he had arrived there, the story he'd sold *Tribune* was published, payment for it only finding its way to him via his old unit. An eight guinea cheque from *Lilliput*, who had belatedly accepted one of the stories he'd sent them, also turned up. Added to which, *Horizon* purchased *This Mortal Coil*, a blackly humorous tale of a soldier who walks, talks, and fights in his sleep.

He had now sold the majority of the army stories he'd completed, his earnings from them providing an invaluable war-chest with which to fund his divorce proceedings. Though these stories tended to "show everyone browned off",[23] the other soldiers in his unit were just as anxious as magazine editors to get hold of them.

The ten-hour-a-day slog in the Orderly Room didn't leave him much opportunity for writing, yet he capitalised on what little spare-time he had at his disposal. Mostly this was in the evenings when he used the Orderly Room as a study. Eager to establish his all-round literary credentials, he spent the initial nine days or so shuttling between three different projects. First, there were the lucrative army stories which he hoped Rupert Hart-Davis would publish in the same volume as *The Simple Life*, the latter providing "an effective contrast between the playboy life of the 30s and now."[24] Then there were two much more substantial projects, his "ambitious leanings [... fired by] being in love".[25] With these, he hoped to create a big splash and, in the process, raise the money he needed to begin married life in comfort. The longest-running of his two large-scale projects was *They Can't Give You A Baby*, progress on which was steady. To accompany the expanded versions of *I Had To Go Sick* and *Y-List*, already incorporated into it, he was writing a chapter "on the difference between actual experience and the same when arranged as a story."[26] In parallel to all this, he was also working on a new novel — new in every sense. For him, it was a fresh departure, in that it veered away from both the straightforwardly autobiographical fiction he'd hitherto favoured and the type of dry comedy with which he'd become synonymous. He conceived it as a dark, Graham Greene-like spy thriller. Clear as his conception of the finished novel was, he had trouble implementing his design because he was "very diffident about trying to write anything in this genre."[27] His mind wasn't, in any event, entirely focused on his writing. Smitten by Scylla's charms, he couldn't concentrate. Early in October, he submitted a request to the Commanding Officer of the Bedfordshire and Hertfordshire Regiment, to which he'd just been transferred, for seven days' leave with her in Norwich, stopping off in the capital "to see people on business."[28] His request was granted.

On Monday 12 October he went off to see Scylla who, in a reference to his nom-de-plume of J. Maclaren-Ross, had taken to calling him "Jay". Passing through London en route back from Norwich to Southend, he fixed up his first meeting with the gaunt, Teutonic John Lehmann. Despite Lehmann's homosexuality and all their other differences, they got on very well, mutual respect easing them into an improbable friendship. This cushioned the revelation that Lehmann had rejected *Are You Happy In Your Work*, along with the two stories Julian had sent him.

When he was in London, Julian also attended an interview at the War Office, secured with the help of friends — Woodrow Wyatt, himself an ex-employee there, providing a likely point of contact. Julian, who was still pining after "a job where [he] could use some intelligence",[29] was interviewed by two pleasant, middle-ranking officers. Unfortunately they were at a loss to suggest any appropriate vacancies for him. But they assured him "that something would be done sometime, if humanly possible."[30]

While he'd been away from the Orderly Room, the paperwork had been piling up. To clear this alarming backlog, he had to work "every night till 12 for a fortnight".[31] Right in the midst of this frantic catch-up operation, he had *The Mine*, another of his army stories, which he rated "the best so far",[32] featured in *Tribune*. Its publication encouraged him to spend part of his time off-duty that Sunday parcelling up a fresh submission for them. And he sent Kaye Webb, the editor of *Lilliput*, a brief parody of pretentious art criticism, comparing the Pre-Raphaelite painter John Everett Millais's *The Blind Girl* with a construction by the overbearing Toni del Renzio, the in-joke being that del Renzio abhorred English art. Julian also found time to reply to a note he'd had from Lehmann, saying that Penguin's solicitors were worried about potential libel actions arising from *Y-List*. In an effort to dispel their fears, Julian gave them "a definite assurance that the characters and the names in the story [were] fictitious."[33]

Between tedious stints in the Orderly Room the following week, Julian read the most recent issue of *New Writing and Daylight*, a Lehmann-edited anthology which he may well have been given when the two of them met in London. As someone struggling to write a thriller, Julian felt that his efforts were endorsed by Lehmann's essay asserting the cultural significance of thrillers and spy fiction. In the essay, Lehmann quoted a resonant phrase from Virginia Woolf's *Between the Acts*, referring to "the fields of [...] night",[34] which Julian decided to use as the title for his thriller-in-progress. Jubilant, he wrote to Lehmann to thank him for his unwitting assistance.

But Julian doesn't appear to have got far with his novel, its composition still hamstrung by self-consciousness. He had, however, found time to revise the opening pages of *They Can't Give You A Baby*, describing his life in the run-up to conscription. He submitted these to Rupert Hart-Davis, who wrote back expressing interest in the book. News of this cancelled out Julian's disappointment at discovering that Hart-Davis wanted to delay publication of his army stories until there were enough of them to make up a conventional-sized collection. The latest edition of *English Story*, meanwhile, showcased *Happy As The Day Is Long*, his low-key, atmospheric pre-war short story. In his haste to make the jump from being a successful magazine writer to having a book in print, he told Hart-Davis that he'd be prepared to sell his collection for "a very small advance".[35] To this offer, he attached only one condition: that the stories had to be released under the Guild Books imprint, an affordable paperback series produced by Jonathan Cape and the other members of the British Publishers' Guild. But Hart-Davis, who now combined his role as a publisher with a commission in the army, resisted the offer.

Casting round for other means of raising money, Julian made "a frightful fuss"[36] about how he was a Private performing a job normally assigned to a higher-paid Lance-Corporal. In about the second week of November, the Adjutant for whom he worked finally buckled. By arranging to have his promotion to the rank of Lance-Corporal backdated, the Adjutant even ensured that Julian received the accompanying pay-rise straightaway. It was a gesture which persuaded Julian that his demanding boss was "rather nice really".[37]

Not entirely mollified by the appearance of a Lance-Corporal's stripe on his shoulder, he pursued his contacts at the War Office by writing a long statement of his case. But he received no response, the officers in question having been transferred shortly after his interview with them.

His morale was further lowered by the discovery, only a week or two after his promotion came through, that Eileen, furious with him for his defection to Scylla, had destroyed the only copy of his Jack Sheppard script, which he'd left with her for safekeeping. He was in such a state of shock that he contemplated trying to obtain leave on compassionate grounds. His situation wasn't helped by the fact that, despite his recent promotion, he still found himself short of cash: so short he had to chivvy Lehmann into paying the five guineas owed for *Y-List*.

Its publication in the December issue of *Penguin New Writing* brought his talents to the attention of a much larger readership. The impact of *Y-List* and his other army stories was considerable and far-reaching. Reading them at boarding school in Ireland, the future literary critic Anthony Cronin was struck by the "tiny shrugged off undertones of loneliness and pain"[38] beneath their "acerbic, brittle, funny"[39] surfaces, and by their technique which "was so spare and unerring as to constitute, in however small a way, almost a new kind of writing."[40]

Awareness of the J. Maclaren-Ross trademark was reinforced that month by the inclusion of two more of his pieces in leading magazines. Having bought another three of his army stories, *Lilliput* printed his first published parody, sniping at Toni del Renzio. In the meantime, *Horizon* carried *This Mortal Coil*, its daringly authentic barrack-room language triggering a last minute panic. Concerned that the liberal use of the words "bugger" and "sod" might lead to prosecution for obscenity, Colonel Connolly dragged Peter Watson, his financial backer, and Janetta Woolley, one of his secretarial assistants, over to the printers on the night *Horizon* went to press. Together they inked out the offending words. As tiredness set in, they sometimes ended up underlining these instead. To save time, the printer eventually altered the typesetting, replacing Julian's perceived obscenities with discreet dashes.

Keen to continue widening the scope of his output, which now ranged from parody to drama, Julian wrote to Evelyn Waugh asking him to sanction a critical assessment of his work. But Waugh responded with a flippant letter telling Julian to wait until he'd died.

*

Julian kicked off 1943 in much the same successful vein in which he'd finished the previous year. Alongside F. Scott Fitzgerald, V.S. Pritchett, and Graham Greene, he had *They Put Me In Charge of a Squad* printed in *Modern Reading*. His inclusion in such an illustrious line-up must have seemed like a prelude to his induction into the upper echelons of the literary world.

Always glad to have several projects simmering at any one time, he began to fill the government-issue notebooks he'd salvaged. He used them to revise and restructure his mid-Thirties novel, *House of Cards*; to draw up the partial outline of a childhood memoir, entitled *The Snows of Yesterday*; to draft a list of books he planned to write, the length of it attesting to his immense ambition; and to make a number of abortive attempts at finding the apposite tone of voice for his vacuum-cleaner novel, briefly dubbing it *The Lost* before reverting to its earlier jocular title.

Things took an unforeseen turn, though, around the New Year. Hearing that all the clerks at the Infantry Depot were due to be replaced, he guessed that he'd "be drafted as a private to some other unit".[41] The way he saw it, there were three feasible destinations, all of them unappealing. He might find himself part of an infantry unit, condemned to "sweep out the Naffy."[42] Or else he might be posted to a Maritime Anti-Aircraft Battery, where he'd "have to go sick a million times before they found [he] was useless to them on account of [his] leg."[43] Above all, he feared the possibility that the ORSM (Orderly Room Sergeant-Major), who disliked him, might implement a previous threat to have him "sent abroad, to a depot where [he'd] spend [his] time demobilising men for 2 years after the war ends."[44]

If any of these grim scenarios came true, he felt he'd "go crazy",[45] so he decided to dedicate his impending nine-day leave to finding himself a job at the War Office or the Ministry of Information, "where [he] could be of real use."[46] With that goal in mind, he drew up a lengthy list of friends and acquaintances who might be able to help. This featured not only a girl serving as secretary to General de Gaulle, but also the writer, Arthur Calder-Marshall, who worked for the Films Division of the Ministry of Information, and Aneurin Bevan, the maverick Labour politician, editor of *Tribune*, and outspoken critic of the wartime government.

About thirteen days into January, Julian gathered together his manuscripts and writing-case, then travelled up to London, where he'd arranged to meet Scylla, whose leave overlapped with his. For safekeeping, he sent his prospective father-in-law a box full of the government-issue stationary he'd acquired.

Once he was in London, Julian started working his way through his contacts list. Even though he found plenty of people willing to take an interest in his difficulties, they were unable to assist him, because "they had no influence or the influential persons they knew were themselves handicapped by red tape or other obstructions."[47] More to the point, he was told that, eminently employable though he was, "the Ministries etc. had definite instructions not to take anybody out of the army if it could be avoided."[48]

His plan hadn't yielded results by the time both he and Scylla had exhausted their leave-allocation. Yet he was still a long way from completing his itinerary, so he made up his mind not to return to Southend until every possible contact had been explored. Together with the devoted Scylla, who was due back in Norfolk, he sheltered in a flat somewhere in the vicinity of Golders Green, most likely belonging to a girl by the name of Mishka. Using that as a base, he continued his quest.

Without the requisite pass, he could easily have been picked up by the hated Military Police. Known as "Red Caps", they combed the crowds at railway stations, stopping anyone who looked faintly suspicious or slightly scruffy, even a badly tied bootlace serving as a suitable pretext. Each journey across London becoming as potentially nerve-wracking as a scene from a classic thriller, he dodged them for several days.

By Tuesday 2 February, he still hadn't achieved his objective. Nonetheless, there were a few people on his contacts list, such as Aneurin Bevan, whom he hadn't yet seen. Probably sensing that the chances of success were receding with every fruitless discussion, he tried a different tack. That day, he quickly penned a detailed statement justifying his desertion, which he described as "the only thing to do."[49] He gave it the self-referential title, *I Had To Go Absent*. "I merely want to satisfy myself," the piece concluded, "that an intelligent man of 31, travelled, educated abroad, sophisticated and an anti-fascist, a writer who can write over 17 stories in spare-time and get them published, cannot be utilised, owing to his medical category, in any better capacity than an office boy in an orderly room."[50] To publicise his case and, perhaps, shame the authorities into action, he offered the piece to Tom Hopkinson, editor of the popular *Picture Post*, who agreed to print it.

A day or two later, having found that Rupert Hart-Davis was stationed at Wanstead, where he was an Adjutant with the newly created Sixth Battalion of the Coldstream Guards, Julian phoned him to ask for help. But Hart-Davis had gone out.

Next morning, when Julian and his girlfriend were still in bed together, the police raided the flat where they'd been staying. He soon discovered that his arrest, fourteen days after he'd first gone absent-without-leave, had been the result of a tip off received by Scotland Yard. His suspicions as to the identity of the informant appear to have fallen on a woman at the War Office: an organisation about which he proceeded to make unsubstantiated allegations, claiming they'd been infiltrated by fascist-sympathisers.

Handcuffed, he was taken to Golders Green police station, where he spent the rest of the day in the cells. Two guardsmen then turned up to escort him to Great Scotland Yard. He insisted that the Corporal in charge should show him the warrant for his arrest. When the Corporal obliged, Julian scrutinised it carefully. As someone whose egocentricity and incipient paranoia made him prone to divining covert manoeuvrings, he may not have been all that surprised to read that the warrant had been authorised by someone he knew.

In an implausible, appropriately novelistic coincidence, the officer who had sanctioned his arrest turned out to be none other than Rupert Hart-Davis. Most days Hart-Davis, now responsible for supervising the battalion police force's search for deserters in north and east London, routinely signed a large stack of warrants without looking at the names on them. The name of "Lance-Corporal Ross, J." had been among them.

Striving to extricate himself from this tight corner, Julian persuaded the Corporal to let him write a note to Hart-Davis. The note explained that he'd been placed under close arrest, and appealed for assistance.

After a day at Great Scotland Yard, his appearance transformed by a close-cut convict's haircut, he was taken back to the Infantry Depot in Southend to face the consequences of his desertion. Not that he thought of himself as a conventional deserter.

Imprisoned in what passed for the Regimental Gaol, a small, chilly back-room in one of the numerous barrack-huts, he had plenty of time to brood over his predicament. According to his knowledge of military procedure, he thought they'd simply strip him of his recent promotion. Instead of which, he heard — via the guards — that the CO was planning to have him court-martialled. A spell in the Military Detention Barrack appeared the likely outcome. The one consoling thought was that he could exact revenge on the army by recounting the whole sorry saga in *They Can't Give You A Baby*. Yet, at the back of his mind, he had doubts as whether he'd ever finish it.

"What infuriates me," he wrote in another letter to Hart-Davis, "is that I honestly did it because I really hoped to be more use to the war effort in one of the ministries than sitting at a desk correcting the spelling and grammatical errors of my superior officers and now they're going to pile it on."[51] The charges against him had, indeed, multiplied within a few days of his arrival at the Regimental Gaol. "Out of spite",[52] his girlfriend's disapproving father had returned the salvaged box of government-issue stationery to the Orderly Room, prompting a charge of stealing army property. There also seem to have been possible charges arising from his having written to the press about military matters, even though *Picture Post* hadn't fulfilled their commitment to publish his statement. Confronted by the prospect of what now seemed an inevitable court-martial, Julian abandoned the tough and imperturbable persona he prided himself in presenting. In its place, he became increasingly distraught and depressed, leading to the proposed involvement of a psychiatrist.

On Julian's second Sunday back in Southend, Hart-Davis drove across the icy wartime countryside in the hope of visiting him. The careworn old CO, who was entitled to veto such a visit, granted the request. As soon as Julian was alone with Hart-Davis in his makeshift prison cell, he rushed up to him, thrust a tiny bundle into Hart-Davis's hand and said, "Here are my manuscripts."[53] These appear to have consisted of all nineteen pages of *I Had To Go Absent*, which the nonplussed Hart-Davis stuffed into the pocket of his great coat with some difficulty. Julian then set about describing the circumstances surrounding his supposed theft of the stationery and ensuing desertion. Because he had no confidence in any of the potential Defending Officers who might be allocated in the event of a court-martial, he asked the articulate and well-connected Hart-Davis to take on that role. Hart-Davis, who was beginning to wish he'd never got involved, reluctantly agreed to act on his behalf. Before leaving the unit, Hart-Davis informed the CO that he was prepared to defend Julian should the case result in a court-martial.

Julian's sense that he was being persecuted by the army, that "regulations were being especially tightened for [him]"[54] gradually increased. As well as being denied the opportunity to see Scylla, who visited him the following Tuesday, he became convinced that the ORSM was deliberately delaying the process of censoring and releasing letters addressed to him, making it difficult for him to collaborate with Hart-Davis. In order to bypass the ORSM, he arranged for "one of the chaps"[55] to smuggle out his next letter.

But Hart Davis's involvement backfired. Like Thomas Pollok who, four generations earlier, had broken army regulations in a bid to help the state, Julian fell foul of military justice. To avert a potentially embarrassing, closely fought trial, the CO reacted by sentencing him to the stiffest penalty available — 28 days' detention. This seems to have thrown Julian into a "state of incoherent agitation",[56] exposing the fragility beneath the armour-plated image he liked to project. Alarmed by his sudden breakdown, Major Lock, the Area Psychiatrist, was summoned. On examination Julian was deemed to be "medically unfit for the ordeal"[57] of detention.

Northfield Military
Hospital, 1940-42
(© Mrs Simmons)

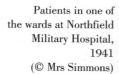

Patients in one of
the wards at Northfield
Military Hospital,
1941
(© Mrs Simmons)

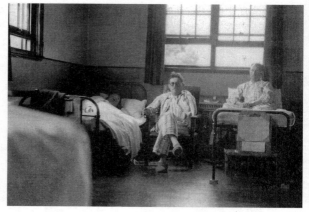

Hospital Blues

Now that the threat of an impending court-martial had been lifted, Julian seems to have calmed down. In what at first appeared to be a reprieve, he was told that he was being sent to a hospital in Birmingham, where he would undergo more rigorous psychological evaluation. "A little nervous"[1] about what awaited him, he left the Regimental Gaol on Thursday 18 February 1943, only the day before another of his stories was due for publication in *Tribune*. As a precaution against him deserting again, he was assigned an escort. They were, however, easy-going enough to let him break the monotony of their cross-country trip by browsing at a station bookstall.

The hospital was in Northfield, a comparatively prosperous suburb on the south-western fringe of Birmingham. To get there from the city centre, dominated by grand but gloomy Gothic Revival buildings, he and his escort would have taken a tram. Ahead of them lay a noisy and uncomfortable five-mile journey, the tram juddering, pitching, and occasionally jerking to a standstill. As it passed through Northfield and down the busy Bristol Road South, street after street of modest inter-war houses spooling past, the immense redbrick water tower that marked Julian's destination would have loomed on the horizon, its verdured cupola and leaded lantern giving it an incongruously Renaissance appearance.

Alighting at the nearest tram-stop, his escort would have marched him almost a mile uphill in full kit, then through the entrance to the hospital. It was guarded by two military policemen in sentry-boxes, who checked the passes of everyone entering or leaving. The hospital's imposing wrought-iron gates, which would have been unlocked by the sentries, opened onto a sinuous, tree-lined drive, bordered by fields. About two-thirds of the way along the drive, there was a large, austere-looking lodge. Julian's escort would have used the telephone outside to announce his arrival.

Further down the drive, the huge Edwardian hospital building would have slowly hoved into sight, the view of its symmetrical, prison-like façade at first blocked by the squat chapel. Formerly the civilian Hollymoor Hospital, a purpose-built annexe of the Rubery Hill Asylum, it had, only the previous year, become the Northfield Military Hospital. Housing in the region of five-hundred patients, its ultimate goal was to reintegrate them into the army.

Once Julian's escort had delivered him to the Guard Room in the main building, he would have been ready for his induction into a strange and surreal world. The procedure would have started with a Royal Army Medical Corps Orderly placing Julian's bulging kit-bag on a trolley and leading him down a series of long corridors, paved with cheap, badly cracked mosaics, their patterns patchily illuminated by low-wattage bulbs, locks meanwhile clicking ominously behind him. Each of these corridors was denoted by a London street-name so as to make it simpler for people to navigate the sprawling building. No sooner had Julian given his details to the clerk in the Admission and Discharge Room than he would have been shown into another room and told to strip naked in preparation for a brief medical examination by a nurse. His next stop would have been the Linen Store, where new patients were issued with a plate, basin, mug, cutlery, towel, some pyjamas, and a pair of socks, as well as the often ill-fitting Sick Soldiers' Uniform. On exchanging his normal khaki clothing for this, he would have accompanied the Orderly down yet more corridors. When they got to the Pack Room, he would have been instructed to leave his kit-bag there, first removing his bathroom things, his plimsoles, boots, shorts, T-shirts, gas-mask, and anything else he needed.

He and the Orderly would then have resumed their trek, eventually passing through what was known as the Day Room. Assuming he arrived at the hospital in the late afternoon, he would have found twenty or thirty ostensibly sane men there, playing cards, or sitting by themselves frowning over jigsaw-puzzles, or writing letters. More than likely greeted by the usual welcoming smiles and nods, he would have been ushered into the adjoining ward, reserved for new arrivals. Allocated one of the narrow, iron-framed beds that lined the reception ward, approached via either Cheapside or Petticoat Lane, Julian would have been told to leave his possessions there before proceeding to the bathroom, where a steaming bath would have awaited him. Afterwards, he would have returned to the crowded Day Room for his evening meal.

As he was changing into his regulation striped pyjamas, just before lights out at 9.00pm, he would probably have had an inkling that the reception ward was not the tranquil place it might have seemed. To reduce the risk of patients hanging themselves, the cords had been removed from all the hospital-issue pyjamas.

At 6.15am the following day, the Night Orderly would have gone round waking each of the other men in the ward, then weighing them and hustling them down the corridor to the bathroom. Julian, on the other hand, would have been told to stay in bed until a psychiatrist had come round and interviewed him. When this was over, he too would have been weighed and led to the bathroom. There the anti-suicide safeguards were especially prominent. Not only were the light-bulbs protected by wire cages, but the lavatories had no chains, relying instead on what were, at the time, innovative push-button flushes.

Freshly washed and shaved, Julian would have rejoined the other occupants of the reception ward. For the duration of their two or three day sojourn there, they had to comply with a strict programme. At 7.00am they gathered in the Day Room for breakfast, served by an Orderly and a Ward Sister. Half an hour later, the breakfast things were cleared away. Under the supervision of an Auxiliary Territorial Service nurse, the patients were set to work polishing the floor in the ward and the Day Room. This continued until 8.30am when they were required to stand beside their beds for the Orderly Medical Officer's tour of inspection.

That morning Julian would have commenced the programme of interviews and tests carried out by the Head Psychiatrist and Chief Medical Officer. These included an intelligence test and a detailed medical examination, in the course of which samples of his blood and urine would have been taken. Depending on the results of these, he would have been assigned the most appropriate of seven grades of physical training, ranging from "Relaxation" to the arduous "Hardening Course", carried out in the cavernous gym, each session coordinated by a team of trained instructors.

On his return to the ward, he would have found a diet-sheet and a coloured card hanging from the clipboard at the bottom of his bed. The colour of the card indicated the psychiatrist entrusted with his case. It also told him which of the echoing, curtainless, sparsely furnished psychiatric wards he'd be transferred to at the end of the mandatory induction period.

Julian was placed in the care of his near-namesake, Major Charles M. Ross. And he was posted to a ward beyond a row of psychiatrists' offices, nicknamed "Harley Street". Like the reception ward, you entered it through a Day Room. On one side of this, there were high windows, the lower half of them bricked up to prevent patients from jumping out. Distributed round the room, there were half-a-dozen hexagonal tables, numerous wooden chairs, a long settee and three armchairs, upholstered in green leather. Through a tall, glass partition, you could see the main body of the ward, its bare floorboards so thoroughly buffed that they glinted in the light.

His fellow patients, for whom the prospect of never being released from Northfield was a nagging possibility, tended to spend most of their free-time in the Day Room. There they warmed themselves by the fire while they wrote letters or made leather trinkets. When they weren't in the Day Room, they entertained themselves with billiards, snooker, bingo, cards, darts, and table tennis. Alternatively, they congregated in the NAAFI (Navy, Army, and Air Force Institute), where they could buy sweets and exchange coupons for a ration of 40 cigarettes-a-week. Or else they played football, went swimming, attended a packed itinerary of trips to the Birmingham Ice Rink, film and stage shows, gramophone concerts, whist drives, tea parties, and boxing tournaments. Friday night dances were also laid on, the generally uncommunicative patients partnered by a much smaller contingent of local girls, otherwise starved of male company. Amorous couples were, however, prevented from sneaking off by military policemen who patrolled the corridors.

But the initial impression of relative normality was misleading. To some extent, the patients were all neurotics, afflicted by states of anxiety, depression, terror, and hysteria, many of them mute and withdrawn, many of them prone to twitching and stuttering, their condition, in certain cases, brought on by the trauma of what they'd seen in combat. Far from being the haven it appeared, the hospital was somewhere that exuded menace. Beneath the surface calm, there lurked the worrying threat of violence, heightened by the knowledge that the majority of the inmates were trained in the techniques of creeping up behind enemy soldiers and silently despatching them.

Equally deceptive was the unrepresentative warmth and homeliness of the Day Room. In the rest of the ward, conditions were a good deal less comfortable. The bathroom was crowded; the marble-floor of the toilets was awash with urine; the lavatory seats were sticky with it; the cubicles were fitted with chest-high doors that enabled Orderlies to peer over them; and the dormitory was glacial, due to the rule that the windows had to be kept open at night. As if it was not already hard enough for the patients to get to sleep, there was always a great deal of talking and horseplay which persisted until the 11.00pm patrol by the Ward Sister, the Orderly Sergeant, and the Orderly Medical Officer, who were empowered to discipline anyone found smoking in bed.

Woken by reveille at 6.30am, on his first morning in the ward Julian witnessed what would become a familiar scene. This consisted of the daily struggle to rouse another of the patients, a punch-drunk ex-boxer with a cauliflower ear, who, though he was still asleep, invariably forced the hapless Orderly to dodge a flurry of punches.

The main event of the morning was scheduled for 10.00am when all but the most severely drugged and incapacitated patients were assembled for a parade which would have been noisier and untidier than any Julian had previously attended. For these shambolic affairs, the conventional standards of military etiquette were abandoned, the only rule being that patients remained in their blue hospital uniforms. Even so, there was little in the way of uniformity. Some of the patients wore brown plimsoles, others favoured army boots. Some were Privates, others NCOs, their stripes fastened to their sleeves with safety-pins. Some had black Tank Corps badges on their khaki caps, others displayed the insignia of different regiments. A lot of the patients, the bulk of whom had long-standing problems conforming to military regulations, exploited the relaxed rules by neglecting to polish either their buttons or their boots. A few of them even remained unshaven. As the Corporal Orderly worked his way through the roll-call, ward by ward, he could scarcely be heard above the din of conversation. If anyone failed to reply when his name was called out, it would be repeated until the patient responded, or another of the men replied for him. While all this was going on, a steady stream of people drifted past: hospital staff; medical orderlies; patients from the training wing; those who weren't required to attend the morning parade, the majority of them walking with the aid of sticks; and men in the enviable position of having just been discharged, their crudely cut civilian demob suits proclaiming their freedom.

When the roll-call was over, the patients who were excused marching fell out. The remainder divided into two sections, the good and the bad walkers, Julian joining the latter. Before setting off on their daily constitutional, many of them donned army great-coats, either because of the cold or because they were ashamed of their distinctive hospital clothes which, at times, provoked hostility from the locals. The Sergeant in charge made them march in rows of three, an order they implemented with calculated indiscipline. The moment they were clear of the hospital grounds, they were permitted to abandon their formation and walk at their own pace. Their route took them round the edge of the hospital boundary, towards the distant Lickey Hills and on to the Bristol Road South, the air filled with the rumble of heavy lorries, army convoys, trams, and the occasional private car. From the doorways of neighbouring shops, apprehensive shoppers eyed them nervously. The road was soon flanked by the vast Longbridge factory. Owned by the Austin Motor Company, it was now being run by BSA, the Birmingham Small Arms Company, who were using it to produce Browning guns. Hence the sporadic, disconcerting rattle of machine-gun fire that could often be heard coming from the testing-range.

Past the factory, they stopped off for their regular morning cup of tea at a row of shops which had been knocked together to form an enormous café, its frontage brightly painted, its forecourt dotted with rustic benches and tables. Most of the other customers were boiler-suited workers from the factory. Forming a separate queue, the hospital patients, among whom there was an infectious feeling of dissatisfaction, would buy themselves spam sandwiches, hot dogs, scones, cakes, and strong cups of tea with real milk and plenty of sugar. Their hunger assuaged, they walked the remaining mile or so into Northfield, where they were free to wander round, provided they returned in time for the 11.45am parade outside the Dining Hall.

Julian and the others would then have trooped into the big, brown-walled, brown linoleum-floored Dining Hall for lunch. Because the hospital had been exempted from rationing restrictions, the food was better than average, meat being a recurrent ingredient. The rest of the day was punctuated by a programme of gym sessions, entertainments, ward meetings, group therapy sessions, and psychiatrist's appointments. Between Julian's arrival and the beginning of the following week, Major Ross concentrated on familiarising himself with the background to the case, which he considered "most interesting [...] but at the same time unusually difficult [...requiring] a considerable amount of study."[2] Besides reading Julian's short stories, Major Ross got him to talk about his life before he joined the army. Julian found the Major "entirely sympathetic and amenable"[3] to the notion that he'd acted out of the best of motives. "Very depressed"[4] though Julian was, the Major's opinion that "there was a good chance of [...] ameliorating the court-martial business"[5] offered some comfort. As did the hope that, if the court-martial was dropped, Arthur Calder-Marshall — who had promised to help — would find him a job at the Ministry of Information.

In his spare-time, Julian was free to read and write. But he couldn't afford all the books and magazines he wanted, not on his meagre 10/- per-week Sick Soldiers' salary, a problem exacerbated by the shortage of interesting material in the Hospital Library. Also, the frequent interruptions made it "practically impossible"[6] for him to carry on with *They Can't Give You A Baby*. If he was going to write anything while he was there, he suspected it would have to be "short stuff",[7] nothing that required his unbroken attention.

He did, however, maintain the flow of letters to Rupert Hart-Davis, who had already contacted the hospital's Registrar to plead Julian's case. Hart-Davis even assisted his "flat broke"[8] friend by cashing two cheques Julian had just been paid by magazine editors.

During his next interview with Major Ross, Julian suggested that he should be released from the army for six months while he finished his book and found himself a job in either the War Office or a government ministry. But Major Ross was unwilling to recommend him for release until he had a firm job offer.

Worries about his immediate prospects proliferating, these worries combined with longer-term concerns about how he'd support himself once the war ended, his gloom had swiftly deepened. So much so that when reveille sounded on the morning of Wednesday 17 March he had trouble getting out of bed. His tardiness led one of the hospital staff to shout at him and threaten him with being placed on a charge.

Unable to stomach any more of the army's "petty discipline",[9] he was now more determined than ever to return to civilian life, where he could "be of some real use to the war effort."[10] Through Major Ross, he obtained an interview with the CO, Lieutenant-Colonel Pearce, who had the power to decide whether or not he should be discharged from the army. Julian came away from the interview with cause for optimism, the CO having demonstrated himself to be a reasonable man.

To help secure the desired result, Hart-Davis arranged to visit the hospital on Friday 26 March. As well as talking things over with Major Ross, he saw Julian during normal visiting hours. The warm and sunny weather enabled the two of them to sit outside while they chatted, Hart-Davis's continued interest in publishing a collection of Julian's army stories probably offering an agreeable distraction. Before leaving, Hart-Davis assured him that he would do what he could to assist. But Julian's optimism about securing a discharge was soon dispelled.

The following Tuesday, in the aftermath of the CO visiting the War Office to discuss his case, Julian had another session with Major Ross, who now seemed bent on keeping him in uniform. Such a sudden and inexplicable change of mind made him suspect that "somebody with some pull [was] trying to do [him] harm."[11] Despite Julian's protestations about how he was "incapable of carrying on",[12] how it "would benefit nobody",[13] and how it would only precipitate a full-blown nervous breakdown, Major Ross talked about him being posted to another army clerical job. The mere thought of this plunged him into an even more profound depression than before. When he realised that his only hope of avoiding a return to the army lay in persuading the CO to overrule Major Ross, he wrote to Hart-Davis, urging him to argue for a discharge. "I'd sooner work in a factory or on munitions [...] rather than have anything more to do with the army [...]," he explained. "I feel worse than when I was awaiting trial, since it seems that this, like every help I have been promised in the army, is leading nowhere — or rather to another bloody orderly room."[14]

Five days later, as part of his campaign to circumvent Major Ross, Julian managed to obtain a second interview with Lieutenant-Colonel Pearce. The outcome of it proved such an "awful shock [...he] nearly broke down completely".[15] Instead of contradicting Major Ross, the CO "said there was not only no chance of getting a War Office job but that [Julian] would also have to return and face the court-martial",[16] after which he'd probably have to go back to more clerical work.

That same day, Julian penned the next of his regular letters to Hart-Davis, confessing that he'd "come to the end of [his] tether."[17] Lonely, frustrated, and in a "pretty black"[18] mood, "the suspense and alternate hope and despair"[19] starting to undermine his mental health, he followed this with a phone-call and yet another letter, embellishing the conspiracy theory he'd evolved. "It's quite possible," he confided in Hart-Davis, "that there is someone who has connections at the War Office who wants me out of the way".[20]

Again, Hart-Davis did his best to help by writing to the COs of both the hospital and the Infantry Depot in Southend, stating that Julian "would only be an expensive liability in the army and they would do well to discharge him."[21] But Hart-Davis's efforts had no discernible impact.

For the time-being, Julian's frenzied state of mind precluded him from writing anything other than long, impassioned letters. He did, however, have the chance to catch up on his reading, thanks to the surprisingly well-stocked branch library in Northfield, from where patients could borrow books provided they paid a deposit amounting to the price of whatever they borrowed. The locker beside his bed became a treasure trove of contemporary literature, containing the latest works by Graham Greene, Evelyn Waugh, Carson McCullers, Georges Simenon, and Francis Stuart. These were augmented by magazines and new anthologies, their purchase subsidised by the sale of more of his short stories.

One of his army pieces was bought by *Tribune*, and two others were purchased by hardback anthologies. Through John Lehmann, he was put in touch with the editors of the soon-to-be-launched *Bugle Blast*, who wanted to include a piece by him in their compilation of writing by members of the armed forces. He gave them *Subject: Surprise Visit*, a short, typically satirical sketch about the panic caused by the news that a General was due to inspect his unit. His other sale came courtesy of

Colonel Connolly, who had prepared *Horizon Stories*, an anthology —
released by Faber & Faber — of the best fiction to appear in the
magazine to date. *A Bit of a Smash*, its title and setting (but not its
censored language) reinstated, was among the chosen few, its selection
earning Julian £5.

Prompted by the increasing likelihood of Jonathan Cape publishing
his army stories, a contract for which seemed imminent, he sought Hart-
Davis's advice on an appropriate follow-up, the hope being that his
prospective publisher would issue him with an advance. Because Julian
felt that he "should stop writing about the army for a while",[22] he shelved
They Can't Give You A Baby. And he also set aside *The Fields of Night* on
the grounds that he was too close to the experiences he'd be describing.
He was left with two alternatives: either to write a novel set entirely on
the Riviera, or else to attempt "something which [...would] present a
complete background of life as [...he] knew it during the changing years
from money and the Riviera to vacuum-cleaners and the first days of the
army."[23] On Hart-Davis's advice, he made plans to go ahead with the
second of these. Yet circumstances continued to prevent him from
"having [...the] clear mind"[24] he needed to implement his plans.

Uppermost in his thoughts was, of course, the looming prospect of
being forced back into the army which, he feared, would mean his
"finish as a person and a writer."[25] Though he was trying not to let
things get him down, the rigid strictures of hospital life were also having
an adverse effect on his already frayed nerves. Twice within the space of
a week, he was placed under arrest by officious staff, his absence from a
scheduled stint in the gym being the first of his transgressions. Each
time, the charge was later dropped, the hospital authorities claiming it
was the result of a "misunderstanding".

The "absolutely heartbreaking"[26] uncertainty about his future was
amplified by the sudden revelation, during the penultimate week of
April, that both Major Ross and Lieutenant-Colonel Pearce would soon
be replaced. Before Major Ross departed the following Monday, Scylla
travelled from Norfolk to Northfield. While she was there, she spoke to
the Major, who revealed that "he had recommended Julian's discharge
from the army as he did not consider him to be temperamentally
suited."[27] First, though, Julian — who was deemed "quite responsible
for his actions"[28] at the time of his desertion — would have to face a
court-martial and serve whatever sentence was deemed appropriate.

Near the end of April, Julian's sense of isolation — expressed in letters
to Mac — was alleviated by the fortuitous arrival of Raynor Heppenstall,

a fellow writer, fellow Francophile, fellow misfit, and almost exact contemporary. A sardonic and cynical working-class Yorkshireman with a predilection for poker-faced witticisms, Heppenstall also turned out to be an ardent admirer of his work.

Haggard with worry, Julian, "walking rapidly but with steps articulated, as it seemed, only from the knees [...] three or four library books under his arm",[29] was on his way to see his psychiatrist when one of the patients pointed him out to Heppenstall and said, "He don't give a damn."[30] It was in the Dining Hall, where two or three-hundred men usually sat, eating, drinking, and gossiping to the accompaniment of an inmate who played swing-style fox-trots on the piano, slapping out the bass with his fist, that Heppenstall next sighted Julian. Extending across the room, there were four parallel queues. At the head of each of these, there was a tea-urn, tended by a bespectacled, diminutive girl in a blue uniform. Behind her, there were tables laden with scones, sandwiches, rock-cakes, and jam tarts. When Julian reached the counter, he scanned the goodies and said, "Tea and two pieces of jam tart, please."[31]

"Jam tart's finished," the girl responded defiantly.

"Nothing of the sort," Julian insisted, pointing towards what he wanted. "I can see two whole tarts over there."

"That's not my table."

"I really don't care who's table it is. Please cut me two pieces from one of those jam tarts."

"Come on, mate," the man behind Julian said. "We all want to be served."

"Is it my fault if these girls adopt a policy of wilful obstruction?" Julian replied before renewing his duel with the girl at the counter. "I want two pieces of jam tart and a cup of tea. Fetch the manageress, will you?"

Shooting him a venomous glance, the girl presented him with his tea and jam tarts. To exact revenge on her, Julian poured a handful of coins back into his pocket and pulled out a note instead. With a show of annoyance, his adversary flounced over to the till and changed it, leaving Julian to turn to the man behind him and say, "I'm very sorry to keep you waiting, chum. But somebody had to make a fuss. These girls act like God Almighty. Anyone would think they were doing you a favour to serve you at all."

He waited for his change, then manouevred out of the queue, careful not to spill his tea. Since there were no empty tables, he took a seat at one already occupied by a cadet from the training wing.

"Excuse me," Julian said, peering mischievously at the pristine white band round the cadet's cap. "The blood is seeping through your bandage."

His victim flashed him a dubious smile.

"I have often wondered," Julian mused, "what operation is performed on those at OCTU, so that they must all wear a bandage about the head. Do they trepan you and take something out, or do they put something in?"

Still smiling, the cadet got up and walked away.

It was in the same venue that Julian's first meeting with Heppenstall took place. He was sitting by himself at one of the linoleum-topped tables, its surface spattered with crumbs and tea, when Heppenstall came over and engaged him in conversation. At this, his "peevish haughtiness folded back and revealed a charm and friendliness his physiognomy had not promised."[32] Glad to have someone who shared his passion for writing and contemporary literature, he was soon lending Heppenstall books from his amply-stocked locker and "lovingly exhibit[ing] his collection of notebooks and writing paper."[33]

The scope for literary conversations widened when, around this time, possibly at a hospital-sanctioned tea party thrown by a well-meaning local resident, he met another admirer of his work, the Birmingham-based freelance critic and novelist Walter Allen, whose earnest expression was accentuated by buck-teeth and heavy, black-framed glasses. Dissimilar as the two men were, they had enough in common to kindle a friendship. Anxious not to lose touch with Julian after he obtained his anticipated discharge from the army, Walter promised to look him up in London where, lured by the Soho pubs and the presence of the film and publishing industries, he had already made up his mind to settle. He told Walter that "he didn't know where he would be living but he could be found from six to eleven most evenings at the lefthand side of the Saloon Bar in the Wheatsheaf."[34]

In his desperation to avoid the stressful trial that appeared the inevitable prelude to his return to civilian life, Julian pondered a possible legal loophole. By consulting military regulations, he was able to confirm his suspicions that the army hadn't followed proper court-martial procedure. Reassured by this newfound knowledge, he had, by the first week of May, recovered his composure sufficiently to start writing again. Whenever he got the chance, he'd position himself in the Day Room, his back to both the fire and the other patients encircling it.

The adjoining wall-seat piled with books and a cardboard box of letters, writing-paper, and notebooks, he would sit there, sucking on his cigarette-holder, the draught from the window blowing the smoke in his eyes as he resumed his disrupted career.

Dismal though the hospital was, its absurdities furnished him with fresh material whose comic potential he belatedly recognised. Roused from sleep one night by a mob of irate, broom-wielding patients, clutching the loose waistbands of their pyjamas as they pursued a mouse round the ward, he speedily processed the incident into a story called *We've A Rat In Our Ward*. He also wrote a short, very funny piece called *I'm Too Old To Learn The Violin*. He was far from pleased with this, disparaging it as a mere sketch, yet he permitted it to be featured in *Psyche*, a mimeographed hospital magazine that had just been launched. Outside Northfield, meanwhile, Julian's literary reputation continued to grow. In a review of the latest issues of *Penguin New Writing* and *Modern Reading*, *The TLS* focused on his contributions, highlighting their cynicism, and crisp, photographic style.

But it wasn't long before all the same old worries reasserted themselves. Following Major Ross's departure, Julian's case was taken over by a new psychiatrist who, he'd heard, was determined "to keep everyone on in the army, even those recommended for discharge."[35] In a blatant contradiction of everything Major Ross had told Scylla, Julian was suddenly fetched from his ward on the morning of Monday 10 May by a heavily armed three-man escort. They issued him with his infantry uniform and the rest of his equipment. Without even giving him a chance to gather together his books and manuscripts, they marched him to the Guard Room. While he waited for the relevant paperwork to be completed, his over-zealous escort kept watch over him.

Hearing what had happened, Heppenstall hurried over to the Guard Room to see Julian. The normally affable Sergeant in charge wouldn't let them talk, so Heppenstall could only give Julian an encouraging smile, a thumbs-up gesture, and make a scribbling movement with his hand. Julian nodded and smiled back, but his mind was elsewhere.

Under armed guard, he was hauled off to the railway station and taken back to Southend. On the train he scrawled a panicky note to Hart-Davis, appealing for assistance. When Julian completed his journey, he appears to have been reinstalled in the Regimental Gaol, the consequent solitude driving him to despair. That Friday morning, he was seen by the MO, whom he "rather annoyed".[36] Perhaps as a means of needling Julian, the MO talked about having him committed to an asylum: a possibility that terrified him, partly because he didn't want to be tarnished by "the stigma of insanity".[37] At their next meeting, the day afterwards, the MO frightened him still further by saying that the army had categorised him as a psychopathic personality. Mention of this made him fear they'd "try to certify [...him] directly after discharge."[38]

Despite repeated calls for help, issued via another letter, a telegram, and even a message relayed by Scylla, he heard nothing from Hart-Davis. Powerless to influence the army's machinations, he was left to await a decision. Midway through the following week, he at last received a response from Hart-Davis who had, it transpired, been posted elsewhere. Hart-Davis informed him that the CO at Southend had reached a favourable decision. Besides shelving court-martial proceedings, he'd decided to suspend Julian's original 28 day prison sentence, subject to a re-examination by a psychiatrist. On Wednesday 19 May, however, Julian discovered that the CO had changed his mind. Now Julian would have to serve the prison sentence, after which a Medical Board would decide whether or not to discharge him. His paranoia fed by what the MO had told him, he was convinced "this was only the beginning of it".[39] Should his suspicions be proved correct, the Medical Board would then refuse to grant his recommended discharge, trapping him in what had become a bureaucratic nightmare.

Two days after the CO's revised verdict had come through, Julian was taken to the grim Military Detention Barrack in Colchester, where he was due to serve his sentence. Though military prisons had a reputation for excessively harsh treatment, the Commandant took pity on Julian and gave him "a light job in the office".[40] Nonetheless, there seems to have been no escaping the regime's "tyrannically enforced discipline",[41] which extended to a ban on cigarettes. Being such a heavy smoker, he must have suffered severe nicotine-withdrawal symptoms. What's more, each day he was quick-marched round the parade-ground, carrying a full pack. And when the air-raid siren went off during the night, he was woken and ordered to put on his battle-dress, together with a gas-mask. Even his morning trips to the toilet became a basis for anxiety. If he was still sitting on the lavatory beyond the permissible three minutes, the warder would thrust his grimacing face in front of Julian's and shout, "Come on, man, come on! What do you think you are? A woman having a baby?"[42]

With generous remission for good behaviour, Julian was released from the Detention Barrack on Friday 11 June. Instead of slotting back into his previous role in the Orderly Room, he was assigned to C Company while he awaited the promised Medical Board, experience breeding scepticism about whether it would ever take place. Against all logic, his new CSM declared him fit to perform any duties, the likelihood of further humiliation on the parade-ground inducing in him understandable alarm. But the MO, in view of Julian's knee problem, soon excused him from most parades. Due to his poor physical condition, he was adjudged suitable for nothing more demanding than so-called sanitary duties. Each morning at 9.00am, Julian — now stripped of his Lance-Corporal's stripe — would cross the barrack square, clutching a tin of disinfectant and a bucket containing brushes, soap, and a cloth. For the next two hours he'd submit to the indignity of cleaning the lavatories.

Only four days into his latest posting, he was instructed to report to the Area Psychiatrist. In the absence of Major Lock, who was ill, Julian saw a colleague of his. The man's blunt and detached manner made Julian fear the worst. Yet he came away feeling much less pessimistic, the psychiatrist having assured him that his discharge was a formality.

His thoughts no longer monopolised by the army, he was free to turn his attention back to his writing. As well as struggling to produce an account of life in the Detention Barrack, he once again started to consider more ambitious projects. While he'd been performing menial jobs in the Colchester, he had had an idea for the thriller he'd long been wanting to write. Its title altered from *The Fields of Night* to *The Hunted Man: A Melodrama*, he now drew up a basic outline, which he sent to Hart-Davis in the hope Jonathan Cape might commission it. As he envisaged it, the novel would depict "the individual against the machine (in this case the army)."[43] Replete with autobiographical references, its settings encompassing a deserted funfair, an army psychiatric ward, and a detention barrack, the book would follow the hunted man of the title, a writer by the name of Severn who, while in London on leave from the army, becomes the victim of a fascist conspiracy. But the ruthless conspirators, one of whom dies in a fall down the escalator of a tube station, are challenged by Severn, his resolve hardened by the ordeal.

For all the psychiatrist's assurances, Julian still harboured suspicions that someone at the War Office was plotting against him. In consequence, he half-expected either to be posted abroad, or to be discharged from the army, then certified insane, "railroaded into the nuthouse",[44] and prevented from writing. These suspicions were only relinquished when the Telephone Orderly, with whom Julian was on friendly terms, mentioned that he'd eavesdropped on a call between the CO and Major Lock. The conversation made it clear that Julian was about to be discharged.

An additional indication of his probable release came when he received orders to attend a Medical Board on Monday 5 July. In advance of that, he spent at least part of his latest allocation of leave in Felixstowe. The evening before his big day, he seated himself in an alcove in the bar of the giant Felix Hotel where, cigarette-holder protruding from his mouth, he hurriedly wrote up another army story. All of a sudden, he was interrupted by a girl he knew. The girl — Zoë Hicks, a daughter of Augustus John — introduced Julian to her friend Joan Wyndham. To make a good impression on his companions, both of whom were in WAAF uniform, he bought them all double-whiskies and told them he was about to be invalided out of the army after a stint in the Officer Training Corps. When he found out that Joan and Zoë were going down to London the following day, he arranged to travel with them, saying he wanted to see his publisher and visit the Soho pubs.

Next day, he swapped his unflattering army clothes for his old cream corduroy jacket and teddy-bear coat, his malacca cane completing the costume. But he was mortified to discover his outfit looked a little shabby. And it no longer fitted properly. Since he'd been in the army, he'd put on weight, a prominent pot-belly jutting out from his otherwise slender frame.

On the train with the two girls, whom he'd instructed to "call him Jay because everyone else does",[45] he talked about his literary ambitions and about the appalling time he'd had in the Suffolk Regiment. From the station, he whisked them off to the Fitzroy, where he got into a game of Spoof with some other people he knew. Feeling neglected as well as bored by his incessant self-absorption, the girls soon abandoned him in favour of the poet Dylan Thomas.

That afternoon he travelled back to Southend for the crucial Medical Board, at which he was handed his passport to civilian life. Declaring that he'd "ceased to fulfil army physical requirements",[46] the doctors regraded him "E" — unfit for military service. Yet he still had to wait until his official discharge papers came through. As a final reminder of the cumbersome and inflexible bureaucracy that had so exasperated him, the days drifted past without any sign of these.

Much as he yearned for a return to civilian life, he was apprehensive about it, a lack of money being the prime cause for concern. To bring in the cash he needed, he attempted to raise advances for the books he'd been planning, and to resolve the question of whether Hart-Davis would be publishing his collection of army stories, the title of which was undecided. Along with that, he also urged Hart-Davis to pay him an advance that would support him while he wrote either *The Hunted Man* or *They Can't Give You A Baby*. So far, though, the only positive commitment had come from the editor and journalist, Leonard Russell, who commissioned him to write a short novel for inclusion in *The Saturday Book*, the hardback miscellany which Russell edited. Entitled *Hangover*, the proposed novel would, Julian felt, contain "a lot of stuff [he] want[ed] to get rid of before [his] mind [could] be free."[47]

In parallel with his efforts to sell his work, he was allowed to make frequent trips to London, where he tried to find employment. Before leaving the depot late in the morning, he'd change out of his army uniform. During his afternoons in London, he touted his scriptwriting talents round the Ministry of Information, the BBC, and various film companies. Despite his optimism about his job prospects, nothing materialised. He had more luck, however, with arranging accommodation. This appears to have consisted of a flat at 19 Park Place Villas, a squat Regency mansion in Maida Vale, rimmed by a narrow balustraded garden, only the breadth of the adjoining road separating it from the Regent's Park canal. Once the tenancy had been sorted out, he wrote to Raynor Heppenstall and asked him to post the pile of manuscripts and notebooks, left behind at the hospital, to his new address.

By mid-July, Julian's discharge papers still hadn't appeared, yet his frustration must have been tempered by the news that Hart-Davis had decided to publish his collection of stories. Hart-Davis had, moreover, committed the company to taking out an option on *The Hunted Man*, which Julian saw as a "Hitchcockian melodrama... [portraying a world in which] the individual has as little chance of survival as a sparrow striking a high tension cable."[48]

The deal hadn't yet been tied up when Hart-Davis was granted compassionate leave from the army to travel to America to fetch his two eldest children, who had been evacuated there earlier in the war. In his place, Julian had to negotiate with G. Wren Howard, co-founder of the company, who floated the idea of expanding the collection to include Julian's civilian stories. Faced by Howard's notorious parsimony, dislike of authors, and reluctance to discuss financial terms, Julian's vague distrust of publishers rapidly crystallised into a conviction that they exploited and misunderstood writers. Still, he managed to strike an acceptable bargain with Howard. The arrangement was formalised on Monday 26 July when Julian signed a contract securing an immediate £100 advance on the royalties from his debut collection of stories. As a mark of gratitude for all Hart-Davis's help, Julian dedicated it to him. In his eagerness to see the book published as soon as possible, he obtained a promise that it would be released the following January.

A fortnight after these negotiations had been concluded, the galling wait for his discharge papers finally came to an end.

Annie Allchild behind
the bar of The Fitzroy
Tavern, during the
1939-45 war
(© Sally Fiber)

Phil Lindsay,
late 1930s
(© Cressida Lindsay)

Count Potocki of
Montalk, c.1940

J.M. Tambimuttu (right)
giving a talk about
T.S. Eliot, 1942
(© BBC Photo Library)

Bronia Kennedy, c.1944
(© Mrs Bronia McDonald)

Ironfoot Jack,
drawing by Ruth Willetts, c.1955
(© Paul Willetts)

Dylan Thomas, 1940s
(© BBC Photo Library)

London Calling

Freed at last from what he saw as "the crazy, petty atmosphere of army life",[1] Julian left the depot at Southend on the morning of Monday 9 August 1943, which he thought of as "Release Day".[2] He then made his way to the station and boarded the London train. Its hypnotic rhythm soon lulled him to sleep, his slumber apparently animated by an exhilarating dream in which the entire plot of *The Hunted Man* reeled through his head. Scene after scene were visualised with the clarity of a movie. All that remained now was to capture the whole thing on paper.

As planned, he moved into the flat he'd found. To celebrate his emancipation, he treated himself to an extravagant shopping spree, unwittingly reprising his father's youthful improvidence. Of the money Jonathan Cape had paid him, he spent most of it on a flashy new wardrobe. Reacting against such a prolonged period of being confined to drab army uniforms, he kitted himself out with a crimson jacket and cream suit, both in corduroy, plus a black astrakhan-collared coat, a maroon cummerbund, a mustard-yellow waistcoat, and a silk Schiaparelli tie with a bold pattern of French newspaper headlines on it. He also acquired a pair of sunglasses, a rare accoutrement then, rendered doubly unusual by their American aviator-style frames. He took to wearing these most of the time, even when he was groping through the blackout, his unwillingness to remove them provoking wearyingly repetitive enquiries as to whether he was blind, or disfigured, or wore them "to hide behind because of a psychological need."[3] The desired gangsterish connotations were diluted by the rest of his outfit, the cream suit more evocative of the Riviera, the malacca cane more redolent of the fin-de-siècle foppishness he'd embraced as a teenager. In an era of uniformity, of wartime austerity, his appearance ensured that he was as conspicuous as a Technicolor interloper in a monochrome movie. And it aroused inevitable suspicion that he was, in the parlance of the day, queer.

Proudly attired in his latest get-up, his coat habitually draped round his shoulders in the style of a smooth but sinister Hollywood hoodlum, he passed the long summer evenings reacquainting himself with the riotous wartime Soho pub scene. Sometimes he went to the huge, high-ceilinged Swiss Tavern on Old Compton Street, its subdued lighting lending it a murky intimacy. Normally abbreviated to "the Swiss", it had a raffish ambience that made it popular with painters and writers — Julian's old acquaintance Mulk Raj Anand among them — who didn't mind the tarnished walls and the barman's dirt-soiled white mess-jacket. Unable to afford pricey bottles of black-market booze, he had to rely on the normal quota of, at most, two pints of beer each night. Drinking there one evening, Julian got into conversation with the wiry, lean-featured conscientious objector, would-be writer, and fellow Graham Greene afficionado, Stephen Fothergill, who made the mistake of telling him the story of how he'd been banned from a nearby pub "on account of his staggering."[4] From that moment onwards Julian, quick to reduce people to the status of eccentric supporting characters in his personal drama, called him "Staggering Stephen".[5]

On another night there, soon after his arrival in the capital, Julian was buttonholed by the flamboyant, ruthlessly egotistical Sinhalese editor of *Poetry London*, Jim Tambimuttu. Slim and somewhat pale-skinned with sinuous black hair, his appearance made even more distinctive by his battered calf-length blue overcoat, buttoned to the chin against the cold, its velvet collar turned up, "Tambi" — as he liked to be known — was then at the height of his renown as a literary impresario. Appropriately enough for the man who claimed to have coined the term Fitzrovia, Tambi squandered the majority of his time in pubs and cafés, seldom without a flock of awestruck hangers-on, captivated by his bohemian glamour, his courteous, disarmingly relaxed and cordial manner, not to mention his deep and melodious voice, the vowel-sounds elongated, the confiding phrase "y'know" peppering his speech. Within a few minutes, Julian too had been swept along on one of his nightly pub-crawls, their departure supposedly prefaced by Tambi's solemn warning against the danger of contracting "Sohoitis",[6] of "stay[ing] there always day and night and get[ting] no work done ever."[7]

It was not to the Swiss but to Soho's northern annexe that Julian more often gravitated. Since he'd first got to know the area, the Fitzroy Tavern had remained physically unaltered, yet it had lost its bohemian cachet, its decline hastened by the annoying number of gawping sightseers who converged on it. Indeed, it was well on the way to becoming more famous as a homosexual pick-up joint, mainly frequented by sailors. The reputation of the place, sufficient for it to be declared out of bounds for army personnel, was confirmed by the presence of Paul, the bearded, kilt-wearing pianist — ears adorned with little gold earrings, wrists sheathed by bangles — who played stride-piano and sang bawdy songs in a camp, high-pitched voice. Conscious of the Fitzroy's associations, Julian preferred the Wheatsheaf. In the run-up to 6.00pm, he'd be waiting outside the front door. When opening-time at last arrived, he'd breeze through the Public Bar and into the Saloon Bar, always making a beeline for the extreme lefthand end of the counter, where it was easiest to get served. One elbow propped on the back of the tall settle to his right, he would stand there, casting an ironic, surprisingly observant eye over the noisy, jostling throng, his upright posture emphasising his height, his already precise and inhibited gestures constricted by the paucity of space. Neither the faint smell of food filtering down from the upstairs billiard-cum-dining room, nor the plangent wail of air-raid sirens, nor the dull thud of exploding bombs and the accompanying stutter of anti-aircraft fire could dislodge him from the Saloon Bar, its reassuringly cosy atmosphere enhanced by the tight-fitting blackout boards over the windows. Periodically, though, he had to relinquish his spot, wriggle through the crowd and up the packed stairs to the gents'. If he returned to discover that his spot at the bar had been usurped, he would slowly but inexorably shoulder aside the intruder.

Finding himself in the company of devoted drinkers, nursing their precious pints, he began to increase his alcohol intake. Most of the time he drank acidic, suspiciously watery Scotch Ale, served by an ill-assorted trio of bar-staff. The landlady was a short, plump spinster named Mona Glendenning, who ran the place in conjunction with her similarly rotund brother, Redvers, and his wife, Frances, a spindly woman in a tweed suit and pince nez. Except on Sundays when he wore a battered-looking suit, Redvers — "Red" for short — favoured shirtsleeves and braces, his stomach spilling over the waistband of his trousers. In recognition of Julian's growing value as a customer, Red started favouring him with extra beer and the odd additional measure of strictly rationed White Horse whisky.

Unlike the Fitzroy, the clientele of the Wheatsheaf tended to be a less boisterous, more diverse group. The predominantly middle and upper-middle-class artistic and literary types, whose appearances tended to coincide with when they were on leave from the military, coexisted but seldom interacted with a fluid blend of businessmen, civil servants, black marketeers, criminals, deserters, elderly locals, and the occasional whore. While the pubs in the southern sector of Soho were overrun by foreign soldiers, sailors and airmen as well as male and female prostitutes taking a breather from servicing the servicemen, the Wheatsheaf's comparative distance from the West End meant that few of the foreigners or the whores found their way there. An exception was the demure-looking prostitute nicknamed "Sister Ann". Outside the evening rush-hour, when she stood on Tottenham Court Road, snagging prospective clients as they walked towards the tube, she was often to be seen loitering in the corridor between the two bars, her subdued appearance giving no indication of her trade.

Two of the Wheatsheaf's most loyal customers were Wilf, an ancient member of the Home Guard, a line of medals arrayed across his chest, some of which dated from the Zulu War; and a tiny, cantankerous octogenarian named Mrs Stewart, rumoured to have been a beautiful streetwalker in her youth. Always neatly clad in an anachronistic black dress, she would, like Julian, arrive punctually at opening-time and head for the Saloon Bar. In a voice so garbled she was barely intelligible, she'd buy herself a bottle of Guinness and sit on the settle directly behind him, a newspaper spread out across the table, timing herself with an alarm-clock as she ploughed through a crossword-puzzle. As Julian was to discover, she'd take umbrage if anyone tried to help her with a tricky clue. She could also be offhand with well-meaning people who volunteered to stand her a drink. But Julian was so solicitous of her welfare, his attitude towards her chivalrous if a shade condescending, she soon accepted him, along with the drinks he bought her.

In the course of his visits to the Saloon Bar, he came across all its other stalwarts. There was the strapping, overtly lesbian novelist, Kaye Dick, emphasising the aptness of her surname with mannish clothes. There was Charles Wrey Gardiner, the amiable, bespectacled, formally attired proprietor of the Grey Walls Press, which Julian dubbed "the Grey Balls Press".[8] There was the venerable, floppy-hatted Augustus John, sitting at the other end of the bar, eavesdropping on whatever was going on around him. There were the two Roberts, Colquhoun and MacBryde, very different painters from Augustus John, both Scots, both belligerent and caustic yet as inseparable as the most devoted young married couple. There was the drug-addicted, homosexual John Booth-Palmer, secretary to the theatre critic James Agate. There was the charismatic, long-faced young artist John Minton, boyishly diffident"[9] in "the blue reefer jersey he usually wore."[10] There was the sardonic hack-writer James Graham-Murray (better known by the sobriquet, "James the Shit"), respectable-looking were it not for three or four missing front teeth, the legacy of a misjudged quip. And there was the exhibitionistic, sexually undiscriminating painter Nina Hamnett. Then in her late fifties, her face mottled and puffy, her teeth decayed, her figure concealed beneath fetid and shapeless secondhand clothes, her helmet-like hairstyle topped by a beret she never seemed to remove, she carried herself with panache, undaunted by her miserable circumstances or meagre finances, greeting friends and acquaintances with a jaunty "Hullo, ducks!" Every so often she'd go round rattling the tin where she kept her money, soliciting donations with the well-worn phrases, "Got any mun, dear?" or "You couldn't buy me a drink, could you, love?" For the price of a beer, she would tell oft-repeated anecdotes about her outrageous and happy-go-lucky existence in Twenties Montparnasse, about modelling for Gaudier-Brzeska, hobnobbing with Picasso, dancing naked for Van Dongen, meeting James Joyce, and chalking up affairs with Rodin and Modigliani. "Modi said I had the best tits in Europe," she was fond of remarking. At the faintest provocation, she'd peel back her pullover to reveal breasts far better preserved than the rest of her. "You feel them," she'd say. "They're as good as new."[11]

Other intermittent patrons of the Saloon Bar included the abstemious, thirtysomething Quentin Crisp, dressed in the functional uniform of wartime women, a jacket worn over a blouse, trousers and medium-heeled lace-up shoes, hair meticulously coiffed and hennaed, fingernails glossy with lacquer, face subtly made-up. Equally irregular visitors were Toni del Renzio, spewing tall stories about being related to the Romanoffs and having inherited the Italian title, "Count del Renzio"; Stephen Spender and John Lehmann, both radiating a palpable sense of unease in such flamboyant company; George Orwell, taciturn and watchful, pausing just long enough for a quick half; the ageing aesthete, Norman Douglas, sheltering in England for the duration; as well as the notorious Aleister Crowley, now overweight and seedy, his speech hesitant and doped. Aside from del Renzio and Crowley, the latter of whom claimed to have set fire to the lining of Julian's coat by putting a spell on it, Julian came to be on good terms with all these part-time Wheatsheaf-ites.

Whereas most of the regulars affected a heavily stubbled, self-consciously rumpled look, Julian was always scrupulously clean-shaven and fastidiously turned out. To go with his cigarette-holder, cane, and furled gloves, he took to wearing a fresh pink carnation in his buttonhole and dispensing pinches of snuff to his acolytes. All part of the persona of "Julian the Writer"[12] which he'd created. Such was his aura of impending literary stardom, of someone possessing a privileged insight into the world, a huddle of admirers, many of them girls, attracted by his poise and good looks, would indulge him. They'd buy him drinks, play Spoof with him (which earned him yet more free drinks), and challenge him to name the characters and publication details of obscure novels. His memory was so exceptional, his reading so phenomenal, spanning nineteenth and twentieth-century English,

French, and American fiction, he'd invariably meet the challenge.

The group clustered round Julian also provided a convenient audience for his waggishly outrageous pronouncements and interminable monologues, punctuated by long drags on his cigarette-holder. Brushing aside any attempts at small-talk, he'd hold forth about the books and films he admired, quoting passages or acting out scenes with no effort to distinguish the characters by modifying his voice or gestures. He'd talk about the mechanics of publishing. He would, assuming there were no women within earshot, tell smutty stories and brag about his sexual exploits — something he'd never been prone to do in the past. He'd eulogise the suave villainy, the scene-stealing brio of the Hollywood actors Sydney Greenstreet and Eduardo Cianelli. He'd discourse knowledgably on the careers of infamous murderers such as Henrik de Jong and Eugen Weidmann. And he'd proclaim the books, plays, and film-scripts he planned to write, Weidmann forming a recurrent subject.

At other times he'd recite anecdotes, culled from his experience, their cast often recruited from among his fellow drinkers. Each anecdote would be told again and again, every retelling accruing embellishments and carrying it further from its source. Bit by bit, it would gain authority as well, the drama becoming more distilled, the dialogue terser and more incisive. Eventually it would reach a point where it stopped evolving. At which it was ready to be transcribed in his obsessively neat handwriting and then submitted to the editor of a magazine, the story's title as carefully considered and well-tested as the tale itself.

His ostentatious bearing and seemingly impenetrable force-field of affectation alienated numerous Wheatsheaf-ites, who restricted their dealings with him to distant nods and mimed hullos. Yet he could be "genuinely kind and approachable".[13] When he was introduced to the young aspiring writer Derek Stanford, who had published what, Stanford himself conceded, was a "bogus"[14] essay on Wyndham Lewis in the *Fortune Anthology*, he could have made some sneering comment. Instead, he congratulated Stanford "in the most genial fashion."[15]

Apart from the way his normally unobtrusive eyelids lowered as the hours drifted by, Julian was capable of consuming any available alcohol with no tangible effect. He was so inordinately proud of this, he often used to boast about it. Slowly but steadily soaking up the booze, he'd cling tenaciously to his spot at the bar until closing-time approached. Or until the supply of beer ran out: a common occurrence on particularly busy nights in most wartime pubs, where chalked signs declaring NO DRINK would spring up.

Once last orders had been called just before 10.30pm, the familiar cry of "time gentlemen, please" cutting across the hubbub, Julian would take advantage of a fortuitous discrepancy in the licensing laws. Due to the different regulations operated by the two boroughs of Holborn and Marylebone, the boundary of which ran right down the middle of Charlotte Street, the pubs on the opposite side of the street from the Wheatsheaf closed half-an-hour later. As did those on the other side of Oxford Street, the main section of Soho falling under the aegis of the City of Westminster. Picking his way past the fights that raged most nights in the street outside, past the swaying drunks who shouted slurred insults in his direction or launched unprovoked attacks, his trusty cane coming in handy as a means of defending himself, Julian would sometimes simply transfer to the Marquis of Granby or the Duke of York. Unless, of course, they had run out of drink already.

Positioned at the tip of the diagonal intersection between Rathbone Place and Rathbone Street, the Marquis had a well-deserved reputation for rowdiness. Its sleazy clientele mostly comprised small-time gangsters, bookies, guardsmen, and homosexuals on the lookout for rough-trade, their amorous advances often precipitating punch-ups. If Julian wasn't in the mood to brave the hurly-burly of the Marquis, he'd navigate his way through the blackout — fragments of shrapnel crunching underfoot — to the other end of Rathbone Street, where the Duke of York offered a less hectic alternative. While its Public Bar tended to be packed with the bearded, heavy-fringed, proto-beatniks whom Julian termed "Bums",[16] the posher Saloon Bar was occupied by the literary crowd. Behind the counter, staffed by the irascible "Mad Major" — Major Alf Klein — and his wife Blanche, an orthodox Jew who insisted on the pub closing during religious holidays, there was a large placard proclaiming the landlord "The Prince of Good Fellows". Not that he displayed much fellowship towards some of his bohemian customers, his high-handed attitude towards them earning Julian's dislike.

Alternatively, Julian would join the column of laughing, shouting, shrieking revellers lurching southwards into Soho proper. Beyond the funereal Black Horse, on the final stretch of Rathbone Place, its narrow frontage giving no indication of its roomy, unalluring interior, he and his drinking buddies would turn right onto Oxford Street, then left down Dean Street, arriving at the vibrant, scruffy Highlander just in time, if they were lucky, to squeeze in an extra pint.

When the two Roberts weren't in the Wheatsheaf, they were frequently to be seen amid the perspiring crowd that jammed into the Highlander's pair of tiny, smoky bars. It was there that Julian first nerved himself to speak to "the wolfishly lean and sullen"[17] Robert Colquhoun.

Having seen the latest exhibition of his paintings that afternoon, Julian went up to Colquhoun to congratulate him, only to be branded a phoney by the "gloweringly offensive",[18] Glaswegian-accented painter.

After the Highlander closed, Julian would move on to one of a plethora of cheap, handily placed cafés and restaurants. Occasionally he ventured down St Giles High Street, its pavements dotted with predatory homosexuals loitering near a French-style pissoir. Signposted by the obligatory heterosexual couple enjoying a quick knee-trembler against the wall, there was an unpromising doorway leading to the spacious, seedy basement that housed the strangely-titled Coffee An'. There you could get coffee an' something else, though its impoverished clientele tended to miss the point, assuming instead that it was really called "the Café Anne". Its brusque and swarthy staff, renowned for their readiness to threaten unruly customers with knives, served nothing more sophisticated than horse-meat steaks and salami sandwiches. These were eaten at long refectory tables, a couple of scrawny alsatians loping hungrily round them. Against the backdrop of a large, crudely executed mural depicting a contemporary reinterpretation of the crucifixion, the Roman soldiers portrayed as jackbooted Nazis with swastiki armbands, their faces concealed behind sinister gas-masks, writers and artists sat side by side with crooks and deserters, drawn to Soho because they could survive there without a ration book by purchasing unrestricted foods like salami, horse-meat, pigeon-meat, and even sparrow-meat.

On his visits to the Coffee An', Julian would have seen the New Zealand-born Count Potocki of Montalk, who was there most nights, gorging himself on what was reputed to be the cheapest food in Soho. Not content with asserting that he was the rightful heir to the throne of Poland, Count Potocki also claimed to be the Grand Duke of Lithuania, Hospidar of Moldavia, and High Priest of the Sun. His waist-length hair plaited and tied with a girlish bow, he wore sandals, a billowing scarlet medieval robe with a silver star emblazoned on the front, and a heavy-looking gold chain round his neck with an ornate medallion on the end, the whole risible ensemble topped by either a crown or a velvet cap. He always carried with him a small stack of *The Right Review*, the hand-printed magazine that he hawked round the West End streets, its pages filled with a bizarre combination of decorous woodcuts, poems by writers such as Lawrence Durrell, mad anti-semitic tirades, and convoluted genealogical justifications for his wide-ranging titular claims. Anyone prepared to pay for the Count's meal would be granted a knighthood, the recipient forced to kneel down while the ritual was performed. Only a few months earlier, the Count had been lambasted by the national press for ennobling a deserter.

As a rule, Julian tended to patronise three of the fractionally more upmarket eateries in the environs of the Wheatsheaf. One of these, at 91 Charlotte Street, was Tony's, an unsalubrious ground-floor café and cramped cellar restaurant where black market steak and eggs were served. Mainly patronised by spivs, huddled together in furtive conversation, plus pimps and their heavily made-up girls, each clutching a cheap handbag, "it was a place of 'deals' settled by a nod"[19] and "money exchanged at the exact moment a parcel slipped surreptitiously under the table."[20] Downstairs, braving the reek of fried onions and dry-rot, Julian and a lot of writers, artists and misfits, notably Quentin Crisp, would sit at dirty white tables, eating and chatting. His other favourite post-pub destinations were a small Greek restaurant on Rathbone Place, and the rough-and-ready, sparsely furnished Scala, on Charlotte Street, where nothing cost more than about half-a-crown. The Scala's speciality was the misleadingly titled Vienna Steak, in truth a particularly unedifying form of rissole. As a satisfying epilogue to his night's drinking and socialising, he'd order goose pilaf from the Greek restaurant, Welsh Rarebit from Tony's, or spaghetti bolognese from the Scala, washed down by a carafe of cheap, astringent red wine, and a cup of strong black coffee.

Considering how he'd come to detest service life, it is ironic that Julian's first publication after his discharge was a comic tale called *I Like It In The Army*, featured in the second issue of the hardback anthology, *Bugle Blast*. From his stockpile of army stories, he also sold two more to Kaye Webb, editor of *Lilliput*. Besides which, he succeeded in placing *Mandrake*, an appealing piece about his childhood in the south of France, with *John O'London's Weekly*, the literary tabloid newspaper.

Despite racking up all these sales, he was soon running short of cash. In pursuit of a screenwriting job, he made use of his existing connection with the Films Division of the Ministry of Information. He arranged to meet the bulky, floppy-haired Arthur Calder-Marshall and his radiant wife Ara straight after they'd finished work one evening. The venue was the Horseshoe Tavern, a huge, spartan hotel-turned-pub next to the Dominion cinema, right on the junction between Oxford Street and Tottenham Court Road. On hearing that Julian wanted to take up the earlier offer to find him work at the Ministry, where he had set his sights on a screenwriting job, the Calder-Marshalls whisked him from there to the Highlander, intent on helping him to make some useful but unspecified contact. In its sedate early evening incarnation, the appetising aroma of sausage-rolls and other hot snacks permeating both bars, the Highlander was scarcely recognisable. Its proximity to the offices of the many small documentary film companies, now flourishing under the patronage of the Ministry, ensured a high proportion of young film industry employees among the drinkers. The majority of these were earnest recent graduates whom Julian referred to as "Slithy Toves",[21] "the girls in white blouses and slacks with shoulder-slung bags",[22] the boys in "tweed jackets with leather inserts in the elbows",[23] their university scarves coiled round their necks.

While her husband was ordering their drinks, Ara introduced Julian to someone he'd never met before, though they were more or less the same age and inhabited the same alcohol-fuelled bohemian milieu. His new acquaintance, who had a "narrow white papery clown's face of despairing gaiety"[24] and thick glasses that gave his eyes a lunatic intensity, was the pipe-smoking Scots poet Ruthven (pronounced "Riven") Todd. Ara's husky voice made it sound as if she had introduced Julian to the "Reverend Todd". There was, in any case, something clerical about Ruthven's demeanour.

In "a characteristic Ruthven conversational ploy",[25] he said that he was responsible for Julian's discovery as a writer, having persuaded Cyril Connolly to publish him. Julian didn't believe Ruthven, yet he may have been telling the truth. Ruthven was, after all, helping out at *Horizon* at just the time Julian submitted *A Bit of a Smash in Madras*. Intriguing as Julian found him, Ruthven's competing talents as a monologuist were destined to prevent them from translating mutual curiosity into friendship.

Clearly awaiting someone's arrival, the Calder-Marshalls kept watch over the open door of the pub. Their vigilance was rewarded by the entry of a thick-set man in his early thirties. Arthur Calder-Marshall guided him over to where Julian and Ara were standing. The newcomer was Donald Taylor, the blandly personable Managing Director of the Strand Film Company.

By securing a contract with the Ministry of Information, Strand had established itself as Britain's leading producer of documentaries, their morale-raising message imbued with a socialist vision of a more equitable future. Through his meeting with Donald, who made a habit of recruiting talented writers irrespective of whether they had any screenwriting experience, Julian was offered the job he needed.

*

For a healthy salary of about £10-a-week, payable every Friday, he started work at Strand towards the end of August. The company had a clutch of upstairs offices at 1 Golden Square, wedged right in the corner of a large, verdant park near the southern fringe of Soho. There, amid the clacking and chiming of typewriters, he became part of a triumvirate of screenwriters. His colleagues comprised Dylan Thomas and Phil Lindsay, the heavy-drinking Australian novelist, who was collaborating with Donald on a feature-film script about the murderous Dr Crippen.

Julian's new boss paired him off with the short, tubby figure of Dylan, assigned them a shared office, and set them to work on a screenplay about the Home Guard. He and Dylan skirted one another warily at first, only establishing a rapport when they went drinking that evening. From the office, they adjourned to the conveniently positioned Café Royal. A revolving-door at the back of the building was screened by some heavy velvet blackout curtains. Fumbling through these in the darkness, they'd have found themselves at the foot of a shallow, dazzlingly lit flight of stairs. These led up to the smoky, red plush-upholstered Back Bar, where bohemians rubbed shoulders with American servicemen and their giggling girlfriends. Julian and his new colleague plundered the Back Bar's abundant supply of Irish whisky, its availability a perk of Ireland's neutrality. After a few drinks there, they headed off to the Wheatsheaf, pausing for a glass or two in their favourite Soho pubs, Julian gradually coming to appreciate Dylan's exuberance, his charm, his ribald sense of humour, his relish for the lurid and macabre.

Except at weekends when Dylan frequently went off to Wales, where his wife Caitlin and their baby daughter were sheltering from the bombing, he and Julian now tended to spend their evenings together in the Wheatsheaf. Incompatible as they were in so many ways, not least in their potentially conflicting predilection for monopolising conversations and their constant need for admirers from whom to cadge money, they formed an unlikely alliance. With their loud voices and even louder clothing, Dylan affecting the style of check-suit and matching cap favoured by illegal off-course bookies, they dominated the Saloon Bar. Often they'd discuss their screenwriting work. Or else Dylan would reminisce fondly about Fred Farr, his mentor on *The Swansea Evening Post*.

It was probably through Dylan that Julian got to know his friend and near-contemporary, the critic John Davenport. A broad-shouldered, chubby former wrestler and poet manqué, he was customarily to be seen with a cowlick of thick black hair drooping over his forehead and a cigarette protruding from his pneumatic lips. Davenport had a well-earned reputation for being bellicose, embittered, tactless, and tetchy. Nevertheless, he struck up another unexpected friendship with Julian, whose narcissism he found endearingly absurd, whose essential generosity and tolerance excused his "didactic arrogance",[26] whose "independence of mind",[27] critical acuity and literary gifts Davenport considered worthy of respect.

But Julian didn't take to Dylan's other chum, the equally corpulent Gilbert Wood, who worked as a scene painter on film sets. Timid when sober but acerbic when drunk, he had what Julian felt was an undeserved reputation as a trenchant wit. Together with Julian, Dylan and Davenport, he formed part of the core of a sizeable Spoof-playing contingent. This was also made up of the cheerful, beer-bellied Welsh poet Keidrich Rhys and his smartly-clothed wife Lynette, her face often haloed by a big black hat; the pudgy-featured Phil Lindsay; and the habitually tousled, unshaven Canadian-born, English-educated Paul Potts, inveterate scrounger, fervent left-winger and self-styled "People's Poet From The Canadian Prairies". Like Julian and Keidrich, Paul had been ignominiously discharged from the army, though he still dressed in a tatty army-issue greatcoat which flapped open to reveal a stained red shirt, worn with sandals and black corduroy trousers.

Two other integral members of the clique were Tambi and his Sinhalese sidekick Alagu Subramaniam, always abbreviated to "Subra". The antithesis of Tambi in most respects, Subra was dumpy, indolent, equable, and so reticent he seldom mentioned the short stories he wrote. Whatever the weather, a long red scarf dangled from his stubby neck. A lawyer-turned-loafer, Subra supported himself by working in a bookshop on Southampton Row, where he told people he was the General Manager. In reality, he was no more than a dogsbody, his income supplemented by stealing books on request.

Via Tambi, Julian also met the abstract-expressionist painter Gerald Wilde. Tambi would sometimes sweep into the pub, trailing Gerald behind him like some faithful but badly fed mongrel, a startled expression on his prematurely grisled countenance, his attenuated face wreathed by twin fronds of shaggy ginger hair, his clothes so dirty they looked as if they belonged to a tramp. Requisitioning a hat from someone, which doubled as a begging-bowl, Tambi would work his way round the pub. His double-jointed fingers pointing in the direction of Gerald, whose unkempt appearance spoke eloquently of bohemian penury, he'd solicit contributions for "a poor but brilliant artist [...] who lacked not only food but also the materials to express his genius."[28] The contents of the hat would then be decanted into Tambi's pocket, the hat returned to its owner, and a round of drinks purchased. If Gerald was lucky, Tambi might treat him to a pint of bitter and a Scotch egg from the restaurant upstairs.

Every so often Julian and his entourage were joined by Walter Allen, now living in London. Adept at straight-faced teasing, Julian convinced the gullible Walter — who found him amusing company — that his cane was really a swordstick he carried in case John Davenport attacked him. Moreover, in a casual display of what he referred to as his "absolutely photographic memory",[29] he dumbfounded Walter by reciting the entire concluding chapter of Walter's pre-war novel, *Blind Man's Ditch*.

Two other intermittent members of the group, their appearances restricted to whenever they were on leave from the military, were Mac and a tall, debonair young naval officer, Oxford cricket blue, and poet by the name of Alan Ross. For him, Julian offered a welcome respite from months of stultifying naval conversation, though the fascination palled once Julian had exhausted his extensive repertoire of anecdotes and started to repeat himself.

At closing-time, Julian would often join Tambi, Subra, and whoever else was still in tow for a late night meal in one of the Indian restaurants on St Giles High Street. Huddled together in the darkened street after they'd downed their last pints of the evening, he showed them the lucky bullet he had, with such equivocal results, been carrying round since the summer before last, its mangled shape momentarily spotlit by someone's torch. But it slid through their fingers and dropped down an adjacent gutter, from where all attempts to retrieve it failed.

On nights when Julian wasn't with Tambi, he'd head for his old haunts, Alan Ross accompanying him on one of these visits to the Scala, his image of himself as a successful writer dictating that he should treat the place as if it was the Ritz. Its menu, spattered with food-stains, was sparse and unvarying, but even that didn't deter him from studying it with all the eyebrow-flexing care of a gourmet wavering over an array of tempting and esoteric dishes. At length he opted for his current favourites: soup, followed by roast beef and vegetables. In dictating his order to the Greek waiter, he gave detailed instructions as to how he wanted the vegetables and beef cooked. When he'd finished, the incredulous waiter "ambled across to the serving-hatch and bellowed 'Roast and two veg for His Nibs and his mate.' Similar consideration was given to the matter of the wine, at the end of which House Red was selected with the same deliberation that others might have given to a rare Mouton-Rothschild."[30]

Though the easy-going nature of the documentary film world meant there was no pressure on him to keep normal office hours, both he and Dylan showed up at Golden Square each morning, regardless of how heavy a night they'd had. Facing one another across their desk, the narrow window beside them framing the spire of the otherwise devastated Soho church of St Anne's, they swapped notes on the latest movies they'd seen. And they made a tentative start on the Home Guard script they'd been allocated. Neither of them knew anything about the subject, so they painstakingly constructed a comedy-thriller set in an imaginary village, possibly a precursor of Llareggub in *Under Milk Wood*. The village was peopled by *Dads' Army*-like eccentrics, who had to contend with a German parachutist and a group of Nazi collaborators. Reliant as ever on first-hand experience for his writing, Julian modelled one of the villagers on Wilf, the ancient Home Guard who drank in the Wheatsheaf.

As a sideline, they were encouraged by Donald Taylor, who was planning to move into feature film production, to discuss the formal possibilities of screenwriting and come up with ideas for scripts. Julian managed to interest his boss in producing an adaptation of his army stories. And, together with Dylan, he devised the outline of a script which they were going to call either *The Whispering Gallery* or *The Distorting Mirror*, inspired by their shared passion for thrillers and Gothic horror movies. Anticipating Ealing Studios' masterful *Kind Hearts and Coronets*, which exploited an identical premise for blackly comic purposes, it told the story of a distant relative of the owner of a stately home, who plots to eliminate everyone in the long path to succession.

Provided their morning's work had gone well, Julian and Dylan would join Phil Lindsay on a trip to the Horseshoe Club, one of many afternoon drinking venues that thrived because pubs were prohibited from opening between 3.00pm and 6.00pm. Located in a basement at 21 Wardour Street, it was approached via a litter-strewn staircase down to a door with a spy-hole in it, through which the doorman vetted prospective customers. To Dylan, who went there on a regular basis, this lent it the low-life frisson of a gambling den or speakeasy. The more worldly Julian found the place disappointingly tame. All that awaited them inside, slouched on the club's cracked leather sofas, were bookies' touts, elderly lesbians, and a regiment of bulbous-nosed old men. Because of Dylan's tendency to confuse "age with sage",[31] he was on the best of terms with most of the old boys, particularly the art critic Tommy Earp, remarkable for his wiry physique, red face, quavering voice, and absurdly exaggerated upper-class accent. Dylan often used to extol his "subtle deadpan wit",[32] but Julian found him boring and a little creepy. Baffled by his friend's tolerance of Earp and his ilk, he stopped going to the Horseshoe. From then on, he and Dylan came to an arrangement whereby they'd take turns manning the office after lunch, enabling Julian to devote alternate afternoons to his complicated love life. By his own admission, he was dating "various young women"[33] at the same time as Scylla, any potentially awkward phone-calls to the office tactfully fielded by Dylan.

One of his harem, whom he appears to have met in the Highlander, was a tiny, self-assured, pertly attractive brunette in her early twenties, a prominent scar on her neck detracting from her prettiness. Despite her carefully made-up face, she looked far younger than she was, an impression accentuated by the way she wore her longish hair tucked schoolgirlishly behind her ears. Such was her youthful appearance, which belied the rackety life she'd been leading, the landlord of a London pub once refused to serve her because he assumed she was under-age. Her name was Monica, though Julian — whom, like Scylla, she addressed as "Jay"[34] — introduced her to his friends as "the Pinchables".[35] Unlike Eileen or Elizabeth, there was nothing maternal about her. Pleasant as she could be, she had a harsh and assertive streak that equipped her to see off her rivals for Julian's affections. Not that Julian gave her any "real idea what [he] felt about [her]."[36]

In the evenings she would often go straight from her job at the Ministry of Information to the Wheatsheaf, where she'd place her handbag on the bar and perch proprietorially on a bar-stool beside Julian, her head only reaching up to his shoulder, all the while sipping glasses of gin and tonic or brandy. Whenever the opportunity arose, she'd drop references to her student days at Oxford, a habit that peeved Julian, who was sensitive about his lack of a university education.

If he could afford it, after the pubs closed he'd take her to the Gargoyle, an expensive and famously rumbustious Soho club where several of his friends, who were members, made a habit of signing him in as a guest. The club was situated above a printing works on Meard Street, a grimy, cobbled thoroughfare sometimes facetiously mispronounced as "Merde Street". Run by the Hon. David Tennant and his wife, the revue star Hermione Baddeley, it had been launched in the Twenties to provide a meeting place where artistic and theatrical types could mingle with members of London high society. By then, its fashionable status was waning, though it continued to attract a loyal and disparate clientele that encompassed John Minton, Nancy Cunard, Augustus John, and Bertrand Russell.

From the street outside, you could usually hear the sound of laughter and music leaking through its open windows. Beyond the burly doormen who guarded the narrow entrance and greeted guests with a salute or a deferential touch of their peaked caps, there was a short, dingy passageway that led to a claustrophobic cage-lift, not much bigger than a phone-box. Creaking and rattling as it made its ponderous ascent, it would jerk to a halt on the top-floor, where a uniformed member of staff would slide open the squeaky lift door and politely shepherd its occupants across the large, wood-panelled vestibule, the walls of which were hung with Henri Matisse lithographs. At the reception desk, customers would sign the guest book before being relieved of unwanted coats and scarves. They were then free to explore the warmly lit club, its patinated fittings conveying an impression of tarnished opulence. Past the reception desk and the cloakrooms, there was a bar, a chintzy lounge, and a dining-room where, in spite of wartime constraints, the chef upheld its reputation for serving delicious yet relatively inexpensive French provincial cuisine. Even the dried egg omelettes were more palatable than those served elsewhere. The bar, not the dining-room, was nonetheless Julian's preferred destination. Eschewing the banquettes along the edge of the room, the low tables in the middle, or even the bar-stools, he liked to stand, more often than not flanked by Dylan Thomas and John Davenport, at the polished mahogany counter, which spanned the width of the building.

Only on rare occasions would he allow himself to be chivvied down the stairs connecting the bar with the low-ceilinged, L-shaped ballroom. Designed by an incongruous pairing of Matisse and the architect Edwin Lutyens, its windows were hung with leather curtains decorated with African motifs, its ceiling was encrusted in gold-leaf, and its walls were tessellated with glittering mirror-glass. All but a fraction of the floorspace was taken up by tables and chairs, bounding the miniscule, generally heaving dance-floor. As the night wore on, Alex Alexander's nattily kitted out four-piece house-band would play louder and louder, the dancing becoming progressively more unrestrained.

The Home Guard script, which Julian and Dylan had been having such fun with, was abruptly cancelled around mid-September. Their brief partnership over, Julian was redeployed to another project. Still relishing the freedom of civilian life, his work for Strand was juxtaposed with both the social whirl of Soho and spells of working on his novel. In contrast to the rigid routine and predictability of the army, "every day seemed a great new adventure."[37]

He wasn't making much headway as a screenwriter, but his career in the short story genre continued to flourish. *Y-List* was selected for inclusion in the forthcoming *Little Reviews Anthology*, scheduled for release during the build-up to Christmas. Added to which, on the first Friday of September, *Tribune* published *A Sentimental Story*, his portrait of an abortive wartime romance. Two more of his stories also made it into print during October. Alongside pieces by Frank O'Connor and William Sansom, he had one of the brief sketches already sold to *Lilliput* reprinted in a short-lived pocket magazine called *Writing Today*. And he had *Are You Happy In Your Work* published in *The Saturday Book*, whose editor, Leonard Russell, maintained "a high opinion"[38] of his writing despite his apparent failure to deliver the novel he'd agreed to write. Better still, Russell — displaying what Julian regarded as a "sympathetic understanding"[39] of the problems he faced — was prepared to pay promptly.

His sense of himself as a rising star was given further endorsement when Nina Hamnett asked if he'd sit for a portrait. One afternoon, in between pub opening-hours, he went back with her to where she lived at 31 Howland Street, only a short walk from the Wheatsheaf. Under the prying eyes of her landlady, who observed the comings and goings with a mixture of suspicion and envy, he tramped right up to her sordid top-floor flat-cum-studio, its two rooms littered with unprimed canvases, stretchers, and empty tubes of paint. There he posed for her while she executed a watercolour portrait of him.

With the onset of winter, Donald Taylor was summoned by the board of directors to repeated crisis meetings at Strand's studios in Boreham Wood, an air of uncertainty consequently suffusing the company. Donald, however, remained buoyant about the future, predicting that they'd soon be making features instead of documentaries. The portents were less encouraging, though. Films scheduled to go into production were halted, the offices becoming a waiting-room for bored cameramen and directors. Yet Julian, who worried that Donald had grown disenchanted with him, somehow clung on to his job and kept up his boozy regime.

On the evening of Friday 10 December he and Keidrich Rhys were at the bar of the Wheatsheaf. As one of them handed a fresh Guinness to Mrs Stewart, who was poring over her crossword, Keidrich became aware of a dark-haired, high-cheekboned Major in the New Zealand army peering at Julian, outraged perhaps by his longish hair and flashy yellow waistcoat. The stranger was sitting with another Kiwi: a small, stockily built woman a few years older than him. They were positioned at the table next to Mrs Stewart. Glass in hand, Keidrich stared at the Major. In his soft Welsh accent, a seldom-heard tinge of antagonism audible, he invited Dan "to agree what a dirty game of rugger the All Blacks played."[40] He went on to recall "a notable, if exceptional, defeat by Wales at Cardiff [...] with provocative satisfaction." The Kiwi's mild retort only served to rile Keidrich, whose attitude became even more threatening.

Indifferent to either sport or nationalism, Julian initially remained aloof from the burgeoning argument which showed signs of escalating into a bar-room brawl. For all his occasional verbal aggression, his love of violent stories and his sense of himself as someone formidable, someone not to be trifled with, he was terrified of violence, invariably beating a surreptitious retreat whenever a fight started. "His pen was," as Mac put it, "always mightier than his sword",[41] yet that didn't deter him from goading the Kiwi. Noticing that the Major had an old edition of *Penguin New Writing* with him, Julian said, "But look. He can read."

Far from initiating the anticipated fracas, his comments gave the Kiwi a chance to diffuse the situation by saying, "It's got a short-story of yours in it."

"You know my name?" Julian replied. Pacified a shade, but still circumspect, he said, "Perhaps you'll tell us your name."

The butt of their comments turned out to be the up-and-coming short-story writer, poet, and essayist Dan Davin, who had lived in London and knocked around Fitzrovia before the war. On discovering Dan's name, Julian said, "Didn't you write a story, *Under the Bridge*, in *New Writing* Number 13?"

Dan admitted that he had.

"Why didn't you tell us you were a writer?" Julian demanded. "We thought you were an officer. Have a drink."

So began his friendship with Dan and his wife Winnie, who were snatching a few days together before Dan's next posting to an unknown destination.

As the year approached its conclusion, Julian should have been preparing to celebrate the release of his first book. But Wren Howard had fallen several months behind schedule. Now he'd decided to print only Julian's army stories. Borrowing the title of the military memoir conceived earlier in the war, Julian wanted to call the book *They Can't Give You A Baby*. The staff at Jonathan Cape, however, vetoed the title because they feared that booksellers would think customers were asking for contraceptives. On a provisional basis, the collection was, instead, given what Julian regarded as a dreary title — *Are You Happy In Your Work.*

Even though Wren Howard had infuriated Julian by shunting back the book's publication date until early July, his writing was in wider circulation than at any previous juncture. In the space of only a month, four different publications carried work by him. The most well-established of these was *The Strand Magazine*, recently relaunched in the voguish pocket format. With the publication of *It Won't Be Long Now* (later retitled *Through the Usual Channels*), his story about his protracted struggle to obtain a divorce while still in the army, Julian joined a roster of big-name authors such as C.S. Forrester and Agatha Christie. He also had another army story featured in *Lilliput* and two more included in the opening issue of *The First Eighteen*, co-edited by "the intriguing and attractive Patricia Joan Bruce",[42] its contents selected from work "by men who are serving — or who have served — in the Forces during the present war."[43] And, furthermore, two of his sketches made it into *Christmas Pie*, the latest of a series of charity fund-raising magazines published by Hutchinson and edited by Leonard Russell, who modelled them on *Lilliput*. Minus the pin-ups.

Russell's playful foreword to the magazine parodied the casual, apparently effortless style of Julian's army stories and, at the same time, poked gentle fun at the way he contrived to smuggle references to Eugen Weidmann into the most unlikely conversations. "Really this style of writing is ridiculously easy," Russell declared. "No wonder Maclaren-Ross writes six stories a day. (Interruption by J. Maclaren-Ross: I write four-and-a-half stories a day, not six. To paraphrase Weidmann, [...] let us at least have accuracy on the part of the editor.)"[44]

Yet Russell remained a staunch admirer of Julian's work, his enthusiasm affirmed by his acceptance of two more stories for inclusion in *Spring Pie*, the next edition of the magazine. Of these, one was set in the army, the other in the civilian world, reflecting Julian's altered circumstances and yielding his earliest published writing about the Soho scene in which he'd already become such a noted personality.

Doodlebugs and Green Bombs

Inured to all the talk of a financial crisis at Strand, when Julian returned to work after Christmas, his routine enlivened by meeting Nancy Cunard, he was fretting not about his job but about the delayed publication of his collection of stories. Its eventual release, he feared, might coincide with the inevitable backlash against army fiction. Soon, though, he had to cope with a more urgent problem, the cue for which appears to have been the resignation of Donald Taylor from his post with Strand.

At the start of 1944, just as the German air-raids on London resumed after an interval of several months, the company went out of business. This brought to an end what, for Julian, had been a carefree and cathartic period. On a more practical level, it deprived him of his only reliable source of income. Yet he didn't expect the situation to last long, having been assured that he'd be employed by the feature film company Donald planned to launch.

Until then, he had to find a way of covering the rent on his flat. He responded by writing to G. Wren Howard at Jonathan Cape to ask whether they "would be willing to help [him] with money in any way."[1] But Howard turned down his request. Purely because he had to generate some quick cash, Julian set aside his novel and went back to writing short stories. Two of these appear to have been despatched to Leonard Russell, who accepted them for publication in the forthcoming *Summer Pie*.

After the best part of six jobless weeks, Julian had run up a £35 debt — most likely with a money-lender — that had to be settled "very soon or else."[2] He was confident that he could pay this off by writing more stories. The trouble was, he felt totally bereft of ideas. And he was reluctant to agree to spend time on them: time that might otherwise be devoted to his novel, which he was now thinking of calling either *Company of Shadows* or *Conspiracy of Silence*.

Just when he needed it, towards the end of the second week of February, he found himself another scriptwriting job, apparently working from home. The job seems to have consisted of producing a screenplay of Graham Greene's *The Confidential Agent*, his instructions being to omit all potentially controversial allusions to the Spanish Civil War.

His position was further improved in April by the arrival of the final £50 instalment of the advance for his collection of stories, the final proofs of which were enclosed. Right at the last minute, the book's title had been changed from *Are You Happy In Your Work* to *The Stuff To Give The Troops: 25 Stories of Army Life*. Glad as he was of the money, he was annoyed that Jonathan Cape couldn't have paid it a few months earlier when he was most in need.

At Donald Taylor's suggestion, Dylan Thomas had taken refuge with Caitlin in Sussex. Once or twice-a-week, though, he continued to come up to London. Now that Julian was neither writing in tandem with Dylan, nor seeing him on a daily basis, a welter of in-jokes and shop-talk papering over their fundamental differences, the intimacy between them dwindled.

The decline of their friendship was, to some extent, counterbalanced by the unforeseen revival of another, much older association. After a twelve-year hiatus, Julian re-encountered Peter Brooke, who had meanwhile abandoned his thespian ambitions and embarked on a tentative career as a writer. Their chance meeting took place in Torino's, a cheap, perennially crowded café at the intersection between Old Compton and Dean Streets. Known as "the Café Madrid" because it had long been a haunt of exiled Spanish anarchists and black-berreted veterans of the Spanish Civil War, it was ostensibly an Italian restaurant. Yet the couple who ran it didn't mind their customers lingering for hours at a stretch over nothing more substantial than cups of coffee. From the marble-topped table where Julian was sitting, he spotted the khaki-clad Brooke. Hand outstretched, he greeted his flabbergasted friend, who was enjoying a few days leave from the army, in which he was serving as a junior officer.

"My last memory of you," Julian announced, "was when you fell into the orchestra at the Méditerranée in Nice, during your rendition of Algy in *The Importance of Being Earnest*. It was a brilliant performance, by the way. You were quite drunk, and you fell, sensibly, on the drum."[3]

But Brooke remembered nothing of the incident. Only later did he come to realise that Julian "had a trick, mostly harmless, of adorning the experiences of his friends with a dramatic flourish."[4]

After a drink together in the Swiss, Julian took him on a northward stroll through his Soho kingdom, an area with which Brooke was unacquainted. "Interesting country for the likes of you and me," Julian told him. "Writers' material all around you aching to be put on the page."

They inevitably ended up in the Wheatsheaf, where Julian introduced him "to a number of people who were mostly disciples of [his]. 'You'd better stand second to the right,' said Julian. 'You're an army man, which won't be well accepted, but you've published a book. I stand at the corner, and you're next to me except when my girl arrives, and then you're third.' "

Entranced by Soho, Brooke spent the next day in the Wheatsheaf with Julian, who had let him sleep on the couch in the upstairs sitting-room of his flat. For the final weekend of Brooke's leave, he invited Brooke to join him and Monica —who seems to have usurped Scylla's place in his affections — on a visit to her parents' house in Windsor. It was an invitation Julian may have lived to regret, due to his friend's refusal to tone down his extrovert behaviour.

Probably because Julian recognised that the current script-writing job was far from secure, he made a bid to market his own prose fiction more vigorously. To plug the hole left by his one-time agent Bill Makins, who had long since been conscripted, he got himself taken on by a major literary agency, A.P. Watt & Son. Between mid-April and mid-May, they submitted three of his hitherto unpublished army sketches to the BBC's Home Talks Department with a view to having them read on the radio. But the BBC rejected them all.

By mid-May, Julian found himself out of work again. His predicament appears to have prompted him to contact Charles Wrey Gardiner in the hope of selling *The Simple Life*, the novella he'd written three years earlier, the manuscript of which had, in the interim, "absented itself from [his] possession for long intervals".[5] He and his prospective publisher, who found him "interesting to talk to",[6] got on well. Despite the "prejudice in the publishing trade against books under 70,000 words in length",[7] Charles was keen to bring out *The Simple Life*, now retitled *Bitten By The Tarantula*, under the Grey Walls Press imprint, run from his mother's house in Billericay. Somehow, though, the deal fell through.

Julian realised that he was still many months away from earning anything from his expansive novel-in-progress, he looked round for a less long-term project. He decided to offer Jonathan Cape a wholly revised and abbreviated version of another unplaced but seemingly completed novel, *The Salesman Only Rings Once*. But Howard declined the offer. He did, however, phone Julian to ask him to visit the firm's Bedford Square offices. When Julian went round there, Howard told him that it might be possible to pay him an immediate advance if he submitted a one-page synopsis for a suitable-sounding novel. In order to boost the odds on Howard stumping up an advance, Julian drafted two brief plot outlines. He sent these to Jonathan Cape, along with a letter informing Howard of his financial position. Unmoved by Julian's plight, the cautious and pragmatic Howard wrote back on Friday 2 June, turning down his request and expressing concern that his difficult circumstances might militate against him producing the novel he was already contracted to deliver.

Necessity compelled Julian to try another angle. The following week, he phoned Howard and offered him, in exchange for an immediate advance, a collection of civilian short stories, twenty-five of which he'd so far completed. Again, Howard remained resolute, declining to commission more short fiction until the projected novel had been published. Angry with Howard, whose attitude he considered "monstrous [...and] consistently unhelpful",[8] his annoyance intensified by the delayed release-date of *The Stuff to Give the Troops*, the delays having adversely affected both his career and finances, Julian contemplated taking legal action.

An alternative idea for raising some cash presented itself to him when, presumably browsing in a bookshop, he discovered that *Horizon Stories*, the two-year-old anthology featuring his work, had gone into its third impression. Scenting a royalty payment, he rang up the accountant at Faber & Faber, who revealed that royalties were, indeed, owing. On the accountant's advice, he wrote to Colonel Connolly, asking for a cheque and explaining that he was "rather pressed for money at the moment".[9]

The cheque can't have amounted to more than about £5. Certainly not enough to keep Julian in drink and cigarettes for long. In pursuit of a far bigger payment, he sent his collection of short stories to another large publisher, this time Hutchinson, the company behind both *The Saturday Book* and *Pie*. They agreed to buy the collection, but his financial position compelled him to strike an unconventional and potentially disadvantageous deal with them. Forsaking his right to any future royalties, he accepted a flat-rate fee. Even so, Hutchinson soon had second thoughts about publishing such racy material. Out of the £150 that he was paid by them, he had to settle some of the pre-war debts he'd incurred while he was on the dole. Still, there seems to have been enough left in the kitty to tide him over for a while.

No sooner had his money worries abated than he was faced by a far more serious threat to his well-being. In the third week of June, only days after the successful Allied landings in Normandy, the Germans initiated the so-called Little Blitz, bombarding London with flame-tailed V-1 rockets, launched from the Low Countries. Variously nicknamed "flying bombs", "buzz bombs", "doodlebugs", or "bumble bombs", they arrived at the rate of about 100-a-day, reducing everyone to a state of incessant anxiety. At any moment you might become aware of an angry insectoid drone which would suddenly stop when the rocket's engine cut out. You then had about twelve seconds in which to shelter in a doorway or fling yourself to the ground. Most of the rockets fell south of the river, unleashing explosions so powerful they were capable of shattering glass within a radius of a quarter of a mile. One such explosion blew out all the windows in Julian's flat, the consequent cold draught forcing him to sleep in the cellar until he could get the glass repaired. No easy task in wartime.

Perhaps as a way of calming his nerves, Julian's alcohol consumption escalated sharply, earning him the tag of "Hollow Legs". During the opening weeks of the bombardment, he took to spending most lunchtimes with his recently acquired friend, the critic and verse-novelist Philip Toynbee, son of the historian Arnold Toynbee. They'd meet in the Saloon Bar of the Museum Tavern, which the perpetually sozzled Philip, himself an ex-serviceman with a similar animus against military bureaucracy, used as a surrogate office, a sheaf of manuscripts invariably fanned out across the table next to the fireplace. And in the evenings Julian, swathed in his white scarf and old teddy-bear coat despite the midsummer heat, would yield to the magnetic pull of the Wheatsheaf, Red's tolerance of his Spoof-playing leading him to declare Red "the best landlord in London".[10]

Since the turn of the year, Julian's circle of cronies had undergone a radical transformation. He was still joined on a regular basis by Monica (whom he liked to introduce as his wife), as well as by Keidrich and Lynette Rhys, not to mention Subra, usually escorting Jackie Stanley, Tambi's buxom, good-natured blonde ex-spouse. Yet neither Dylan Thomas nor Tambi himself, whose charm had worn thin, retained their places in his entourage. On his visits to London, Dylan would often call in at the Wheatsheaf, only he tended not to linger in Julian's territory. Part of the reason was that he was embarrassed by Donald Taylor's decision to re-employ *him* and not Julian when the new company, Gryphon Films, was set up. Pausing for a few minutes with Julian, Dylan would gravitate to a table in the far corner, occupied by a group that normally included Tambi, Nina Hamnett, Augustus John, and the poet George Barker, wearing a stained overcoat and an old flat cap. From there, Dylan would exchange the occasional friendly wave with his erstwhile colleague.

Julian's rival clique was now reinforced by Charles Wrey Gardiner; by Peter Brooke, who visited whenever he was on leave from the army; by the young Air Ministry employee, Anthony Curtis; by Willia Willetts, a lean, verbose, vaguely mysterious man with a passion for Chinese art; and by Eric Lyng, who was always soliciting contributions for a literary magazine that never materialised. The fresh intake also encompassed the former burglar, Jim Phelan, now a fellow writer; the rugged-featured Glaswegian poet Sydney Graham, dressed in a rumpled tweed jacket and baggy flannel trousers; the independently wealthy John Hartcup, distinguished-looking, if slightly bloated, a sandy quiff belying his ostentatious manner; and Noel Sircar, a Eurasian who worked at the India Office but wanted to be a children's writer. The lecherous Noel was, as he proclaimed, always on the look-out for "a bit of C",[11] his favourite prank being to accost arty women with the unceremonious chat-up line, "I'd like to fuck you. I wouldn't half shove it in",[12] though he'd flee in panic if any of them wanted to accept his offer. In contrast to most of Julian's other literary admirers, who treated him with the reverence he seemed to demand, Noel took great pleasure in gently debunking him.

That summer the throng radiating out from Julian expanded to encompass the tall, thin, intimidatingly erudite poet John Heath-Stubbs, weak eyes magnified by round glasses, dark, neatly parted hair flopping over his protruberant forehead. Julian was amused to hear that Heath-Stubbs, who worked in the Encyclopaedia Department at Hutchinson, had recently been consulted by one of his colleagues regarding a story in the collection Julian had sold them. Set in Paris, it featured a passage where the young narrator strides past a prostitute who tries to tempt him, only to be met with a shrug and the word "fauché". The editorial staff were worried this might be obscene, but Heath-Stubbs reassured them that it was merely slang for "broke".

More temporary membership of Julian's clique was accorded the handsome sixteen-year-old Bruce Bernard, who was going through a priggish and reproachful teenage phase that led to him being widely known as "the Head Prefect".[13] Yet Julian treated him like the sophisticated adult he imagined he was.

Anthony Curtis's friend, the youthful novelist Peter Vansittart was another of the typically high turnover of short-term communicants at Father Julian's Saloon Bar altar. For several weeks Vansittart hovered shyly on the edge of the crowd that flocked round Julian every night, standing him drinks and listening obediently as he held forth. At that period Julian mainly talked about his mooted novel, its proposed title regularly changing, current favourites being *The Night People*, *Company of Shadows*, and *The Fields of Night*; about his dealings with John Lehmann and Cyril Connolly; and about his admiration for the American character actor, Laird Cregar, whose versatile and charismatic performances in *This Gun For Hire*, *Joan of Paris*, and the remake of *Blood and Sand* he dissected with fanatical relish. When Vansittart finally mustered the courage to engage him in conversation, he was pleased to discover Julian had read his first novel, *I Am The Word*. But his pleasure was undercut by Julian's brusque, telegraphic dismissal of it: "Chatto book. Yellow cover. Title blocked in blue. Very pompous."[14]

Chastened, Vansittart underwent the inevitable rite of passage by meekly asking whether Julian wanted a drink. Not even glancing in his direction, Julian — who endeavoured to emulate Laird Cregar's vocal mannerisms — replied, "Indubitably. Pints all round. A double brandy for Monica."

However club-like the ambience may have been, the Soho circuit wasn't without its rivalries and bitter feuds. What united all its many factions, though, was a respect for individualism, even when that spiralled into rampant eccentricity. Of the area's ample cast of eccentrics, one of the most prominent and ubiquitous was the self-proclaimed "King of the Bohemians", Iron-Foot Jack, so named because he wore an iron patten on his right foot to correct a six-inch imbalance between the length of his legs which, he liked to tell people, was the result of a shark attacking him in the Coral Sea. He also claimed mystic powers and, in the Thirties, had founded a cult through which he'd extracted money from his affluent adherents. An ex-fairground performer, he retained the mischievous and self-conscious air of a showman, favouring a strikingly stagey get-up, his black suit habitually worn in combination with a florid scarf, tied like a cravat, a stiff-brimmed black hat, and a cloak draped over his broad shoulders.

A more sinister and malign brand of eccentricity was represented by the well-known illustrator whom Julian christened "Hammerhead".[15] Not because of any physical deformity, but because of the tiny hammer he carried round in the pocket of his jacket. After the pubs closed, he'd position himself in some secluded alley or doorway and wait for a suitable victim. Stepping out from there, he'd ask for a light. While the stranger was busy fishing out a cigarette-lighter or some matches, Hammerhead would knock him unconscious with a single swift blow, then stride hurriedly away.

For other famous Soho figures of the period, eccentricity shaded into tragedy, high life tapering into low life. As in the case of Countess

Eileen de Vigne, the destitute ex-wife of a South American aristocrat, who subsisted on coffee, jam puffs, and benzedrine, paid for by selling discarded possessions scavenged from the dustbins of wealthy households. Yet, in common with Nina Hamnett and a number of other unfortunates whom drink or drugs had pushed into a slow downhill slide towards destitution, she maintained a precarious dignity, an appealing air of triumph in defeat that made her a patron saint of the Soho cult of failure.

Further ratification of Julian's status as a rising literary star came with the sale of another story to *Lilliput*, followed by his delayed hardcover debut. Publication of the collection had been scheduled for the beginning of the month. But it wasn't until Monday 24 July that it appeared.

Due to the wartime paper shortage, Jonathan Cape was able to print an edition of only 4,000, the book's brevity accentuated by compact typesetting. Its fresh tone of voice and unusual subject matter nonetheless succeeded in grabbing widespread attention, not so much among the literary establishment as among Julian's peers, for whom its impact rivalled that of the rockets that continued to pound the capital. Walter Allen, a shrewd literary adjudicator, rated it as one of the two "best and most accurate rendering[s] of the military existence of the day."[16] Anthony Powell came to a similar conclusion, calling it "as good a series of sketches of army life as has yet appeared."[17] And John Lehmann was struck by Julian's "intuitive sympathy for those who have fallen foul of The Machine; for those who are too simple in their eccentricity as well as for those who are too complex and sensitive, to fit into the conventional set-up."[18] In Lehmann's opinion, he had "the makings of a Dickens in him — a Dickens who had read Dashiell Hammett."[19]

For the most part, the reviewers were just as congratulatory. *John O'London's Weekly* acclaimed *I Had To Go Sick* and *This Mortal Coil* as "two little masterpieces, stamped unmistakably: J. Maclaren-Ross".[20] And *The TLS* praised the collection for being "bright and amusing reading" and highlighted its "lively use of army slang", its "air of spontaneity", its "acute and pointed truthfulness [and] descriptive zest and vigour".[21] But all this was trumped by *The New Statesman and Nation*. "Mr. Maclaren-Ross has given not only the funniest but, imaginatively, the truest account I have yet read of army life in this country," Philip Toynbee wrote. "As a humourist I would rate him very high indeed, and it is long since I have read anything funnier [...] It is a rich and subtle humour to distort the possible by a hair's breadth, to colour real events by that faintest exaggeration which converts the merely tiresome into the uproariously farcical. Of all methods this would seem the best for dealing humorously with the army, and Mr Maclaren-Ross uses it deliciously. Red tape is seldom funny in experience, yet how close to experience is a story like *Through the Usual Channels*, and how exceedingly funny [...] These stories [...] give reason to hope that Maclaren-Ross may prove the considerable satirist of whom we are in such evident need."[22] It was a point of view that wasn't, of course, shared by the War Office, from where disapproving noises emanated.

Hazardous as the V-1 rockets had made life in London, they were nowhere near as terrifying as their successors, the much larger, faster, and more destructive V-2s, the first of which fell on Friday 8 September. Entire houses were razed, craters ten feet deep and fifteen feet in diameter marking where they'd stood. What was most frightening about them was that they struck with little or no warning. Seeking a break from the unremitting anxiety they induced, sometime around then Julian and Monica made plans to get out of London for the weekend. Monica, who was keen to give Julian a guided tour of her old stamping-ground, suggested they go to Oxford. Never having visited the city, it was an idea that appealed to him, so he splashed out on first-class train tickets there for them both.

From the moment they entered the city, Oxford proved an enormous let-down for Julian, who had expected "to see from the window a perspective of dreaming spires." Instead, he saw a gasworks, "immediately blotted out by an advertisement for timber and a line of trucks filled with coal."[23]

Burdened by heavy suitcases, he and Monica set about finding accommodation. As they tramped along rows of hotels and boarding houses, he had an unpleasant flashback to his footsore days as a vacuum-cleaner salesman. None of the hotels or boarding houses had any vacancies. Even the phone-boxes were full, RAF personnel and American airmen spilling out of them, in the process preventing Monica from contacting a friend who might have put her and Julian up for the night. To salvage something from the trip, Julian decided to take Monica for a drink. But even that went wrong, because the pub had run dry. Thwarted at every turn, they took the last train back to London, Julian's disappointment superseded by outright hatred of the city, his animosity towards the place fed by his resentment of academics and students. On their return, the bleakly humorous tale of their ill-fated trip was incorporated into his battery of Saloon Bar anecdotes, ultimately evolving into a short story called *The Oxford Manner*.

The Wheatsheaf had, by now, become the focal point of Julian's daily regimen. Each morning he'd take a taxi there, an extravagance he justified on the grounds that his injured knee ruled out walking or public transport. Like an actor poised to venture on stage, he used the journey "to prepare in comparative calm for the ordeal ahead",[24] and to get into character, his "inner-self [discarded] through the taxi-window."[25] As the cab pulled up outside the pub, there would occasionally be an altercation over the fare, climaxing at least once in Julian instructing a police constable to "take that man's number."[26] Bang on opening-time, Julian would make "his entrance, pushing the doors open with his malacca cane with the pinchbeck top. He entered, head held high like a king, King Julian."[27]

When the pub closed for the afternoon, Nina Hamnett would periodically invite him and one or two of the other Saloon Bar regulars back to her flat, where they could carry on talking. From time to time, he would, alternatively, take a taxi back to Maida Vale. Not to return home, but to visit Bronia Kennedy, a short-haired, corduroy-trousered former Land Girl in her mid-twenties, whose friendship with the painter Feliks Topolski and family connections with Fitzrovia impressed him. Julian had chatted her up during a recent session at Tony's, where they laughed themselves silly swapping reminiscences of Hoover's Regent Street sales school, which an ex-boyfriend of her's had also attended. On each visit to her flat, Julian entertained her fatherless baby daughter with some of the tricks he had picked up while he was living with the Jaegers and their child. Once, arriving at Bronia's unannounced, he was surprised to find Quentin Crisp drawing comical pictures for her daughter, Hilary, on a roll of lining-paper. With mannered charm, Quentin dispensed a few amusing anecdotes before beating a tactful retreat. Yet Julian's short-lived flirtation with Bronia, who sensed that her lack of "glamour-girl looks" precluded her from being "proper girlfriend material",[28] never progressed beyond a couple of kisses prior to him taking the tube back into the West End.

Usually, however, the awkward hours between pub opening-times were spent elsewhere. Either Julian would go to the cinema or, if none of the current releases appealed to him, stroll down Rathbone Place and onto Charlotte Street for a late lunch at the Scala. Over a helping of fatty roast beef, the rim of his plate piled with horse-raddish sauce, he would make notes on the conversations he had overheard in the Saloon Bar. To fill the remaining three hours or more until the Wheatsheaf reopened, he'd wander along Charing Cross Road, browsing in the bookshops that lined it. Determined to keep up with contemporary fiction, he would purchase every new novel that interested him the day it came out. He'd then read it overnight and sell it to a secondhand bookshop under the pretence that it was a review copy, allowing him to recoup half the cover price. Even so, his book-buying placed yet another unnecessary financial burden on him. Well-meaning Walter Allen "once hinted that he could save a lot of money by joining a public library. Those at Hampstead and St Pancras, [Walter] said, were especially good."[29] But Julian greeted his advice with a disdainful look that conveyed the impression that Walter had shown himself to be "irredeemably bourgeois".[30]

Of the Charing Cross Road bookshops, Julian's favourite was Zwemmer's, then under the fastidious management of the tall, pinstriped and pedantic Rudolph Friedmann, whose ban on smoking Julian took delight in flouting. Walking into the shop one afternoon, Julian found Friedmann talking to Charles Wrey Gardiner. Watched by Derek Stanford and Ruthven Todd, Julian winkled Charles away from Friedmann and escorted him round the room, all the while delivering a plausible critique on an imaginary exhibition of contemporary art. Everyday objects were assigned grand titles, a bucket and brush being transmuted into *Coming of Spring*.

Before going back to the Wheatsheaf at the end of each afternoon, Julian always stocked up on the pricey American brand of jumbo-sized Royalty cigarettes that he now preferred, unmistakable in their chunky tinfoil wrapping. The smoke from these soon contributed to the dense smog enveloping the Saloon Bar. It was there that he ran into Dan Davin again. In the nine months or so since he'd first met him, Dan had been serving with the New Zealand Division in Italy. Now part of the army's General Staff in London, Dan was able to visit the Wheatsheaf some lunchtimes and most evenings. Frequently primed with "too many pints elsewhere",[31] he would head for Julian's end of the bar where, scowling and ignoring introductions to the assembled acolytes, he'd inveigh against the "bloody pommies"[32] and initiate arm-wrestling contests. Much as Julian resented what he considered Dan's "coarse 'colonial' behaviour",[33] he didn't show his annoyance. Nor did he let it mar the deepening friendship between him and Dan.

They were sometimes joined by Dan's wife, Winnie, her mental alacrity and vibrant personality endearing her to Julian. More often, though, Dan was accompanied by New Zealand army friends such as the learned but boisterous Paddy Costello. Julian's instinctive dislike of Costello was exacerbated by the embarrassing incident that occurred when the drunken Costello "started to bang his fist on the counter and [shout], at the top of his voice, about the fucking English."[34] Red wanted to have him chucked out. Because he was a friend of Dan's, Julian intervened on his behalf and had a quiet word with the landlord, whom he treated with the condescension he reserved for those outside the artistic world. At this, Red backed down, not wishing to alienate his most valuable customer.

On a separate occasion Red entrusted Dan, by then a prized customer himself, to throw out a inebriated Canadian soldier who'd been causing trouble. Sprinting for safety across Rathbone Place, the soldier avoided Dan's knockout punch. When Dan returned to the Saloon Bar from his fruitless chase, Julian treated him to "a blow-by-blow playback of the brief encounter, as though [Dan] had not been a party to it — except for instructions on how [Dan] might have settled [his] man more effectively."[35]

So constant was Julian's presence in the Wheatsheaf, the Gargoyle, and his other West End haunts, that it was a topic of considerable speculation as to when he found the time to write the stories that seemed to form a staple of every literary magazine. The truth was hard to believe.

Near midnight, after his habitual post-pub or club meal, he would set off for the Goodge Street tube, where a raving blonde nicknamed "the Goodge Street Whore", mistaking him for a homosexual, made a point of screaming abuse at him until the last train pulled into the station and he made his escape. Back at his flat in Maida Vale, he'd uncap the Hooded Terror, light up the first in a succession of cigarettes, and open one of the notebooks in which he did most of his writing. The rest of the night would be spent copying out the stories he'd rehearsed earlier in the day, his handwriting as lilliputian and fanatically neat as ever, his faculties apparently unimpaired by the booze he'd consumed. Only at dawn would he grab a few hours sleep before summoning the taxi that would carry him back to the Wheatsheaf.

To ward off fatigue, he began using benzedrine, a stimulant that could be obtained without a prescription. Like several of his Soho friends, among them John Heath-Stubbs, he would buy inhalers intended for hayfever and asthma sufferers. He'd then break the container open, scoop out the benzedrine-soaked cottonwool inside, and steep it in a cup of coffee. It wasn't long before he'd graduated to the vastly more potent methedrine capsules, only available on prescription. He got these from an unscrupulous doctor who drank in the Wheatsheaf and was prepared to prescribe unlimited quantities of what Julian lovingly referred to as his "green bombs".[36] These, he explained to Dan Davin, "had the useful property of [...] simultaneously 'pepping you up and calming you down'."[37] Yet when Julian persuaded him to try one, he found it so strong that it kept him talking manically for a day-and-a-half, at the end of which he lapsed into a profound depression.

Dissatisfied with the fruits of A.P. Watt & Son's efforts, Julian made up his mind to switch to another literary agency. Such was his soaring reputation among critics like Alan Pryce-Jones who, writing in *The Observer*, hailed him as a young writer "with something to say",[38] he seems to have had no difficulty in being signed up by Curtis Brown, the prestigious Covent Garden-based agency. It was probably through them that he succeeded in selling the Swedish and French translation rights to *The Stuff To Give The Troops*, netting an invaluable £50.

Over the ensuing weeks, his connection with Leonard Russell also yielded useful rewards. During October, his work appeared in both the miscellanies Russell edited. *The Saturday Book* included a comic story of his called *The Two Retired Chess Champions and The Girl Who Preferred To Play Draughts*, while *Autumn Pie* featured a gentle, digressive piece in which he portrayed himself sitting in an uncomfortable chair musing on the past. Somehow Russell managed to persuade him to pose for a picture to go with it. Stiff and self-conscious in his suit and tie, his hair carefully combed away from his forehead, he was photographed in profile, the unflattering angle drawing attention to his elongated jawline.

The V-2 explosions which had formed an unpredictable counterpoint to the last few weeks reached a new intensity that month. An average of four of them struck the capital every day, the eastern and north-eastern suburbs bearing the brunt of the assault. Like so many other Londoners, Julian did his best to carry on as before despite the ever-present danger.

In the second week of October, he was invited, most likely by Nina Hamnett, to a lunchtime private view in the palatial galleries of the Royal Academy at Burlington House in Piccadilly. As a member of the renowned London Group of artists, she was exhibiting three portraits — including a watercolour of Mrs Stewart — in the latest of the Group's annual exhibitions. Julian found himself sharing a sofa with Nina, who sat cross-legged, her hairy legs sheathed in tatty stockings, while she watched people looking round the exhibition.

That winter Julian began to secure even wider exposure for his work. As well as having a story about his adolescent chess craze published in *Selected Writing*, he pulled off the improbable feat of selling a couple of stories to the tub-thumping populist weekly newspaper, *John Bull*. On

Thursday 4 November they printed a piece from *The Stuff To Give The Troops*. And the following week they featured a previously unpublished army story. Julian must have been overjoyed by the way it was billed as having "the real Maclaren-Ross touch".[39]

His literary success nourishing his egotism, he lost no time in introducing himself when the eighteen-year-old Anne Valery, who resembled a cross between Ingrid Bergman and Veronica Lake, hourglass figure sheathed in a black velvet dress, wandered into the Saloon Bar of the Wheatsheaf one night. "I'm Julian Maclaren-Ross, I'm a genius, I write short stories, and I've been waiting for you…,"[40] he told her. Suitably impressed, she stayed with him until closing-time. Afterwards they strolled past the lightless doorways of the restaurants that lined Charlotte Street, ending up in the basement of Tony's. Taken by Julian's casual references to the likes of Graham Greene, Dylan Thomas, Augustus John, and Stephen Spender, Anne agreed to go with him to the Gargoyle, where he'd been granted honorary membership. Arm-in arm, they rode the lift upstairs and then made for the ballroom, Julian nodding to the band-leader Alex Alexander as they passed him. But Julian, relishing the role of the metropolitan sophisticate, was disconcerted to discover that Anne, who worked in the MI13 wing of army intelligence, knew so many of the other members. He became even more peeved when she showed less interest in listening to a lengthy synopsis of his latest short story than in ogling the famous, immaculately turned out photographer Cecil Beaton.

Later that night, just as they were preparing to leave, Julian startled her with an unexpected revelation. "I say, this is a bit embarrassing," he announced. "I don't seem to have enough to pay the bill." Reluctantly, Anne pulled out two pound notes from her purse. These had no sooner been proferred than David Tennant, whom she vaguely knew, came over and told them that the evening was on the house.

Intent on accompanying Anne back to her room at the famously indulgent and eccentric Cavendish Hotel, Julian clung onto her as they exited the club. "When the war's over," he mumbled in an attempt to charm her into bed, "I'll carry you off to a castle in Spain. I'll cover you with mimosa and we'll have scrambled eggs for breakfast."[41]

After agreeing to meet him in the Wheatsheaf at 7.00pm the following night, she kissed him, then forcefully disentangled herself and hurried away down the blacked out street. Next day, however, she didn't show up at the agreed time. As a result, Julian must have assumed that he had been snubbed, so he was in a foul mood when she eventually appeared at about 8.00pm. "You're a spy," he said. "I always knew you were a spy. You're late because of your grubby little war work."[42]

Only a few hours earlier, Anne had, unknown to him, been caught in an air-raid, the force of an exploding parachute-mine blowing her off her feet and demolishing the café where she'd been due to meet a friend, now presumed dead. Shock rendering her inarticulate, she picked up a convenient half-pint of beer and very carefully tipped it over Julian's head. Rivulets of it coursed down his dumbstruck face and trickled under his astrakhan collar.

Anger unabated, she swivelled round. The uniformed and be-spectacled but still attractive Peter Brooke, currently enjoying minor renown as a popular song lyricist, was standing behind her. "Would you be very kind and escort me out of here?"[43] she asked him. He gallantly obliged by taking hold of her elbow and guiding her out of the pub. When they reappeared together the evening after that, she was firmly installed as his girlfriend. As such, Julian was willing to accept her into the group that routinely surrounded him in the Wheatsheaf. His crush on her having survived the previous night, he maintained an amorous and protective attitude towards her. On discovering she'd met Augustus John, he warned her "that Augustus was famous for seduction."[44] And, in Monica's absence, he kept repeating his offer to take her to Spain. Besides which, he bought her presents of blue eye-shadow and white face powder to help her achieve the fashionable night-owl look that she so coveted. Yet she refused to succumb to his advances.

A touch of jealousy tainting his friendship with her new boyfriend, he was appalled when he caught them having noisy sex in the ladies' toilet, commonly termed "the doxy-box". "Bloody hell, Brooke," he said, hammering on the door. "Try the Bricklayers' Arms — there's more room in there." No reply was forthcoming, only more groaning. "This won't do, Brooke," he called out angrily. "This certainly won't do."[45]

Rounding off a year in which Julian's career had made such forward strides, Leonard Russell published another of his uncollected army stories in *Christmas Pie*. *The Mine*, one of the pieces from *The Stuff To Give The Troops*, also made it into *World Digest of Fact and Comment*, a monthly pocket magazine that specialised in reprinting stories and articles by people ranging from Orson Welles to Karen Blixen. Aided by all this publicity, sales of his debut book were healthy enough to justify Jonathan Cape putting in an order for a second edition of 1,000 copies.

Altogether he had, so far that year, earned the by no means negligible sum of £283. Yet his intemperate way of life tended to consume money faster than he could make it. By around the beginning of December he was so hard-up that he had to relinquish his flat in Maida Vale. The sense of crisis was redoubled when he received a letter from the Inland Revenue demanding the income tax he owed on his past three years' earnings, which he'd never bothered to declare.

As a temporary measure, Edward du Cros — a friend from the Wheatsheaf — agreed to put him up in his third-floor flat at 185c Cromwell Road, a gloomy four-storey terrace on the Earl's Court section of one of west London's biggest and busiest roads. Though Julian resented having to trudge up several flights of stairs, he must have been relieved to have somewhere to stay. While he was there, he devoted his time to working on another novel, which he envisaged finishing "next winter, at the earliest".[46] Not the wisest of moves for someone in his situation.

During mid-January 1945, he submitted an application for financial assistance from the Royal Literary Fund, who dispensed grants to writers undergoing material hardship. In support of his application, he persuaded Leonard Russell and John Lehmann to supply references. They both came up with effusive testimonials to his literary abilities. Russell expressed his conviction that Julian "might easily write a really remarkable novel"[47] if he could only "overcome his financial difficulties".[48] But even that was exceeded by Lehmann. "His sense of human comedy in our age is ruthless and bitter," Lehmann declared; "and he is continually achieving effects on the border of the tragic, a very rare power in so young an author and one that removes his best work very far from the category of the clever documentary with which it has sometimes been hastily confined."[49]

The next meeting of the committee responsible for assessing Julian's application wasn't scheduled until early February. In the meantime, his only traceable income came from the publication of two of his civilian stories in *John Bull*, the shortfall probably covered by consulting the precious black pocket-book that he had filled with the addresses and phone numbers of people who might loan him cash — cash he could seldom afford to repay.

On the advice of the publisher Sir John Murray, who had been delegated to file a report on *The Stuff To Give The Troops*, which Murray condemned for its vulgarity, the Royal Literary Fund turned down Julian's application, so he had to look round for an alternative means of generating the money he needed. His solution was to tout a book of his civilian short stories — extending from early examples like *Five Finger Exercises* to *The Mine* — round several London publishers. The small, recently founded company of Lawson & Dunn, who were delighted to have been approached by such a comparatively well-known author, seem to have been the only firm prepared to table an offer. In lieu of the orthodox advance on future royalties, they offered him a single cash payment of "no more than about £25"[50] which, they told him, was "better than a kick in the pants":[51] a comment that provided the book's eventual facetious title. Desperate for a quick return, he went ahead and sold the collection to them.

Like Jonathan Cape, they were based in Bedford Square. But that's about as far as the resemblance between the two firms went. Julian was the first and only fiction writer signed up by them, the rest of their list consisting of out-of-copyright poetry and compilations of cartoons. Perhaps because of their lack of experience or the paper shortage, they arranged to produce Julian's collection jointly with the Hyperion Press, an altogether more successful and established company dedicated to producing art books.

For Julian "every offer from a fresh publisher was," as Walter Allen recalled, "like the beginning of a new love affair: it was ecstatic, and the relation was to be for life. Then he would discover that this publisher, like all the others, was an exploiter of authors [...]".[52] Even by his exacting standards, a sense of grievance against Lawson & Dunn blossomed quickly, thanks to the paltry advance and their subsequent refusal to purchase *Bitten By The Tarantula*.

Hoping he might be able to sell his much-rejected novella to the small firm of Eyre & Spottiswoode, which employed Graham Greene as a part-time director, he contacted Graham and fixed up another of their sporadic meetings. When he explained his position, Graham offered to put him in touch with someone who might be interested in publishing the book.

Towards the end of February, Graham took him to the offices of Allan Wingate Ltd. These were on the ground floor of a large late Georgian house at 64 Great Cumberland Place, near Marble Arch. Not unnaturally, Julian went there expecting to meet the eponymous Mr Wingate. But he was intrigued to discover that no such person existed. For fear of alienating people by trading under a German-sounding surname, the firm's founder had picked a name from the London phone directory. In place of the reticent, middle-aged Oxbridge-educated Englishman Julian had anticipated, Graham introduced him to André Deutsch, a diminutive, fidgety, and boyishly voluble twenty-six-year-old Hungarian emigré, whose crinkly hair was already receding, whose accent imbued even the most mundane transaction with a dash of exoticism. The introduction, which took place in the large marblechimneypieced front room André shared with several colleagues, was a great success. Julian and André conceived an instant liking for one another.

André had set up Allan Wingate as a sideline from his salaried job with the much larger rival firm of Nicolson & Watson. Prior to meeting Julian, he'd issued only two titles. Since he wanted to diversify into publishing fiction, he was keen to read the manuscript Julian had brought with him. Only a few evenings after it had been handed over, Julian — hearing that André preferred to conduct business discussions away from the company's cramped premises — arranged to meet him in the Bricklayers' Arms on Gresse Street. Echoing the design of the nearby Wheatsheaf, the Bricklayers' was built in the mock-Tudor style, its façade imitating a traditional coaching inn. According to two local legends, one which credited Nina Hamnett with finding a jemmy on the billiard table, the other which told of a gang of burglars breaking in and sleeping there, leaving behind a stack of empties, Nina had dubbed it "the Burglar's Rest". It was a pub whose character veered from the sombre to the riotous, later in the evening playing host to a horde of loud, drunken old women. Earlier on, when Julian scheduled his meeting with André, it was a lifeless place, whose patrons sat quietly beneath its dusty chandeliers enjoying the rare choice of four different beers, munching on cold cocktail sausages, or playing billiards in the Saloon Bar, the sound of muted voices seldom rising above the click of billiard balls. In that guise, Julian came to regard it as being "useful for a business talk or [as somewhere] to take a young woman whom one did not know well."[53]

Secure in his conviction that Julian was "a supremely talented writer",[54] André offered him a contract with Allan Wingate. As always, in his determination to extract the maximum possible payment and obtain the fastest possible publication, Julian quibbled over the terms of the contract. But he soon signed it. The deal provided him with two £100 advances: for *Bitten By The Tarantula* and his next collection of civilian stories. This was to be called *The Weeping and the Laughter*, its title a quotation from Waldo Lydecker, the waspish protagonist of the hit Hollywood movie *Laura*, who was, in turn, quoting the decadent poet Ernest Dowson. On top of these two advances, André committed himself to paying a further £200, due on receipt of the manuscript of a full-length novel, provisionally entitled *The Lunatic Fringe*, which Julian said he'd deliver in August that year.

His latest earnings appear to have enabled him to tackle his tax arrears by engaging the services of an accountancy firm that employed a specialist in helping writers resolve just such problems. The money also gave him the chance to move out of his friend's flat and into the swanky 350-room Imperial Hotel in Russell Square, its jagged neo-Gothic skyline vying for attention with the similarly striking Hotel Russell. Incorporating a fussily decorated Turkish bath in the basement, a winter garden, a restaurant, a dance hall, a bar, and a lift which, Julian claimed, was essential because of his damaged knee, it represented the height of Edwardian luxury. Just the type of august establishment where he believed a professional writer should live, his preconception of the appropriate material rewards fostered by his earlier visits to the plush homes of Frank Harris and Graham Greene.

Within days of penning an author's note for inclusion at the front of *Bitten By The Tarantula*, he began to wonder whether the deal might be in breach of his existing contract with Jonathan Cape. As a panicky afterthought, he spent some of his advance on hiring a solicitor to clarify his legal position.

Between 11pm and midnight on Tuesday 14 March, he was drinking coffee at a window-seat in the Scala with Dan Davin. Midway through one of his anecdotes, Dan heard a V-2 rocket land in the direction of Russell Square. Battle-hardened as he was, Dan reacted by shoving Julian under the table and diving on top of him. The window behind them was immediately blown out, shrouding them in a blackout blind, splintered glass raining down on them. Gingerly picking themselves out of the debris, they found that Julian had sustained the only wound, having cut his palm on a shard of glass. Once the blinds were reinstalled, and the lights were switched on again, he and Dan were served fresh cups of coffee.

Another coupon from his ration-book of good luck was torn out the following week when his solicitor contacted him to say that Jonathan Cape had agreed to release him from the contract he'd signed the previous summer. There was now no obstacle to Allan Wingate bringing out an edition of 5,000 copies of *Bitten By The Tarantula* that August, as promised. But Julian soon heard that its publication date had been put back to November. To compound his disappointment, he was told the paper shortage had caused the size of its first-edition to be scaled down.

Because the war's victorious outcome had been so widely predicted ever since the successful D-Day landings, news of Germany's surrender that spring came as something of an anti-climax. In spite of both this and the prevailing war-weariness, Londoners were determined to burn off some of their accumulated frustrations through a giant party. From the rubble-strewn East End to the dowdy West End, bonfires were lit in the streets to mark V-E Night, the sky streaked and stippled not by shellbursts and arcing tracers but by celebratory fireworks. Only a few miles from Buckingham Palace, outside of which a vast, swaying crowd had gathered, revellers poured through the brightly lit Soho streets. Julian joined in the raucous Saloon Bar celebrations, yet — little did he realise — he had less than most to celebrate.

For him, the war had played a paradoxical role in his life. Disagreeable though he had found his military service and subsequent hospitalisation, it had, in many ways, been the making of him as a writer. It had "rubbed his nose in the stuff of humanity".[55] It had presented him with inherently dramatic and often bizarre raw material. It had enmeshed him in a nightmarish bureaucracy which offered an ideal focus for his satirical instincts. And the wartime resurgence of interest in short fiction had provided the catalyst for his burgeoning literary career. In a sense, Julian was among the few beneficiaries of the war. He had, by the time hostilities were over, "already established a reputation, not only as a wit and a character, but as the author of some brilliant short stories [...] Everything seemed within his grasp, and he was tipped as one of the most promising young authors, likely to make his mark in films [...] and on the air as well."[56]

How to be Bohemian

Metropolitan life changed rapidly after the euphoria of V-E Day. Gone were the intensity and danger of the war years. Gone, too, was the invigorating sense of London as the hub of the free world. Gradually the continental troops, who had given the city an unaccustomed cosmopolitan atmosphere, began to vanish. As did the Americans, their absence casting a desolate hush over once rowdy night-time streets. Another slower, more subtle transition also impinged on the literary world. Book sales had boomed during wartime, but the new distractions, notably the triumphant, crowd-pulling return of professional sport, may have been responsible for curtailing the boom. Now that readers had more time for the sustained attention demanded by novels, the flourishing short story market, in which Julian had achieved stardom, went into a slow decline, the circulation, influence and, indeed, quality of magazines such as *Penguin New Writing*, *Horizon*, and *English Story* dwindling.

Even Fitzrovia itself was not exempt from the transformation. With its official reclassification as an "industrial" rather than "residential" district soon after the war, businesses displaced the artists, writers, and students who had traditionally lived and worked there. The clientele of the neighbouring pubs began to change as well. Many of the writers who had been Fitzrovian regulars, lured there by the area's hedonistic wartime ambience, found employment with the now expanding BBC, consequently switching their allegiances to the pubs within the shadow of Broadcasting House. Others merely drifted away. But Julian, like some old India hand, unable to wrench himself free from colonial life, stayed on, content to linger in the circumscribed, claustrophobic world of the Soho pubs and clubs. There he carried on as if nothing had changed, still cadging drinks, still borrowing money from friends and acquaintances, still talking about his favourite movies, *The Mask of Dimetrios* and *The Maltese Falcon* above all.

It was in the Wheatsheaf that Julian enjoyed a surprise reunion with Raynor Heppenstall who, following his recent discharge from the army, was living in Hampstead with his wife and two young children. Unaware that they'd entered Julian's domain, Raynor and his wife walked into the Saloon Bar. From the far end, Raynor was taken aback to hear Julian's distinctive voice and glimpse his head of dark hair, his pale hand clutching his cigarette-holder. Slaloming through the dense evening crowd, Raynor greeted the flashily attired Julian, who was quaffing brandy in the company of Subra, a girl in a WAAF uniform, and a short, redheaded man with a moustache. The sight of Julian's Schiaperelli tie and the proximity of Keidrich Rhys and Paul Potts, two other former inmates of Northfield Military Hospital, seated nearby, inspired Raynor to joke about how they ought to commission someone to design an Old Northfieldians tie.

Survival as a freelance writer had, for Julian, become "a sort of test, a challenge",[1] his avoidance of the conventional nine-to-five grind becoming a point of pride. Like Graham Greene before him, he sought to extend his literary range from fiction into film criticism. Only a week after V-E Day, John Lehmann purchased *A Mirror to Darkness*, his pioneering essay on the literal and metaphorical darkness of what is now termed film noir. This featured in the summer edition of the hardback miscellany *New Writing and Daylight*, edited by Lehmann and published by Leonard Woolf's Hogarth Press. At the same time, Lehmann agreed to pay £25 for an option on his next three stories. The option was soon exercised on a long story Julian had shown him, which Lehmann adjudged "a masterpiece of humorous observation".[2] Entitled *The Swag, the Spy and the Soldier*, it was an expanded version of an uncompleted story about Micky Hopper's court-martial, the additional material chronicling their pre-war friendship.

Julian also sold the intriguingly titled *Welsh Rabbit of Soap* — a poignant tale of the early days of his romance with Monica — to Leonard Russell for inclusion in *The Saturday Book*. And he netted a small fee for the right to use one of his army pieces in the forthcoming anthology, *Stories of the Forties*, co-compiled by Woodrow Wyatt.

Despite the increase in his literary earnings, he was back in trouble by the final week of May 1945, his prospects not helped by his acrimonious split with Curtis Brown, the literary agency he'd engaged only a few months earlier. Relinquishing his expensive room at the Imperial Hotel, he moved to the fringe of Shepherd Market, a seedy, prostitute-infested yet picturesque district of Mayfair, where he rented a tiny flat in a three-storey townhouse at 3 Queen Street, not far from where his father had lived as a young man. Besides being handily placed, the flat had its own telephone, which Julian considered an essential tool for dealing with publishers.

He attempted to extricate himself from his financial problems by producing an article he'd promised Lehmann about the films of his long-standing hero Alfred Hitchcock. Punctilious as always about payment, Lehmann, who had earmarked the essay for *Penguin New Writing*, handed him a cheque for £25 when they met for a drink a few nights later. But the money didn't last long. Still, having gleefully monitored the disappearance of every copy of *The Stuff To Give The Troops* from all the West End bookshops, he assumed that he would be receiving some royalties. Though the terms of his contract specified that these weren't due until September, he wrote to the eponymous Jonathan Cape to ask whether the firm would be willing to advance whatever they owed him. It seemed a straightforward way out of his current impasse, yet he was disappointed to discover that his book's healthy sales were a fraction short of covering what the firm had already paid him. For the time-being at least, no royalties were due, so he had to hunt for an alternative source of cash.

Remembering André Deutsch's offer to bail him out if he got into financial difficulties while writing *The Lunatic Fringe*, he decided to hold André to his word. Not that Julian had even started work on the novel in question, the deadline for which was imminent. When he went round to the offices of Allan Wingate and asked "for an extra £50 to help complete it",[3] André refused. On account of the current paper shortage, André even asked Julian to postpone delivery of the book. Indignant at what he saw as the latest in a series of broken promises, he chased André round his desk, wielding the famed malacca cane. Over subsequent days, he took to ringing him up and haranguing him about the money he needed. All to no avail.

His annoyance stoked by the conviction that André's "uncertainty and procrastination"[4] was damaging his career, Julian felt entitled to look for a new publisher. John Lehmann was the obvious person to approach, not only because he held an editorial post with the Hogarth Press, but also because he had plans to set up his own company.

Just as Julian had hoped, the efficient and increasingly powerful Lehmann was keen to add him to the company's roster of authors. Buoyed by this latest upturn in his fortunes and by the concurrent mood of cheerful expectation arising from the delayed announcement of the Labour Party's emphatic General Election victory, which came through on Thursday 26 July, he spent that night downing alternate glasses of beer and scotch in the Wheatsheaf. Later in the week, when he met John Heath-Stubbs there, Julian asked whether he too had got drunk to mark the occasion. To his amazement, Heath-Stubbs revealed that he'd voted Conservative. Shaking his head in disbelief, Julian said, "Who'd have thought it? A promising young poet who votes Conservative... Is that what the future holds for us?"[5]

In Julian's case the immediate future held a deal with John Lehmann, finalised at the start of September. For an instant advance of £50, half what he'd originally asked for, Julian undertook to provide either the Hogarth Press or Lehmann's new firm with two collections of stories and a novel, at least one of which had to be delivered by the beginning of March 1946.

Less than three weeks afterwards, his sense of well-being was thrown out of kilter by a worrying letter from Lehmann's secretary. It announced that the solicitors acting on behalf of Penguin Books were apprehensive about *The Swag, the Spy and the Soldier*, due for inclusion in the end of year issue of *Penguin New Writing*. They wanted Julian's assurances that the story was "not founded on facts that may lead readers to identify the characters with real people."[6] And they wanted him to tone down some of the language in order to reduce the likelihood of someone instigating a prosecution for obscenity. Bristling at the idea of his work being tampered with, Julian wrote back to say that there was nothing libellous in the story and that no concessions should be made that might "encourage a similar kind of puritanism to that which prevailed after the last war."[7]

The advance from Lehmann supplementing a useful four guinea fee from *World Digest* for the rights to reprint a condensed version of *A Mirror to Darkness*, he found himself a larger flat, again equipped with a telephone. At the end of the second week of October, he moved into his new place at 59 Bayswater Road, right next to Lancaster Gate tube station, the building's front windows facing Kensington Gardens.

He was in the Wheatsheaf when Peter Brooke, greying at the temples and dressed in a navy blue demob suit, suddenly entered the Saloon Bar. Sighting his old friend, Julian used his cane to point towards the spot next to him, the regulars shuffling along to make room. Julian then embarked on an apocryphal anecdote about Brooke, who merely nodded and smiled in response, though he was unnerved by the way Julian had started to reinvent him, endowing him with a "false personality".[8] He knew only too well, however, that there was no point in protesting. Once something had been incorporated into Julian's repertoire, it became, for Julian at least, an irrefutable fact. As Staggering Stephen, himself an intermittent visitor to the Saloon Bar, was to discover, no matter how misinformed Julian might be, he'd always defend his position with unyielding tenacity. And so, when he declared that Fred Astaire had been born an Englishman, Stephen was unable to persuade him otherwise. On another occasion he casually referred to Stephen's "drug addiction".[9] When Stephen denied that he'd ever been a drug addict, Julian said, "But you *were* once, and now you're cured."[10] Even more vehemently than before, Stephen denied it. "Yes, yes," Julian insisted impatiently, oblivious to his denials; "you were a junkie for a time, and you kicked the habit."[11] At which Stephen abandoned his futile protestations.

Peter Brooke instantly slotted back into Julian's clique, back into the comic, accident-prone persona he'd been allocated. Briefly stepping out of this role, Brooke confided in Julian about the unhappy conclusion to his affair with Anne. "My dear chap," Julian replied as he clapped his hand on Brooke's shoulder. "Don't mention this again, and I will never mention it. I thought it was the sort of thing we all got over in Nice. The appalling waste of time, I mean. The mooning."[12]

Julian's refusal to listen to Brooke talk about his amorous troubles did nothing to ameliorate them. His doleful mood heightened by a spate of rejection letters from magazine editors, Brooke slid down the Saloon Bar pecking order. Before long, he found himself tenth in line from Julian, sandwiched between Willie Willetts and "a bearded gentleman who was supposed to be a German or Russian spy."[13] Meanwhile, Julian regarded the once ebullient Brooke with consternation. "You must pull yourself together, old chap," he said, prodding him with his cane. "If you go on like this, you'll come to a bad end. You'll have to get a job."[14] Lacking Julian's resourcefulness and indomitable optimism, Brooke temporarily abandoned his literary aspirations, accepted employment with the Inland Revenue, and deserted the Saloon Bar.

Of all the many post-war absentees from the Wheatsheaf, Dan Davin was the one Julian missed the most. In the aftermath of V-E Day, Dan and his wife had moved to Oxford, where he'd landed a demanding job with the Clarendon Press, the scholarly imprint of the Oxford University Press. Yet Dan stayed in touch with Julian, his affection for him magnified by his respect for his writing and gratitude for the literary advice he'd so generously dispensed. During periodic business trips to London, Dan would make a point of popping into the Wheatsheaf to see Julian. Among the earliest of these visits took place one Saturday lunchtime, probably in either late October or November. When the pub closed for the afternoon, Julian, Dan, and Nina Hamnett took a taxi from Rathbone Place to the Plaza cinema where they attended the matinee of *The Lost Weekend*. It was an apt choice of film for the now alcoholic Julian. Adapted from Charles Jackson's grim, much-admired novel, it starred Ray Milland as a dipsomaniac writer wrestling with his addiction. Whereas Nina was so shaken by the movie she needed a stiff drink before she felt up to joining the others on their hunt for a taxi back to the Wheatsheaf, Julian remained strangely impervious. Far from identifying with Ray Milland, he saw himself mirrored by the hardboiled figure of Bim, the male nurse in the hospital's alcoholic ward. For "the rest of that night's wanderings",[15] he savoured Bim's minor contribution to the movie, "recalling with ever-increasing vividness and pleasure the imaginary mouse which had terrified the alcoholic's delirium and caused Bim such agreeable chuckles."[16]

Whenever Julian saw Dan, he'd talk incessantly about what, he hoped, would be his masterpiece — *The Fields of Night*, its title altered to the MacBeth-inspired *Night's Black Agents*. The book now starred "Rickard, the revolutionary intellectual, [who] finds himself in revolt against [...] army-routine",[17] his desertion causing him to be hunted by both the army and a "crypto-fascist organisation".[18] As he conceived it, *Night's Black Agents* would articulate his "notions of conspiracy, of evil forces constantly gathering and plotting."[19]

Its synopsis had already been written and re-written. Its intricacies had, moreover, been expounded so often Dan "almost knew the plot by heart",[20] so often Dan began to suspect that Julian preferred talking about it to writing it.

Through Dan, he got to know two other New Zealand expatriates. There was the dapper poseur, Geoffrey Flavell, a pre-war friend of Dan's, who was working as a surgeon at several London hospitals. His interest in literature and the visual arts, his exuberant and self-deprecating humour, his taste for hyperbole ensured that he and Julian hit it off. Soon they were meeting for regular roast-beef dinners in Soho restaurants, Julian invariably wolfing down the discarded fat from Geoffrey's plate.

Dan also introduced him to the ex Kiwi serviceman Jack Gillies, who had a deserved reputation as a raconteur. Jack loved to tell the story of how he and a friend had liberated a huge black Mercedes coupé, formerly owned by the Munich gauleiter. They had, so the story went, smuggled the car into England and kept it in a barn somewhere in Surrey. As if to banish the inevitable suspicion that the whole thing was pure fabrication, Jack would occasionally drive the car into Soho and manouevre it down the narrow passageway that ran through the Wheatsheaf into Percy Mews, the cul-de-sac at the back. On seeing it, Julian christened it "Black Beauty". Jack sometimes took him out for a spin in it, the enjoyable illusion of chauffeur-driven, elegant-living sustained for the all-too-brief duration of the ride.

It was around then that Julian became friendly with John Gawsworth (assumed name of the poet and editor Terence Armstrong), an even more idiosyncratic character whose dark, neatly trimmed moustache and slicked back hair contrasted with everything else about him. Demobbed from the RAF, he was living on a tiny income from some rented houses in Ireland. He'd often come into the Wheatsheaf, dressed in incongruous outfits, bought from secondhand clothes stalls on Portobello Road, a black bowler hat, for instance, worn with a purple velvet jacket. Alongside his self-conscious sartorial eccentricity, Gawsworth boasted in his bluff, Sergeant-Major's voice of being the heir to the Kingdom of Redonda and literary executor to the West Indian-born popular novelist M.P. Shiel — a man who wrote lavish fantasies, set in worlds where it was perfectly feasible for an embalmed corpse to be transmuted into a gigantic vermillion-feathered cat. According to the legend perpetuated at every opportunity by the garrulous Gawsworth, Shiel's wealthy father had been piloting his yacht through the Caribbean when he'd sighted the minuscule, uninhabited island of Santa Maria la Redonda. On discovering that the British crown had annexed the rest of the Leeward Islands but neglected to do the same to this rocky outcrop, Shiel claimed it in the name of his son, later arranging for the Bishop of Antigua to crown his fifteen-year-old offspring "King Felipe I of Redonda". Unmarried and childless, M.P. Shiel had, in 1936, decreed that Gawsworth should succeed him as monarch, his proclamation endorsed by pricking their right wrists and pressing them together.

As a connoisseur of the outlandish, Julian was bound to find it appealing. Though the tale sounded far-fetched (and has since been largely discredited as a publicity gimmick conceived by Shiel to bolster his diminishing reputation), Julian lent his uncritical support to the concept of Gawsworth being a King-in-waiting.

Unlike the tortured protagonist of *The Lost Weekend*, Julian managed to combine high alcohol consumption with high literary productivity. During November, *Better Than A Kick In The Pants*, his latest collection of short stories, its opening pages carrying a dedication to Monica, was released by Lawson & Dunn, whose scant resources meant they couldn't even afford to advertise it in *The Bookseller*, the trade's principal journal. In a fate shared by the follow-up books of so many other widely praised debutant authors, it suffered a critical backlash. *The TLS* condescendingly acknowledged Julian's talent for slangy, often inconsequential dialogue, but complained about the absence of any other redeeming attributes. Even that was restrained in comparison to the mauling it received from the poet and satirist Henry Reed. Writing in *The New Statesman and Nation*, he condemned some of the stories as "no more than pub anecdotes"[21] and went on to suggest the book should have been called "Any Bloody Thing Will Do."[22]

From about the time his second collection was published, Julian, in grudging recognition of London's reconfigured literary map, began making frequent lunchtime appearances in the Stag's Head. Otherwise known as "the Head", it was a relatively small pub at the base of an office block near Broadcasting House. In common with several of the other pubs in that vicinity, chiefly the George, the Dover Castle, and the Yorkshire Grey, the latter nicknamed "the Whore's Lament", the Head functioned as an alternative staff-room for members of BBC radio's Drama and Features departments. However much Julian disliked the majority of its clientele, he felt obliged to go there in the hope of making useful contacts.

The main door to the Saloon Bar was at the junction between Hallam and New Cavendish Streets. Like the Wheatsheaf, the Head was owned by Younger's, who had furnished it in much the same style. The wooden panelled walls were inset with glazed squares of tartan, faded Gothic lettering identifying the appropriate clan. The settles, chairs, and bar-stools were upholstered in green rexine. And the floor was covered in red lino, imprinted with squares to mimic terracotta paments. Among the dominant BBC contingent were the poets Roy Campbell — notorious for his pugnacity and his unfashionable, stridently expressed right-wing sympathies — and Louis MacNeice, who always sat at the same chair in the corner. Mingling with the BBC staff, the irregular click and rumble from the pinball table underscoring their conversation, there was normally a smattering of writers, composers, and actors. Such sporadic visitors included the composers Constant Lambert, Humphrey Searle and Elizabeth Lutyens; the poets Dylan Thomas, Kathleen Raine, Alex Comfort, Robert Conquest, Henry Reed, and David Gascoyne; as well as the prose writers C.P. Snow, Pamela Hansford Johnson, Angus Wilson, Laurie Lee, and Rose Macauley.

Impossible to miss in either his teddy-bear coat or his black astrakhan-collared number, Schiaparelli tie, sunglasses, and cane, these now combined with a mustard-coloured velvet jacket, chocolate brown trousers and suede shoes to match, his posture confident and composed. Julian would make a grand entrance into the Saloon Bar. A lot of the BBC crowd would ignore him lest they end up on the receiving end of one of his monologues. An exception was Raynor Heppenstall, who had recently joined the BBC's boozy ranks. Irrespective of Julian's manifest faults, Raynor maintained a soft spot for him because of the longevity of their friendship, their shared experiences, and what he saw as Julian's "generous and vigilant appreciation of other people's work, to say nothing of his own merits as a writer."[23] From across the crowded bar, Raynor usually greeted Julian with a guarded smile, its reticence testimony to his divided loyalties.

Once he'd entered the pub, Julian would make for the bar and order the first of many gin-and-peps. It was at the bar that he probably encountered David Thomson from the Features Department. Late in November, on the understanding that payment would be prompt, Thomson commissioned him to script a dramatised biography of the pirate Captain Kidd for a new radio series they were planning. His visits to the Head paying further dividends, he was also approached by a member of the BBC's French Section, enquiring whether he'd allow them to translate and abridge a story of his for broadcasting in France. But he refused to countenance it unless he had final say over the translation — something they weren't prepared to sanction.

In the space of only a couple of weeks, Julian researched the life of Captain Kidd, polished off a script, and submitted it to the Features Department, who agreed to a 30 guinea fee. Yet the eagerly anticipated cheque wasn't forthcoming.

A well-timed morale-boost was provided by the re-publication of *I Like It In The Army* in *World Digest*, not to mention the inclusion of Nina Hamnett's portrait of him in the latest London Group show, which opened at the Royal Academy on Wednesday 12 December. As an avid follower of contemporary painting, he would surely have relished its presence in the same room as pictures by Victor Pasmore, David Bomberg, and William Roberts.

Maybe because he was behind with the rent on his flat, he hatched a plan to move out and head down to Bognor for the holiday period. In preparation, he phoned Mac to ask if it'd be okay for he and Monica to spend Christmas Day with them. Mac knew his wife would be annoyed, nonetheless he went ahead and said that he and Lydia would be delighted to see them. Julian "told him to order some plum pudding, turkey, and all the trimmings. 'And I'll pay for the lot…,' he added."[24]

When Lydia found out what had happened, she was incensed. But her anger abated in the weeks leading up to their arrival. Just before Christmas, Julian and his girlfriend vacated their flat and travelled down to the south coast. Arriving in Bognor, they registered at the Bedford Hotel.

On Christmas Day, he and Monica took a taxi from their small hotel to the Jaegers' house at 13 Jubilee Parade in Elmer, a suburb familiar to Julian from his blissful sojourn there as a child. Despite his previous assurances, he made no effort to contribute to the cost of all the goodies Mac and Lydia had laid on. Naturally, this did nothing to assuage the resentment Lydia already felt towards him. She was too polite a hostess, however, to let that spoil their Christmas, which offered "a nostalgic reminder of the old days: full of laughter."[25] Even so, Mac couldn't help noticing the detrimental changes two-and-a-half years of big city life had wrought on Julian, the softer side of his character having been buried beneath a layer of toughness and cynicism "that made even verbally dexterous Fleet Street journalists wary of him."[26] Sensing that his alcohol-dominated way of life was destroying him, that "he was going to pot or, more precisely, to whisky",[27] Mac pleaded with him to stay in Bognor for good. But the ambitious Julian said he had to get back to London if he was ever going to make it as a successful writer.

The promised cheque from the BBC still hadn't arrived by the third week of 1946, so Julian, who "saw himself as a sort of frightful celluloid gangster who went round talking to editors out of the side of his mouth",[28] sent a stroppy telegram to the Features Department, demanding his money. That Friday, he followed this up with a trip to London to visit Rothwell House, the former block of flats near Broadcasting House, where Reggie Smith, the producer of his script, had a pokey office. Reggie was a close friend of both Walter Allen and the Davins, yet this seems to have been the first time Julian had met him. As a blunt, working-class Brummie, whose behaviour was governed not by social convention but by his principles and loyalties, Reggie could hardly have been further removed from the stereotype of the suave, public school-educated BBC producer. Reggie's other distinctive trait was his gargantuan, round-shouldered physique, any hint of menace dispelled by his relaxed, cheerful, affectionate, and voluble personality. Though he was a famously astute judge of scriptwriting flair, subsequently demonstrated by his support for the young Harold Pinter, Reggie is now best-remembered as the model for the character of Guy Pringle in *The Balkan* and *Levant* trilogies, his wife Olivia Manning's celebrated sequence of novels. Right from the start, Reggie appears to have felt an instinctive sympathy for Julian and admiration for his literary gifts, for what he called his "special talent for making apparently trivial dialogue carry the weight of character."[29] Because of this, he was prepared to tolerate and even indulge Julian's truculence.

Confronting Reggie in his office, Julian was informed that he would get his fee once he'd made some alterations to the script and written an additional scene. Instead of being placated by their meeting, next day Julian drafted a testy letter to the BBC, accusing them of "slipshod methods of payment"[30] and threatening to withhold permission to use his script if he didn't receive his full fee by the following Thursday. His letter seems to have done the trick.

Now he was back in Bognor, Julian renewed his friendship with Martin Jordan, who had survived a gruelling spell as a Japanese prisoner of war. Heartened by the BBC's purchase of his Captain Kidd script, Julian revived his pre-war collaboration with Martin on *The Newgate Calendar*, their play about Jack Sheppard. When he left Bognor sometime around the end of January, he and Martin continued their scriptwriting partnership by post, reshaping the material into a dramatised radio documentary, retitled *The Bowl of St Giles*. At the third attempt, they finally succeeded in selling their script to the BBC.

From Bognor, Julian went to stay with Edward du Cros again in Earl's Court, his return to the capital coinciding with the twice-postponed publication of *Bitten By The Tarantula: A Story of the South of France*. For its cover, André Deutsch had commissioned a three-colour illustration by the surrealist painter John Banting, whom Julian knew from the Swiss. The book's flyleaf carried a condensed and candid biography of Julian, written by André, together with a brief statement by Julian himself. His waning belief in this latest addition to his oeuvre all too evident in the apologetic tone of his statement, Julian presented the book as no more than a lighthearted piece of entertainment which, on rereading, he found "funny in parts". To back up his claim, he made a spurious confession that he'd written the book in 1942 "as a relaxation from writing the series of army tales afterwards published in a volume called *The Stuff To Give The Troops*." He also seized the chance to caution people against assuming that the narrator was a self-portrait.

Like its predecessor, *Bitten By The Tarantula* attracted some scathing reviews. And, once more, the severest of its detractors was Henry Reed, whose hatred of Julian's work was fortified by a hatred of Julian himself. "Mr Maclaren-Ross's book," he wrote, "is very well bound and generously, though not elegantly, printed; but its last three pages increase their number of lines from thirty-four per page to forty-one, thereby giving a peculiar stretto effect to the narrative which is, in fact, its sole interest. [...] The point of Mr Maclaren-Ross's novel is not obscure. It has none."[31]

Thanks, perhaps, to an almost diametrically opposed review in the influential *New Novels* section of *The Sunday Times*, describing it as "high spirited and [...] highly diverting",[32] the powerful Boots chain of lending libraries placed an order for 1,000 copies. *Bitten By The Tarantula* went on to score Allan Wingate's first commercial hit, allowing André to dedicate himself to the business full-time. But the firm's inability to obtain additional supplies of paper meant that the book couldn't be reprinted, denying Julian the opportunity to chalk up really substantial sales. Its relative success did, however, validate André's decision to bring forward the release date for *The Weeping and the Laughter* from 1947 to the coming autumn. Along with the change of publication date came a change of title. Even though its contents were by no means focused exclusively on the narrow bohemian world Julian inhabited, he decided to call it *The Nine Men of Soho*. Out of enduring affection and respect for his one-time girlfriend, Eileen Cooke, he dedicated it to her.

Seeking to capitalise on the mystique of Fitzrovia, André paid Nina Hamnett to provide a drawing of the Fitzroy Tavern for the book's dustjacket. But Julian, sensitive to the homosexual connotations, protested vociferously, claiming — quite inaccurately — that he wouldn't be seen dead in the place. His protestations led to André commissioning a replacement cover illustration by John Banting, whose work Julian admired. In the meantime, *Second Lieutenant Lewis*, a touching memoir of Julian's friendship with Alun Lewis, who had been killed in the war, appeared in the April edition of *Penguin New Writing*.

On Thursday 2 May, Julian consolidated the bright start he'd made to the year. That evening, his protracted quest to become a broadcast radio playwright culminated in the transmission of his play about Captain Kidd, which formed the first episode of the series, *Rogues and Vagabonds*. Maintaining his winning streak, Julian persuaded John Lehmann to commission an article he wanted to write for *Penguin New Writing* about British feature films, examining their inadequacies, their fatuous exoticism, their patronising depiction of working-class characters, and their futile attempts to rival Hollywood epics. Lehmann, whose faith in Julian's good intentions remained undented by experience, advanced him £10 in cash. Julian responded by delivering the completed article on time, its crisp prose and punctual arrival gleaning him a £25 advance on his next three publishable short stories.

The recent handsome returns from his writing permitted him to reinstall himself at the Imperial Hotel. Posing as, "Mr and Mrs Maclaren-Ross", he and Monica took a room on the top-floor where, as they made their way down the interminable corridors, the floorboards creaked and the once sumptuous Oriental-style carpets were worn thin. Their room, fitted with a bedside telephone, central heating, hot and cold running water as well as a coin-operated radio, overlooked Russell Square. From there, the restful cooing of pigeons in the trees was audible early in the morning before the drone of traffic blotted it out.

While he and Monica were at the Imperial, Julian made good use of its other facilities. Between lunchtime and evening sessions in the pub, he'd sit in the heavily furnished lounge, playing chess with a Chinese resident. And when his taxi had delivered him home after a hard night's drinking and talking, he'd settle down with a notebook in the same, now deserted lounge, and write with the fluency of a secretary taking dictation.

Itching to free himself from his contractual obligations to André Deutsch, whom he still owed a full-length novel, he resuscitated the idea of producing a revised version of *The Salesman Only Rings Once*. On the strength of the chapter-plan he'd drawn up, André gave him an advance of about £100. Julian was able to make swift progress on the book, cutting it heavily and replacing the earlier third-person narration with an appropriately laconic and colloquial first-person style, perfect for portraying his sometimes comical, sometimes grim experiences, these counterpointed both by a tale of adulterous romance and the portents of impending war.

Around then, possibly at the bar of the Wheatsheaf, Julian first came across Bobby Roberts, who turned out to be a great fan of his stories. A loquacious, moon-faced, bespectacled man, always clad in the same muted check suit, Bobby revealed that he was a friend of Anthony Powell, one of Julian's literary idols. As a favour to Julian, he said he'd fix up a meeting between them.

Already the victim of too many such introductions to the often tedious eccentrics Bobby cultivated, Tony Powell was reluctant to agree to the arrangement. By sheer persistence, Bobby eventually set up a meeting in a pub on Great Portland Street, most likely the George. Prior to arriving there, Bobby had warned Tony and his wife, Lady Violet, about his egotism. With a sense of foreboding, the lean, smartly dressed, patrician-mannered Tony, some six years Julian's senior, stepped through the door of the pub where Julian, his demeanour verging on the aggressive, was sitting. Speedily confirming Bobby's ominous assessment of him, Julian launched into an unstoppable monologue, covering the usual well-trodden territory of books and gangster movies. So jealously did he defend the conversational ball, he even evaded the lunging challenges of Bobby, who attempted to shout him down.

Tony nevertheless found him sufficiently engaging to want to remain in contact. As the two of them got to know one another, Julian revealed more about himself and his background, hinting that his peripatetic father had been a spy. In his fondness for projecting a false image of stoical, unselfpitying resilience, he fed Tony mendacious stories about how he'd served his full sentence in the Detention Barrack, and how he'd been reduced to sleeping on the Embankment before the war. Impressed by Julian, Tony introduced him to another of his literary heroes: the wealthy novelist, Henry Yorke, who wrote under the name of Henry Green. His pleasure at coming face to face with the crotchety Yorke was, however, unrequited.

Soon Julian started dropping round to the Powells' tall, elegant house at 1 Chester Gate on the eastern fringe of Regent's Park where, on one occasion, he was roped into a game of Happy Families with their young son, Tristram. Together with Monica, he also became a recurrent dinner guest. Monica's presence only encouraged him to play up to the audience, his egotism killing conversation. Towards the end of the evening, he'd slip into his Sidney Greenstreet impersonations. Practice taught Tony that this was the signal to steer him towards the exit.

Julian's run of good luck had petered out by the summer when he confessed he was at his "wits end to know which way to turn for money",[33] that he was desperate to "sit down and concentrate on writing a novel in moderate peace of mind."[34] Of course his precarious position wasn't helped by his self-destructive and obstinate insistence on living with Monica in the pricey Imperial Hotel, the management of which impounded his laundry to prevent him from leaving without settling his bill.

Drinking in the Wheatsheaf one lunchtime, the equally hard-up James Graham-Murray regaled Julian and John Heath-Stubbs with the story of how he had, in desperation, gone to the Jesuit church on Farm Street and said, "Father, I'm a Protestant. And I've no intention of converting to Catholicism. I just need you to help me out by lending me £5…"[35] The astonished priest responded by saying he wished everyone's problems were so easily solved. He then despatched a minion to fetch the money. On hearing this, Julian said, "My God, they did that for *you*, and you're a Protestant. Perhaps I should try it too. Since I'm a Catholic, they're bound to help me."[36] After the pub closed, he went over to Farm Street and trotted out the same spiel. This time, though, the priest merely gave him the address of the nearest Labour Exchange.

A more effective solution to his difficulties was provided by John Lehmann, who paid him an extra 10 guineas for revising his previously submitted article on British feature films. Lehmann also hired Julian to write at least eight detailed reports on French novels he was thinking of publishing. And he obtained a generous fee on Julian's behalf from the French literary magazine, *Dialogue*, for the right to reprint *The Swag, the Spy and the Soldier*. Yet Julian's hefty running-expenses meant that he was back in trouble by August.

Aggrieved at what he regarded as the injustice of his situation, he had no qualms about publicising his plight. He did this through a questionnaire sent to him that month by Sonia Brownell, who was managing *Horizon* while Cyril Connolly was on holiday. The questionnaire was intended to canvas the financial expectations of leading writers. His response to its initial question, asking the recipient to name a figure, was characteristically forthright and uncompromising. "A writer needs all he can lay his hands on in order to keep alive," he replied.

"How much he should actually have depends on the writer himself: his tastes and habits. In other words, he should be able to live comfortably, in a style that suits his temperament. If he is a drinker he shouldn't have to worry whether he drinks beer or spirits or wine, though he shouldn't necessarily have enough to get sozzled every night. If he is a smoker he shouldn't have to buy Woodbines if he prefers Perfectos. If he wants to buy a book he should be able to buy it, not wait until it is sent to him for review or lent to him by a friend. If he doesn't drink, smoke, read books or go to the cinema, then he almost certainly has other vices, or else a wife or mistress to spend money on; well, he should have enough to spend. A writer's standard of living should be at least as high as that of a solicitor, or any other professional man.

"I am a metropolitan man and I need a minimum of £20 a week to live on, given the present cost of living; and that's not including rent."[37]

Answering the survey's request for advice that could be given to anyone who wanted to write for a living, he voiced all the cynicism and hostility he felt towards publishers: "(a) Don't attempt it. (b) If you are crazy enough to try, be tough; get all you can. Price your work high and make them pay. Don't listen to your publisher's sob-stories about how little he can afford. He'll have a country house and polo ponies when you are still borrowing the price of a drink in Fitzrovia. Remember, he makes the money; make him give you as much as you can extort, short of using a gun or pincers. Art for art's sake is all cock, anyway.

And, by the same token, please pay promptly for this contribution, because I am broke."[38]

Julian's response to the questionnaire featured in the September issue of *Horizon*, alongside replies from a cross-section of other writers. Next to the modest expectations of most of them, aside from the upper-crust Elizabeth Bowen, his aspirations were unrealistic. He had certainly never come close to fulfilling them. That year his earnings amounted to £324, well short of the target he'd set himself, though that didn't stop him from living in the profligate, taxi-hopping style he felt he deserved, the yawning gap between his actual earnings and what he considered his rightful income creating a mounting sense of injustice.

In October he succeeded in disentangling himself from his contract with Allan Wingate by delivering the novel on which he'd been working. He called it *Of Love and Hunger*, a phrase plucked from the W.H. Auden/Louis MacNeice collaboration, *Letters From Iceland*. In testament to his durable friendship with Mac and Lydia Jaeger, along with the salient borrowings from their life together at Greenleaves, he dedicated the book to them.

When he showed up at André Deutsch's office to drop off the manuscript, he found André deep in conversation with a business partner, the sardonic, bushy-eyebrowed cartoonist Nic Bentley. So taken was Bentley by both Julian's appearance and minute script, afterwards likened to "the handwriting of a prep school art mistress",[39] he sketched an affectionate caricature of him, which he toyed with using as an illustration to one of George Mikes's best-selling *How To Be ...* books.

About a week later, André contacted Julian to express his delight with the manuscript. All the faith he and so many other people had placed in Julian's literary potential had at last been triumphantly repaid. Out of the raw material of his life, filtered through the disparate influences of not just the hardboiled writers but Patrick Hamilton too, Julian had created something fresh, exhilarating, and commercial.

Other episodes from his time in Bognor, as well as Soho and the Riviera, formed the core of *The Nine Men of Soho*, his third collection of stories. Released that month, it was preceded by a playful note, stating that "The 'I' in these stories is always Me. All other characters are imaginary." Like his previous book, it enjoyed brisk sales, aided by some excellent reviews. Writing in *The Daily Telegraph and Morning Post*, Anthony Powell praised it for being "the lively and original" product of "an author of unusual promise".[40] In her column for *The Tatler and Bystander* magazine, Elizabeth Bowen identified him as a "writer due for the first rank". Besides finding it "extremely funny", she asserted that "Better, and more dire, pictures of the Bohemian extremity—in pubs and the Soho purlieus, in dun-beleaguered bungalows along half-made roads, in and out of bookshops and under the duress of the Army—are not [...] to be found."[41]

Well though the book did, it would have sold in even greater numbers had it been published by a larger, more established company. But Allan Wingate had neither the budget to advertise it properly, nor the influence to procure sufficient quantities of paper to print the large edition it merited.

Julian consolidated his growing renown with the ensuing publication in Leonard Russell's *Winter Pie* of *The Days of the Comet*, his amusing, anecdotal memoir of his childhood introduction to the cinema. "For some time I'd been seeing films in which the heroine was threatened with Being Ruined," the best of the anecdotes began. "Occasionally this process was described as a Fate Worse than Death. I had never seen the threat carried into practice, as the arrival of the hero always prevented that, so I decided to write a script where the heroine was really Ruined. This incident I was obliged to cut down to a mere caption, as the actual nature of Ruination eluded me [...] All went well until my sister got hold of the Prodigious exercise-book containing the script.

"It amused her enormously, and she gave it to my father to read. My father was less amused. In fact he was furious".[42]

For all the comparative success Julian had been enjoying, he was still short of money. If he was to have any hope of fulfilling his contract with John Lehmann and delivering a book by the beginning of next March, he knew he had to raise more cash: enough to allow him to approach it with the "absolutely concentrated effort"[43] his working methods demanded, any sustained interruptions to the process usually proving disastrous.

Following his father's example, he sought to exploit his bilingual background by working as a translator. A timely commission came from John Lehmann, who had just launched the publishing firm, John Lehmann Ltd. Only recently Julian's friend had rejected an unsolicited translation of Raymond Queneau's picaresque comedy, *Pierrot mon ami*, submitted by the then unknown Iris Murdoch. In a sneaky manouevre, Lehmann now hired him to translate that same novel for the firm's Modern European Library series. With its clipped, idiomatic style, low life characters, racy plot, and garish amusement park setting, its hapless hero's antics echoing his own fleeting stint at Butlin's, the material was perfect for Julian. Sympathetic towards him but wary of his record of failing to abide by contracts, Lehmann was only prepared to advance half the translation fee, the other half payable on delivery, the deadline for which was the best part of a year away. But the fee soon evaporated.

Such was his confidence in the sales prospects of his most recent novel, Julian went back to André Deutsch to ask for another advance on the royalties. At the start of November, André gave him £100, but made him sign a contract pledging to pay £50 interest on it. For the moment, his money worries were alleviated, enabling him to devote his full attention to the novel he planned to write for John Lehmann. The novel was either *Threnody on a Gramophone* (about a "dispossessed Russian exile, living by his wits in the South of France 1931-32.")[44] or, more likely, *Night's Black Agents*.

Imprudent as ever, Julian wasted no time in destroying the financial status quo by squandering the money André had given him. To thank the Powells for the hospitality they'd shown he and Monica, Julian insisted on treating them to dinner at the Café Royal. There they were joined unexpectedly by a tall, good-looking, loose-limbed friend of Tony's, dressed in the uniform of the United Nations Relief and Rehabilitation Organisation. The interloper, squiring his latest girlfriend, was John Heygate. In view of Julian's penchant for divining hidden, often tangential connections between himself and well-known personalities, he would — if he'd been aware of it — have relished the link Heygate provided with the young Evelyn Waugh. The libidinous Heygate was, after all, the man who ran off with Waugh's first wife. Heygate's current, lovestruck girlfriend kept passing her lover notes under the table. Julian later told Tony that he'd glimpsed one of these and deciphered the upside-down handwriting. Referring to Julian, the note said, "He is too esoteric..."[45] It was a perceptive comment. As Tony conceded, Julian *was* "too esoteric; certainly too esoteric to find life easy."[46]

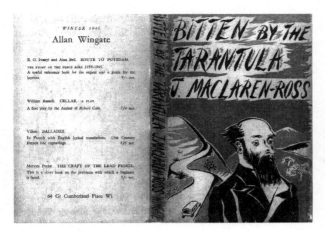

John Banting-designed
dustjacket for
Bitten By The Tarantula,
1946

Portrait of
Julian Maclaren-Ross,
published in
Autumn Pie, 1944

Illustration from
News From The Lesser Burrows,
1947, showing Bertram Badger,
the character modelled on
Julian Maclaren-Ross

The Bizarre Life Of Julian Maclaren-Ross

Into the Red

By the middle of November 1946, Julian began to run short of cash. As an economy measure, he and Monica swapped their room at the Imperial Hotel for one at the less prestigious, much more modern County Hotel on Upper Woburn Place, close to Euston Station. They were, he admitted, soon living a "hand to mouth"[1] existence there. Hoping to earn himself a little more time in which to work on his novel, Julian attempted to sell a short story to the ailing *Penguin New Writing*. But its theme — an attack on racial prejudice against black people — scared off John Lehmann, who was concerned it might antagonise the magazine's white readership in the southern states of America.

To eke out their remaining funds over the fag-end of what he had come to regard as a "terrible year",[2] Julian and "Mrs Maclaren-Ross" left their hotel and spent Christmas and the New Year in Elmer with the Jaegers. Yet this offered only a fleeting reprieve. When they checked back into the County Hotel, the nagging financial worries resumed. These denied Julian the peace of mind he considered a prerequisite to writing the novel he'd promised to deliver to John Lehmann by mid-April — a good six weeks later than his contract stipulated.

He averted penury by persuading John to commission a piece for *Penguin New Writing*. The commission appears to have been for a short, promptly completed memoir of his childhood fascination with the puppeteer Monsieur Félix. Only a few days afterwards, his 15 guinea fee for it almost if not entirely exhausted, he endeavoured to extract another, altogether larger advance from his friend. Implying that he wouldn't be able to meet the deadline for his novel unless John agreed to his proposal, he tried to raise £120 for a book of his previously uncollected critical articles and short fiction, beefed up by two long, as yet unwritten stories. But John turned it down.

His financial position worsening, Julian was, by the final week of January 1947, resigned to the notion that he and Monica would have to move out of their hotel. As a stopgap, necessity overcoming his lingering dislike of Oxford, he arranged to stay with Dan and Winnie Davin while Monica — who may well have been unable to get time off work — remained in London. Just before departing, "now left all but destitute",[3] he contacted Captain Broadbent, the Honorary Secretary of the Royal Literary Fund, to ask for an application form to be sent to him at the Davins'.

From the beginning of February, Julian joined Dan, Winnie, and their three daughters — six-year-old Anna, two-year-old Delia, and one-year-old Brigid — in their narrow but capacious three-storey, semi-detached Victorian house at 103 Southmoor Road, no more than a short walk from the Oxford University Press, where Dan still worked. On arrival there, Julian filled in the Royal Literary Fund's application form and returned it, his self-belief braced by the imminent publication of a French edition of *The Stuff To Give The Troops*. Together with his application form, he submitted an expansive covering letter that outlined his pitiable plight. "I have no idea how I am going to get through the next week or so [...]," he concluded. "To say my need is urgent, would, I can assure you, be a masterpiece of understatement."[4] His application was supported by wholehearted references from Tony Powell, who stressed his "extremely straitened circumstances";[5] from the critic Frank Swinnerton, who testified to his "exceptional and original"[6] talent; and from John Lehmann who, despite Julian's failure to honour the contract he'd signed only a few months earlier, hailed him as "a writer of remarkable gifts".[7]

In the depths of the coldest winter in memory, Julian must have had difficulty adjusting to the Davins' freezing house, a coal-fire in the living-room providing the main source of heat. While Winnie looked after the children and Dan kept his normal office hours, these prefaced by an early morning run, Julian most likely continued his own well-established routine, only staggering to bed after he'd put in a marathon stint on his novel, the deadline for which was approaching. Immersed in the type of secure family life he always seemed to hanker after, he probably enjoyed his visit, though he knew it had to come to an end soon. Over the penultimate weekend of February, he popped down to London to make arrangements to move back there in a couple of weeks.

The Royal Literary Fund hadn't yet reached a decision on his application by the beginning of March when he rejoined Monica at the County Hotel. Even more desperately short of money than ever, he reluctantly shelved his novel. In its place, he set to work on his translation of *Pierrot mon ami*, the incentive being that he could get hold of the second half of his fee once he'd finished it. To preserve the book's original colloquial flavour, he eschewed pedantic exactitude, preferring to search for English equivalents to Queneau's plentiful slang. As a means of putting this to the test, he already appears to have read sections of his work to Dan Davin, instilling in Dan a passion for Queneau. Julian seems to have wrapped up his translation and collected his fee by the second week of March. It was only then that he received a reply from Captain Broadbent, sent to him via Allan Wingate. The letter contained a cheque for £100 from the Royal Literary Fund. He was now free to go back to writing his novel, yet "however hard [he] tried," he found himself "utterly unable to complete [it],"[8] his concentration having been broken.

Putting the novel to one side, he turned his attention to several smaller, short-term projects. Over the next few weeks he penned a blurb which he had been commissioned to write for the dustjacket of *Pierrot mon ami*, declaring that the book "gives the lie to the widely held belief that all modern French writers are exponents of despair and cynicism". He also produced an unsolicited essay on Queneau and a short story intended to fulfil the previous summer's commission from John Lehmann. Both pieces were tactfully rejected by John. News of their rejection coincided with Allan Wingate's decision to postpone publishing *Of Love and Hunger*, even though it had already been advertised as part of the firm's spring list, attracting substantial orders from bookshops.

Through April and the early weeks of May, Julian's grant rapidly dwindled, much of it guzzled by the ravenous cash-registers of various pubs and clubs, among them the Stag's Head. His earlier exasperation with Reggie Smith now forgotten, the Brummie producer became the nucleus of his Stag's Head drinking circle, an infrequent member of which was the pursed-lipped poet and critic John Betjeman. More regular participants were John Davenport; the BBC Features producer, Tommy Waldron, a burly, florid, rugby-playing Irishman with a loud manner made even louder by his heavy-drinking; and the taciturn, undemonstrative, and physically unattractive Olivia Manning who, from the vantage point of her bar-stool regarded the others with an expression of amusement, mingled with contempt.

Enjoyable as Julian found the company of his Stag's Head circle, he seldom stayed there long because he disliked the pub's smug university common room atmosphere. Pausing for a quick word with Raynor Heppenstall, he'd move on to the nearby Marie Lloyd Club, generally known as "the ML". Like so many other drinking clubs, it was a bare, shabby, and uncomfortable place, housed in a cheerless basement. Scattered round hard seats and filthy tables, tended by surly bar staff, groups of seasoned drinkers, mainly from the rag trade and the BBC, wiled away protracted lunch-hours. Amid these surroundings, the well-groomed Julian was conspicuous, the battered condition of his brown suede shoes affording the only indication of his current poverty. After about an hour, Reggie would join him in the ML, picking up where they'd left off, each vying for the conversational initiative.

When the altruistic Reggie discovered how hard-up Julian was, he helped him by casting him in an undemanding minor role in a radio play, something he often did to familiarise potential scriptwriters with the technicalities of the medium. The play, for which Julian earned a handy fee, was being broadcast live from the BBC's Grafton Studio, just off Tottenham Court Road. During the rehearsals that preceded the broadcast, he met another friend and protégé of Reggie's: a diminutive, jobbing actor several years his junior by the name of Tony Van den Burgh. After the broadcast, the need to get everything right first time rendering it simultaneously frightening and invigorating, Tony joined Reggie and Julian for a night of sustained boozing in the Wheatsheaf. Not possessing their prodigious capacity for alcohol, he ended up blind-drunk. His instinctive liking for Julian deepening into outright admiration when he got hold of a copy of *The Stuff To Give The Troops*, the second edition of which had been held up for over a year, presumably by the prevailing paper shortage, Tony was soon drinking regularly with him. They'd meet in the Stag's Head, the ML, the Café Royal, or the Fitzroy, where the emaciated figure of Sylvia Gough, once a celebrated beauty who had traded gossip with Ronald Firbank, danced in the Ziegfield Follies, and modelled for John Singer Sargent, would cadge drinks from them. Other favourite afternoon haunts of theirs were the Club des Caves de France, a dingy venue that consciously imitated a French wine bar, and the Mandrake, only a few doors down from the Gargoyle, yet catering for a very different clientele.

Ostensibly a chess club, the Mandrake occupied a dusky basement, reached via a precipitous flight of steps. Prior to opening-time, the door was protected by a rusty metal grille, around which impatient customers gathered. Through the door, there was an anteroom that matched the unprepossessing exterior. In the evenings this was pressed into service as a restaurant. It adjoined a much larger room with a piano in the righthand corner and an angled bar dead-ahead, behind which a pageant of uniformly pretty waitresses and barmaids were to be seen. Beyond this area, there was a room reserved for people who wanted to read magazines and drink coffee. And, beyond that, there was the Quiet Room and the Chess Room, set aside for a handful of serious chess players. The rest of the club was populated by an ill-assorted, polyglot crowd, all of whom had coughed up a nominal membership fee. There were off-duty waiters; professional pickpockets; shady businessmen; the occasional writer; and an ample complement of idiosyncratic personalities. Nina Hamnett, liable to burst into slurred renditions of traditional Cockney ballads, was often to be seen there. So too was Mr

Mendelsohn, owner of the chaotic antiques shop opposite the Wheatsheaf, chaperoning his radiant daughter, a showgirl whom he aimed to marry into the aristocracy. Of the club's quirkier clientele, perhaps the most unavoidable of them was the wealthy, alcoholic Brian Howard, the inspiration behind at least one of Evelyn Waugh's most memorable characters, his potent charm cloaked by a propensity for venomous put-downs.

In order to get round the licensing laws, specifying that alcohol could — outside normal pub openings hours — only be served with food, the Mandrake's customers had to buy a token sandwich. Normally this was a dry and inedible specimen. Whenever someone had the temerity to complain about it, the proprietor would march over to their table and, in the voice of a teacher lecturing an obtuse child, explain, "This is a sandwich for drinking with, not for eating..."[9]

The Mandrake was run by the hospitable but hot-tempered Boris Watson, formerly Boris Protopopov, his Bulgarian parentage disguised by his commonplace surname. Most days the mountainous, dishevelled Boris, who had previously operated the even less salubrious Coffee An', was to be found hunched over a chess board, his eyes fitfully scanning the club. Boris and Julian were to become firm friends, their friendship cemented by their overlapping enthusiasm for chess as well as their contempt for Count Potocki, a vituperative letter from whom Boris had framed and hung from the wall. If Julian or any of the other regulars needed to cash a cheque, Boris would oblige on condition half its value was paid in the form of a credit-note from the bar.

Over drinks in the Mandrake with Tony and Reggie, who often steered the conversation in the direction of sex, Julian would talk about his erotic misadventures. These he recounted in sharply focused detail, their pornographic potential blunted by his startling reliance on prim euphemisms, a puritanical streak coexisting with a seemingly incompatible level of prurience. Whenever Tony or Reggie introduced a more bluntly anatomical, matter-of-fact tone, deploying words like "fuck" and "cunt", the fastidious Julian would recoil with an expression of mild effrontery.

Financially "things [had] reached [...] a new low"[10] by mid-May, Julian's refusal to compromise, his determination to pursue his vocation come what may, dragging him towards the financial precipice. Though he felt that he needed "a complete rest and not more work",[11] he had to look for another commission. With that in mind, he wrote to John Lehmann, tabling a new proposal. For an advance of £60, he offered to write one of the pseudonymous John Chapter thrillers he had, for many years, been contemplating as a potentially remunerative sideline. Or, if that didn't appeal to John, he suggested he might translate another French novel for him.

As it happened, neither of his proposals appealed to John, so he turned to his other old ally, Graham Greene, who had, by then, become a full-time Managing Director of the publishers, Eyre & Spottiswoode. During a visit to their cramped offices on Bedford Street, near the Strand, he tried to talk Graham into giving him an advance for his long-pondered novel dramatising Eugen Weidmann's life and crimes, the action transplanted from Paris to Soho and Southend. Graham's uncommon willingness to help less established writers, his taste for just such vernacular thrillers, and his determination to revive his firm's moribund fiction list ensured a positive response to the sales-pitch. Julian was given a £300 advance, later topped up by a succession of small loans. At a time when the average advance was between £75 and £100, this was a substantial investment that reiterated Graham's faith in his friend's talent.

Prudence not being a component of the Maclaren-Ross character, Julian used his newfound resources to reinstall himself and Monica in the Imperial Hotel. That summer, secure in the knowledge that he now had enough cash to see him through the composition of the entire novel, he made a start on the book, the original title of which, *Death and His Sweetheart*, had been scrapped in favour of *The Dark Diceman*. For Julian, it presented a chance to reinvent himself as the thriller-writer he yearned to become, his conscious intentions working against the grain of his comic gifts. Abandoning the supple, conversational manner that was his hallmark, he chose to narrate the novel in a conventional third-person style. Yet he continued to draw extensively on his own experiences, strewing autobiographical references across the opening scene, set in a rural Sussex pub where the locals, watched by the psychopathic Weidmann-figure, Walter Dockert, are playing Spoof.

Fresh from sustained sessions of toiling over his novel, he would head off to the Wheatsheaf, where he'd recite extracts from it at the faintest encouragement. The impression that things were, once again, going his way was lent added credence by the broadcast of *The Bowl of St Giles* on the BBC's Home Service at the start of August, its cast including the young Denholm Elliott. Now that it had at last been transmitted, the BBC released the second half of his fee, his uncharacteristically healthy finances permitting him to press ahead with *The Dark Diceman*, undistracted by the usual concerns.

He was still working on it that autumn when he had an atypical story called *Quoth The Raven* — a humorous fantasy in which he imagined the disagreeable consequences of training a pet raven to talk — published in Leonard Russell's *Winter Pie*. And, in early October, Allan Wingate finally brought out *Of Love and Hunger* to widespread acclaim. *The TLS* felt that it broke American fiction's recent monopoly on laconic prose and graphic characterisation; *The Sunday Times* marvelled at its skilful compression, its readability, and urgency; and Anthony Powell, writing in *The Strand Magazine*, selected it as one of "the Thirty Books of the Year", an elite group that included Patrick Hamilton's *The Slaves of Solitude* and F. Scott Fitzgerald's *The Crack-Up*.

Alone among the up-market weeklies, *The New Statesman and Nation* refused to perceive its manifest virtues, maintaining their snooty disdain for his idiomatic prose. Its sales were nonetheless so healthy André Deutsch soon recouped the initial advance he'd paid Julian. But the company's allocation of paper, still the subject of wartime restrictions, remained meagre. The book's print-run was therefore comparatively small, limiting the scale of its commercial and cultural impact.

His mood lifted by all the attention *Of Love and Hunger* was bringing him, Julian reacted with unexpected equanimity when one of his Wheatsheaf cronies published an anthropomorphic children's book featuring an unmistakable, mildly derogatory portrait of him. In Noel Sircar's *News From The Lesser Burrows*, he was transmuted into Bertram Badger, an "amusingly pompous",[12] egotistical, long-haired, periodically penniless actor, "clad in a long moth-eaten fur coat"[13] and carrying "in his paw a tall walking stick".[14] Instead of flying into the glowering rage everyone in the Wheatsheaf had dreaded, he took coy, smirking pleasure in people addressing him as "Bertram".

Unknown to Julian, his closest and longest-standing friend had also written a novel with a pivotal character modelled on him. As someone who knew Julian better than anyone else, Mac was ideally placed to produce an accurate portrait. The result was even more irreverent. So obvious was the resemblance between Julian and his literary alter ego, Mac's prospective publisher, Charles Wrey Gardiner, had turned it down on the grounds that the Grey Walls Press would be laying itself open to legal action if it published the book. In the hope Julian might be talked into signing an undertaking to refrain from litigation, Mac sent him the manuscript of *The Man In The Top Hat*.

Like Julian's newly released novel, it depicted their experiences as vacuum-cleaner salesmen. Unlike *Of Love and Hunger*, however, its chosen literary form was not naturalism but a brand of proto-magic realism, the quotidian details of everyday life dovetailing into an incongruous fairy-tale world populated by wizards and elves. In Mac's lush fictional universe, Electrolux was transformed into "Samo", a religious cult whose adherents preached "the Gospel According To Samo"; the Wheatsheaf became "the Golden Cockerel"; and a succession of their mutual friends and acquaintances, such as Dylan Thomas, Paul Potts, and Eileen Cooke, made guest appearances, Dylan doubling as "Fish the Poet".

While Julian was happy to be cast in the starring role of the writer-turned-book reviewer "Uncle Julian", who carried a malacca cane, wore a teddy-bear coat, smoked through a cigarette-holder, and wrote laconic reportage about low life subjects, he was upset by Mac's portrayal of him. For all the pervasive fondness with which Mac painted him, it was not the flattering portrait he might have anticipated. Far from presenting him in the way he "liked to be seen [... as an...] aristocrat with a claim to literary fame",[15] the book portrayed him as a likeable but lazy, egotistical, selfish, rakish, "dangerously ambitious",[16] drunken reprobate, his innate vanity leading him to produce a novel simply entitled *Julian*. The book also poked fun at his craving for fame. "Placards now proclaimed his genius," Mac wrote. "A huge and impressive portrait of Julian appeared in the towns. A sophisticated and immaculate Julian, smoking from an elongated cigarette-holder [...] A playboy, a man about the literary world. A king [...] Tailors prepared new fashions 'as worn by Julian' [...] And the rabble bowed when he appeared in his yellow landau drawn by four white horses."[17]

Understandably apprehensive about his friend's reaction to the book, Mac took the train up from the south coast to discuss it with him. Julian suggested they meet in his favourite Greek restaurant on Rathbone Place. As arranged, he brought with the manuscript Mac had sent him. Over his habitual plate of goose pilaf, he told Mac that he should have consulted him before writing it. At which Mac reminded Julian that *he* hadn't asked permission to base one of the characters in *Of Love and Hunger* on him.

Furious at what he saw as a betrayal of their friendship, Julian hurled the manuscript across the restaurant and threatened to sue Mac for libel if he went ahead and published it. Leaving Mac to gather together his typescript, he sidled out of the restaurant, the tough cords of their relationship apparently severed.

About that time, his friendship with John Davenport almost came to an end, too. Still reeling from the effects of "an hysterical hangover brought on by drinking all the previous day and night",[18] Julian had had a sudden urge to see him, so he headed for the pub in Fulham where Davenport often went. Julian found him sitting at a table with Sidney Graham and his wife, Nessie. Positioning himself opposite Davenport, Julian was soon in full flow, treating his mute friend to either "a lengthy précis of a French novel"[19] or "a foot by foot, appallingly accurate, account of an old German film."[20] "Stupified by boredom,"[21] Davenport eventually let out a pained groan.

"What's the matter?" Julian enquired.

"Julian, you are such a bore sometimes," Davenport replied.

Giving Davenport "an incredulous, haughty stare",[22] he said, "You must be drunk." Then he resumed his disquisition.

Through that autumn, Julian's bulging wallet steadily lost weight, assisted by frequent visits to Better Books, a recently opened shop on the Charing Cross Road. Already this was a popular meeting place for everyone from the nudie photographer Harrison Marks to the writers Denton Welch, Sir Osbert Sitwell, and Gerald Kersh. Besides buying the latest novels, he'd sometimes join the shop's young, ebullient owner, Tony Godwin, and his handsome, equally youthful business partner, John Clarke (a moonlighting actor soon to find fame under the stage-name of Bryan Forbes), for a cheap Italian or Greek lunch in one of Soho's many cafés.

Another drain on his finances was provided by daily trips to the Stag's Head. From time to time, Dylan Thomas, who had just returned from Italy, would peel himself away from his predominantly Irish clique and wander over for a chat with Julian and Co. He and Julian were now on good but not close terms, fostered by Julian's success in getting Graham Greene to stump up an advance for a travel book Dylan had proposed. During one such encounter with Dylan in the Head, Margaret Taylor — the hulking, bossy wife of the historian A.J.P. Taylor — swept into the Saloon Bar, looking for Dylan, who was embarrassed by her sexual and literary devotion to him. Glimpsing Margaret, Dylan ducked beneath the flap at the end of the bar, his hand snaking stealthily up to retrieve his pint. Julian, who found it hard not to laugh, was left to deflect her frantic enquiries about whether he'd seen Dylan.

The inevitable cash crisis struck around the beginning of December. It was just the scenario Julian had been anxious to avoid. With five chapters, amounting to about 18,000 words of *The Dark Diceman* down on paper, he had to take a break from it. He knew from previous experience that this would be likely to scupper the entire project.

Help was forthcoming from Tony Powell, who had become part-time

Fiction Editor of *The TLS*. Only a few weeks before Christmas, Tony invited him to review novels for their fiction section. It was an invitation Julian had reservations about accepting. Not least because, at the outset of his career, more experienced writers had warned him "to avoid reviewing books at any price".[23] And because he had little respect for most critics. "In this benighted country [...]," he once complained to Mac, "the actual creator is given less respect than the pompous asses who are paid to 'adjudicate' upon his work."[24] Economic expediency, however, dictated that he enlist in the army of pompous asses.

His recruitment by Tony was an astute, symbiotic move. He brought to *The TLS* not just a refreshing approach but a knowledge and partiality for contemporary French literature that echoed the cosmopolitan interests of its debonair incoming editor, Alan Pryce-Jones, who was bent on challenging its renowned stodginess and cultural insularity.

Julian's initial assignment was to produce short reviews of two new novels, allocated by Tony on the basis that they might interest him. For this, he was paid £15. His first review appeared in the next issue of *The TLS*, published on Friday 20 December. In common with every other contribution to its pages, his piece went unattributed, the principal being that anonymity enabled many writers to be far more objective and sincere.

From the outset, Julian proved himself a discriminating and fair-minded critic, his reviews distinguished by an unexpected largesse and breadth of appreciation. Satisfied with Julian's work, Tony commissioned further reviews. By the New Year, Julian had consolidated his position as a regular contributor to the resurgent *TLS*. Each Thursday, he'd make his way to the newspaper's offices in Printing House Square, a cobbled quadrangle near Blackfriars Bridge, rimmed by elegant buildings. From there, he would collect that week's parcel of review-copies, left just inside the heavy front door of Private House, the former family home of *The TLS*'s Victorian founder. The following Monday he would put in a jovial and punctual return appearance, typically dressed in a linen jacket, its collar concealed by his hair. This time he would venture into the main offices, where he'd hand his scrupulously neat, handwritten copy to either Tony or Arthur Crook, the Deputy Editor. The accepted arrangement in the literary world was for payment-on-publication, but his perpetual need for ready-cash led him to insist they pay him "cash-on-delivery".[25] For Tony and Arthur, the consequent disruption to the paper's accounting system was justified by the lively, readable quality of his prose. Under pressure from Julian, they even took the rash step of sometimes paying him in advance. And twice he "achieved the rare feat of failing to deliver the articles for which he'd already been paid."[26]

A less contentious means of supplementing his income was offered by the standard practice of selling the review-copies he was given each week, these consisting of anywhere between two and seven novels. Every so often, he'd take consignments of them round to Gaston's bookshop on Chancery Lane, where he was paid half the cover price, assuming the volume was in mint condition. Though his work for *The TLS* kept him just about solvent, it was a source of considerable frustration, because it soaked up the time he might have devoted to finishing *The Dark Diceman*, short-term needs taking precedence over long-term ambitions.

When Julian heard that Tony had commissioned Walter Allen to write what was known as a "middle" — a long essay that straddled the centre pages of *The TLS* — he took Walter, his wife, and their four-months-old son round to Chester Gate to meet his friend. Most of the evening was devoted to talk of silent movies, Tony and Julian swapping impassioned reminiscences of the vampish Theda Bara.

Shortly after their trip to Chester Gate, Walter joined the slow leakage of literary talent from London, in his case moving to Romney Marsh. Yet even that didn't remove him from Julian's orbit. Now and then, often on a Saturday afternoon, Julian would send him a telegram, "invariably asking for five pounds immediately, to be wired to him at such-and-such a post office."[27] Walter shared this role of surrogate banker with Dan Davin, who didn't mind stumping up the occasional loan. These tended to be made during Dan's infrequent visits to London when he joined Julian in the Wheatsheaf, where the hard-core of the wartime crowd was still to be found: the increasingly disreputable-looking Paul Potts side by side with John Heath-Stubbs, Dylan Thomas, Tambimuttu, Sidney Graham, Johnny Minton, James Graham-Murray, George Barker, Anthony Curtis, Peter Vansittart, and John Hartcup, who had set up a small literary agency which counted Julian among its clients. A newer but equally stalwart addition to the Saloon Bar set was the once handsome and highly rated poet, John Waller. Like Julian, he would, at the slightest dip in temperature, appear in a capacious camel-hair coat. Witty and unashamedly homosexual, John was a baronet with a big house in Kensington, to which he'd sometimes invite Julian and friends. Outrageous though Waller could be, he was a model of restraint in comparison to John Gawsworth, another recent, less regular recruit to the cast of bizarre characters who patronised the Saloon Bar. On the death of M.P. Shiel the year before last, Gawsworth had proclaimed himself King Juan I of Redonda, the title he liked to be known by, pals like Julian usually abbreviating it to "the King". Taking his position very seriously, he would don robes and conduct ceremonies at which he'd issue elaborate, specially printed state papers, conferring peerages on drinking buddies such as the actor Michael Gough. As part of the initial batch of ennoblements, that year Julian became Duke of Ragusa, a facetious title that alluded to Julian's predilection for red wine from the region around the Sicilian town of Ragusa.

No doubt inspired by Subra's tale of how he'd persuaded Peter Vansittart to pen a cheeky begging letter to the Prime Minister, which yielded a £150 grant from the Royal Bounty, Julian decided to follow suit. In January 1948, he wrote to Clement Attlee, explaining his dilemma and appealing for money to help him finish his novel. But there was no response from Downing Street.

By the end of January he and Monica had, again, been forced to transfer from the Imperial to the County Hotel. In the meantime, he'd placed a short story with Roy Campbell, the abrasive South African BBC producer, whom Julian knew well from the Stag's Head. Campbell also wanted him to read it on air. Unfortunately the story — a lame black-market satire, revelling under the whimsical title of *The Two Fish Spivs and the King of the Goldfish Called Garth* — turned out to be too long for the Light Programme's 15-minute *Mid-Morning Story* slot. Still keen to use it, Campbell asked Julian to abridge the manuscript, which he went ahead and did.

His total fee for the story was £20, payable after it was broadcast. Since that wouldn't be until late February, he remained "short of dough",[28] as he liked to put it: so short he was unable to pay the hotel bill he and Monica had run up. In real danger of being kicked out and having their laundry seized by the management, he wrote to Dan Davin on Thursday 19 February, asking if he could borrow £15, his recent complimentary review of Dan's new collection of short stories offering emotional leverage. As requested, Dan wired the money to the Euston Post Office, enabling Julian and Monica to extend their stay at the County Hotel. But the cheque from the BBC, with which he planned to repay Dan, remained tantalisingly out of reach. No sooner had Dan loaned him the money than the broadcast was pushed back by almost a month.

Just when his perennial money problems must have been reasserting themselves, towards the end of February he received a letter written on behalf of Clement Attlee. It informed him that the Prime Minister — unaware of the ghoulish nature of the book Julian wanted him to subsidise — had authorised a confidential grant of £200 from the Civil

List. On the pragmatic advice of John Betjeman, who warned the Prime Minister's office that Julian might blow the whole lot on drink, and that it was "no use expecting him to be practical about his affairs",[29] Downing Street decided against issuing the grant as a lump-sum. Instead, they made special provisions. These entailed the appointment of the Royal Literary Fund's Captain Broadbent as a trustee, his role being to dispense the grant in four £50 instalments, spread over the next eight months. The first of these was despatched to Julian on Thursday 5 March. When the cheque arrived at his hotel, he found himself unable to make use of the much-needed money. Since he didn't have a bank account, he had to beg a favour from a friend, who agreed to cash it for him. But his friend's bank refused to accept the cheque because it was crossed, so he posted it back to Captain Broadbent with a hastily written note, appealing to him to send either cash or a replacement uncrossed cheque. The dependable Captain Broadbent received Julian's note on Monday, contacted Coutts & Co, the exclusive bank on the Strand, and arranged for them to cash the cheque.

When Julian got his hands on the money in mid-week, he immediately made plans to travel to a villa in the south of France which Gerry Fisher, his accountant, had offered to lend him. Sequestered there, he intended "to settle down and complete *The Dark Diceman*."[30] Before he could leave the country, though, he had to fulfil an engagement at Broadcasting House. On the morning of Thursday 18 March, he turned up there to read his contribution to *Mid-Morning Story*. Sitting in a small studio, overlooked by Roy Campbell and the rest of the production team, he spent an hour rehearsing his reading. Then, at 11.00am, he gave a nerveless rendition of it, broadcast live on the Light Programme.

Next day, he checked out of the County Hotel. Equipped with his passport, still under his baptismal name, he went to stay with a friend in the country. His host was likely to have been Gerry Fisher, who had a cottage in Cookham Dean, near Maidenhead — a handy staging-post en route to the Channel ports. At such short notice, Monica may not have been able to obtain leave from her job at the Central Office of Information, meaning she had to stay behind. In Julian's absence, she decamped from the County Hotel to their friend Edward du Cros's flat. Assuming the mantle of dutiful wife and personal assistant, she dashed off several letters to Captain Broadbent to ensure there were no hitches with the payment of the next instalment of "her husband's" Civil List grant, due in May.

From the south of France, Julian kept in touch with her by phone.

While he was there, he devoted some of his holiday to studying further accounts of Weidmann's crime spree. But his novel-writing plans were thrown into disarray by what he read. Many of the facts contradicted the material on which he had based his book. Reluctantly re-evaluating the novel, he reached the disheartening conclusion that he would have to expand it substantially, scrapping and re-drafting whole swathes of his manuscript. As he knew only too well, the task was bound to require far more time than the outstanding instalments of his grant could buy him.

During the last week of April, he returned to London and took a room at the County Hotel. Initially at least, he doesn't appear to have let Monica know that he was back in town.

Though the trip to France had proved counter-productive for his work, it had given Julian, normally so proud and intractable, a chance to brood over the row sparked by *The Man In The Top Hat*. Averse to simply writing off such an important friendship, he got in touch with Mac and made peace. To placate him, he promised to write a letter to the Grey Walls Press, formally denying any grounds for a libel claim. He even asked Mac for permission to produce a screenplay of it, sensing that it might provide an entrée into the film world. Ensconced in his hotel on Tuesday 27 April, he penned some sample dialogue, as well as a five-page treatment. With masochistic relish, he duplicated Mac's scabrous depiction of him as someone on the brink of insanity, an isolated, drink-ravaged, and forgotten writer whose selfish pursuit of literary fame had alienated him from everyone, his own daughter included. He then pitched the idea to a succession of film companies. But none of them expressed any desire to commission a full screenplay, its lack of a strong narrative, its blend of realism and fantasy placing it well outside the parameters of mainstream cinema.

On Friday 14 May he belatedly consummated his promise to Mac and wrote to Charles Wrey Gardiner, stating that "To my mind there is nothing of a nature to libel me in C.K. Jaeger's novel *The Man in the Top Hat*, nor shall I institute any proceedings against the author, agents, or publisher."[31] The threat of legal action lifted, the Grey Walls Press accepted Mac's novel for publication.

Somehow Julian met and befriended the charming businessman and aspirant movie mogul Rudolf Cartier. In mid-to-late August, Rudolf put him in touch with Everest Pictures, a newly founded film company, who were on the lookout for viable subjects for feature films. Eager to sell them the rights to *The Dark Diceman* and to see the Weidmann case portrayed on celluloid, Julian got in touch with the three founding directors of the company. Though they expressed interest in filming his novel when it was finished, they made it clear that they were unable to pay the high asking-price. As an alternative, they offered him £800 to write a screenplay adapted from another novel, the rights to which they had already acquired. In his keenness to break into the movie business and to fund the uninterrupted composition of *The Dark Diceman*, he accepted their offer without even bothering to obtain a contract.

Everest Pictures's first film was to be produced by Nelson Scott, who also happened to be on the board of directors. He was a tall, handsome, smooth-talking Canadian with golden, curly hair, and a taste for elegant, expensive clothes, these lending substance to his high-falutin talk of how he was putting together a major movie with international stars and a publicity budget to match.

The book that Julian had been asked to adapt was the French writer Louis Hémon's debut novel, *Maria Chapdelaine*. When it first came out in 1916, it had scored a huge critical and commercial hit. As well as going on to be published in numerous English and French editions, it had been filmed in France during the Thirties, and Alexander Korda had financed an abortive English-language version of it, directed by the playwright Rodney Ackland. Based on several months Hémon had spent in the snow-covered Canadian wilderness, it tells the story of a beautiful young girl's return from her convent school to her isolated home village, where she is wooed by three contrasting suitors. But its pastoral subject matter, its quasi-Victorian sentimentality, its clumsy authorial intrusions, its leaden dialogue and long, often portentious descriptive passages, evoking the desolate grandeur of its setting, weren't to Julian's taste.

Much as he needed the money and the screenwriting credit, he found himself unable to carry out the brief. With the deadline closing in, Julian phoned Mac and asked him to help out in exchange for a slice of the fee. Only too happy to earn some extra money at the same time as reasserting their friendship, Mac quickly processed the novel into a screenplay, to which Julian contributed no more than a few snatches of dialogue.

On delivering the script to Nelson Scott, he and Mac were invited to a series of meetings scheduled over the next few months. These were held in the well-appointed townhouse at 1 Culross Street, off Park Lane, which Nelson shared with a fellow director of the company. Arriving there each morning with Mac, who was commuting from Bognor, Julian got to know Nelson's butler. "Count Rex", as he insisted on being known, claimed to be a genuine blue-blood, his claims buttressed by an unlikely roster of titled friends. Yet it became apparent that Julian's new chum was even worse off than him. When Count Rex offered him and Mac a cigarette, snapping open an ornate case, there was only a single Woodbine inside. This, Count Rex nonchalantly snipped into three pieces. As Julian became better acquainted with him, he confessed that he was reduced to living in a cubicle in the Turkish Baths under the Imperial Hotel. Whenever Julian could afford it, he'd give Count Rex the money he needed to pay for that night's ticket to the baths.

At the script conferences, Julian and Mac were joined by Nelson, his house-mate, and a number of people already hired to work on the film. There was the Irish leading man Kieron Moore. And there was the benign, bespectacled veteran Swiss-born director Marc Allégret, nephew of André Gide and collaborator with Marcel Pagnol. His best years far behind him, Allégret had been based in England since the previous year. Also in attendance was Allégret's assistant, the youthful Roger Vadim. Tobacco smoke filling the flat, they discussed the script and made minor changes, pausing periodically for food and drink. During these breaks, they would, weather permitting, wander out into the wintry garden and relax beside the shallow ornamental pond. At Nelson's suggestion, they'd play a game where you tossed pennies into the water. If you could land yours on top of any of the others, you won the rest of the coins in the pile. Nobody could get the hang of it, the bottom of the pond gradually becoming dotted with copper coins. Over the half-term break, Mac brought his daughter with him. He gave her a stack of pennies so she too could play. Unlike everyone else, the pre-pubescent Karel demonstrated an uncanny knack of hitting the target. Little by little, she emptied the bed of the pond. Both Mac and Julian were tickled to see how petulant it made the fiercely competitive Nelson.

In between script conferences at Culross Street, Mac drafted two fresh screenplays, incorporating only the odd line of dialogue written by Julian. For each draft, Nelson promised them an additional fee. Despite all the time he and Julian had devoted to the project, neither of them had received any payment so far. The persuasive Nelson's explanation was that "they could not be paid until the first shooting day, when the backing for the film would be released."[32]

So much of Julian's time was absorbed by *Maria Chapdelaine*, he had to take a sabbatical from his reviewing work for *The TLS*. He did, however, accept a commission to write a middle on Henry Green. To suit the context in which it would be appearing, he exchanged his normally succinct, casual style for one that was punctilious and ruminative. Additional much-needed cash was raised by selling *The Episcopal Seal*, a short story about a West End spiv, to *The Strand Magazine*, who promoted it as "A Story of London's Underworld By A Master of The Picaresque".[33]

Near the end of November, possibly as a means of trimming their budget, he and Monica moved into a seedy furnished flat at 17 Holland Park Gardens. The furniture was upholstered in red and all the walls had been painted the same colour, creating a hellish glow. Still, Julian and his girlfriend weren't in any position to be choosy. Had it not been for the final instalment of his Civil List grant, which Monica persuaded Captain Broadbent to send out slightly ahead of schedule, they would have faced "a very lean time"[34] in the run-up to Christmas.

Early in January 1949, Julian heard that Everest Pictures had clinched a deal with the powerful British Lion company, who had agreed to distribute *Maria Chapdelaine*. Further encouragement came with the news that Everest had signed the photogenic French actress Michèle Morgan, then in her late twenties, for the title role. Because she'd already starred in not only Marcel Carné's classic *Quai des Brumes* but also *Joan of Paris*, opposite Laird Creagar, Julian was excited by the prospect of meeting her when the film went into production in the summer.

That March, Everest paid Julian £100, only a fraction of what he expected. The situation was made even worse when he heard they'd passed on responsibility for the entire film to British Lion. He and the even more irate Mac repeatedly visited and phoned Everest's offices on Shaftesbury Avenue, but Nelson Scott was never available to discuss the matter with them.

Eventually Julian resorted to approaching British Lion and explaining the situation. Since he and Mac had no written contract, the company felt under no obligation to pay them the massive sum they demanded. The two of them were left powerless to do anything, except trade stories with other embittered screenwriters, who informed them that it was "a fairly common experience".[35]

Still reeling from the grievous financial impact of this, Julian was, within a matter of weeks, floored by an even harder blow. In all probability tiring of his perilous, self-destructive way of life, his nocturnal working habits, poverty, drinking, and drug-taking, Monica announced that she was leaving him. When the news broke, he was in the Fitzroy Tavern, his usual circle supplemented by a rare appearance by Arthur Crook. Prompted by Julian, they were poised to embark on a game of Spoof to determine who bought the next round of drinks. The game was delayed by Monica's sudden arrival. Bursting through the door, she marched angrily over to the bar, where he was holding court. "Julian, I'm leaving you,"[36] she told him.

"Really?" he replied with all the insouciance of his hardboiled heroes. As she flounced out of the pub, he went back to his game of Spoof, seemingly undisturbed by the scene that had just taken place. But that, like so much else about him, was only an act. In reality, her departure from their flat pushed him "to the edge of a nervous breakdown".[37]

Plunged into a deep depression, he couldn't generate the necessary energy and confidence to remould and complete his much-disrupted novel. More worryingly, he developed symptoms of persecution-mania, nourished by all the amphetamines he'd been taking. When Mac came up to London to stay with him, Julian glanced warily up and down the street as he opened the door. "Come in to the red,"[38] he said with more than a hint of irony as he ushered Mac into his flat. Later on, they went to the Wheatsheaf together. Before Julian would set foot outside, though, he made Mac walk down to the corner of the street and check nobody was watching the building.

A welcome diversion from his troubles arose around the end of May. Perhaps because Nelson wanted to appease Julian and Mac, he invited them to join the group gathering at Victoria Station to greet Michèle Morgan when she arrived on the boat-train. It was too good an invitation to refuse. The welcoming party also comprised Marc Allégret, Kieron Moore, and Rudolf Cartier, who had invested in the film. On disembarking from the train, the high-cheekboned, blonde actress, her English beguilingly accented, was whisked to the luxurious Dorchester Hotel, where a suite had been booked for her. Julian and the others joined her at the table Nelson had reserved in the hotel's grand restaurant. Luckily, when it came to settling the enormous bill, Nelson announced that Everest would be paying.

Soon afterwards, rumours reached Julian that insufficient money had been raised to allow *Maria Chapdelaine* to go into production. But these were swiftly disproved. During the second week of June, shooting got underway at the otherwise empty Alliance Riverside Studios in Hammersmith. The principal supporting roles were taken by the distinguished French actress Françoise Rosay, and the plummy-voiced Jack Watling, ludicrously miscast as an illiterate backwoodsman.

Curiosity triumphing over their resentment at the way they'd been treated, Julian and Mac spent a lot of time on set over the ensuing nine-week shooting schedule. And they travelled to Virginia Water, just outside Epsom, where some of the outdoor scenes were filmed, vast quantities of salt being distributed in lieu of snow. Both of them took a schoolboyish delight in the lengths to which the cameramen had to go in order to make Michèle Morgan's bulging haunches appear less prominent. Whenever she wasn't required on set, she'd be cloistered in her hotel suite with the director Marc Allégret, who delegated authority to Roger Vadim. Mac was shocked to find Vadim using his mentor's absence to alter the script as he went along.

Most evenings Julian still managed to find his way to the Wheatsheaf, where he usually drank beer with whisky chasers. A fan of snappy Americanisms, culled from books and movies, he'd ask for "scotch on the rocks" rather than plain old whisky and a dash of water. It was there that he got into a fierce debate with John Heath-Stubbs about George Orwell's newly published *1984*, which had been greeted by a wave of critical approbation. "What's the Soviet Union ever done to *him*?"[39] an outraged Julian asked, his low opinion of Orwell's work intensified by sexual jealousy. Literary London was, after all, awash with malicious gossip about how Sonia Brownell had captivated the terminally ill Orwell, and how the character of Julia, Winston Smith's lover in *1984*, was modelled on her.

Trading on his still youthful good looks, his hair dense and merely flecked with grey, Julian sought consolation for his rejection by Monica in a series of transcient relationships with girls he picked up at the bar. These included a worldly twenty-year-old art student, who had dark hair clipped in the fashionable gamine style, who "was not tall, but sturdily built, with sloe-black eyes in a round, healthily attractive face",[40] and who wore what she described as "Existentialist clothes".[41]

Joined by a couple of her friends, she took Julian to a be-bop club "which lay beyond a no-man's land of bomb-craters and blitzed buildings somewhere north of the Tottenham Court Road."[42] But the club, located in the basement of a bombed building, only served soft-drinks. Not something guaranteed to endear it to Julian. He was also unimpressed by the conformism of its predominantly teenage customers, all desperate to avoid appearing "Square".[43] The boys mostly went for pompadour hairstyles and powder-blue drape-coats, while the girls dressed, like Julian's lover, in ski-pants and white blouses, their faces devoid of make-up, their bodies unencumbered by any jewellery. Even the music was a disappointment. What the band played was not, in his opinion, "jazz at all, as [he] knew it, but a meaningless jangle of reiterant noise."[44]

Sometime after their unsatisfactory night out, he and his latest girlfriend split up. Setting the seal on their rancorous separation, she broke into his gas-meter and stole the contents.

*

When filming on *Maria Chapdelaine* had finished in late July, Julian succeeded in re-focusing his attention on *The Dark Diceman*. By the beginning of September, he reported to Captain Broadbent that it was "now nearing its final phase".[45] Just when he needed domestic stability, he had to leave his flat, most likely because he fell behind with the rent. In his haste to leave, he forgot to gather together the sheaf of manuscripts Mac had left behind when he visited earlier in the year.

An air of fortitude in adversity augmenting his proven attractiveness to the opposite sex, he had, by then, found a new girlfriend, whom he probably met in the Wheatsheaf. Her name was Barbara Wimble. Like her predecessor, she was much younger than him. And, like Monica, she regularly joined him in the Wheatsheaf, treating him with maternal solicitude that belied the age-gap between them. Unlike Monica, though, she had no particular literary leanings. Nor did she possess Monica's self-assurance or sophistication. Then again, she had a tall, slim figure, long dark hair, very pretty eyes and a gentle, placid temperament that endeared her to old friends like Dan and Mac.

From Holland Park, Julian transferred to Barbara's less conveniently located flat. This was on the top floor of a modern, four-storey block at 29 Lee Court, halfway along Lee High Road in Lewisham. It was not long, however, before he found himself owing rent-money to Barbara. "Almost penniless"[46] now, he worried that his failure to contribute to the rent might lead to him being thrown out.

In a twist reminiscent of the formulaic adventure serials he used to follow as a child, rescue from the financial mire came at the last moment. His saviour was Tony Powell who, during late September, started employing him again as a contributor to *The TLS*. At Tony's behest, he cranked out a succession of reviews, plus an enthusiastic middle marking the publication of Joyce Cary's *A Fearful Joy*.

Financed by his work for Tony, he continued to patronise the Wheatsheaf. One lunchtime right at the end of October, Barbara phoned him there to tell him that he and the other regulars were the subject of a malicious article published in the latest issue of *The Leader Magazine*, a glossy rival to the more famous *Picture Post*. The article's unfamiliar author, "Anthony Carson", had renamed the pub "the Load of Hay"[47] and made a half-hearted attempt to disguise the identities of the people he was lampooning, people who "lived on air, on suckers, on perpetual credit".[48] While Gawsworth appeared as "The King of Abyssinia",[49] Julian was depicted as "The Writer",[50] for whom "this claustrophobic pub was his South Sea Island, his mistress, his theatre, his club and his cloister."[51] Julian didn't mind being caricatured as "a Literary

Gangster",[52] or a "pistol-packing Oscar Wilde",[53] but he drew the line at being called a "megalomaniac [...] Prospero equipped with no Ariel or Caliban, only the shipwreck."[54] His indignation tempered by pleasure at the publicity the article had given him, he set about unmasking the author. He soon discovered that "Anthony Carson" was the pseudonym of none other than Peter Brooke.[55] It was a discovery that resulted in the dissolution of their always uneasy friendship.

Upsetting as Brooke's treachery must have been, Julian had other much more pressing problems, chief among them his struggle to survive as a freelance writer. Perhaps because he and his girlfriend were having trouble keeping up with the rent, they had, by the second week of November, moved out of the flat in Lewisham. Their new home was a small boarding house at 55 Eardley Crescent in a run-down part of Earl's Court, a mere five doors away from where the future comedienne Hattie Jacques lived.

Through November and December, Julian kept himself afloat by reviewing a weekly batch of novels for *The TLS*, boosting that year's earnings to a mere £200 — well under a quarter of what he saw as his rightful income. It was an ignominious way to shuffle out of a decade that had held such promise.

Kieron Moore and
Michèle Morgan in
The Naked Heart,
1949
(© The Ronald
Grant Archive)

Reggie Smith, 1940s
(© BBC Photo Library)

Alan Ross (left), 1946 (© Jane Rye)

Cash-on-Delivery

So highly evolved was Julian's capacity for self-deception that he liked to imagine he never contracted the Soho-itis Tambi had supposedly cautioned him against. By the beginning of the Fifties, he was, however, already exhibiting symptoms of that debilitating disease. Like several other veterans of the Fitzrovian Front, he clung stubbornly to his chosen territory and the way of life that went with it. Still sporting his teddy-bear coat, cigarette-holder, cane, snuff-box, and carnation in his buttonhole, he continued to frequent his old haunts. At lunchtimes and in the evenings, he was normally to be found in the Wheatsheaf, knocking back so much red wine the future art critic and fellow Spoof-enthusiast, David Sylvester, christened him "Maclaret". And, on those all too rare occasions when his finances permitted, he rode the rickety lift up to the Gargoyle. Typically, his afternoons were frittered away in the Mandrake, where he'd hobnob with casual acquaintances "who were more often than not neither amusing nor talented and who were tolerated by Julian himself for the only loan they could afford, their ears."[1] Whenever Dan Davin was in town on business, Julian would always receive a phone-call from him, fixing up a rendezvous there. Reunited in the club's crepuscular confines, its greatly expanded network of rooms echoing to the sound of a trio of musicians playing sentimental Neopolitan tunes, Dan would stand Julian drinks and lend him money. Though Julian was unable to repay these loans, they cost him dearly in other respects. Now that the balance of power in their friendship had shifted so decisively, Dan felt entitled to lecture Julian on his "stupidity in dealing with publishers".[2] He also aroused Julian's unspoken resentment by addressing him as "Monster",[3] a nickname Julian didn't mind Dan using in Oxford, but hated hearing in London, where he feared it might dislodge his mask of waspish dignity.

Less than five years had passed since V-E Day, yet Soho had changed immeasurably in that short space of time. The Mandrake had been invaded by would-be rebels, enticed by adverts hailing it "London's Only Bohemian Rendezvous".[4] The cafés and one or two of the pubs, the Duke of York in particular, had been colonised by the hirsute, duffle-coated, "pseudo-artistic"[5] beatniks whom Julian despised. And a new, more raucous clientele were flocking to the Gargoyle, evening-dress becoming the exception rather than the rule.

For a while at least, in its comparative immunity to change, the Saloon Bar of the Wheatsheaf seemed to buck the trend. Most of the wartime artistic regulars had gone, among them George Barker, Dylan Thomas, and Subra, but Nina Hamnett, now a flea-ridden drunk, prone to leaving a wet patch where she'd been sitting, carried on drinking there. So too did James Graham-Murray and Johnny Minton, the latter by turns reticent and manic, melancholy and exuberant, a crocodile of predominantly male hangers-on, known as "Johnny's Circus", usually in tow, attracted by his wealth, charm, generosity, and growing renown as an illustrator.

In company with the other Saloon Bar survivors, self-consciously idiosyncratic characters who had become "like actors impersonating themselves in a long run",[6] Julian kept up his well-established routine. Making sure he arrived first, he'd stake his customary spot, from where he'd dispense pinches of snuff, ensnare gullible newcomers in protracted games of Spoof, and hold forth in his clipped, slightly nasal voice to a diminishing circle of cronies. New recruits, once so plentiful, were now hard to find. People were increasingly wary of him, not just because of his reputation for delivering stultifying monologues, or the fear he might portray them unfavourably in one of his stories. Consistent as his dandified appearance was, his wardrobe undergoing only subtle seasonal adjustments, he'd grown far less approachable, his manner becoming brusque and bombastic. "At the sound of his booming voice, the habitués of the back tables, accustomed though they were to its nightly insistence, looked up in dull horrified wonderment. There was no getting away from that voice. On the noisiest evenings, above the rising conversation, above the shuffling of feet and the rattling of glasses, above the protestations of inveterate boasters, [...] above it all the voice of [Julian] went its own implacable way. Presumptuous strangers, casual, uninitiated visitors had at times tried to drown that voice, to interrupt it and disconcert its owner. But in vain: [Julian] was an old hand, too tough, too knowing, too experienced, to allow anyone or anything to ruffle his composure."[7]

As he left the Wheatsheaf at closing-time one night, "pulling on his gloves, adjusting his coat, contemplating his stick",[8] Peter Vansittart witnessed him being accosted by a menacing gang of youths who challenged him to "Say something witty."[9] His face tightening into a mirthless expression, his myopic eyes narrowing contemptuously, his voice taking on a deadpan timbre, he replied, "Noël Coward."[10] At which the flummoxed youths drifted away.

From being a rising literary star, Julian had imperceptibly turned into something of a relic, an object of bemused curiosity. His tendency towards self-dramatisation and paranoia, intensified by the side-effects of the amphetamines he'd been taking, led him to blame his misfiring career not on himself but on malign forces, on night's black agents arraying themselves against him. In blatant disregard of all the unpropitious omens, most obviously the way his books had dropped out of print, he shared the indomitable optimism of what Peter Brooke called Soho's "pending men":[11] actors, writers, painters, boxers and gamblers, who were just biding their time until their endlessly discussed plans came to fruition. He was "always about to make a killing, often from a film he would write. Before a word of the script was written, much less a producer found, he had cast it completely. 'Of course,' he would declare grandly, 'Dennis Price will play the lead.' "[12]

Additional grounds for misplaced confidence were provided by *The Dark Diceman*, though it remained unfinished, his will to complete it possibly sapped by the realisation that the finished book would never live up to the unattainable perfection of the novel he'd been musing over for so many years. Yet Julian still talked about it with such animation listeners could have been deceived into assuming it was already on display in all the bookshops.

During the opening months of 1950, various attempts at raising fresh advances from publishers having been rebuffed due to his failure to honour previous contracts, Julian's only source of income remained his work for *The TLS*. A few years earlier, he could have fallen back on writing short stories, but even that option was denied him now, the magazines on which he used to rely, such as *Horizon*, *Penguin New Writing*, and *English Story*, all being on the brink of collapse.

More than likely because he and Barbara had fallen behind with the rent, they moved out of the boarding-house in Earl's Court. At her instigation, instead of taking an exorbitantly priced hotel-room together, the two of them — posing as a married couple — had, by mid-March, rented a flat in bohemian Paddington. For the purposes of the electoral register they became "Andrew and Barbara Maclaren-Ross", Julian's alias indicative of his mounting anxiety about the Inland Revenue carrying out another investigation of his tax affairs.

Their comfortably furnished three-room flat was on the first-floor of 29 Norfolk Square, his normal objections to living anywhere without a lift overruled by Barbara, whose practicality and commonsense had triumphed over his native extravagance. The front window opened onto a balcony, facing what was less a conventional London square than an elongated park, its miniature lawns bordered by mature trees. In a move symbolic of what, he hoped, would be his newfound domestic stability, he and Barbara acquired a white tomcat whom they named Rashomon after Akira Kurosawa's great samurai movie.

The formerly grand, stucco-fronted building in which they were living had been carved into a warren of flats and bedsits. These housed more than two dozen tenants, who shared a communal pay-phone in the hall, invaluable for Julian's business calls. The majority of the four guinea-per-week rent, paid to their non-resident landlady, was covered by Barbara's salary as secretary to the Managing Director of Films de France, a Mayfair-based distribution company. Julian, in consequence, only had to worry about defraying his everyday expenses through his earnings as a reviewer and occasional essayist for *The TLS*. Even so, he remained chronically short of cash.

Both his novelistic and screenwriting plans having stalled, he began to seek alternative means of easing his money worries. With that in mind, he hatched two schemes. First, he hired the Bodley House Literary Agency to re-sell his play about Captain Kidd to one of the nascent commercial radio companies. And he wrote to Reggie Smith proposing that he adapt a play by Nasir Shangi, an Asian pal of his. Neither of his schemes came to anything, though.

Sometime near the end of April or the beginning of May, he was approached by the impressive-sounding Vandyke Picture Corporation. In keeping with its ostentatious name, the company had a swish Knightsbridge address. There Julian encountered Roger and Nigel Proudfoot, the company's production team, who lived up to its jaunty logo: a cartoon silhouette of the society portrait painter Van Dyke. While Nigel concentrated on the company's financial affairs, Roger focused on the practical side of the business. Contrary to everything its credentials implied, Vandyke was a tiny outfit dedicated to churning out low budget second-features. Often referred to as "quota quickies", these were produced to satisfy the artificial demand for homegrown movies, created by legislation that dictated a minimum percentage of indigenous films in British cinemas.

On Julian's first visit to the firm's offices at 1a Cadogan Place, Roger Proudfoot told him that they'd read his work and wondered whether he had "any original stories suitable for filming. Not scripts: just a few lines on paper. Synopsis form."[13] Baulking at his request for money up front, Roger suggested, instead, that he should write a screen adaptation of *Four Days*, a short play Nigel had heard the previous November on

BBC radio's *Saturday Night Theatre*. Ever since then, the Proudfoots had been trying to acquire the screen rights from its moderately well-known author, Monckton Hoffe. When Nigel summarised the plot of this hackneyed domestic drama about the unfaithful wife of a successful, workaholic businessman, whose marriage is saved by the amnesia he sustains during a failed suicide attempt, Julian's reaction was unenthusiastic. He didn't expect to hear from the Proudfoots again. There he was mistaken.

Over subsequent weeks Roger phoned several times, "his excitement mounting progressively at each separate stage: negotiations were afoot; author being tricky; agent bluffing; distributors ready to sign: then — crescendo — they'd got the rights at last".[14] Once that had been sorted out, Julian was left to haggle over the fee with Nigel. Taken aback by Julian's stipulation of a fifty-percent downpayment, Nigel said that he'd "go into a huddle"[15] with his brother and see what could be done. Certain that this marked the end of any involvement in the project, Julian went back to his work for *The TLS*, who continued to supply him with a weekly batch of between two and four novels for review. To fulfil these commissions, he toiled away most nights until 3.00 or 4.00am, only catching up on his sleep during the day.

To exploit his facility as a literary critic, he proposed that the BBC pay him to do a talk on Edward Sackville-West for *The Contemporary Novel* series, currently being aired on the Home Service. Should Sackville-West be considered too recondite, he put forward Anthony Powell and Eric Ambler as alternative subjects. But the BBC chose not to take up his proposal.

Because the obligatory three year period had elapsed since he'd been awarded his grant from the Royal Literary Fund, Julian — whose work had netted him only about £140 that year — was free to make another application. In late June he requested a form. Before filling it out, he sought to soften up Captain Broadbent with a long letter, setting out the reasons for his latest impasse. "What I need is a lump sum of money which would enable me to get something done, and also to rest from my present hand-to-mouth existence," he explained. "I would like also to have a change of scene from London; a few weeks in France, without financial worry, would I think do me, psychologically, the world of good."[16]

His plea for a second grant was backed up by letters from Tony Powell and John Betjeman, who wrote that "I have long had a high admiration for his short stories and [...] I regard [*Of Love and Hunger*] as one of the few modern novels at the top of the first-class [...] I do not see how writing so closely wrought and subtle as his can be produced without the peace of mind which financial stability can bring".[17]

At the start of July, Julian submitted an application, along with a note to Captain Broadbent, enclosing a letter of endorsement from a third, even bigger literary name. The letter was from Evelyn Waugh, whom Julian may well have visited at the Knightsbridge hotel where he was staying. "I have followed Mr Maclaren-Ross's work since the first publication of a sketch of military life which I read in *Horizon* [...]," the letter declared. "I think now that he has developed his talent well and that, given proper opportunities, he shall develop into a first-class writer. I believe that one of the things he needs most is financial support during this crucial stage of his career. I therefore greatly hope that you will be able to give him the freedom from immediate anxiety which is needed to mature his undoubted talent."[18]

Julian's impoverishment was relieved by a commission from *The TLS* for a front-page essay on surrealist writing, though it can't have kept him going for long. Almost a fortnight passed without him hearing anything from the Royal Literary Fund. Impatient to find out whether he could expect another grant, he contacted Captain Broadbent again, asking him to phone as soon as a decision had been reached. It transpired that the committee had already opted to award Julian £100, but the cheque had been sent to the wrong address. Not that it would have been much use to him, because he still had no bank account. Obliging as ever, one morning midway through July, Captain Broadbent arranged to meet Julian at Coutts, where he cashed the cheque for him.

If the sudden gap in his busy reviewing schedule during late July is anything to go by, he used the money to pay for the trip to France he'd been hankering after. He then resumed his regular reviewing duties for *The TLS*, duties that left him with little time to complete *The Dark Diceman*, his faith in which seems to have finally flagged.

In the penultimate week of August, three months after he had last heard from Vandyke, Julian was phoned by John Guillermin. His Cockney accent contrasting with the plummy cadences of the Proudfoots, Guillermin announced that he'd be directing *Four Days*. Shooting was due to take place at Nettlefold Studios at Walton-on-Thames over the second and third weeks of September. The central role was to be taken by Kathleen Byron, who had achieved big screen fame through her performances in *Black Narcissus* and *The Small Back Room*. According to Guillermin, the script, adapted by the novice screenwriter Lindsay

Galloway, needed some polishing. And that was where Julian came in.

As requested, he took a taxi straight over from his flat to Cadogan Place, where Guillermin was waiting for him. An ambitious man in his mid-twenties, Guillermin[19] had made his directorial debut only the previous year. Handing Julian a copy of the script, he said they wanted him to tighten up the dialogue which was "a bit slow in patches".[20] Before accepting the meagre payment the Proudfoots offered him, Julian insisted on reading the screenplay over lunch, then meeting Guillermin and their employers back at the office that afternoon.

The script was even worse than anticipated: so bad he told them that the whole thing needed re-doing. For a fee of £50 cash-on-delivery, he agreed to rewrite it by the end of the week. Appropriately enough, that left him with a mere four days in which to draft a viable shooting script. Denied the necessary time to hone the dialogue to the standard to which readers of his work were accustomed, he could do little more than create a fluent, professional dramatisation of the play's ludicrous, moralistic plot, any surviving vestiges of its clumsy, information-laden style sensibly expunged.

That Friday, as arranged, Julian went round to Vandyke's offices to deliver his handwritten script. But nobody was there apart from a secretary, who didn't have the money they owed him. Cautious after his costly experiences with Nelson Scott, he refused to hand over the script to their outraged secretary. When Nigel Proudfoot phoned him that night, Julian demanded his fee immediately, his resolute stance yielding a cash payment.

Three-and-a-half years on from the delivery of his translation of *Pierrot mon ami*, John Lehmann Ltd published it as part of the company's handsome Modern European Library imprint: a ground-breaking series which already included the first English-language publication of Jean-Paul Sartre's *Nausée*. Retitled *Pierrot* for British consumption, underlining the allusion to the identically named Commedia dell' Arte character, Julian's translation appeared in October. Like so many of the books produced by the company, it was accorded a positive reception, *The TLS* applauding its "quite unusual liveliness".[21] But this didn't boost the book's sales sufficiently to warrant a reprint. Nor did the extra publicity it obtained, courtesy of Walter Allen who, in late November, invited Julian to discuss the book on *What Shall I Read?*, a Monday evening programme on the Midland Home Service.

Some of the pleasure Julian must have derived from *Pierrot's* publication was diminished by the release of another very different novel by John Lehmann's firm. Written under the nom-de-plume of "Roland Camberton", *Scamp* was a roman-à-clef by Henry Cohen, depicting the youthful bohemian scene that was slowly taking over Soho. Such was Julian's distaste for these bearded and corduroyed interlopers, whom he dismissively termed "bums",[22] he was bound to dislike the book. What clinched it, though, was Cohen's biting portrayal of him as the former travelling salesman, Angus Steerforth-Sims, author of *Gotcher Mate*, *Shooting the Line*, and *Autobiography of a Pickpocket*. A one-time star of English fiction and ubiquitous patron of the "Corney Arms",[23] where he inveigles newcomers into expensive games of "Scrag",[24] Steerforth-Sims's career has failed to live up to expectations, his short stories becoming "stale and second-rate",[25] mere "rehashes of his earliest and most original work."[26] Cleverly concealing the wounded pride Julian must have felt at being so cruelly caricatured, he treated the book to a dismissive notice in *The TLS*.

The Maclaren-Ross finances were again at a low ebb as he entered 1951, though his flow of reviewing assignments carried on unabated. In mid-January, he was able to recompense Tony Powell's many acts of kindness with a perceptive essay on his novels, coinciding with the release of *A Question of Upbringing*, the first volume of *A Dance To The Music of Time*.

Valued as Julian's contributions were, not only by Tony but also by Arthur Crook and Alan Pryce-Jones, he was desperate to escape from the inexorable demands of literary journalism. To that end, undaunted by his two previous exasperating brushes with the film world, he tried to find further screenwriting work. His hopes were raised when he obtained an appointment to see Sidney Cole, one of the Associate Producers at Ealing Studios. He and the influential Cole, an amiable man in his early forties, had a lengthy meeting at the company's offices in Ealing Green. But Julian was bitterly disappointed to hear that all the studio's films for that year had already been scripted.

His disappointment was, however, offset by some news that filtered through to him during March. He heard that John Grierson, the famous documentary film-maker, who had set up Group 3, a "new Government-sponsored film unit [...] for making low-budgeted features",[27] might "need script-writers and ideas".[28] Grierson's company, based at Southall Studios in Ealing, should have been ideal for Julian, with its avowed emphasis on offbeat stories and films with a free and flexible style, yet nothing appears to have come of his enquiries.

Left feeling "buggered and bewildered"[29] by his money problems, by the way his career had become so becalmed, he wrote to Mac proclaiming that "London's a desert as far as I'm concerned."[30] To give himself a respite from his troubles, he asked Mac whether it would be alright for he and Barbara to stay with them at the beginning of April. Failing that, he begged Mac to visit him in London. He even used the lacklustre promotion by the Grey Walls Press of Mac's most recent novel to chivvy him into a visit, saying, "If I were you, I'd come and kick up hell at the Grey Balls."[31]

Sympathetic as ever, Mac told Julian it would be fine if he came down to Bognor. Soon after his arrival, he was joined by Barbara. Away from London and its attendant pressures, away from his bibulous routine, he was "an altogether different person",[32] relaxation banishing the strident side of his character that had become so dominant.

Given his dispute with Nelson Scott, it can't have come as any surprise when Julian discovered that neither he nor Mac had been invited to the premiere of *Maria Chapdelaine*, now renamed *The Naked Heart*. Justice, he concluded, had been served by the damning reviews it received. Under the influence of the trade press — whose principal publication, *Kinematograph Weekly*, described it as a "doubtful 'British' booking"[33] — it had to wait until Sunday 22 April before its West End opening. Even then, it was only booked by two of the less prestigious cinemas: the Astoria and the Tivoli.

Morbid curiosity overriding his sense of disenchantment and indignation, Julian arranged with Mac to go to a screening of it at the Astoria one night, only a matter of days after it had opened there. Seeing its title plastered across the front of the cinema, they both felt an unforeseen surge of excitement. While they were standing on Charing Cross Road staring up at the stars' names, spelt out in lights, someone tapped Mac on the shoulder. He swivelled round to find a grinning Kieron Moore positioned behind he and Julian. The three of them chatted amicably for a few minutes. At an opportune moment, Keiron asked Mac if he'd lend him a few shillings. Nonplussed, Mac nodded towards the posters and glossy black-and-white film stills on display, and said, "What about all the money from the film?"[34] With a resigned shrug, Keiron admitted that he'd squandered it all. So Mac delved round in his wallet and gave him what he could spare. Keiron thanked him, then disappeared into the early evening throng.

When Julian and Mac went in to the empty foyer to buy their tickets, they quizzed the cinema manager about how *The Naked Heart* was doing at the box office. They listened gleefully as he admitted that ticket sales were so poor he'd been pleading with his Head Office to let him drop it from the programme. But Mac's delight quickly shaded into anger. Sitting in the cinema, watching the credits unroll in front of row upon row of vacant seats, he was dismayed to see that his name had been relegated to the foot of the list of screenwriting credits. Beneath the names of Marc Allégret, Roger Vadim, and Hugh Mills (someone Nelson Scott had never even mentioned), he'd been bracketed together with Julian, the two of them credited with the "Original Treatment". Worse was to follow.

The film turned out to be every bit as bad as the reviews had led them to expect. Mac was furious not just about the credits, but about the way the director had, as he saw it, mangled his script. Julian, in contrast, was merely peeved at having his name on the credits of such a turgid movie. Not that many people would have noticed. Only a week after its low-key opening, *The Naked Heart* had vanished from West End screens.

His friendship with Mac rejuvenated, Julian went down to Bognor during the summer. This time work prevented Barbara from accompanying him. On the Sunday of Julian's visit, Mac was already committed to playing cricket for his local club. Rather than stay by himself in Bognor, Julian accompanied Mac, Lydia, and their infant son Nicholas — whom he always treated with avuncular kindness — on their jaunt down the coast to Bournemouth. Since Julian had come to detest sport, once the match got underway he took Lydia and her son on a nostalgic pilgrimage to the house in Southbourne which he remembered so fondly.

As they approached it, trolley-buses instead of trams clattering downhill past the familiar buildings, past the arcade, past the local pub, he experienced a feeling of distortion common to all such visits, the scale of everything failing to measure up to how he visualised it. Though he'd always thought of the hill as being steep, it was, in fact, only a gentle incline. Likewise, when they reached the house where he used to live, the conservatory was much smaller than he had envisaged. Even the house itself was almost unrecognisable, its brickwork sheathed in a layer of grey stucco, its front gable embellished with faux Tudor beams. Crestfallen at how mundane it looked in comparison to his burnished recollections of it, Julian returned to the cricket ground with Lydia and her son, consolation coming in the form of cheap whisky, available from the club-house bar.

Revisiting his childhood home nonetheless inspired him to start writing a memoir of his early years. He showed the opening section to

Rupert Hart-Davis who had, by then, founded Rupert Hart-Davis Ltd, a small yet adventurous publishing house. Though Rupert was interested in buying the book, he was unwilling to hand over any money until he'd seen the completed manuscript. Without such a payment, however, Julian wasn't in a position to settle down to write the rest of the memoir.

Hard-up once again, he began to borrow money from Walter Allen, who had risen to prominence as the presenter of the Sunday afternoon discussion programme, *Talking of Books*. Unlike Walter's previous radio programme, this was broadcast across the entire country on the BBC's Home Service. Julian must have tuned in, because he suddenly started ringing Walter at the studio and leaving messages with the girl on reception. These said he needed to speak to him "about something extremely urgent"[35] and "would [Walter] telephone him as soon as [he] came out of the studio"?[36] Walter didn't always return his calls, but, when he did, Julian would ask him for a loan.

With the same objective, Julian invited him back to Norfolk Square one evening. Despite all the yarns he had, over the years, spun Walter about his gammy leg, he climbed the stairs that led to the flat he and Barbara shared. There he plied their susceptible guest with rum and Coca-Cola. Once Walter was suitably relaxed, Julian got "down to the real business of the meeting, which was to borrow a fiver."[37]

Motivated more by financial necessity than creative fervour, at the beginning of October Julian wrote to Mr Hamilton, the Managing Director of Hamish Hamilton, requesting an advance for the new novel he wanted to write. *Death and Business*, as he planned to call it, would chronicle his experiences between 1944 and 1949. Its focal point was to be his ill-fated stint on *The Naked Heart*, which would masquerade under the title of "The Accursed Hunter".[38] Being someone who generally exacted ample revenge for wrongs committed against him, he must have been attracted to writing about Everest Pictures because it offered such an irresistible opportunity to settle old scores. In his letter to Mr Hamilton, he predicted the book would be ready by the end of the year. Just in case Hamilton hadn't come across his work, he enclosed copies of all his published books. For good measure he also sent two favourable reviews he'd received from Elizabeth Bowen and John Betjeman.

On the recommendation of a member of the company's specialist team of readers, who rated Julian a gifted writer well-worth backing, Hamilton okayed the payment of an advance. Julian then experimented with all sorts of different ways of beginning *Death and Business*, but none of them felt right. Until he'd cracked that conundrum, he couldn't get more than a few pages into the book. His self-imposed deadline for delivering the completed manuscript just over a month away, he broke the news to a jittery Mr Hamilton that he might not be able to hand in the manuscript on schedule. In a cryptic aside, he put the delay down to the fact he was expecting "a piece of news affecting the book's development [...] next week, which promises to be a turning point in various ways."[39] This mooted turning-point appears to have revolved round the final instalment of the Vandyke debacle, something he must have wanted to incorporate into the novel.

After considerable equivocation, *Four Days* had finally been released, garnering respectable notices. "The 'let bygones be bygones' sentiment is a trifle far-fetched, but there is more than enough red meat to counteract the sugar," opined the critic of *Kinematograph Weekly*. "Reasonably well staged and acted, it puts quite a kick into its modest 55 minutes."[40] When Julian at last got a chance to see it during the first week of December, he was horrified to discover his contribution to the film had been marginalised. In the opening titles, he was given only second-billing behind Lindsay Galloway, his name printed in much smaller lettering under a credit for "Dialogue". As if that was not infuriating enough, his surname had been mis-spelt, lending credence to his view of himself as the blameless victim of the machinations of film producers and publishers alike. To cap it all, in the course of a bar-room conversation with another screenwriter, he heard that "one of the big shots"[41] at Group 3 Productions had taken a liking to *Four Days*. On the basis of Lindsay Galloway's screenplay credit, they'd signed him up.

Julian's money problems meanwhile deepened, a demand from the Inland Revenue for income tax arrears complicating the situation. That winter he was in such penury he found himself incapable of replacing the famous teddy-bear overcoat which, after a decade-and-a-half's sterling service, had become unwearable. Its demise may well have acted as the harbinger of the illness that confined him to bed during early December. So serious was his condition, a doctor had to be summoned. True to form, instead of using the National Health Service, he relied on a costly private medic.

Not only was he lumbered with an invoice way beyond his slender means, but his writing schedule was now set back. In response to Mr Hamilton's request for a progress report on *Death and Business*, he pretended that work on it was being delayed by the need to take on extra reviewing from *The TLS* to pay his medical bill. And, as a supplementary excuse, he used the imminent arrival of the proofs for a brief novel he'd written.

The novel in question had, most likely, been sold to Derek Verschoyle, the gin-steeped owner of the embryonic firm of Derek Verschoyle Ltd, whose offices were at 14 Carlisle Street, off Soho Square. For some reason, the book — nothing of which seems to have survived, not even its title — progressed no further than the proof-stage. At that point, perhaps due to concerns about the potentially libellous nature of the manuscript, it became "frozen in a publishing limbo from which [Julian] was unable to summon up sufficient will or dexterity to extract [it]."[42]

He didn't have to wait long, though, before his next hardcover appearance. That came in January 1952 when his melancholy account of his friendship with Alun Lewis was included in *The Pleasures of New Writing*, an anthology of pieces from John Lehmann's acclaimed magazine. Yet he was left wondering where he'd gone wrong over the past three years, and how he could reinvigorate his career. "This year [...]" he resolved to deliver a novel — possible candidates including *Death and Business*, *Night's Black Agents*, and *The Dark Diceman* — "or else write one really good original film story"[43] that would propel him back into the spotlight.

Once the advance from Hamish Hamilton had run out, Julian set about trying to find a film company prepared to commission him to write an updated adaptation of *The Suicide Club*, Robert Louis Stevenson's episodic novella about a group of squeamish would-be suicides who form a club, the members of which arrange to execute one another. Circumstances compelling him to set aside his grudge against Nelson Scott, he approached Everest Pictures with the idea. But Nelson wasn't interested. The concept was, however, taken up by Alexander Korda's British Lion-London Film Productions conglomerate, who planned to start shooting it in mid-March. They paid him £25-per-week, enough to cover his income tax arrears and fund the composition of the screenplay which, quoting from a John Dryden poem, he called *The Beast in View*. While "preserving the cynical atmosphere" of Stevenson's novella, he endeavoured to make his script "as different from the original as Hitchcock's *39 Steps* was from Buchan's book."[44]

Far from setting him on the road to achieving his Orson Welles-inspired goal of "writ[ing], and act[ing] in, and finally direct[ing] [his] own pictures",[45] the script never made it into production, denying him the additional £1,000 fee that had been dangled in front of him. Still, the money he'd already received kept him solvent and subsidised his daily forays into Soho. There he divided his time between the Wheatsheaf, the Mandrake, the Club des Caves de France, and the diminutive York Minster, near the corner of Old Compton and Dean Streets. Better-known as either "the French Pub" because of its popularity with the Free French forces during the war, or simply "Berlemont's" on account of its emigré French landlord, the extrovert, handlebar-moustached Victor Berlemont, its walls were decked with a collage of framed photos of boxers, movie stars, cyclists, and politicians, some still famous, others long-forgotten, all dedicated to Victor. The singularity of the place was emphasised by its stock of exotic drinks such as sloe gin, arak, and pastis. Fixed to one end of the bar, it even boasted a contraption originally designed for dispensing water onto a sugar-cube, balanced on a special spoon, held over a glass of absinthe.

It was in Berlemont's celebrated pub that Julian first fell into conversation with the tall, dryly humorous former conscientious objector, Conan Nicholas, whose public relations job at the Turkish Embassy enabled him to spend extended lunchbreaks there every day. Charmed by Julian's erudition, eccentricity, impeccable manners, generosity of spirit, ability to quote impressive chunks of writing (the closing paragraphs of *Middlemarch*, for instance), and fondness for sweeping pronouncements, among them "Loud laughter betrays the vacant mind",[46] Conan became a recurrent drinking partner.

Experience may have purged Julian of his earlier boastfulness, yet he still enjoyed behaving as if Soho was his personal fiefdom. Jabbing the tip of his malacca cane in Conan's direction soon after they met, he declared with unsmiling gravity: "If I lift this stick up and point it at you, you're in trouble. I'll never speak to you again."[47]

Around then, he began making periodic, unannounced afternoon visits to the top two floors of the house on Thayer Street where André Deutsch's eponymous new publishing company, set up after André had been ousted from the chairmanship of Allan Wingate, was based. His breath stinking of booze, the tipsy Julian would try to cajole his former publisher into stumping up some cash for a novel. While André retained enormous respect for him as a writer and a sneaking fondness for him as a person, he was loath to grant his request because he knew the novel would never be written. When the inevitable, tactful refusal came, "Julian would become quite aggressive, muttering threats and swishing his cane menacingly"[48] as André and his right-hand woman, Diana Athill, coaxed him towards the exit, approached via a grimy corridor, flanked by brown-paper parcels.

Despite his growing notoriety among the publishing community, against whom he now took an embittered and hostile stance, he succeeded in winkling an advance out of another small firm that spring.

The firm was Phoenix House, who paid him £125 or thereabouts, probably for a short thriller called *The Nameless*. "If the suspense [could] be made to proceed from character and not from situation," he felt that there was "nothing bad in writing such a book."[49]

But he didn't get far with it, his attempts at producing fiction paralysed by a tortuous psychological block. He suspected this had been engendered by his growing self-consciousness, "preoccupation with technique",[50] and urge to "find a new style altogether".[51] His critical faculties prevailing over his creative instincts, he'd write the same paragraphs over and over again, subtly modifying them as he groped towards an inaccessible ideal.

Whatever the cause of the writers' block that afflicted Julian, it also prevented him from getting on with either *Night's Black Agents* or *Death and Business*, now retitled *Business and Desire*. Though he sensed the latter "should be the easiest"[52] to write, he just couldn't seem to organise his material and get it down on paper. A similarly "dark cloud of difficulty"[53] descended when he made a fresh start on *Night's Black Agents*. He was confident that it had "a good exciting story"[54] which "should be great fun to write,"[55] but he couldn't decide on the style or point of view best suited "to convey the particular atmosphere"[56] he envisaged. Nor could he recapture the excitement he'd once felt about the material (or, for that matter, about life in general). Even if he *could*, he still faced another major obstacle.

Because he considered he'd been shabbily treated by publishers, he felt justified in behaving badly towards them. Over the years he had accepted so many advances from different companies for *Night's Black Agents*, a furious legal melée would have broken out if he had tried to publish it. Since no one firm would be willing to buy out all the others, he had to resign himself to the fact that the masterpiece he'd dreamt about on Release Day would remain unwritten.

Alex C. Snowden (far right)
and Lee Patterson (centre right)
filming *The Key Man*
on location in Soho, 1957

Advert for the
Mandrake Club, 1953

The Mandrake Club

4, Meard Street, Soho, W.1

Tel.: GERrard 4444

Open 3 p.m. to Midnight

This is London's only Bohemian rendezvous and
the largest Club. Application for membership
(10/6 p.a.) must be made to the Secretary in
advance and the fact of advertising does not mean
that everybody is accepted.

Music Nightly   Good Food & Good Wine
NO DANCING

Soho pub-scene,
drawing by Ruth Willetts, c.1952
(© Paul Willetts)

Balancing the Books

Stymied in his ambitions as a novelist, Julian decided to abandon fiction for the moment and revive the concept of writing a childhood memoir. Instead of soliciting advances from potential publishers, he decided he'd get a better deal if he offered them the finished manuscript. To enable him to take that route, he had to conserve his financial resources. Through August and into September 1952, living on a self-imposed ration of one meal and 10 cigarettes-a-day, he toiled over the book without interruption, gradually expanding the chapter-plan he'd drawn up during the war. By avoiding any of the scriptwriting or journalistic assignments he usually relied on, he was able to focus all his energy on the task. No distractions were allowed to intrude on it, not even the occasional trip to the pubs and clubs where he'd been such a fixture.

Almost as fast as his manuscript accumulated, so too did his rent-arrears. He was fortunate in having an understanding landlady. When he told Mrs Lyle about his commercial expectations for the new book, which he was banking on to cancel out his debt, she didn't press him for payment. The mounting financial pressure temporarily relieved by a £5 gift from John Lehmann, Julian pushed ahead with his memoir, stinting on sleep and venturing out so seldom that he began to be afflicted by bouts of agoraphobia.

On one of his rare excursions into the outside world, he went round to the offices of Rupert Hart-Davis's publishing firm. These were located in a Georgian building in Soho Square, its wide front-door topped by an elegant fanlight, its two front windows devoted to displaying books from an eclectic list. In view of Rupert's earlier interest in the memoir he was writing, Julian offered the company first refusal on it.

His immense powers of concentration enabled him to finish the book by the penultimate week of September. He called it *The Weeping and the Laughter*, the title he'd originally assigned to his third published collection of short stories. He then submitted it to Rupert, his covering letter requesting a whopping £250 advance, payable by the end of the month. Desperate for a decision, having run so short of cash that he'd "scarcely eaten anything for 2 days",[1] he followed up the letter with another visit to Rupert's offices. While he was there, he inadvertently gave his friend the impression that he was threatening him with a pistol. Unwilling to be placed under duress, Rupert gave him back the unread manuscript. That day or possibly the day after, Julian endeavoured to repair the damage by sending his friend an apologetic letter.

Nearly two months of solid work on his book, followed by a middle *The TLS* commissioned on William Faulkner, had left Julian drained, broke, and "in urgent need of relaxation and congenial company."[2] Dan Davin and his wife offered the most obvious source of this, so he wrote to Dan, asking whether they would put him up for ten days or perhaps a fortnight. Never one to refuse Julian's periodic appeals for sanctuary, Dan said it'd be fine. Leaving Barbara behind in their flat, Julian took the train up to Oxford later that week.

As ever, Julian relished the stability, the sense of purpose, and the reassuring routines of family life. Parenthood being, in his opinion, incompatible with his single-minded pursuit of literary celebrity, he was reluctant to admit how much he liked children. Not that he had any particular rapport with them. Yet he revelled in the company of Delia, Anna, and Brigid, whose shrill voices filled the rambling old house. Whenever Dan and Winnie were unavailable, he'd press-gang the children into listening to his monologues, their youth exacting no concessions in either subject matter or tone of voice. He also taught them to play what, for a while, became their favourite game. By tightly rolling up a newspaper and bending one end, he made them each blunt swords with which they fenced until the loser's weapon disintegrated.

Both Dan and Winnie went to great lengths to make his visit an enjoyable one. Awkward as he was to integrate into groups because of his demanding and prickly personality, his resentment of academics, his intermittent hostility towards strangers, and his intolerance of conversations which veered onto topics that didn't engage him, Dan and Winnie introduced Julian, who was at his most genial in these circumstances, to their friends. And they also made a great fuss of him, leaving him to spend many blissful hours by the fire, their beloved Big Cat purring on his lap, a regularly replenished glass in his hand.

When Dan heard about his enormous rent arrears, he came up with a business proposition designed to help him. Dan's suggestion was that Julian should expand the middles he'd written for *The TLS* into a book on modern novelists, appropriate for publication by the Oxford University Press. Julian approved of the idea, though he was far keener to discuss what had happened with Rupert Hart-Davis, "more for the pleasure of getting [Dan's advice] and the pleasure of disputing it than from any intention of taking it."[3]

Refreshed by his stay in Oxford, the brevity of which had prevented him from annoying the Davins, Julian headed back to London on

Saturday 18 October. Barbara, who had evidently missed him, was there to greet him as his train pulled into Paddington station.

His position strengthened by favourable verdicts from Walter Allen and Leonard Russell, both of whom had now read *The Weeping and the Laughter* in manuscript form, he got back in touch with Rupert. Because he "require[d] ready money urgently",[4] Julian was prepared to accept a lower price for the book on condition Rupert paid up straightaway. Within only a few days of contacting Rupert, who wanted to add the book to the firm's spring list, they'd negotiated an advance of £150, the contract also providing an option on the planned sequel. Conscious of his massive debt and aggrieved by his conviction that publishers exploited authors like him, Julian was disappointed he hadn't obtained more.

Half the advance went straight to Mrs Lyle, who had been so forbearing. Much of the other half was swallowed by the unforeseen medical expenses that hit him at the start of November when he was stricken by an attack of piles. These were so excruciating he had to retire to bed, his condition monitored by his doctor, who visited every day. An operation was recommended, but the cost of it and the potential loss of earnings while he was in hospital made him decide to postpone surgery for as long as he could.

In a bid to extricate himself from his financially beleaguered position, during the early part of December he attempted to get some screenwriting work from Norman Collins. Since Julian's encounter with him before the war, Collins had left the publishing industry and become Deputy Chairman of the recently created Associated TeleVision Company, which was yet to make its first transmission. Besides sending him some "very friendly letters",[5] Collins appears to have passed him on to a colleague, with whom he met to discuss a proposed television version of a film script he'd previously written. The script in question was a free-spirited adaptation of the novelist Hugh Walpole's atypically bleak Thirties thriller, *Above the Dark Circus*. But nothing tangible had come of the idea by the third week of December when the handsomely printed proofs of *The Weeping and the Laughter* arrived for correction. Julian was now so penniless he applied for financial assistance from the Society of Authors.

After what must have been a notably grim Christmas and New Year, his prospects began to improve, this new trend prefaced by a letter from the Society of Authors. They announced that he'd been awarded £30 from the Gertrude Page Fund, due to be sent to him in a week's time.

More good news came from both Norman Collins — who said he'd let him know whether there was any work for him by late January — and from Leonard Russell. In the role of Literary Editor of *The Sunday Times*, Russell hired him as a fiction reviewer to fill in for the celebrated writer C.P. Snow's two week absence, spanning the last week of January and the first week of February. The only drawback concerned Russell's attitude towards payment. Making no secret of his disapproval of what he termed Julian's "habit of 'dunning editors' ",[6] of demanding prompt payment-on-delivery, the hitherto indulgent Russell wouldn't countenance bending the paper's system. This precluded cheques from being issued until a week after the end of the month in which the reviews appeared. Infuriated by such a delay, Julian planned to show up the system's patent iniquity in *Business and Desire*, the book he still intended to write for Hamish Hamilton.

Besides reviewing a clutch of four novels and a collection of essays by V.S. Pritchett, which he praised for their refreshing absence of academic jargon, he spent at least part of the middle of January 1953 on another money-making scheme. In the absence of the expected cheques from either the Society of Authors or *The Sunday Times*, it was becoming imperative that he raise an advance from somewhere. Having already expressed an interest in his mooted book of essays, Dan Davin was an obvious target for Julian, who began mulling over themes for a volume covering writers as diverse as Eric Ambler and Dashiell Hammett. On Sunday 18 January he wrote to Dan announcing his intention to "pick out a few authors who've either not been mentioned enough or, in my opinion, not examined in the way they should be — the connecting link being the fact that they show characters in action rather than through introspection or psychological analysis."[7] An immediate advance-payment for the book wasn't, however, forthcoming.

By mid-February, neither the Society of Authors nor *The Sunday Times* had paid him the £60 or more they owed him. Their tardiness left Julian in such dire straits that he sought help from Rupert Hart-Davis. Though he sensed that Rupert considered him a "temperamental, self-willed, wrong-headed fool"[8] who created his own problems, he was prepared to endanger their professional relationship by requesting a loan to keep him going until the missing cheques arrived. But Rupert refused, saying he had no intention of becoming Julian's banker. His refusal provoked a self-justifying reply from Julian, whose financial position was deteriorating by the day. An energetic correspondent despite his avowed hatred of letter-writing, Julian followed this with another appeal for money. Trying hard to play on Rupert's sympathy, he explained that he couldn't afford the tube fare into the West End, and he was "feeling half faint with hunger".[9] Again, Rupert resisted his pleas.

The crisis was alleviated during the final week of April by a return to writing for *The TLS*. Tony Powell had just vacated his post there, yet Julian remained on good terms with Arthur Crook, who commissioned him to produce a middle on Georges Simenon.

Resigned to the necessity of taking whatever commissions came his way, instead of working on the books he wanted to write, he joined the many talented people being recruited by Norman Collins's company, not least the brilliant film directors Robert Hamer and Edgar G. Ulmer. His contract required him to write a "short television film"[10] rightaway and to become, at some unspecified later date, a salaried scriptwriter for the company. Due, in all likelihood, to the exorbitant asking-price for the screen-rights to *Above the Dark Circus*, Julian's earlier proposal hadn't got anywhere. In its place, he appears to have been assigned to produce a sample script for another literary adaptation, the most plausible candidate being a series of self-contained half-hour mystery films based on John Dickson Carr's stories about Colonel March of Scotland Yard, "Head of the Department of Queer Complaints".

It took Julian until mid-March to fulfil this first part of the contract. After he'd handed in the script to Collins, he went off to stay with the Davins again. Dan wanted to discuss the book of essays, but soon discovered that it had slipped down his friend's list of priorities. Julian was now more interested in writing the second volume of his autobiography, evoking "the formative years of adolescence".[11] Happy to allow Julian's creative writing to take precedence over his critical output, Dan let the project drop from the agenda.

As a thank-you to Barbara for everything she'd done for him during an extremely demanding period, Julian dedicated *The Weeping and the Laughter* to her. Emblazoned with an oddly understated blurb, billing it as "sad and elegant", the book went on sale on the last Friday of March. But Rupert had trouble persuading certain West End booksellers to stock it, because they disliked Julian who, though his money problems had reduced him to the status of "an ex-bookbuyer",[12] remained "a pretty constant bookshop visitor".[13]

Over the next few weeks *The Weeping and the Laughter* attracted a succession of outstanding reviews. Writing in *The New Statesman and Nation*, the popular humorist Arthur Marshall described it as "charming, vastly amusing and well-written."[14] And *The Times* was even more fulsome in its praise, labelling Julian as "one of the most gifted writers of his generation"[15] and going on to praise it as "an exceptionally civilised and amusing book."[16] The only discordant note was struck by Julian's friend, John Betjeman, who appraised it for *The Daily Telegraph and Morning Post*. While he concurred with the other reviewers, he treated it as fiction rather than autobiography. Such was Julian's irritation, he wrote to John asking him to arrange for the paper to carry "some sort of disclaimer".[17]

Neither the enthusiastic reception by the press, nor another appearance on the BBC's influential *Talking of Books* programme, where Julian was joined in the studio by Angus Wilson and Arthur Marshall, were sufficient to generate the high sales necessary to redeem what was fast becoming a commercially disastrous year for Rupert Hart-Davis Ltd. Sales of Julian's book were, indeed, struggling to recoup the advance he'd already been paid. Annoyed by the way Rupert's firm had handled the book, he wrote them a string of irate letters, complaining about the lack of advertising, about their poor distribution outside London, and about the mix-up that had prevented a review from appearing in *The Sunday Times*.

With no more money coming in, his debt to Mrs Lyle began to increase again, making it hard for him to concentrate on *The Rites of Spring*, the second volume of what he saw as a sequence of autobiographies, whose outline he'd already submitted to Rupert. In pursuit of ready-cash, he neglected it in favour of commissions from *The TLS* for middles on Nigel Balchin and P.G. Wodehouse, as well as a single batch of reviews. Meanwhile, he was receiving regular treatment from a local doctor, who diagnosed a "nervous disability"[18] and "anxiety state",[19] brought on by stress, his money-worries compounded by Barbara's current poor health and their cramped living conditions. To add to his problems, Anthony Gibbs, the new Bertie Wooster-like Chairman of Allan Wingate, was threatening to sue him unless he repaid the extra cash André had advanced him on unrecouped royalties from *Of Love and Hunger*.

Now firmly established in the role of guardian angel, Tony Powell did what he could to help Julian out. Only a few months earlier, Tony's friend, the opinionated and forthright journalist Malcolm Muggeridge, had taken over the editorship of the weekly magazine *Punch*. Entrusted with the task of re-energising this flagging, stuffy publication, Muggeridge had persuaded Tony to accept the role of Literary Editor. No sooner had Tony moved into the magazine's offices at 10 Bouverie Street, just off Fleet Street, than he began to institute subtle changes. Most conspicuous among these was his imposition of "a relatively highbrow standard of book-reviewing on a magazine with a long and obstinate tradition of active philistinism."[20] He also set about recruiting new contributors who would transform its dowdy image. Since Julian had already demonstrated his value and versatility on *The TLS*, Tony Powell had no qualms about adding him to an illustrious roster of freelance writers. These included Noël Coward, Angus Wilson, Lawrence Durrell, Elizabeth Bowen, Kenneth Tynan, Joyce Cary, and John Betjeman, their work interspersed by cartoons and illustrations by draughtsmen of the calibre of Ronald Searle and Mark Boxer.

At last fulfilling the ambition he'd harboured nearly twenty years earlier, Julian made his debut in the pages of *Punch* with an amusing parody of P.G. Wodehouse, which featured in the Wednesday 20 May issue. Its publication elicited a letter of congratulation from Wodehouse himself. A little over a week afterwards, Julian also had an appreciative essay on Wodehouse's work featured in *The TLS*. Wodehouse responded to this by sending him another "charming"[21] letter, expressing gratitude for the article, which had pushed Penguin into sanctioning paperback editions of five more of his novels.

Just under a month passed before Tony Powell — who paid Julian cash-on-delivery, sometimes out of his own pocket — found space to publish the next of Julian's long comic pieces. Composed in the form of a screenplay about a film company called "English Leopard",[22] it ridiculed Sir Claude Dansey and Sir David Cunynghame, two of the directors of British Lion, whom he held responsible for the scrapping of his adaptation of *The Suicide Club*. Well-paid as he was for these contributions, half the £25 fee from which went to his landlady, they didn't solve his wearisome debt problem. By June he owed a massive £280 in overdue rent. All the same, Mrs Lyle remained sympathetic to him because she thought he'd "been dogged by misfortune."[23]

On Friday 19 June he wrote to Captain Broadbent at the Royal Literary Fund, announcing his intention to make another grant application. But Captain Broadbent informed him that his appeal was unlikely to be successful because he'd already received two previous hand-outs.

A further reversal occurred a few days after that when Barbara was rushed into St Mary's Hospital on Praed Street, probably suffering from some form of gynaecological condition. Without her, Julian was lost, his normally well-concealed vein of self-pity resurfacing. "I've had a filthy time recently, with Barbara ill and in hospital, so I could do with a lucky break,"[24] he admitted in a letter to Dan Davin. His hope was that the Royal Literary Fund would provide it.

Aware that his publisher was on the committee scheduled to adjudicate on his application, Julian may have been concerned that the current dispute with Rupert might prejudice their judgement. To bolster his case, he managed to get Mrs Lyle to write to them on his behalf. He also obtained a doctor's certificate, stating that he was still being treated for the nervous condition which had been so hampering his work. And he persuaded Dan Davin to supply him with a reference, testifying to him being "in want or distress".[25] When he submitted his application during the last week of June, he even enclosed a recent, unrelated letter from John Betjeman proclaiming him a "genius".[26]

In the run-up to the next meeting of the committee of the Royal Literary Fund, Julian's old comrade-in-adversity, Raynor Heppenstall, published *The Lesser Infortune*, a documentary novel about their spell in Northfield Military Hospital. Though Julian was, in a pertinent allusion to Dorian Gray, allotted the name of "Dorian Scott-Crichton", the likeness was unmistakable. Heppenstall regarded it as "wholly affectionate",[27] yet he was well enough acquainted with Julian's exhibitionism and "symptoms of persecution mania"[28] to be worried about the possibility of him filing a lawsuit.

Sure enough, Julian was hurt and appalled by Raynor's portrait which, he felt, misrepresented him "as a monster".[29] Too broke to resort to litigation even if he had wanted to, he camouflaged his true feelings, lest they expose the vulnerability he found so embarrassing. Under the pretence that he was flattered by Raynor's depiction of him, he went round bragging about how *he* was the real Scott-Crichton. And when the novel was reviewed in *The New Statesman and Nation* on the first Saturday of July, he despatched a lengthy and indignant letter to the magazine, defending the book against the few minor criticisms levelled at it. The real subject of his letter was, however, not *The Lesser Infortune* but his own experiences, from which he was still smarting. In his letter, he railed against "the stupid malice"[30] of the hospital authorities, the "McCarthyish"[31] tendencies of the army, and "the indiscriminate waving of white feathers at men of intelligence who, through no fault of their own, spent the recent war struggling to free themselves from the nightmare fly-trap of a Kafkan bureaucracy."[32]

He was rewarded for his magnanimity by the arrival on Thursday 9 July of a note informing him that the Royal Literary Fund had, contrary to Captain Broadbent's predictions, awarded him a £100 grant. But there was no sign of an accompanying cheque. To his dismay, the committee turned out to have paid the money directly to Mrs Lyle.

As was so often the case, the revival in Julian's fortunes didn't last long. The following Tuesday evening, Barbara suffered a haemorrhage, maybe owing to a miscarriage. This precipitated her return to St Mary's Hospital, though the doctors said she was in no danger. A week later, they discharged her. She then went on holiday — back to her family, perhaps — to recuperate.

Lonely without her, Julian spent a few days with Gerry Fisher in Cookham Dean before resuming his stopgap work for *Punch*, who paid between 10 and 15 guineas for each of his contributions. Since this wasn't enough for him to survive on, he made an effort to find additional sources of income, his aim being to raise the cash to bankroll an unbroken stint on a novel. Not *Business and Desire* (which seems to have been quietly forgotten), but possibly a new novel.

Noticing that *The Weeping and the Laughter* had disappeared from the bookshops and no longer featured in the adverts placed by Rupert Hart-Davis's company, he assumed that the original 5,000 print-run must have sold out. According to their contract, Julian would regain the copyright unless Rupert printed a second edition. By threatening to offer *The Weeping and the Laughter* and *The Rites of Spring* to another publisher, he tried to force Rupert into ordering a reprint. But Rupert scuppered the plan by pointing out that less than half the first edition had been sold. This only served to stoke Julian's lingering anger over the perceived mishandling of his book, and over Rupert's frequent willingness to criticise his behaviour.

It wasn't until late August that his efforts to find fresh sources of income began to pay dividends. Most likely over a drink in the Stag's Head, he succeeded in interesting John Davenport in broadcasting three extracts from *The Rites of Spring* on the BBC's Third Programme. One of these was to be a memoir of his meeting with Frank Harris, earmarked for a 30-minute reading. Through a recommendation from Davenport, he also landed a commission to provide a separate extract for *Encounter*, the new magazine co-edited by Stephen Spender.

From the second week of September, he was so busy striving to fulfil these commissions he couldn't even spare the time to write to friends or visit his usual West End watering-holes. Shutting himself away in his flat, he immersed himself in his writing, working continuously for up to 62 hours without sleep. For Spender, he wrote about his introduction to formal education at the hands of the despotic Monsieur L'Abbé: a period he did not "like to look back upon, or would care to live through again."[33] And for Davenport, instead of writing about Frank Harris, he decided to produce a reminiscence about the bullying that had flourished while he was a pupil at Le Châlet.

A fortnight went by without any news from John Davenport regarding

The Gondolier of Death, Julian's memoir of his time at Le Châlet. In the interim, Leonard Russell re-employed him on *The Sunday Times* as one of a panel of reviewers that included Cyril Connolly. His initial review for the paper, assessing five new novels by writers as varied as John O'Hara and James Hanley, appeared on the third Sunday of that month.

Exhausted by nearly seven weeks of unremitting work, Julian headed for the familiar haven of the Davins' house. On the afternoon of Sunday 18 October, not long after his arrival back in London, Julian went to the Mandrake, where he ran into Dylan Thomas, whom he still regarded as a friend. He and Dylan, who was due to leave for New York the following day, enjoyed "quite a long talk"[34], focusing on Donald Taylor and their screenwriting.

Several weeks had elapsed since Julian had submitted *The Gondolier of Death* to John Davenport, yet he'd heard nothing about the BBC's plans for it, so he wrote to Davenport asking if they'd made up their minds whether to broadcast it. But he discovered they'd decided against accepting it because it was too long.

To finance his extravagant drinking habits, Julian had taken to playing Spoof for money, his aptitude for the game ensuring that he won far more than he lost. Gambling was illegal in British pubs, yet the bar staff of the Wheatsheaf turned a blind-eye until other customers started to complain. Fearful of losing his license, the new landlord Arthur Harrodine (who had taken over the tenancy from Red) prohibited Julian from playing Spoof. And when Julian ignored him, Arthur banned him from the pub.

His exile from what had, for so long, been his Soho headquarters coincided with his becoming a frequent lunchtime and afternoon visitor to the now notoriously sleazy Club des Caves de France at 39 Dean Street, only a few doors away from the more salubrious Colony Room, favoured hangout of Johnny Minton and Francis Bacon. Except for its name, little remained of the Caves's original Gallic theme. It was entered via a dark doorway, guarded by two hefty bouncers who half-heartedly quizzed people as to whether they were members, though proof never seemed to be required. Inside the street-level bar, where "perpetual twilight reigned at any time of the day",[35] it took a while for your eyes to adjust. It then became apparent you were in an elongated, low-ceilinged, smoke-wreathed room. Beyond the short flight of steps leading down to the tiny basement bar, there was a counter of such prodigious length it was more like a runway than a bar. Hanging above it, there was a string of coloured lights. Along the facing wall, a line of drink-stained seats were positioned, the floor around them flecked with cigarette-butts. In between the seats, there was a row of wine barrels, a series of small plastic-topped tables, and a wooden dais with an upright piano on it. Each of the tables had a filthy-looking jar of pickled gherkins in the centre, the contents deliberately doused in salt so as to make the customers thirsty. Displayed on the wall behind, there was a row of elaborately framed but inept surrealist daubs, painted by an ageing, monocled sot who called himself "Baron von Schine". Despite the implausible list of international galleries where he'd supposedly exhibited, they never seemed to sell. Most days the Baron was to be seen slumped beneath them, often sound-asleep.

Studiously averting his eyes from a painting of "a headless white horse rising from a pyramid of pink sand"[36] that hung over the piano, and "which [he] believed brought [him] bad luck if squarely confronted",[37] the increasingly neurotic and compulsive Julian would saunter to the far end of the bar, his dark glasses rendering the place even murkier than it already was. In his dapper get-up, sponge-bag trousers worn with a silver-buttoned burgundy blaizer and a replacement for his teddy-bear coat, he stood out from the classless, uniformly shabby clientele. Many of the regulars, lured by the ambience, the cheap wine, and the management's readiness to let them nurse a single drink for hours, were people he knew: Monica, James Graham-Murray, the two Roberts, Caitlin Thomas, Nina Hamnett, Paul Potts, and Stephen Fothergill. There was also Elizabeth Smart, the intense, darkly attractive Canadian writer and former lover of George Barker; the sedately attired, amusingly camp publisher and bookseller, David Archer; and the slight figure of the writer, Philip O'Connor, ingratiating when sober, otherwise surly or aggressive.

The place where Julian liked to stand, just about as far from the entrance as it was possible to get, was marked by a risibly Freudian picture of a giant snowman sitting on a rock, clasping a furled red umbrella, the object of an awestruck nymphet's pop-eyed gaze. There Julian would be served by whichever of the club's four mainstays was behind the bar that afternoon. Sometimes it was the surprisingly refined Frenchman and his wife who owned the club, the antics of their customers accounting for their expressions of perpetual bewilderment. Sometimes it was Frank, a thickset ex-naval officer who behaved with the weary resignation of a kindergarten teacher supervising an unruly class. But more often it was the giant yet placid and accommodating Italian barman, Secundo Carnera, younger brother of the heavyweight boxer Primo Carnera.

Here in the Caves, Julian offended Staggering Stephen by turning his back on him when he was halfway through telling him something. Grabbing him by the shoulder, Stephen spun him back round. Incensed by what Julian considered an act of gross impertinence, he glowered menacingly at Stephen, then threatened him with the swordstick he'd taken to carrying.

Another afternoon, James Graham-Murray introduced Julian to his friend, the intriguing but deeply sinister Gerald Hamilton, widely regarded as the model for the title character in Christopher Isherwood's *Mr Norris Changes Trains*. Dressed in a rumpled suit and a Panama hat that concealed his baldness, the elderly Hamilton, his long, jowly face distinguished by moist, rubbery lips, owl-like eyebrows and dark, mischievous eyes, liked to sit opposite the bar, parlaying stories of dubious provenance. Without a hint of levity, he would recount the tale of how, in the last war, he'd offered to assist the government by parachuting into Nazi Germany disguised as a nun.

As the afternoon wore on, the clientele of the Caves became progressively less raffish. This gradual metamorphosis was completed by about 5.30pm when a trio of middle-aged men in evening-dress and bow-ties, one of whom sported an obvious toupée, would occupy the dais in the corner. From there, they'd either serenade the customers with decorous dance music or accompany the club-owner's coy, pouting daughter, who sang extracts from operettas, occasionally preceded by impromptu, maliciously ironic introductions by the impish photographer John Deakin. But Julian and the other afternoon regulars had, by then, normally drifted away to the pubs.

Maigret and the
Writer's Widow

At the start of that winter, Julian maintained his high journalistic output, working under such pressure that he believed it was damaging both his health and his relationship with Barbara. Only days after his next clutch of reviews appeared in *The Sunday Times*, he produced an extended piece commissioned by *Encounter*. The article was about *Clubland Heroes*, the seminal study of boys' adventure stories, for which he still felt a nostalgic attachment. His reading of *Clubland Heroes* led him to consider producing a comparable study of the thriller genre in film and literature. The book would evaluate everything from the novels of John Buchan, Graham Greene, and Eric Ambler to the films of Alfred Hitchcock, and Fritz Lang. But it joined the already extensive list of unrealised projects.

Keeping up this hectic schedule, Julian moved on to another intensive book-reviewing assignment for *The Sunday Times*. Yet the income from his journalism didn't prevent him from falling badly behind with the rent again. He strung Mrs Lyle along by saying this was because he was busy working on a book, about which he had "great financial hopes".[1] Lenient as always, she allowed the debt to accumulate. With the end of the year approaching, it had mounted to a colossal £362. This time, though, there was no chance of him being bailed out by the Royal Literary Fund. In a spectacular betrayal of all the trust and sympathy Mrs Lyle had shown him, Julian plotted to avoid paying her by vacating the Norfolk Square flat on Wednesday 11 November 1953, dragging Barbara with him. The sense of impending crisis in advance of their planned departure wasn't helped by the "terrible shock"[2] and grief he felt when he heard that Dylan Thomas had died in New York.

Full of remorse for what he viewed as his insensitive treatment of Dylan, he tried to make up for his shortcomings. He did so by phoning Stephen Spender at *Encounter* with a suggestion for a long piece about the period he and Dylan had worked together, the idea being that the fee would be donated to Caitlin and their children. Spender agreed to publish it and even arranged for Julian to visit the magazine's offices to discuss it. Right after that, Spender went off to Italy. While he was away, the article was swept aside by a flood of solemn tributes.

Bridling at Julian's plans to leave their flat, Barbara appears to have announced at the very last moment that she'd be staying behind. To avoid embarrassment, Julian confided in his friends that the decision to separate was a joint one. Unhappy though he felt about it, blaming his heavy journalistic commitments, he remained on friendly terms with Barbara. When he moved out, leaving behind not just her but also their cat, on whom he doted, she agreed to store some of his things. These consisted of books, several suitcases full of his possessions, and a stack of back-issues of *Punch*, featuring his work.

By Wednesday 24 November, word of his domestic travails fuelling the Soho gossip-mill, Julian had found himself a flat at 5d Hyde Park Mansions, a decrepit block tucked down a side-street off the Marylebone Road. Opposite the entrance to the street, there was the Blue Hall Cinema, its façade — to his delight — plastered with advertising for the crime movies that formed its staple programme. He hadn't been there long when Dan Davin wrote to him, floating the possibility of him being employed as the editor of an anthology of English short stories planned by the Oxford University Press. Excited by the prospect, Julian — who envisaged featuring Commonwealth English-language writers such as Mulk Raj Anand — speculated on worthwhile, infrequently anthologised candidates for inclusion. But Dan's proposal didn't amount to anything.

In the meantime, Julian's memoir of Monsieur L'Abbé appeared in *Encounter*. He also had two pieces printed in *Punch*, one a science-fiction spoof, the other an anecdotal tale about an occasion when the store detective at Zwemmer's had mistakenly arrested him for shoplifting. And he made four more contributions to *The Sunday Times*, including a rare negative review of Kingsley Amis's *Lucky Jim*. His usually sound, unprejudiced judgment swayed by the rancour he felt towards the fashionable new generation of novelists who were hogging the limelight, he accused Amis of peddling schoolboy smut.

A pleasant distraction from the journalistic grind was provided by the extensive Erich von Stroheim season, hosted by the National Film Theatre during the opening weeks of 1954. The season incorporated screenings of the movies that had established von Stroheim's reputation as a master of silent cinema, among them *Greed* and *Foolish Wives*, the Twenties Riviera setting of which would have struck a chord with Julian. Apprehensive though he was about them failing to live up to his fond memories, he made several visits to the former Festival of Britain "Tele-cinema" on London's South Bank, where the National Film Theatre was housed. He needn't have worried, though, because their impact on him remained undiminished.

The recent split from Barbara triggering a return to his old nomadic existence, Julian was on the move again around mid-February. Straying from his accustomed patch, he took a spacious flat at 12 Regent's Park Terrace, a tall, stucco-fronted building on the seedy Camden Town side of the park.

To subsidise the composition of the second volume of his auto-biography, which he was anxious to complete, he offered to write a self-contained extract from it for John Lehmann's latest publication. That month John had launched the *London Magazine*, edited from an office in the basement of his elegant South Kensington townhouse, where he held regular parties, at least one of which Julian and Barbara had attended. Though John turned down Julian's offer, he liked the idea of having him as a contributor to the magazine, so he gave Julian some work, reviewing a couple of scholarly books on American literature. Julian was a little hesitant about passing judgement over such overtly academic material, yet he soon accepted the job.

Before carrying out his commission, he left his Camden Town flat sometime between the end of March and the beginning of April. Perhaps because he was unable to afford the deposit on another flat, he registered at the Belvedere Hotel, a glorified guest house at 52 Norfolk Square, within sight of where he had lived for so long. Only a few days after his arrival, he submitted his review to John Lehmann, who paid him for it with typical alacrity. His earnings allowed him to take the brief break he had been itching for, the exertions of the past few months having taken their toll. On about Wednesday 7 April, he went down to Bognor, where he spent Easter in a modest hotel, his stay punctuated by get-togethers with the Jaegers. Midway through the penultimate week of that month, he returned to London and checked back into the Belvedere Hotel.

Much as Julian wanted to dedicate himself to writing his autobiography as well as another novel, practical considerations dictated that he had to resume his reviewing chores with *The Sunday Times*. Each week, a daunting stack of new novels descended on him. He was expected to review these in batches of between three and five books, his assessments of them generally appearing on alternate weekends. So wide-ranging were his tastes, he was able to write with genuine zeal about books as disparate as James Baldwin's *Go Tell It To The Mountain*, Herman Hesse's *Siddhartha*, and Davis Grubb's *The Night of the Hunter*, the cinematic potential of which he was prescient in identifying. Between marathon shifts of reading and reviewing, the incessant pressure leaving him tired and dispirited, he found time to produce an article for *Punch* on the adventure stories of José Moselli, the article inspired by his reading of *Clubland Heroes*.

During May, he received a welcome morale-boost when Cyril Connolly selected one of his wartime short stories for *The Golden Horizon* anthology, bringing together what the Colonel regarded as all the best contributions to the magazine. Julian must have appreciated his former editor's decision to dedicate the book to Sonia Brownell who had, several years earlier, married George Orwell on his deathbed.

Early in June, Julian was thrown back into crisis when he lost his job on *The Sunday Times*. Like it or not, journalism — albeit of a more interesting genre — still provided his sole source of income. The hole in his budget, left by his departure from *The Sunday Times*, was partially filled by John Lehmann, who commissioned him to review a group of novels for the *London Magazine*. That summer Julian also produced an evocative reminiscence of his meeting with Frank Harris, which he intended to incorporate into the next volume of his autobiography. Despite John's previous refusal to commission other memoirs that Julian had suggested, he liked the piece enough to buy it. On top of that, Julian sold a Christopher Isherwood parody to *Punch*, and a long essay about the films of Erich von Stroheim and D.W. Griffith to *Encounter*. Versatile as ever, he adapted the tenor of his writing to suit the setting in which it would be appearing, the comic bravado of his piece for *Punch* contrasting sharply with the unflinching erudition of his essay for *Encounter*.

Throughout his adult life Julian had cultivated an aura of imperturbable self-reliance, yet he was left floundering by the break-up of his relationship with Barbara. So he turned to Dan and Winnie Davin for help. His deep-seated, frequently voiced dislike of Oxford overridden by the Davins' reassuring presence there, he asked if they'd be prepared to put him up while he recovered from the trauma of losing "girl, home and everything else at a moment's notice".[3] Steadfast friends that they were, they agreed.

Whatever qualms the Davins had about playing host to him for an indeterminate period, they treated the lean, hangdog Julian to a "magnificent welcome"[4] when he arrived in Oxford on Saturday 21 August. Just as Mac and Lydia had done in the wake of his harrowing separation from Elizabeth seventeen years earlier, they gave him a vicarious taste of the domestic stability he'd lost.

Unlike previous visits, which had never spanned more than a few pleasant, mirthful days, this one lasted far longer, his protracted presence becoming a cause of irritation for Dan, though his host kept it well concealed. Much as Julian relished being the pampered guest of honour, he knew it wasn't a role he could sustain indefinitely. Around the beginning of September, he found himself lodgings with a Polish man who lived about a mile away in the Parks Road area. Nonetheless, the disconsolate Julian continued to benefit from the Davins' hospitality. Most days Winnie would cycle round there, a freshly cooked meal for him stowed in the basket of her bike. Exploiting her maternal instincts, he even persuaded her to cut his nails, a task which, he told her, he couldn't manage himself.

Well before the end of the month, he moved out of his latest lodgings and rented somewhere just down the road from the Davins, who didn't betray even an inkling of the foreboding they felt at having him as a neighbour. His new home was a sparsely furnished basement bedsit at 59 Southmoor Road, a bay-windowed villa where his aged landlord Mr Goodman lived. As part of the tenancy agreement, Goodman said that he was willing to take phone messages for Julian, who needed to maintain contact with the metropolitan literary world. The bedsit had its own entrance, approached via steep steps leading down from the short, chequerboard-tiled front path. Its best feature was a view of the long, narrow garden, running down to the Oxford Canal, beyond which there was a railway line. Passing trains not only left behind spectral whorls of smoke that drifted across the garden, but also sent seismic tremors through the house, even in the middle of the night. Hardly conducive to alleviating Julian's prevailing unhappiness.

For all their misgivings, the Davins made a selfless effort to jolly him along. They gently teased him, their levity playing on the self-deprecating side of his personality. And, at every opportunity, they endeavoured to integrate him into their crowded social life. So frequent were the invitations to their house that an American friend, who was spending a few days with them, commented on how Julian seemed "to live as much with the Davins as by himself."[5] On Sundays he'd join them for their traditional roast lunch. Afterwards, he'd tag along on their dog-walking expeditions across Port Meadow. But he never got further than the hump-backed bridge that led to it. There he routinely claimed to be overcome by agoraphobia, though Delia Davin suspected that he was merely reluctant to get his shoes dirty. Spurning repeated offers from her and her sisters to blindfold him and hold his hand as he crossed the bridge, he'd always turn back.

Needless to say, Dan and Winnie had no such difficulty in persuading him to accompany them on their nightly excursions to the nearby Victoria Arms, where the garrulous landlady, Mrs Clack, nicknamed Dan "the Professor".[6] Each evening Dan liked to sit on the same threadbare, padded settle in the corner of the pub's intimate Tudor Snug, presiding over the conversation like the leader of a seminar. From the walls of the snug hung an incongruous pair of abstract-expressionist paintings by Gerald Wilde, presented to the former landlord by the artist as payment in kind, their swirling patterns and strident colours partially obscured by heavy protective grilles. It was there that the Davins introduced Julian to their circle of about half-a-dozen close friends who, like them, patronised the Victoria on a regular basis. These were recruited from the academic and artistic communities, as well as from among Dan's more congenial workmates at the Oxford University Press.

While Dan and the others drank half-pints of beer, into which Mrs Clack's false-eyelashes had a disconcerting tendency to drop as she operated the pump, Julian's preferred tipple was Moussec, a coarse brand of champagne. In deference to what he hailed as its miraculous restorative properties, he started calling it "Dr Moussadek"[7] or simply "the Doctor".[8] Since each glass of it cost half-a-crown, more than double the price of a pint of beer, he could seldom stretch to buying a round when it was his turn. To avoid these recurrent moments of mortification, Dan — far from wealthy himself — would sometimes offer to lend him a pound or two. Because his wounded pride made him irritable, any such donations had to be tendered with the utmost diplomacy. Dan discovered that the best tactic was to distract him by coaxing him into one of his customary monologues about the perfidy of publishers, life in the army, crime novels, or cherished movies, an esoteric passion for Japanese cinema providing a perennial topic. If Dan's diversionary tactic failed, Julian would lapse into a sulk, his dark, inexpressive eyes hidden behind the new reflective aviator-style sunglasses he'd acquired.

The Davins' fears about the disruptive effect Julian might have on their social life were soon borne out. One Sunday lunchtime, when they were joined in the pub by a university lecturer friend and his glamorous blonde wife, Julian persuaded the woman to try one of his green bombs. It left her "liberated enough to launch into an animated flirtation"[9] with another member of their group. And, on a separate occasion, when the academic John Wain made an unscheduled evening appearance in the Victoria, Julian greeted his arrival with a belligerent silence. He maintained it throughout Wain's euphoric chatter about his dealings with his publishers, who had brought out his debut novel, *Hurry on Down*, to such acclaim the previous year. To Julian, Wain was an unwelcome intruder into both the literary world and the Tudor Snug, soaking up the attention that should have been lavished on a certain more deserving candidate.

After closing-time, Julian got into the habit of stopping off at the Davins for a nightcap. Self-absorbed as he was, it never seemed to occur to him that he shouldn't stay too long. Instead, he tended to linger well into the night, even though he knew that Dan and Winnie had to be up early. Savouring the relaxed and convivial atmosphere, he would sit there quaffing whisky and sustaining an unrelenting but relaxed and generally entertaining flow of talk which lasted until either the whisky ran out, or else his hosts began to nod off.

Unable to postpone his return home any longer, he'd walk the fifty yards or so back to his bedsit, his gait invested with "a kind of stiff dignity."[10] There he'd settle down to his current journalistic assignment, only collapsing into bed in the early hours. His stamina boosted by the large doses of amphetamines he continued to take, he would, if he had an urgent deadline, sometimes work for the best part of two days without sleep.

Despite his departure from London, he continued to write for *Punch*, penning lengthy and, in the main, affectionate parodies of novelists such as Nancy Mitford and Henry Green, his interest in literary parody reflecting his fascination with the art of disguise. He also produced his first couple of thumbnail reviews for their regular *Booking* section, through which he plugged his friend Jack Gillies's debut novel. Living up to their reputation as generous employers, *Punch* paid over £6 for each of these. All the same, his earnings from literary journalism were insufficient to cover his living-expenses.

As part of their campaign to cheer him up, the Davins took Julian with them to parties thrown by their friends. Among these was the novelist Joyce Cary, who held informal, plentifully provisioned gatherings every Sunday at his large house on Parks Road. The Davins included Julian in the not unreasonable hope that he and Cary, irrespective of their temperamental differences, might hit it off. Julian was, after all, a wholehearted admirer of his work, of what he considered Cary's "unique ability to see all points of view."[11] And Cary had, through his championing of the feckless Gerald Wilde, several of whose pictures adorned the walls of his house, shown himself to be tolerant of bohemian excess. Yet Julian's egotism bored and exasperated him. Even so, the good-natured and considerate Cary, aware that Julian was hard-up and lonely, tried to help him by lending him £5 and inviting him to a dinner he'd arranged. This was being held in honour of Cary's influential American friend Jack Fischer, who was spending September holidaying in England with his wife. As the editor of *Harper's Magazine*, Fischer was well-placed to open up a precious new market for Julian's work.

Things did not, however, go according to plan. Far from ingratiating himself with this potentially valuable ally, who knew F. Scott Fitzgerald and had published work by William Faulkner, Julian picked an argument with him about the publication dates of Faulkner's novels. The row was so ferocious it defied even Dan's valiant efforts to appease the warring parties by suggesting that they were both right, due to the staggered English and American release dates. Unnoticed by either Julian or Fischer, the quiet and unassuming Cary, who hated any form of assertiveness, retreated from the room.

When the argument had at last subsided, an atmosphere of mutual animosity persisting, Winnie fetched their host from the basement, where he was recovering his composure by poring over old bound volumes of *Punch*. At the earliest juncture, the Davins said their goodbyes and walked back to Southmoor Road with Julian. Oblivious to either the embarrassment he'd caused them, or the damage he'd inflicted on his own career prospects, he revelled in his perceived triumph over a Yankee upstart.

If he was to stand any chance of solving his current money problems, Julian had to broaden his journalistic repertoire, so he bagged a reporting job with *The London Evening Standard*. The job consisted of writing an account of the recent demise of one of London's leading small publishers, the Falcon Press, which had earlier merged with the Grey Walls Press. But he backed out of it when he heard that the subject was booby-trapped with possible libel suits. These arose from widespread allegations of fraud levelled against Peter Baker, owner of the Falcon Press, who also happened to be a Member of Parliament.

As an alternative means of bringing in some extra cash that would enable him to resume work on *The Rites of Spring*, Julian drew up a contents list for a collection of his humorous and satirical pieces, the added incentive being that it wouldn't incur too much additional work. It was an idea he may well have got from the newly published *Laugh With Me! An Anthology of Contemporary Humour*, which featured Julian in a line-up encompassing Evelyn Waugh, P.G. Wodehouse, and James Thurber. Many of the thirty pieces in his proposed collection were culled from *Punch*, but many others, a memoir of childhood visits to French cinemas for instance, had been rejected by the magazine. Hence the book's provisional title: *Not Good Enough For Punch*. During mid-October he simultaneously circulated the contents list round several London publishers, along with a covering-letter offering the collection for an advance of £120. First refusal was given to Hamish Hamilton. In an attempt to nudge them into accepting his offer, he claimed the advance would free him from the journalistic drudgery that had prevented him from finishing the novel he owed them. But the company politely declined his proposal.

Mention of the novel they'd commissioned almost three years ago prompted Hamish Hamilton to make a counter-offer. Were he to submit a substantial section of it, they said they'd be willing to pay him another advance. The trouble was, he had completed only a few segments of the book, all of them in need of "drastic revision and re-writing."[12] After a week-long interval during which he must have weighed up his next move, he declined their offer on the grounds that he wanted to buy himself enough time to complete the entire novel, not simply another section of it. Lest that appear too flimsy an excuse, he justified his reluctance by adding that he'd vowed "never to accept again an advance on an unwritten work."[13]

Though Julian had, only days earlier, written to Rupert Hart-Davis stating his desire to end their business relationship, he had the nerve to contact Rupert again, requesting a combined £320 advance for *Not Good Enough For Punch* and *The Rites of Spring*. Their recent acrimonious dealings outweighed by Rupert's belief in him as a writer, Rupert expressed interest in reading the material intended for inclusion in *Not Good Enough For Punch*. Because the majority of Julian's back-issues of *Punch* had not yet been forwarded from London, he was unable to show them to Rupert, or to obtain the speedy decision he required.

None of his money-making schemes having got him anywhere, he devised a fresh proposition for Hamish Hamilton. On the strength of his much-admired translation work for John Lehmann, he suggested Hamish Hamilton might employ him to translate one of George Simenon's Maigret novels, the British publication rights to which they'd recently purchased. They reacted by offering to pay him 10 guineas for producing a trial 5,000-word extract from *Maigret et la grande perche*. Provided it met with the approval of Mme Simenon, who was scheduled to arrive in England with her husband at the end of October, they would then commission him to translate the rest of the book.

Once he'd succeeded in securing dispensation from Hamish Hamilton to let him submit a handwritten manuscript in lieu of the preferred typescript, he dedicated the first two days of November to drafting the trial extract. His translation strove to capture the staccato rhythms, the sparse but evocative descriptions, the crisp vernacular language so typical of Simenon, whose writing he had admired ever since he first came across it while he was still living in France. In his view, any notion of slavish fidelity to the original had to be abandoned, the French slang being replaced by analogous English idioms. With that in mind, when he sent off the manuscript, he noted that he'd translated "La Grande Perche" as " 'Long Tina'[...] because this has the correct underworld sound for England (I know of a 'Long Flora'), whereas 'The Beanpole' would sound all wrong."[14]

Taking a break from his exertions, he spent a few days staying with the critic and crime novelist Julian Symons, who sometimes used to join him in the Wheatsheaf. On his return from Symons's cottage near Faversham in Kent, Mr Hamilton contacted him to let him know that Mme Simenon appreciated his abilities as a translator and hoped he'd continue with the rest of the book. But she insisted he abide by the rules she'd laid down for translators of her husband's work. To comply with these, she requested numerous changes to his sample passage. For a start, she demanded that "Long Tina" should be substituted for "Lanky Liz". And she aggravated him still further by stipulating that he should not only follow the original word-order but also steer clear of slang and incorrect syntax. Outraged, he wrote back to Hamish Hamilton, pointing out that "trying to render the 'rhythm' of the original is what makes most translations read unnaturally. The whole point of Simenon's style is its colloquial ease, and this is apt to get lost if one sticks to the order of the French sentences when translating.

"Another difficulty is slang. The book is full of it, and all the pungency will be lost if the treatment is too polite and the English equivalents are not given."[15]

Julian's repeatedly expressed concerns didn't deter Hamish Hamilton from going ahead with the commission. On Thursday 17 November they sent a £40 advance, the remainder of his fee being payable on completion. In a casual aside, they informed him that Mme Simenon would be vetting the completed translation, her comments inevitably leading to a certain amount of revision. Nothing could have been more guaranteed to antagonise Julian. Pouncing on what he clearly regarded as yet another example of the duplicity and fundamental untrustworthiness of publishers, he responded with a peevish letter. It reminded them that the original agreement hadn't mentioned anything about Mme Simenon supervising the entire project. "I think, too, that in view of all this," he added, "a note should be included: 'Translation revised and presented under the supervision of Mme Georges Simenon', because I don't want to take back the can for anything she insists on that I might disagree with — such as 'Lanky Liz'."[16]

Never content to take the pragmatic option, especially where money was concerned, Julian appears to have cashed the cheque from Hamish Hamilton at the bar of the Victoria, then made a bee-line for the city centre. Whenever his finances could stretch to it, having first despatched either Delia or Anna Davin to the market to buy him a white carnation for his buttonhole, he'd indulge himself in the plush, oak-panelled dining-room of the Royal Oxford Hotel on Park End Street. Reacquainting himself with the luxury he'd grown up to regard as his birthright, he would enjoy a solitary dinner, accompanied by wine, cigars, and extravagant quantities of brandy. Straight after these binges, he'd usually pop round to the Davins. Or else he'd corner anyone willing to listen to his latest pipe-dreams, these invariably revolving round some as yet unwritten film treatment destined to make him rich.

His anxiety about the Simenon translation was exacerbated by the unexpected news that Norman Collins had given him the go-ahead to resume the television scriptwriting job to which he'd committed himself almost two years previously. He appears to have resumed work on writing instalments of *Colonel March of Scotland Yard*. One thing is for sure, though: he soon came to dislike the medium and regard what he was doing as "hard plodding hack work"[17] which had no future in it for him. Yet the job brought in a regular £20-a-week salary.

Besides his scriptwriting commitments, he had a commission from Arthur Crook at *The TLS* for some book-reviewing. He now felt so "snowed under with work"[18] he begrudged the extra pressure exerted by the arrival of a contract from Hamish Hamilton, stating that the completed translation should be delivered by Saturday 31 December. As he told Richard Brain, who had been entrusted with overseeing the project, he was confident about meeting the newly imposed deadline, yet he "didn't want to feel pursued by time's winged bloody chariot."[19]

Respite from his various commissions was provided on both evenings that weekend by trips to the Victoria, where he met up with the Davins. But the strain of his continual presence led Dan to let slip a succession of acerbic remarks about him. As well as confessing to Julian that "it had been a bore to put up with [him], and to put [him] up",[20] Dan accused him "of consistent bad manners",[21] of "talking too bloody much",[22] of "colossal"[23] egotism. And he referred to Julian's " 'troubles with [his] girlfriend' as too puerile, really, to be taken seriously."[24]

For Julian, this was "the last straw".[25] The cumulative effects of fatigue, the looming deadlines, and the side-effects of his amphetamine habit leaving him even touchier than ever, he reacted by stomping back to his bedsit. Too angry to concentrate on the reviewing work he'd allocated himself for that night, he composed a long letter to Dan, reprimanding him for his "pompous and lordly tone"[26] and listing examples of Dan's "own bad behaviour and thoughtlessness",[27] dating right back to the war.

The Davins attempted to make rapid amends by asking him round to their house on Wednesday night, but he sent them a terse and formal note declining the invitation "owing to immediate pressure of work."[28] In the ensuing days he steered clear of the Victoria or anywhere he might bump into Dan. His resentment towards Dan outweighed by the need for a loan or perhaps the urge to revisit his local pub, he seems to have shown up at the Victoria later in the week. There he would have gone through his normal ritual, which involved ignoring Dan's "presence in a studied fashion and [standing] at the bar by himself with a drink, emanating menace, and waiting for [Dan] to do whatever the code demanded.

"After a while when it became clear [Dan] couldn't read the code, and he felt the atmosphere of the pub diluting the emanation, he would cross over to [Dan's] table and stare at [him] through [his] dark mirror-glasses [...] At length he would say, 'Did you receive a communication from me?' 'Yes.' 'Are you going to do anything about it?' 'No.' A long silence in which he would be trying to impose his will upon [Dan] after the manner of some admired film actor. Then [Dan] would say, 'Have a drink?' He would graciously accept, not without some relief, [Dan] suspect[ed], at another anti-climax. [Dan] would buy him a 'Doctor' and peace would be restored."[29]

To allay his worries about the Simenon translation, Richard Brain proposed that they get together while he was in Oxford during the final weekend of November. Julian, for whom boozing and talking business were inextricably entwined, recommended the Turl Street Bar in the Mitre Hotel as the venue for their meeting. "You will know me," he wrote in reply, "because I carry, invariably a malacca cane with a silver top."[30] Over drinks, Julian handed Brain the next instalment of his work for the company. "I must say I'm delighted both by the ease and the excellence of your translation," Brain later assured him, "and by the fact that I think there's very little that even Mrs Simenon in her most carping moments could take exception to."[31]

Julian was also successful in arranging for the retrieval of most of his belongings from the flat where he and Barbara had lived, Barbara's subsequent departure from Norfolk Square rendering it a complicated and worrying process. But the hoped for back-issues of *Punch* weren't among the possessions delivered to Southmoor Road, forcing him to purchase replacements. He sent these, together with copies of several extra pieces, to Rupert Hart-Davis, from whom he urged a quick decision. Punctual though Rupert's response was, it didn't bring with it the news he wanted, so he went back to the scriptwriting and translation work that had sustained him lately.

Only a day or two after Rupert had turned down the book, *Punch* published his recent parody of Simenon's Maigret novels, his detailed stylistic awareness braced by his experience as a translator. Its subtlety and comic effectiveness drew praise from both Mr Hamilton and Mme Simenon, who wrote that she and her husband "were very much amused by [... this] delightful piece of spoofing."[32]

That Thursday Julian popped down to London for the day. Whenever he was in town, usually for the purpose of collecting review copies and cash payments from *Punch* or *The TLS*, he relished popping in to the Stag's Head, the Mandrake, the Gargoyle, the Caves, the French, or the Freelance — a small drinking-club on Romilly Street — where he looked up old friends like Raynor Heppenstall, Reggie Smith, Conan Nicholas, and Tony Van den Burgh. But the principal purpose of this particular visit was to attend a meeting with what he called "the Telly Boys":[33] a meeting that marked the beginning of his disenchantment with them.

He was drinking in one of his favourite pubs that afternoon when, only ten minutes before closing-time, he caught sight of a beguiling blonde, who reminded him strongly of his sister. Wearing a short fur coat and a green scarf, her long hair "done like Laura",[34] the eponymous heroine of the Hollywood movie, she was hovering on the periphery of his group of drinking buddies. Instantly attracted to this intriguing stranger, he manouevred himself into the space next to her and, in a soft voice, said, "You're very beautiful. I'm sorry I didn't catch your name..."[35]

"Oh, you don't have to do that to me," she replied, her delivery "hostile and abrupt",[36] her eyes focused on the floor.

"But honestly I didn't catch it," he protested.

Still staring downwards, she said, "You know perfectly well who I am."

"But I don't." He felt a surge of "dawning fear"[37] as she muttered her name. It was Sonia Orwell. Now in her late thirties, her old allure was, for Julian, undiminished by the pudginess that encased her once photogenic features. "My God, I'm awfully sorry," he said, astonished at how much she'd altered in the eight years since they'd last met, an air of unassailable self-confidence having transformed her. "I really wouldn't have known you."

"I've changed so much...?" she replied anxiously.

"Oh, for the better. Don't worry about that. For the better." On that note, he turned back to his friends. He sensed she was staring at him, but she didn't speak to him again. And when the pub closed a few minutes later, she left without saying goodbye.

Her fractious response to him didn't undercut the powerful physical attraction he felt towards Sonia. Contrary to the expectations engendered by all the uncomplimentary tittle-tattle he'd heard about her lately, he also found that he "genuinely like[d] her"[38] in this brusque and assured new guise. Yet beneath her manner, he discerned someone who shared his hidden vulnerability, someone he should "look after".[39] Just when he thought he was done with romance, entrenched as he was "behind his curtness and formality [...] his unsmiling mask",[40] his earlier infatuation was reawakened and intensified, love coming "in the manner of most heart-attacks [...] like a piercing shaft of pain [...] at the moment when he least expected it."[41]

If any event in his personal and professional life can be said to have been pivotal, this was it. When he arrived back at his bedsit during the early hours, he wrote to the Davins about Sonia, the excitement causing his handwriting to degenerate into an uncharacteristic scrawl. In his note, he proclaimed that, for him, "all dates now originate from the [...] day [...] on which I met HER."[42]

On the evening of Day 4 of the new Sonia-centric calendar, he went round to the Davins to tell them more about his encounter. Lingering over her name like a magician mouthing an incantation, he referred to her as "So-nia",[43] his pronunciation copied from the woman herself. The Davins listened patiently, their tolerance meriting a thank-you letter. "I suppose that something like this was bound to happen to me, at my dangerous age,"[44] he confessed, adding that he was "a romantic fool in the grip of an impossibly lyrical attachment."[45] Aware of how much of a nuisance he was becoming, he signed himself, "Bloody old Julian."[46]

Leading up to Christmas, he was in the Victoria with Dan and Winnie when he had to leave early, suffering from a recurrence of the piles that had troubled him intermittently for at least the last two years. Back at his bedsit, he had no food, no cigarettes, and no money to buy fresh supplies. With nothing to take his mind off his excruciating affliction, he found it hard to get any work done, though he persevered for several days. He was soon so weak that he was unable to walk without feeling dizzy. At length he gave in and took to his bed, from where he composed a plaintive note to Dan, delivered by his helpful landlord. It asked Dan to send round a doctor, because he needed a shot of morphine to numb the pain.

Reluctantly condemned to bed for a full week, during which he slipped even further into arrears with his work, Julian wrote more notes to the Davins, appealing for books, cigarettes, and food. Though Julian's extravagance and solipsism irked Winnie, who proclaimed that she could run their entire household for a fortnight on the money he squandered in the space of a day or two, she was too altruistic to ignore his pleas. Her response was to gather together parcels of goodies for him and cook him hot meals which she wheeled down the road in her bicycle basket.

But the Associated TeleVision Company were not so sympathetic. On Christmas Eve Julian received a letter from them, informing him that they'd docked a week's wages from his salary. This left him perilously short of cash. Again, the Davins took pity on him and invited him to spend Christmas with them. It was to prove "a very happy time."[47]

As soon as the Associated TeleVision Company's offices reopened after the holiday, Julian lodged a complaint about the way they'd treated him, the consequent row accentuating his disillusionment with the job. Had it not been for his enforced break, he would have met his end-of-year deadline for the Maigret translation, which Hamish Hamilton planned to publish in April 1955 as part of a two-novel compilation. Putting off the operation he needed to cure his piles, Julian submitted the final two chapters only a couple of days later than specified in his contract. Before Hamish Hamilton was prepared to pay him the remainder of his fee, however, he had to correct the typescript, sent through to him piecemeal, his financial position meanwhile deteriorating.

Even at this late stage, his disagreement with Mme Simenon hadn't been resolved. Obstinately ignoring all his previous advice, she suggested the novel should be called *Maigret and Lanky Liz*. On Thursday 6 January 1955, his annoyance threatening his amicable relationship with Hamish Hamilton, he wrote to Richard Brain saying, "I must dissociate myself from 'Lanky Liz', and have some kind of prefatory note, saying that this title — and the nickname — are the choices of

Mme Simenon, as I simply can't afford to have reviewers pouncing on me for this, when the book comes out. They're bound to, if only because of the parody, which most of them will have seen."[48]

Relieved though Julian must have been to escape from the meddlesome Mme Simenon, the completion of his translation work in mid-January left him with a much reduced income. To supplement his earnings from scriptwriting and from producing parodies for *Punch*, he made an effort to pick up more book-reviewing work. From Tony Powell, he secured a regular commission from *Punch* for at least one short signed review every week. And from John Lehmann, he landed a commission for a longer piece, scheduled to appear in the *London Magazine*. Already a fan of the poet Roy Fuller's prose work, he chose to write a retrospective appreciation of his two detective novels.

With characteristic profligacy, the contents of his wallet melting "like snow in the hot hands of a child",[49] Julian celebrated the payment of his fee for the Fuller article with another Saturday night blow-out at the Royal Oxford. Afterwards he had arranged to meet the Davins in the Victoria Arms. But only Winnie was there. Feeling let down by what he saw as Dan's "selfish frailty",[50] he vented his indignation by writing him another self-righteous letter. "I arrived at the Victoria last night at 9.00, having bolted my dinner in order to be in time," he wrote, "only to be told by Winnie — at 9.30 — that you had 'retired to bed': an explanation which seemed not only inadequate but ironical to a man who'd been nearly two days without sleep. I can't help feeling it might have been more thoughtful to have telephoned either the Royal Oxford or the Victoria and told me that a subsequent appointment with Morpheus prevented you from being there."[51]

Early in March, just over three months into his contract with the Associated TeleVision Company, Julian had an irreparable falling out with them. It was a job he could ill-afford to lose, yet he rashly handed in his resignation.

His only income was now from his book-reviewing. Perhaps with the intention of extracting a cash payment from Tony Powell, he arranged to go down to London on Thursday 31 March. While he was there, he went for a drink with Roy Fuller who, grateful for the flattering comments in his article, published in the previous month's edition of the *London Magazine*, had contacted him. Evidently on his best behaviour, Julian resisted the temptation to borrow money from the dignified, rigidly conventional, smartly dressed Fuller, whose obvious affluence stemmed not from his literary career but from a senior post in the legal department of the Woolwich Building Society.

At 6.00pm that evening, Julian popped round to John Lehmann's house, anxious to solicit his friend's opinion on his brief encounter with Sonia, about whom he was still brooding. John invited him in, and poured him a drink, over which he started to explain what had happened. Though he was careful to edit Sonia's name from the story, John immediately guessed her identity. Not that John knew her well. He did, however, know that she worked for the publishers, Weidenfeld & Nicolson. Hearing this, Julian hatched a plan that would allow him to kill "two birds with one s. [sic]"[52]

Next morning he rang her at work, his plan being to charm her and to obtain advances on *Not Good Enough For Punch*, plus his next two volumes of autobiography. But she wasn't in the office, so he left his name and said he might ring back later. For fear of appearing off-puttingly eager, he resisted the urge to call her again for almost a fortnight. Second time round, he got straight through to her. Neither of them alluded to their previous awkward encounter. All her earlier hostility apparently diffused, she sounded delighted to hear from him. And when he brought up his business proposal, she seemed interested in it. She said she'd give him a response within seven days.

Under the pretext that he wanted to find out if she'd reached a verdict, he rang her the following week. But a decision hadn't yet been made. Still, he suggested they go out to lunch to discuss his proposal. Her voice conveying the impression that she was "pleased and even enthusiastic"[53] about the idea, she said she'd be happy to have lunch with him whenever he wanted. Overjoyed but still cagey, his amorous objectives disguised by a businesslike pose, he told her that he'd contact her to fix up a meeting soon.

Later that same day, he sent her an outline of *Not Good Enough For Punch*. In the covering letter he made a provisional arrangement to see her when he was in town the week afterwards. By then, though, he was so broke he couldn't afford to go down to London and "entertain [her] in the manner to which [he] thought she'd be accustomed."[54] He had, in any case, become convinced that he shouldn't meet her again until he'd conceived a proper plan of campaign and saved up enough money to buy himself a new suit. So he wrote to her to postpone their lunch.

He kicked off his fund-raising drive by trying — unsuccessfully, as it turned out — to persuade *Punch* to buy *Ginger*, an old army story of his in which a fellow conscript cunningly contrives to get himself dismissed from the services. He also wrote *The Bird Man*, a reminiscence about his boyhood acquaintance with an eccentric bird-breeder who lived in an abandoned windmill near St André. When he submitted it to *The London Evening Standard*, they returned it unread. And when he sent it to another publication, they rejected it on account of what they considered its unnecessarily cruel ending.

His financial and romantic hopes were now pinned on the prospect of Hamish Hamilton commissioning him to translate another Simenon novel. To raise the possibility, he phoned Richard Brain, who promised to discuss it with Mr Hamilton. In the meantime, Julian was busy going through the proofs of his self-deprecating memoir of his encounter with Frank Harris. On Friday 27 April he sent the corrected version to Sonia, together with a letter explaining that it would give her a taste of the intended flavour of the second volume of his autobiography.

That weekend he received a note from Richard Brain saying the next batch of Simenon novels had already been commissioned. In passing, Brain mentioned that *Maigret and the Burglar's Wife* — the title given by Julian to his translation — had been rescheduled for autumn publication as a single novel.

Because he wanted to be near Sonia, and because his current lack of work emphasised his geographical isolation from the literary world on which he depended, Julian began talking about moving back to London. The work situation had, however, improved by the spring. Soon he was "up to [his] eyes with more commissions than [he'd] had for years."[55] *Punch* paid him to write numerous short reviews; several parodies, among them a mischievous burlesque of *The TLS*; a short story about a character clearly modelled on Tambimuttu (who had long since left the country);[56] and an amusing account of his experiences as a book reviewer. Added to which, he penned a couple of expansive reviews for the *London Magazine*. With the earnings from these, he planned to go down to London in mid-May and "start [his] little seige"[57] of Sonia.

It was around then that he was offered some additional work by J.R. Ackerley, Literary Editor of the BBC's well-respected weekly magazine, *The Listener*. Ackerley, who admired his contributions to the *London Magazine*, wanted him to take over the *New Novels* column for three months, starting in June. Attracted by the 15 guineas-per-issue fee, the promised absence of editorial interference, and the £4 to £5-a-week extra he could make by selling his review copies, Julian wasted no time in writing to Ackerley to accept the invitation.

His work for *The Listener* raised his earnings back to a healthy level. It also gave him a convenient platform from which to demonstrate his many virtues as a critic, not least an indifference to literary fashion and a talent scout's instinct for discerning genuine flair. Indeed, he was among the first British reviewers to recognise the potency and originality of Flannery O'Connor.

As his journalistic commitments multiplied, the accompanying burden of the attendant deadlines mounting, Julian grew more dependent on his green bombs to enable him to cope. Their sleep-depriving side-effects, combined with his continued Sonia fixation, led him to fear he was heading for a "crack up".[58] So convinced was he that he'd fallen into a trap laid by Sonia, her sole purpose being to inflict as much suffering on him as she could, he aborted his planned trip to London to see her.

The only way he could free himself from his obsession, he came to believe, was by "settl[ing] down and concentrat[ing] on a book to the exclusion of all else."[59] His inability to do just that was blamed on the distractions of Oxford. He therefore persuaded himself that everything would be alright if only he was living somewhere else. It occurred to him that his friend Gerry Fisher's cottage might provide the ideal bolt-hole. Hopeful of coming to some arrangement with Gerry, he spent the last weekend of May there. But his friend baulked at the idea of having him as a lodger. And so, Julian was left marooned in Oxford.

Hy Hazell (left)
and Lee Patterson
in *The Key Man*,
1957
(© The Ronald
Grant Archive)

Rod Cameron (left)
in *Escapement*
(a.k.a. *The Electronic
Monster*), 1958
(© The Ronald
Grant Archive)

A Face in the Dark

The strength of his infatuation prevailing over his suspicions about Sonia's motives, Julian couldn't resist contacting her again. Affecting what he regarded as his "formal, business voice",[1] he rang her on Wednesday 2 June 1955 and proposed they meet for lunch sometime the following week. "Tuesday would be lovely,"[2] she replied, her manner "very friendly",[3] if "a little timid."[4] In an apologetic tone, she went on to reveal that her boss had decided against publishing the comic miscellany Julian had been touting, though she said the firm was still interested in acquiring the rights to the next two volumes of his autobiography. To his surprise and consternation, she then enticed him "into a murmuring intimate conversation of the sort one has with girlfriends of long standing [...] the sort of phone-talk that usually ends with 'I love you.' [...] ('Where are we going to meet?' 'This railway strike's on. Times of trains from Oxford are so uncertain.' 'But you'll come in the morning?' 'I'll do my best.' 'I'll wait for you. When will you ring?' 'When I get there.' 'As soon as you get there? Your very first call?' 'Yes.' 'Promise?')"[5]

Running through things in his head afterwards, he wondered whether she was "forcing the pace"[6] in a callous plot to make him admit his romantic intentions, only to inflict a humiliation by turning him down. These fears combining with his annoyance at her firm's rejection of his book, he considered sending her a curt note cancelling their date. When he discussed the situation with Dan later in the day, Dan — clearly fed up with the whole business — delivered a grim-faced ultimatum. You're going to your lunch-date, he warned Julian, "even if [I] have to knock [you] out and put [you] on the bloody train [myself]".[7]

But Julian fell seriously ill that night, his robust constitution buckling under the strain of his unrequited passion, not to say relentless deadlines, lack of sleep, alcoholism, and a diet mainly consisting of cheese and biscuits, interspersed by the occasional rich meal at the Royal Oxford. Bed-ridden and delirious, his neck stiff and swollen, his jawline disfigured by a huge, unremittingly painful boil that made it impossible for him to sleep, he lay in his room for two days. The Davins' doctor diagnosed blood-poisoning, a diagnosis that ruled out his meeting with Sonia. Unwilling to countenance this, Julian sought a second opinion. According to the other doctor, he was suffering not from blood-poisoning but from a carbuncle which made travelling "out of the question for fourteen days at least."[8] The second doctor, who insisted on monitoring his condition with daily visits, prescribed six *M & B* (an early version of antibiotics), plus six codeine tablets-a-day to ease the discomfort, these augmented by a penicillin injection every fortnight. In order to ensure their effectiveness, Julian was told to avoid alcohol. He was, however, too dependent on it to defer to doctor's orders. Before long, he'd knocked back half-a-bottle of brandy "and started to roar with laughter that the great dream might end like [this], as a bad joke that was on [him]."[9]

The delirium had abated by Sunday, enabling him to write to Sonia informing her that they'd have to delay their meeting due to illness. Within a few days of contacting her, he'd rallied sufficiently to get out of bed. Staggering down the road to the pub, he fell into conversation with a local businessman. Together they drank so much he ended up with a hangover of such percussive ferocity he retreated to bed again.

Next day the carbuncle burst, leaving behind a gaping sore which made it hard for him to shave that side of his jaw. Since he was so fastidious about his appearance that he wouldn't set foot outside without shaving, he found himself confined to his room until the sore had healed over.

His recovery was far faster than predicted. Indeed, he was well enough by the weekend for the doctor to sanction a trip to Gerry Fisher's cottage, where he'd arranged to convalesce. So he wrote to Sonia to let her know the good news, and to suggest they meet a week on Monday or Tuesday.

That Friday he travelled down to the cottage, from where he rang round the London hotels to book himself a room. By checking into a hotel for the night preceding his lunch with Sonia, he intended to avoid the necessity of getting up too early. But none of the hotels had any vacancies until Tuesday at the earliest. Still ensconced at Gerry's place, he called Sonia at work on Monday to notify her of the enforced change of plans.

They agreed to meet at 1.00pm on Wednesday 22 June at Hatchett's, a luxurious and pricey restaurant on Piccadilly. Sonia said she'd like to use the opportunity to discuss his envisaged volumes of autobiography. Inadvertently, though, she let slip that she hadn't read *The Weeping and the Laughter*. His "recent illness [having] made [him] more irascible than ever",[10] he was so affronted by her perceived lack of interest in his work he "quite forgot that [he] was in love with her"[11] and became sharp and patronising, addressing her not as Sonia but as "Miss Brownell".[12]

After a couple of hours, his pique had faded. In its place, there was a sickening sense of regret at having needlessly sacrificed the date he'd coveted ever since he re-encountered Sonia. Hoping his display of bad temper hadn't alienated her, he phoned her back. Luckily he succeeded in repairing the damage he'd inflicted.

To prevent her from seeing the desperation in his eyes, he turned up at Hatchett's in his mirror-sunglasses. He was already encamped at the champagne bar when Sonia arrived. She casually wriggled onto a stool "a fair distance"[13] from him and placed her handbag on the counter in just the way both Monica and Barbara used to do, though "she wouldn't look at [him] at first."[14] Clutching her glass in both hands, she became cheerful and animated. For the next hour they drank and chatted amicably, their conversation undiluted by even the merest reference to the business they were meant to be discussing. Yet he stuck to his "incredibly cautious"[15] tactics. In his determination not to disclose his feelings for her, feelings he still suspected she might exploit, he restrained himself from so much as touching her hand or making "any pass, verbal or otherwise."[16]

It was just after 2.00pm when they were shown through to their table in the main part of the restaurant. Over lunch, Julian kept replenishing her wine-glass, the alcohol exerting no discernable effect on her. To avoid impeding his own judgement, he meanwhile "hardly drank any wine at all",[17] at least not by his dipsomaniacal standards. Throughout the meal Sonia "was quite warm, human and friendly, even affectionate"[18] towards him, frequently "asking [his] advice and opinion on various things."[19] And several times she manouevred the conversation in a more flirtatious direction with lines like "I suppose you feel alone even now."[20] Captivated though he was by her newfound strength of personality, her ability to "hold her own with [him] on any ground (including drinking),"[21] and her enduring beauty, which "struck him silent and dumb, like that of the Medusa",[22] Julian always changed the subject, lest he compromise his non-committal stance.

They were still at their table, enjoying a post-prandial brandy, at 4.15pm. Her reluctance to curtail their tête-à-tête convinced him that she reciprocated his feelings for her. Certain he'd accomplished his prime objective, he raised the question of Weidenfeld & Nicolson publishing the next two instalments of his autobiography. He proceeded to show her the outlines of these, but he "never got the impression that she was interested in the business end at all."[23]

As they were leaving the restaurant a few minutes later, she told him that "she'd like to meet him again, regardless of whether her company took him on as one of its authors."[24] In the taxi they shared afterwards, he made a bid to prove his credentials as a serious writer by showing her the synopses of his next two novels. And he also talked about his screenwriting plans which she appeared to find far more impressive. By the time she slid out of the taxi, he "thought [he'd] got her under [his] spell."[25]

Always keen to recycle his experiences in his writing, he hatched the idea of turning his grand passion for her into a short novel and a screenplay — to be called *The Girl in the Spotlight*.

At her request, Julian phoned Sonia at the office on Tuesday 28 June to find out whether or not her employers wanted to buy the books he'd offered them. When he spoke to her, she was in the middle of an important meeting, so she said she'd call him back, which she did later that day. "Envelop[ing] the whole thing in mystery",[26] she told him that the proposed deal had "gone wrong"[27] for reasons she was reluctant to discuss over the phone. She wanted, instead, to see him again and talk through what had happened. "In [his] kindest most reassuring voice — never known to fail because so seldom heard,"[28] he said "she wasn't to worry, nor was [he] angry with her."[29] He then fixed up a rendezvous with her at 6.00pm the following day, the venue to be decided.

Devotedly traipsing back down to London, he registered at a hotel. That day he rang her to ask where she'd like to meet. She sounded extremely upset, and said she couldn't make it "owing to a sudden personal disaster".[30] She asked him to ring her again next day. In the hope he might, after all, be able to see her, he extended his stay in the capital. When he rang Sonia, he was annoyed to hear she couldn't make it that evening either, though she said she'd like to go for a drink with him when he was next in town.

Bewildered by the way she seemed "simultaneously to beckon and to flee from him",[31] he sought advice from John Lehmann, whom he visited later in the afternoon. He was astonished to discover Sonia, knowing John was a close friend of his, had recently been round there too, fishing for information about him. John remarked on how she was in an "odd state",[32] and urged Julian to ring her at home that evening.

He didn't, however, take his friend's advice, preferring to return to Oxford and wait for *her* to contact him. Several days later, he received a very polite letter from Sonia, "regretfully turning down"[33] the books they'd discussed. He used this as an excuse to send her "what [he] thought was a very nice note, offering help if she needed it for her personal trouble"[34] and enquiring when she'd be free to meet him for the drink she mentioned last time he spoke to her. Since there was no reply to his note, he wondered whether it might, like a recent parcel of review copies from *Punch*, have gone astray.

On his next trip down to London on Tuesday 19 July, he took Sonia at her word and phoned her to ask her out. But she gave him "the cold shoulder; made a few faintly derisive remarks [...] and rang off abruptly."[35]

While he was in London, he met up with John Davenport who said he'd seen her at a party earlier in the month. Apparently she'd made a point of telling Davenport about Julian's infatuation with her and how she didn't know what to do about it. Under the relentless scrutiny to which Julian subjected her every action, he reasoned that "a girl of Sonia's looks"[36] must be accustomed to fighting off admirers. Such talk, he concluded, must therefore be no more than a tactical ploy. With skewed, self-deceiving logic, he convinced himself that the notoriously tactless Davenport, who "always made a mess of everything",[37] must have blurted out something which was responsible for the way Sonia's attitude towards him had suddenly "crystallised into antagonism".[38]

It was probably that evening, just before taking his usual late train home, that Julian consoled himself with a trip to a nightclub where the blind pianist Stanley Hume was performing. A regular in the Soho pubs when not drifting round Europe like some latterday troubadour, Hume got chatting to Julian, who commissioned him to write and record the music to *The Girl in the Spotlight*. As soon as he had a tape of it, Julian imagined playing it to Sonia "over the phone at 2am."[39]

In its scary intensity, its matter-of-fact folly, his infatuation with her was starting to echo the murderous obsession at the heart of one of his most cherished novels — Patrick Hamilton's *Hangover Square*. Primed, perhaps, by the way that those who knew Sonia likened her power over people to that of an enchantress, he jumped to an absurd conclusion. Because she was the antithesis of the type of girl he normally went for, being neither "very young"[40] nor a brunette, he talked himself into believing that she was a witch who'd put a spell on him. Love now mingled with fear, superstition compelling him to avoid any mention of her name "in case it tightened her hold over him."[41]

Though he had a reviewing assignment from John Lehmann to distract him, Sonia continued to dominate his thoughts. His mania was fed by a letter he received from John, informing him that she'd been round again, seeking advice on how best to fend off his amorous interest. Disturbed by this revelation, he went over to the Davins to discuss it. In describing his feelings to Winnie, he quoted Charles

Causley's poem, *Ballad of the Five Continents*, the closing lines of which he'd come to associate with Sonia: "I am the Prince / I am the lowly / I am the damned / I am the holy / My hands are ten knives. / I am the dove / Whose wings are murder. / My name is love."[42]

Coincidentally, the following day he received a fan-letter from Causley, whom he'd never met. He wrote back asking if it would be okay for him to use that part of his poem as the epigraph for a future novel. Flattered, Causley gave "the lines in question to [him] as a sort of present".[43]

Julian repaid the Davins' for their willingness to listen to his problems by agreeing to escort their two younger daughters, eleven-year-old Delia and nine-year-old Brigid, down to London when he next went there on Tuesday 26 July. But he was too busy mooning over Sonia to pay any attention to either of the girls. Instead, he devoted the journey to composing some lachrymose lyrics to accompany one of the tunes Stanley Hume had written for him.

In town that lunchtime he bumped into Monica, now happily married and friendly, bearing no apparent grudge against him. Playing up to his vanity, to his pride in the youthful darkness and density of his hair, she remarked that he "looked exactly the same as when she first saw [him] in 1943".[44] He used the opportunity to tell her all about his current romantic woes and to canvas her opinion on Sonia's motives, an opinion he valued because Monica was a woman who "knows her way about".[45] She replied that Sonia sounded as if she was simply aiming to add him to her collection of "scalps".[46]

Possibly inspired by the gravity with which Monica had addressed the situation, he contacted Barbara in order to find out what she thought about Sonia, too. It was less than a year since she'd left him, but in that time the hitherto callow twenty-six-year-old Barbara had, to his eyes, acquired a sheen of sophistication. She assured him that any woman who went round talking about him to his friends must be interested in him. Speaking with unaccustomed bluntness, she said "it was silly, boring behaviour anyway."[47]

Back in Oxford, his separation from Sonia fertilising his antipathy towards the city and increasing his determination to return to London on a permanent basis, he was gripped by Sonia-mania. His post-pub sessions with the Davins became tedious and embarrassing for his hosts, who had to listen to hour after hour of talk about how he planned to win her over, of analysis of her behaviour, focusing on subtleties imperceptible to anyone but him. Seeking to disrupt these epic ruminations, Dan took to entertaining their lively new kitten with a piece of string.

All the available evidence suggested Sonia was now "quite indifferent"[48] to him, yet he sensed that he "had made contact with her",[49] imbuing him with a residual faith in his ability to win her over. On Monday 8 August he sent an excited letter about her to Mac (who had recently reinvented himself as a writer of children's books). In the letter, he described Sonia as "a girl whom hard-headed, intelligent men say in all seriousness is a destroyer, and even a witch!"[50] Confident of a happy outcome to what he dubbed "an enormous emotional drama [...] with the girl fleeing mostly across London and asking my friends to save her from me,"[51] he wrote that "when the time comes, please send all appropriate wedding presents such as dried heads, wax dolls, voodoo drums, and a large cauldron to stew the children in (though I believe witches cant [sic] have any) c/o Satamax, London."[52]

To achieve his goal, he decided it was best for him to "sit tight"[53] and try to get things "clear in [his] mind before making any further moves."[54] As he explained to John Lehmann in a meandering letter, mostly devoted to an inordinately detailed exegesis of Sonia's "silly and injudicious, if not actually insane and monstrous"[55] behaviour, he had "two very strong feelings: (1) that she may quite simply approach [him] as though nothing had gone wrong, or (2) that she'[d] arrange for [him] to be somewhere she [was], and pick a flaming row [... which would] certainly end in floods of tears and a reconciliation."[56]

Some of the energy he'd been devoting to his pursuit of Sonia was, for the moment at least, redirected into his writing. During the entire middle week of August he concentrated on preparing his final review for *The Listener*. His work for Ackerley had become such a chore he was looking forward to being shot of it, even if it meant he'd be strapped for cash. To fill the shortfall in his finances and provide him with the £20 he needed for a deposit on a flat in London, he resumed his attempt to find a publisher for *Not Good Enough For Punch*, the title of which he'd altered to *Funny Things Happen*. His belief in its saleability unshaken by its recent rejections by both Methuen and André Deutsch, he submitted it to Constable, Patrick Hamilton's publisher.

Work didn't, however, take his mind off Sonia for long. Once he'd got his piece for *The Listener* out of the way, he headed down to London, where he spent Saturday talking about her with John Lehmann and cross-examining other friends and acquaintances who might have come across her. Lately he'd been wondering whether she'd met someone else, but his concerns were allayed by the news that nobody had heard anything about her having a boyfriend. Patience, he resolved, should now be his watchword.

But this was already running out by the following weekend. At 3.00am, after a night with the Davins, conducting a thorough analysis of Sonia's every move, he sat and wrote Winnie a long, sinister letter which he instructed her to destroy after she'd finished reading it. With crackpot candour, he confessed that things were getting "out of control"[57] and appealed to Winnie's sisterly instincts to help him avert Sonia's "destruction"[58] and "save her from what is coming."[59]

Desperate to be near her, he went to London again a few days later to inspect a centrally located mews flat which he intended to sublet from an acquaintance. But it turned out to be too squalid even for his tastes. In the tiny kitchen "plates were piled high with the remains of kippers and an army-issue shaving brush stood clotted with dried soap on the draining-board".[60]

Alongside his flat-hunting, he may well have met up with John Lehmann, to whom he wanted to talk about *The Girl in the Spotlight*. When the pubs closed that night, pining for even a glimpse of Sonia, he loitered outside her flat at 18 Percy Street — right on the edge of Fitzrovia. The street-lighting making his face look even more gaunt and sallow than usual, "he stared wistfully up at the darkened windows."[61]

His escape plans thwarted, he returned to Oxford, where the annual end-of-summer St Giles Fair was being staged. The hatred he felt for the city seems to have been temporarily deflected by the fair's garish presence, its haunted house, gaudy sideshows, and milling crowds lending a welcome dash of vitality to somewhere otherwise so subdued and austere.

He soon had other things to worry about apart from Sonia. Without his reviewing work for *The Listener*, he was broke. His last shilling had been swallowed by the electricity meter; his stocks of food and cigarettes had run out; his piles were threatening a recurrence; and there was no possibility of obtaining any money from either *Punch* or *The TLS* for at least two weeks. "I haven't been so worried in a long time, as all avenues seem to be closing down,"[62] he confided in Dan. After about a day-and-a-half of enforced fasting, he sent a note to Winnie, requesting "fags, bread and books."[63]

One obvious solution to his present problems, he felt, lay in a return to television scriptwriting. He had, after all, already picked up hints that there might be openings with companies other than Norman Collins's. And he sensed that he'd be in demand once his work had been screened. Yet previous experiences had put him off the idea altogether.

In an effort to raise the cash he so urgently needed, he wrote a short story about Sonia that he submitted to John Lehmann, who diplomatically informed him it was "not quite satisfactory in its present form."[64] And he made two more bids to sell *Funny Things Happen*, which had just been turned down by Constable. First, he offered a revised and expanded version of the book to Rupert Hart-Davis, who turned it down, too. Then, remembering an earlier hint that Hamish Hamilton might be prepared to consider a more diverse collection, he embarked on a lengthy reminiscence, intended both for inclusion in his book and for submission to *Encounter*. Though Hamish Hamilton had rejected the book once already, Julian wrote to Mr Hamilton, enclosing the amended contents-plan and an enthusiastic testimonial from Malcolm Muggeridge, praising him as "the best living parodist."[65] He even had the gall to reprise his original ruse by suggesting that the money from *Funny Things Happen* would finance the completion of *Business and Desire*. But the outcome was no different.

None of his schemes having raised any cash, he pawned the books that he had borrowed from Winnie. Because he had neither the necessary funds, nor the pawnbroker's ticket, which he mislaid, he was unable to redeem them.

Meanwhile, independent television had started to transmit programmes. Their schedule featured a regular Sunday evening slot for *Colonel March of Scotland Yard*, starring Boris Karloff in the title role.

Deprived of the lump-sum he had been gunning for, Julian was, once again, dependent on literary journalism. As well as dashing off short book reviews and scholarly essays, he produced extended parodies for *Punch*, the targets of which were authors he admired, such as William Faulkner, Raymond Chandler, H.E. Bates, and Patrick Hamilton. He also came up with the innovative, waggish concept of writing a profile of the fictional master-criminal, A.J. Raffles, that treated him as if he was a real person. Halfway through October, Julian submitted the piece to *Punch*, who accepted it. That week, he went down to London to collect his fee. Besides visiting the magazine's offices, he appears to have popped round to see John Lehmann, whom he was anxious to recruit for an "intermediary role"[66] in his "new plan for approaching the Girl (or at any rate producing a rapprochement)."[67] If he was "to prevent the death of [his] private dream,"[68] Julian admitted to John that he had to raise "extra finance"[69] to fund his return to London and the envisaged courtship. Knowing "this [was] a difficult time for [him],"[70] John was considerate enough to commission an essay on Patrick Hamilton, which

Julian had been mulling over for more than a year. John also gave him advice on finding a publisher for both *Funny Things Happen* and his next volume of autobiography, recent doubts about the financial viability of continuing to write books having been quoshed.

On Wednesday 26 October, just after he'd polished off his Patrick Hamilton article and received his payment from John, *Punch* featured his parody of H.E. Bates. Deploying an exhaustive knowledge of Bates's stylistic quirks, he poked fun at his transition from writing about aviation to writing about rural romance, the piece depicting Bates strapped into a mock-up of an aeroplane cockpit, the control panel replaced by a typewriter. But Bates didn't share the joke. He got in touch with Julian and told him he'd sue for libel if it was ever reprinted. Defiant and unapologetic, Julian announced that he had every intention of including it in the collection he planned to publish, and that Bates should go ahead and sue him if he wanted.

Only a week-and-a-half later Julian, demonstrating his unfortunate capacity for generating trouble, was involved in another confrontation. His adversary, on this occasion, was Dan Davin. Resentful of what he saw as the patronising way Dan — "now that he's a big shot with the Oxford University Press"[71] — felt he had the right to tick him off like an errant child, Julian picked an argument while they were drinking together in the Victoria. His friend retaliated by accusing him of being an egotist who made all his girlfriends unhappy. It may well have been then that Julian, smarting from the vehemence of his friend's counterattack, issued what Dan described as "a tight-lipped and brief challenge, offering [him] swords or pistols."[72]

The following day Julian wrote him a letter of apology, citing tiredness, unhappiness, and being "strung-up"[73] on amphetamines as the causes of his bad temper. Yet his intimacy with Dan didn't really recover, the role of confidant gradually being reassigned to the infinitely forbearant Winnie.

Julian himself was, as always, the principal victim of his own truculence. Without Dan's support, his life in Oxford became even less tenable. Glad of any opportunity to get away, he sloped off to London for two days in mid-November. There he handed in the manuscript of an essay on Jean Cocteau, commissioned by *The TLS*. And he attended a meeting, probably involving Edmund Hughes, the literary agent he'd engaged, and Elek Books, a small publishing house who were interested in bringing out *Funny Things Happen*.

Before returning home, he went on a heavy drinking jag. The resultant hangover was so violent that when he woke up the next afternoon and composed a letter to Mac, his usually unblemished handwriting, perhaps the most reliable barometer of the stress he was under, became slewed and swollen. The letter announced that he intended to leave Oxford the moment he'd tied up his business deal, from which he hoped to make "plenty of dough".[74] He also treated his old pal to a breathless resumé of his relationship with Sonia, whom he still dreamed of living with and devoting "all his time [...] to making [...] happy".[75] Self-dramatising as ever, he proclaimed that "Love comes at last to Julian, as it must to all men (and as death came to Charles Foster Kane)."[76] A hint of perverse, embattled pride seeping through, he informed Mac that "The girl is still running fast. She must have reached Thibet by now. I havent [sic] rung her up for four months. Patience — see?

"[...] The toughest and wisest blokes in London are speculating about the outcome. The betting's on me so far — though this is the most formidable girl I've ever met [...She has] thus far anticipated my every move and outwitted me."[77]

So overwhelming had his obsession with Sonia become, he now regarded her as "the most important thing in [his] life."[78] Moribund though their relationship was, he wanted to use it as the basis for a melodramatic novel called *My Name Is Love*, the title culled from Charles Causley's poem. In the synopsis he drew up, he cast himself as Mr Hyde, a forty-three-year-old film director who becomes besotted by the beautiful widow of a famous writer. And she was cast as "the imperious, golden-haired"[79] widow, Luna Morell, a Hollywood-style femme fatale, "whose upbringing and background remain[ed] so shadowy, and whose influence, even on the men who have loved her, seem[ed] so malign."[80]

It was not until the end of November that Julian's translation of *Maigret et la grande perche* finally hit the bookshops. Since he prided himself at that time in "almost never read[ing] the papers",[81] he was unaware of how the critics had reacted to it. Yet news soon filtered through to him that the fantasy writer, Maurice Richardson, a fellow Redondan titleholder and Soho acquaintance, had reviewed it in *The Observer*. When Julian phoned him to find out what he'd put in the review, Richardson said that "he thought [his] translation [was] the best one to be done of Simenon so far."[82]

If Julian had any lingering worries about its critical reception, these were dispelled by a letter from Richard Brain, which arrived early the following week. The reviews had generally been positive, Brain informed him, several of them echoing Richardson's praise. His spirits were lifted even further by the arrival of "a very amusing letter from William Faulkner."[83] Unlike H.E. Bates, Faulkner had enjoyed being the butt of his talents as a parodist.

The remaining weeks of 1955 proved productive. He wrote several reviews and an astute parody of Patrick Hamilton's freshly completed *Gorse Trilogy* for *Punch*. He penned a preface to *Funny Things Happen*, recently accepted for publication by Elek. And he sold *The Bird Man*, his much-rejected reminiscence, to *Encounter*. At some later date, he aimed to revise the piece, so it could be seamlessly incorporated into *Threnody on a Gramophone*, the retitled sequel to *The Weeping and the Laughter*, which Elek had agreed to publish. These were to form the first half of an autobiographical quartet revelling under the grandiose title, *Lost Atlantis*. The quartet's other volumes were to be *The Sea Coast of Bohemia*, covering his time in Bognor, and *Khaki and Cockayne*, portraying his army days and their carefree aftermath.

Such a plentiful supply of work should have enabled him to keep up with the rent on his bedsit. It should also have distracted him from Sonia. But it succeeded in doing neither. By Saturday 10 December, he was "terribly short"[84] of money. His undiminished passion for Sonia pushing him to the brink of madness, he frittered away valuable time devising publicity slogans for the film he hoped to make about their relationship, which he now planned to call — somewhat ominously — *Until the Day She Dies*. He imagined Sonia herself playing the starring role of Linda, a girl stalked by the menacing figure of "the Terror",[85] a part he had earmarked for himself. Hence the slogan, "The Picture With A Starless Cast, Whose Cast Is Terror Itself!"[86]

When he and Roy Fuller had the next of their intermittent get-togethers around then, he spent their lunch at Chez Victor, a well-known French restaurant on Wardour Street, gabbling away almost exclusively about what he had come to see as his "pretty well hopeless"[87] love for Sonia. His account "was as cross-cut and obscure as the most recherché of the kind of mystery film he liked."[88] Near the end of the meal, throughout which he'd worn his sunglasses, "he said suddenly: 'Don't look round. She has come in.' The implication was that this unachievable goddess had nevertheless some strange drive to pursue him. Was Mrs Orwell really in the restaurant? [Fuller] scanned the place as [they] went out, but the matter remained in doubt. Julian hailed his inevitable taxi, and went off."[89]

*

He was dreading Christmas which he knew would be lonely and miserable without the Davins' support. By contacting Mac and telling him that he'd be "completely alone"[90] in Oxford over the holiday period, he angled to obtain an invitation to spend the holiday with the Jaegers. But they'd already made other plans.

Just as Julian had feared, he ended up alone in his basement bedsit on Christmas Day, his gloom dispersed only by the timely arrival of a chatty letter from John Lehmann. Denied the customary Yuletide diversions, he set to work on a short memoir, tentatively entitled *From Highbury to Horizon*. Early on the morning of Thursday 29 December, "dead-tired"[91] after a night spent finishing off this latest piece, he wrote to John, offering it to the *London Magazine*: an offer John declined.

His obsession with Sonia still dominating his life and making it hard for him to sleep, he wrote some lyrics for another of the tunes he'd commissioned for *The Girl in the Spotlight*. These he conceived as "a sympathetic parody of the Cole Porter-Ted Lewis school,"[92] opening with the verses, "You're the face in the dark, / My one question-mark, / You're why I lie awake at break of dawn [...]"[93] True to the flavour of his lyrics, he was lying awake fretting about "various things"[94] at daybreak on Wednesday 11 January 1956 when he gave up trying to sleep and dashed off a note to Winnie Davin. Though it crossed his mind that she might consider the lyrics he'd written "absolutely puerile",[95] he enclosed both songs, and proposed he come round and sing them to her sometime.

Worried that his "prey [might] escape",[96] later that day he made another of his periodic day-trips to London. Before resuming his vigil outside Sonia's flat, he visited Elek's offices at 14 Great James Street to collect the money they were advancing him for *Funny Things Happen* and for a novel he'd arranged to deliver by the end of the year. He also kept an appointment with Harold Harris, Literary Editor of *The London Evening Standard*, who wanted him to contribute to their daily *Did It Happen?* feature, in which readers were presented with a supposedly factual story and then asked to guess whether they thought it had really happened.

Instead of submitting a fresh piece, Julian sent them *Ginger*, now entitled *Old Ginger Says Goodbye*. For this, they paid him 40 guineas. He could have used the money to settle his rent arrears, which had risen to £15, but he decided to pool it with his advance from Elek in order to underwrite his long-awaited return to London.

When he vacated his bedsit on Sunday 29 January, a relative of Mr Goodman's — whom Julian had never previously met — impounded his small stash of possessions, among them his beloved fountain-pen, as security against what he owed. Promising to make good his debt in weekly instalments, Julian left Oxford with nothing but his malacca cane and the clothes he was wearing.

Hyde and Seek

His regal manner probably nullifying any suspicion aroused by his lack of luggage, that Sunday Julian checked in to the imposing Park Court Hotel at 75 Lancaster Gate, close to the misty expanses of Hyde Park. It was an area he already knew from the period when he'd lived on the Bayswater Road. Two days after his arrival there, *The London Evening Standard* published his contribution to the *Did It Happen?* feature. Beside it, they printed a tightly cropped, postage stamp-sized picture of him, cigarette-holder in hand, his self-possessed posture betraying none of the awkwardness of someone who "hate[d] being photographed".[1] Satisfied he'd succeeded in conveying an air of suave, unsmiling villainy, he informed Winnie Davin that it would give her "some idea of how [he would] look as the Terror in *Until the Day She Dies*."[2]

Making the most of the hotel's facilities and, at the same time, conserving his cash, he often ate all his meals in the dining-room, the cost of these tacked onto his lengthening tab. Between meals, he rejoined the West End pub and club circuit. There he looked up old friends such as Tony Van den Burgh, who was struck by the way his experiences with Sonia had led to an embittered tone infiltrating his references to women. Despite Sonia's rumoured liaison with the painter and wealthy surrealist patron Roland Penrose, Julian continued to brood over her, secure in the conviction that, if only he could see her again, he'd win her love, his hopes fortified by remarks made by Tony Powell and John Lehmann. While Tony had said they were "made for each other",[3] John had, surely with a touch of sarcasm, described Julian's relationship with Sonia as "the greatest love story since Tristan and Isolde."[4]

As Julian disclosed in a letter to Winnie Davin, Sonia remained "the only one who will do".[5] In a move calculated to "bring her out of hiding and into [his] web",[6] he instructed Edmund Hughes to seek her permission to use a quotation from the late George Orwell's work as the epigraph to both his mooted film and a newly conceived radio adaptation of it. But the approach drew no response from her.

Julian's single-minded attachment to her didn't prevent him from consoling himself with a tall, blonde Austrian former actress named Thea, who worked as a club hostess, most likely in the Mandrake or Modernairs, a relatively new drinking club on Greek Street. For a week or so, around the beginning of February, she and Julian were lovers, their brief and, for him, unemotional relationship, marred by at least one quarrel that led to her departing on the verge of tears.

Late at night Julian imagined he was possessed by the malign personality of the Terror, who had a tendency to resort to violence under even the faintest provocation. Once he claimed to have "suddenly [taken] hold of a rude man in a club and half-throttled him with his own scarf".[7] And, on another occasion, he wrote that he found himself "stamping several times at intervals on the ankle of an outrageous scrounger",[8] sending Thea into "a merry peal of laughter".[9]

Wholly disillusioned though he'd become with life in Oxford, Julian soon started to miss the Davins and feel "secretly frightened and very much alone"[10] in London. Perhaps as a means of alleviating the loneliness, he got into the habit of sending numerous telegrams and making long phone-calls from the hotel, where he was running up a disconcertingly large bill.

With no money coming in, he was unable to keep his promise to repay his debt to Mr Goodman. His ex-landlord retaliated by refusing to forward letters. So Julian wrote to Winnie Davin on Saturday 4 February 1956 asking her to go round to Goodman's house, collect any waiting correspondence (ignoring anything from the Inland Revenue), and send it on to him. She did as he requested. Among the wad of letters he received, Julian was irritated to discover some proofs from *Punch* and a commission from *The TLS*, dating back almost a fortnight. In the interim, he knew it was bound to have been re-allocated to another writer: a loss he could ill-afford, especially now *Punch* had built up such a backlog of his parodies they were accepting no new ones.

That week or possibly the week before, dressed in the polo-neck sweater and belted faun overcoat he'd been wearing ever since his return to the capital, he met up with Keidrich Rhys for a lunchtime drink. The setting was El Vino, a combined off-license, restaurant, and wine bar at the Inns of Court end of Fleet Street, its location accounting for its popularity with journalists, its dark bar divided from the eating area by a low balustrade. When Julian inevitably dragged Sonia into the conversation, Keidrich did his best to quell his friend's fixation by coming out with a series of compromising disclosures about her: how she'd exploited Lynette, his ex-wife, how she wasn't the deb she pretended to be, how she was "a truly colossal snob".[11] And he warned Julian that he'd "never earn enough in a thousand years"[12] to fund her supposedly prodigal way of life.

Keidrich's revelations lending weight to what he already recognised as an irredeemable situation, Julian resolved to abandon his pursuit of Sonia, which had for so long blighted his life and work. To signal what he saw as the death of "his big dream",[13] he produced a six-page transcript of his enlightening conversation with Keidrich. He enclosed this with a letter of thanks to Winnie Davin for relaying his letters. The transcript was described as "positively [the] last instalment"[14] of "Julian Loves Sonia!",[15] "a thrilling serial story of heartache and intrigue".[16]

Just under a month after his letter to Winnie, on one of his habitual visits to the Mandrake, he heard that Dan had died. Distressed and shocked by the news that such a physically fit contemporary could have passed away, he rang Winnie. His voice modulated to a timbre of hushed solicitude, he enquired how she was.

Responding with briskness unsuitable to the tragic scenario, she asked Julian how *he* was.

"Don't let's talk about me," he said, "let's talk about Dan."[17]

Winnie was so taken aback by his unprecedented reticence, she sensed something must be wrong. The truth duly emerged. It turned out that Julian's informant in the Mandrake had been confused by seeing an obituary for an Irish politician by the name of W. Davin in that Friday's edition of *The Times*.

At precisely the wrong moment, the flow of commissions from *Punch* almost dried up, only a couple of novels coming his way for review. Handsomely paid as he was, such a reduced workload was insufficient to sustain his free-spending habits. During his stay at the Park Court Hotel, he had accumulated an £88 bill. Unable to pay it, he sneaked out of the building on Friday 9 March and moved across town to the gargantuan, far grander Strand Palace Hotel, diagonally opposite the Savoy Theatre, within easy reach of his favourite bars.

Prospecting for an alternative source of income, he made another stab at breaking into radio drama. Because he couldn't afford to risk investing a lot of time in a new piece that might not sell, he decided to adapt his *London Magazine* article about meeting Frank Harris into a 45-minute play. On Monday 12 March, the poet and BBC producer, Terence Tiller, someone he often socialised with in the Stag's Head, accepted it for broadcast on the Third Programme. By stressing how hard-up he was, Julian persuaded Tiller to circumvent the normal, long-winded payment procedure and hastily procure the entire fee for him.

Karl Halle — owner of the Park Court Hotel — had, meanwhile, tracked Julian down. That Wednesday Halle took out a writ against him for non-payment of his huge bill. Julian now had 14 days in which to set out any mitigating factors either in writing or through a solicitor. Instead, he tried to placate the court by paying off £8 of his debt. Anticipating that the authorities would pursue him, he changed addresses. His new one was a cheap hotel in Bloomsbury.

The prompt sale of his play about Frank Harris spurred him to approach the BBC with a more ambitious idea. On the off-chance that he might be able to barter the story of his obsession with Sonia for much-needed cash, he sent them the synopsis of *My Name Is Love*, together with a letter proposing they pay him to turn it into a radio serial under the title *The Girl In The Spotlight*. But the BBC wasn't interested. At which Julian turned to his other idea of using the same material as the basis for a screenplay. Like the novel, he envisaged it focusing on a beautiful young girl menaced by a sinister, leather-clad stranger on a motorbike, whose infatuation with her culminates in her murder. Far from being terrorised by him, Julian imagined her being attracted to the prospect of imminent death, the countdown to it displayed on a calendar that punctuates the film.

Depressed, alcoholic, and "almost mad",[18] his obsession with Sonia mushrooming, his tendency towards paranoia magnified by the side-effects of protracted amphetamine-dependency, he became convinced that a cabal of female novelists, most of whom he'd never even met, were conspiring against him by modelling their characters on him. When he ran into Bruce Bernard on Old Compton Street, just after the publication of Iris Murdoch's latest novel, *The Flight From The Enchanter*, he launched into a crazy, quickfire diatribe. "Iris Murdoch and her gang are after me," he informed the dumbstruck Bernard, "but they'll never catch me because my mirror-sunglasses make me invisible..."[19]

While he was based in Bloomsbury, he began to intersperse his afternoons in the Caves with sessions in the Horseshoe Tavern. It was there one afternoon in mid-March that he was introduced to the bespectacled, prematurely bald Irish writer Anthony Cronin. A long-time admirer of Julian's work, Cronin had recently been appointed Literary Editor of the flagging weekly magazine *Time and Tide*. Cordial though Julian was, complimenting Cronin on a couple of pieces he'd published, he went out of his way to emphasise his seniority by addressing him as "dear boy",[20] and sprinkling his speech with vaguely patronising references to "you young men"[21] and "people of my age".[22]

Before leaving the office that afternoon, Cronin had scooped up a copy of Aldous Huxley's newly published *Heaven and Hell*, which he hoped Julian might review. When he offered it to him, Julian — short of work as he was — only accepted it with a show of reluctance, implying that Cronin should have written to him first.

Sensing an iconoclastic streak in the young editor, both of whose previously praised articles were hostile to fashionable authors, Julian proposed Cronin should turn his fire on the weighty posthumous reputation of George Orwell. Since there was a study of his work due for publication, Julian urged Cronin to contact Alan Pryce-Jones at *The TLS* and offer to write a middle about him. Even though it wouldn't be signed, he assured Cronin that everybody in the trade would know who'd written it, and that there were "a lot of people waiting to see the end of [Orwell]."[23] Cronin approved of the idea because he considered Orwell to be over-rated, yet he was unwilling to allow himself to be manipulated. When he tried to discover the root of Julian's grudge against Orwell, he was told "that there were a great many things [he'd] learn as [he] went along."[24]

The day after this meeting with Cronin, Julian reviewed *Heaven and Hell*, a study of the hallucinogenic effects of mescalin, which he found "repetitious in the extreme".[25] He despatched his article to *Time and Tide's* offices on Bloomsbury Street, accompanied by a handwritten note requesting rapid cash payment. To tide him over until that came through, he resorted to the desperate expedient of visiting a pawn shop on Gray's Inn Road. There he parted with his two heirlooms from his father — his cane and fountain-pen (which had only just been rescued from his ex-landlord by Winnie Davin) — and possibly his overcoat. But he was still so broke he couldn't afford to pay his hotel bill. As a result, the management threw him out the following morning.

Later on, he phoned Cronin at work, told him he was flat-broke, and asked if there was any chance of him getting hold of at least part of the fee for the Huxley piece straightaway. Cronin explained "that *Time and Tide* was a stodgy journal, most of whose contributors were as a class rather stodgy people, not indigent literary gentlemen like [he and Julian]; that there was no procedure for getting money in advance of publication nor indeed for a week after that, and that there was nothing [he] could do."[26] In response, Julian "became quite high and mighty" and said that Powell, Pryce-Jones, Lehmann, and Spender "were all accustomed to pay him immediately on delivery of his copy."[27] If these men were prepared to do it, Julian enquired, why couldn't Cronin? Emphasising that he had no scope for manouevre, Cronin ploughed through his explanation all over again. Yet Julian was insistent that he should *try*. At Julian's suggestion, they were to meet in the Golden Lion on Dean Street at 5.30pm.

It was an odd choice of rendezvous. Though it was only a few doors down from Berlemont's, it could hardly have been more different. Unlike its near-neighbour, it had a reputation as a virtually all-male homosexual pub, where sailors and guardsmen could be picked-up for the euphemistic price of their "fare home". In practice, the homosexual clientele tended to congregate in the upstairs bar, the main part of the pub being frequented by a more varied crowd.

Cheerful despite everything, Julian was already there drinking brandy when Cronin arrived, full of apologies for his failure to extract any cash from the magazine's coffers. Instead of reproaching Cronin, he amiably brushed aside his regrets and started talking about his plans for the future and reminiscing nostalgically about the Forties. "Of course in those days I had the whip-hand," he recalled. "Sansom and I were quite as famous as all these Wains and Amises and people now. Mind you there wasn't as much paper about in those days, so we didn't get as much publicity and we didn't do as well financially."[28]

As the evening wore on, he launched into a tirade against the management of the hotel where he'd been staying. In recounting the sequence of events leading up to his eviction, he let slip that he now had nowhere to go. His revelation was delivered with unselfpitying candour, yet Cronin felt so sorry for him he offered to put him up.

When they'd knocked back their last drinks of the evening, they made the long tube journey to suburban Wembley, where Cronin lived with his wife Thérèse and their baby daughter. From Wembley Park station, they headed past row after row of identical neo-Tudor houses. The Cronins had recently rented a ground-floor flat in just such a building. On arriving there, Cronin prepared a bed for Julian on the settee in the small, over-furnished sitting-room which they otherwise never used.

Sometime during the night Julian woke up and began to read the big old family bible left behind by the flat's elderly former tenant. So deep was his continued obsession with Sonia, he imagined he only had to open the pages at random to discover what she was thinking of him. He stayed up most of the night studying haphazardly chosen passages, all of which, in his present state, seemed pertinent, none more so, perhaps, than the verse from *The Song of Solomon*: "Who is she that looketh forth / as the morning, fair as the moon, / clear as the sun, and terrible / as an army of banners."[29]

Agitated and impatient to share his discovery, next day he darted out of the sitting-room as soon as he heard the creak of footsteps. Still clutching the bible, he cornered his sleepy and bewildered host, who was getting ready to go to work. In explaining his discovery, he gave Cronin several demonstrations. These were, according to his host, "not unconvincing if you put the lady mentioned in the position of the Lord, stand-offish, but jealous and vengeful all the same, and therefore of course secretly interested."[30]

Julian further delayed Cronin with a wild monologue about Sonia: how she thought he was "one of those bohemians",[31] how she was sure he was "finished",[32] how "a lot of people [had] told her a lot of things about him",[33] and how "the general opinion that she held of him was something like the one Caroline Lamb had of Byron [...,] fascinated but afraid."[34] There followed "intimations of obscure vengeances, sudden appearances, daring coups, turnings of tables, even hints of abduction or worse."[35] With monomaniacal relish, he went on to tell the non-plussed Cronin all about *Until the Day She Dies*, the screenplay which he was writing. He talked as if it was already in production, its cast and director long since signed up. The role of Sonia would go to the plump-cheeked, pertly seductive leading lady Glynis Johns — a dead-ringer for Sonia in her youth. Julian himself would co-star opposite her, a motorbiker's leathers, gauntlets, helmet, and goggles enhancing the desired aura of menace. When he was not wearing those, he'd be dressed in dark glasses, carrying a cane and, like his father, walking with a limp.

Excusing himself, Cronin departed for the office. He left Julian sitting at the kitchen table telling the thin, fragile-looking Thérèse about the film. His description was augmented by designs for its poster, titles, and credits, lovingly sketched on so many sheets of paper they gradually covered the table. He was still there, still blethering on about it to the stupified Thérèse when her husband got back from work a good nine hours later.

Cuckoo-like in his habit of colonising other people's households, Julian soon made himself at home with the Cronins. Since he had no spare clothes with him, when his shirt needed changing he asked his host whether he could borrow one. Being a lot smaller than Julian, none of Cronin's shirts fitted him, so Julian ended up wearing a Cornish fisherman's jumper in lieu of a shirt, his long arms protruding from the sleeves.

Imprisoned in the flat by a bout of agoraphobia, Julian took to monopolising the shared telephone in the hall. To the embarrassment of the diffident Cronins and the annoyance of the spinster who lived with her ancient mother in the flat above, he spent inordinate amounts of time on loud, hectoring calls to agents, publishers, film producers, and their secretarial staff. In between calls, he'd sometimes pop back into the flat to update the Cronins on his conversations, or to flesh out scenes and dialogue from *Until the Day She Dies*. His lofty and belligerent telephone-manner got him nowhere, often provoking arguments that led to him making fierce yet vague threats. These were delivered in the name of Mr Hyde, one of the twin authorial surrogates in his screenplay.

Of late, he'd come to believe his personality was being hijacked by his protagonist's famous fictional namesake: the cane-wielding, luxury-loving Soho-ite, Edward Hyde, villain of Robert Louis Stevenson's great novella, *Dr Jekyll and Mr Hyde*, which provided such a perfect paradigm for Julian's moody, self-dramatising tendencies. Whenever "he was feeling particularly vengeful or sinister",[36] he took on the identity of his fictional alter ego. Like Dr Jekyll, whose height, heavy build, and drug-taking he duplicated, he would transform into the aloof, defiant, nocturnal, agoraphobic, and mysterious Mr Hyde.

Midway through that week, the woman in the upstairs flat was given a stack of cast-offs by her employer, the Boots chain of lending libraries. Among them was a copy of *The Weeping and the Laughter*. Having read and enjoyed it, her attitude towards Julian suddenly changed, respect replacing contempt. He "responded with mirthless, seignorial smiles and bows which she seemed to find perfectly acceptable",[37] though they chilled Cronin to the marrow.

Irrespective of the improvement in the weather, Julian stayed indoors, only venturing out one fine early spring day when Thérèse ushered him into the desolate front garden to show him a solitary crocus. But he bolted back indoors instantly, "declaring that for a lover like himself the sight was too sad."[38]

He was still in residence at the Cronins' about ten days after his unexpected arrival, his prolonged stay imposing a financial burden with which they couldn't easily cope. Then again, nor could they afford to give him a loan large enough for him to re-establish himself elsewhere. Too polite and benificent to ask him to leave, they found themselves serving as a reluctant audience for yet more tiresome soliloquies about Sonia, the inherent lack of drama accentuating the tedium. Nonetheless, Julian remained capable of being entertaining if he could be coaxed onto other subjects, such as "the sense of evil conveyed by Sidney Greenstreet in *The Maltese Falcon*".[39]

In an attempt to turn his extended visit to their advantage, the Cronins tried using him as a babysitter. At about 11.30pm that night, their daughter woke up and started crying. When Julian went to investigate, he discovered her nappy was wet. Since he had scant experience of babies, he took this to be a bad sign. Cradling her in his arms, he opened the front door and positioned himself in the doorway in the hope of getting advice or assistance from a passer-by. But nobody came to his rescue. The Cronins got home around midnight to find him standing there, panic-stricken, saying, "She's wet. She's wet, I tell you. There's something wrong."[40]

With only Anthony Cronin's small salary to support the entire household, they were extremely short of money by the end of March. In a belated gesture of self-denial, Julian spurned all offers of tea, coffee or beer, preferring to drink tap-water. That weekend dragged by, its rigours elongated by the Easter holiday. At one point Julian, in a loopy bid to raise morale, led his hosts in prayers to Sonia: "She is kind at heart. She will send money."[41]

Their prayers remained unanswered, yet things perked up. On the Tuesday after Easter, Julian phoned Tony Powell, who offered to let him review a new American novel for *Punch*. But there was one big snag. And that was Julian's sudden, neurotic conviction that he couldn't write with anything except the Hooded Terror. To generate the cash necessary to redeem it from the pawn shop, Cronin sold some review copies. While he was at work next day, his wife fetched both the pen and the novel. Barely skimming through it, Julian sat at the kitchen table and dashed off the requisite thumbnail review. Accommodating as ever, Thérèse then delivered this to *Punch*'s offices, where Julian had arranged for her to cash his waiting cheque. When Cronin got back from work, Julian reimbursed him with the cost of retrieving the pen.

Julian's agoraphobia temporarily vanquished by the prospect of a night's drinking, he took Cronin out to a pub near Wembley Park station. There he bought them both brandies. Instead of riding the tube into the West End, he summoned a taxi, though the fare was bound to be exorbitant. The tube "is all very well for you young men starting out, but it won't do for chaps like me," he declared grandly, his warped self-image as an affluent writer reasserting itself. "I've been in the game a long time and I'm too old for that sort of thing."[42]

After the pubs closed the following night, he travelled all the way back to Wembley Park, the plan being that he'd resume his sojourn with the Cronins. From there, he phoned them, just to let them know he'd returned. On hearing what, he thought, was the click of his friend lifting the receiver, he said, "Hullo, Cronin? This is Maclaren-Ross here."[43] But he was greeted by a disconcerting silence, which prompted him to assume there was a fault on the line.

Unwilling to exploit his friends' hospitality without speaking to them first, he found himself a bench in the park beside the tube station and spent a cold, uncomfortable night there. Determined to avoid a repetition of this, he lobbied successfully for more reviewing work at *Punch*, the earnings from which were instrumental in him setting up home at the Celtic Hotel on Guilford Street, back on his old Russell Square beat, no more than a ten-minute taxi-ride from Soho.

About a week later, his cane at his side, his buttonhole adorned by a pink carnation, his teddy-bear coat draped round his broad shoulders, he was wiling away the afternoon over a glass of wine in the Caves when he encountered Anthony Cronin again. "I am Mr Hyde today," he announced. "You must call me Mr Hyde." Turning to Secundo Carnera, the barman, he called out, "Have there been any messages for Mr Hyde?"

"No Joolian, no messages for Mr Hyde, so far,"[44] Secundo replied.

When Julian told Cronin about his phone-call and how he'd been inexplicably cut off, Cronin tut-tutted, but kept quiet about what had really happened. At the sound of Julian's voice, he had carefully placed the receiver on the table and muffled it with a rug.

Early one Friday afternoon near the end of April, Julian walked into the Caves and made his way down the bar, superstitiously averting his gaze from the painting of a headless white horse. As he took his usual spot, he noticed a slim, attractive girl sitting on the adjoining stool, smoking a cigarette, her big blue eyes staring straight ahead, her appearance and nonchalant, self-composed mien redolent of Sonia. In all his innumerable visits to the Caves, he'd never seen her there before, though he gradually realised that she had, as a rebellious teenager, been part of Tambi's entourage just after the war.

What first caught his attention was her dyed honey-blonde hair. Unlike most girls who went for fashionably short crops, which Julian considered unbecoming, she "wore hers more than shoulder-length, curling to a point"[45] down the back of her dark red dress. Introducing himself as Mr Hyde, he chatted her up. Then he bought her a drink, served by Jenny, the club's new owner, a vivacious, heavily made-up woman who had taken to calling him "dear", except "when it came to paying up: the passage of money acquiring the rigid formality of any serious rite."[46] A fresh glass of wine in hand, the blonde girl's initial reserve fast evaporated. She said her name was Diana (though she spelt it as "Diane") Bromley, the surname a relic of a recently failed marriage. She revealed that she was twenty-nine years old, and had a daughter. Normally Julian steered clear of "young women with family responsibilities".[47] For her, though, he was prepared to make an exception. A little later on, he invited her to join him when he transferred to the Mandrake.

Until she got up from the bar-stool, he wouldn't have realised she was quite as lanky as she was. Even without the high heels she favoured, she was slightly taller than him. Aside from their height, he soon discovered he had a lot in common with her. Like him, Diana was a heavy drinker and an afficionado of the Soho scene. She too conveyed an air of tarnished gentility, earning her, in bohemian circles, the nickname of "the Duchess". She too had lived abroad, Kenya in her case. She too had an adventurous attitude to life. She too had a literary background, hers supplied by both her widowed mother, who had published a memoir of their experiences in the wartime Auxiliary Territorial Service, and Leonard Woolf, who was her maternal uncle. She too was no stranger to the world of midnight flits and angry creditors. And she too had constructed an identity independent of the one she'd been born with, her original name and Jewish faith having already been jettisoned.

Because Julian needed to go round to the offices of *Punch*, presumably to collect some money, he had to desert Diana earlier than he'd have liked. Before leaving the Mandrake, he secured a date with her that night. But she didn't show up. Her elusiveness only adding to her allure, he asked her out again when he bumped into her the following week. This time she kept her side of the arrangement, and they went for dinner. Afterwards Julian took her to a "negro club",[48] where the resident band may well have been the West African Rhythm Brothers, members of which were often in the Mandrake and the French. It was then that Diana revealed the combative streak that tended to manifest itself whenever she'd been drinking heavily, a disagreement about money inciting the row that soured their first date.

Over the past fortnight Julian had sold only two short book reviews and a longer article to *Punch*. He was now, as he readily conceded, in such "a frightful financial mess [...], the net tighten[ing] closer around [him] from day to day",[49] he wrote to Winnie Davin asking her to pray for him. Yet he was determined to pay off his debt to Mr Goodman and reclaim his possessions. With that target in his sights, he obtained commissions from *The TLS* for middles on John Buchan and Angus Wilson.

It wasn't until he was poised to write his piece on Angus Wilson's new novel, *Anglo-Saxon Attitudes*, that he heard the book contained a disparaging portrait of Sonia, her name changed to Elvira Portway. Julian, whose obsession with her hadn't yet been supplanted by his burgeoning fixation with Diana, was so furious he went round trying to foment anti-Wilson feeling among the younger literary critics of his acquaintance, Anthony Cronin included. And when he settled down to write his essay, he used it as a means of "confounding Wilson and making love to Sonia in print".[50] In a perverse defence of the reprehensible character of Elvira, he made out that she transcended her creator's satiric intentions, emerging not as "a hanger-on to that fringe of the arts where Bohemia and Mayfair meet",[51] but as a "wayward and enchanting creature".[52]

Welcome as it was, his fee from *The TLS* fell far short of what he needed to fuel the necessary financial recovery. Unable to extend his tenure at the Celtic Hotel, he arranged to stay with John Gawsworth. At the beginning of May, he moved into the basement flat which the King shared with his new wife, Anna, a divorcée in her early fifties, known simply as "the Queen". The flat was situated at 85a Warwick Avenue, in pleasant but dilapidated Maida Vale. Since there was no spare bed, Julian had to sleep on the couch.

About a week after arriving there, he was in Berlemont's when he glimpsed Diana walking past. She was "all dressed up"[53] in the bright, idiosyncratic clothes she liked to wear. Rushing out of the pub, he waylaid her and they went for a drink. Though Diana, whom he dubbed "the Tall Girl",[54] resisted his overbearing blandishments, he tried to ingratiate himself with her by lending her £3 to pay for a hotel room.

He was in the Caves next day with the King and Nina Hamnett — hands trembling from years of alcoholism, a pronounced limp obliging her to use a walking-stick — when Diana showed up with someone who was obviously a boyfriend. A row ensued and Julian left in a huff. Two days passed without any further developments, then he received an apologetic letter from her, enclosing the money she'd borrowed. Placated, he got in touch with her and fixed up a meeting in the Caves. There she announced that she'd split up with George Bright, the journalist boyfriend he'd seen her with the other day. Setting the seal on their reconciliation, she and Julian went for a drink. By the end of the night Diana was drunk. Julian exploited the situation by bundling her into a taxi and taking her back to the King's place, where they slept together for the first time. In the morning, after a long lie-in, they joined the King and Queen for a lunchtime excursion to a local pub, in which they met up with Nina Hamnett, who knew Diana already and had a crush on her. That night Diana went back with Julian to Warwick Avenue. Now they were, as he put it, "definitely together".[55]

But the Queen was getting fed up with having them around. When Julian returned from visiting *Punch*'s offices the following day, she kicked them out. With the second weekend of May approaching, they took a room at the Premier Hotel in Russell Square, paid for using some money Diana's comparably cash-strapped and nomadic "Mamma",[56] Mrs "Tabs" Brailsford, had given her. They were there when, unknown to Julian, a Judgement Summons was issued against him by Marylebone County Court on behalf of Karl Halle. The court ordered him to pay off his debt — plus Halle's legal costs — at the rate of £1-5/- per week. The failure of the authorities to locate him, let alone force him to comply with the judgement, meant that a posse of bailiffs were, before long, on his trail.

That same day, Diana went off to visit her mother, only to return in such a foul mood, exacerbated by both booze and her period, that she got into an argument with Julian. She had calmed down by the morning, though. Full of "guilt, remorse etc",[57] she assured him it'd never happen again.

As a gesture of optimism about their future together and, most likely, as a way of cutting down on their expenses, they vacated their hotel and rented a room in Bolton Gardens, parallel to the Old Brompton Road in South Kensington. Just after they had moved there, the proofs of *Funny Things Happen*, now retitled *The Funny Bone*, came through. While Julian was busy correcting them, Diana dutifully kept him supplied with sandwiches. Since her culinary abilities didn't extend much beyond that, it was just as well he preferred nothing more elaborate when he was working.

The prevailing atmosphere of cosy domesticity wasn't, however, destined to last. On Friday 18 May she and Julian had a row in the street about her daughter Sallie, whose father was Peter Baker, the disgraced ex-Member of Parliament and gaoled former business partner of Charles Wrey Gardiner. Through a court-order, declaring Diana to be an unfit parent, Sallie had been placed under the guardianship of Diana's uncle, Philip Woolf. The row between Diana and Julian reached such a pitch that she struck him and then ran away. Expecting her to resurface once she'd calmed down, he went back to their room. But there was still no sign of her by the next day.

For the second time in the space of just over two months, Julian sought help from the King. Once again, the King provided sanctuary for him. Julian's return to the Warwick Avenue flat coincided with a phone-call from Diana, who rang to tell the King she was planning to leave London. That evening, Julian and the King popped over to Bolton Gardens to fetch his belongings. They found Diana there. Having left her keys behind when she ran off, she'd had to climb through the open window. Julian and the King, probably pausing just long enough to collect his things, hurriedly retreated to Maida Vale, where Julian reoccupied his berth on the couch.

Pushed to the verge of insanity by the stress of his separation from Diana, he began to identify more strongly than ever with Mr Hyde. So intense was the identification, he insisted on Bruce Bernard introducing him to a stranger, not as Julian but as "Edward". And when he next ran into Anthony Cronin, he said he was "in the hands of [the] Tall Girl"[58] who was trying to kill him. "But she won't succeed," [he added.] "I'm stronger than she is, you see. I'm taller too, though she is tall, very tall. But that's why I'm being Mr Hyde today, you see. Because she's trying to kill me."[59]

There were no new twists in his fraught relationship with Diana until the following Monday night. Unrepentant for once, Diana turned up at the King's place and levelled all sorts of complaints against Julian before making her exit. These left him so infuriated that when, the Sunday afterwards, she walked into their local pub — the Albert Tavern on Porchester Road — "looking terrible"[60], he ignored her. As did the King, who seems to have grown similarly tired of her histrionics.

Yet Julian's indignation swiftly dispersed. Feeling lonely without Diana, around the beginning of June he contacted her — most likely via her mother — and arranged to meet her. It was a move that seems to have provoked a bust-up between him and the King, which forced him to move out. Before going to the wine-bar where he was due to meet Diana, he called round to Bouverie Street and raised an advance from *Punch*. His differences with Diana settled, they repaired to a hotel somewhere in Kensington. But it wasn't long before they ran out of cash and had to vacate their room. While Diana probably went back to her mother, Julian was left homeless. In his quest for somewhere to sleep, he trudged round to the YMCA and the Salvation Army Hostel, both of which were full. At 2.00am, by now footsore and desperate, he stopped off at a West End police station and asked the Desk-Sergeant if he'd let him sleep in one of the cells. The Sergeant said he couldn't allow that, but directed Julian to the waiting-room at Euston Station. As Julian approached there, "suddenly prey to agoraphobia, daunted by the shining width of the street [he] had to cross",[61] he fell in with an elderly, neatly dressed man, bound for the same destination. His new acquaintance — a toothbrush-moustached officer who had served in the First World War — "took [his] arm and steered [him] across the road towards crimson neon capitals spelling out the station's name."[62] Together, they made their way into the huge Great Hall, "where every cough raised a hollow echo, and where the benches, padded in scarlet leather, were almost all occupied by sleeping people: some huddled in pairs, others — fortunate enough to secure a bench to themselves — stretched out full length with their feet up."[63] Julian positioned himself beneath a statue of the railway pioneer George Stephenson. Though Julian found it hard to relax in the well-lit Hall, he eventually drifted off. Only a few hours later, he was shaken gently awake by the man he'd met the previous night, who guided him towards the cafeteria, which was just about to open. After breakfast, they washed and shaved in the gents, then parted at the entrance to the underground station.

By posing for some nude photos, Diana managed to raise £25, which allowed them to check into another hotel in Kensington. It was while they were there that Diana introduced him to her mother whose relationship with her was equally tempestuous.

In about mid-June, unable to settle their bill, they were chucked out by the hotel's management. That night Julian, who had smoothed things over with the King, stayed at Warwick Avenue while Diana returned to her mother. By the morning Diana had found a flat on Queensborough Terrace, just off Bayswater Road. Roughly a week into their tenancy, most of which they spent in bed together, the housekeeper asked them for their rent which they couldn't, of course, pay. Diana promptly skedaddled, leaving Julian to deal with the irate housekeeper.

So he ended up back at the King's place, where he remained for at least the next couple of weeks. By about the beginning of July, his stalled romance with Diana had been rejuvenated and they'd found a flat in Holland Park Gardens, scene of his break-up with Monica. Apparently unaffected by the potentially grim associations, it was there that he and Diana enjoyed "their happiest time"[64] together.

His spirits must also have been lifted by the publication of *The Funny Bone* early that month, its flyleaf bearing a quotation from the flattering testimonial Malcolm Muggeridge had written for him. Alongside its British publication, it was simultaneously released in Canada by the Toronto-based Ryerson Press. Given how much Tony

Powell had done for Julian lately, it was timely and appropriate that the book should carry a dedication to him.

The defiant inclusion of Julian's parody of H.E. Bates had unfortunate consequences, though. He hadn't expected Bates to go through with his threat, yet the moment *The Funny Bone* appeared in the bookshops Bates instigated a libel action against him, Elek Books, and the firm that had printed it. Because Julian had only a trickle of work from *Punch*, he didn't have the resources to hire a lawyer to defend himself.

On Tuesday 24 July the case came before the Queen's Bench Division of the High Court on the Strand. The plaintiff was represented by Lord Dunboyne, an experienced barrister. Either resigned to defeat or simply disdainful of the proceedings, Julian failed to attend. In his absence, the solicitor representing Elek and the unfortunate printing firm reached an out of court settlement with Bates. This acknowledged that Julian's parody "could reasonably be read in a sense defamatory of the plaintiff personally, which they never intended."[65] Not only did they apologise to Bates, but they also agreed to cover his legal costs, to pay substantial damages to a charity of his choice, and to refrain from reprinting or republishing the offending parody. Details of the settlement were sent to Julian, yet no specific measures were taken against him. The judge did, however, note that the settlement should not be viewed as exonerating his conduct.

In spite of everything, his book remained in circulation. The same day that the outcome of the case was reported, *The Times* also carried a favourable review of *The Funny Bone*, commending Julian as "an ironist who does not allow irony to get the better of humane tolerance."[66] Over the ensuing weeks it received several other positive notices, the best of them from *The Sunday Times*, in which his remarkable skills as a parodist were likened to those of Van Meegren, the renowned forger, "churning out masterpieces to order".[67]

Through the remainder of that summer, Julian paid the rent on their current flat by penning more reviews for *Punch*. He also supplied the magazine with *The Salad of a Bad Café*, a brilliant if merciless parody of Carson McCullers, plus a touching re-evaluation of the neglected work of Frank Harris. All this journalism had another unforeseen consequence. Satisfying as it must have been to see his name regularly appearing in the pages of *Punch*, such widespread exposure had its drawbacks.

When word got round that he wrote for the magazine, a mob of bailiffs convened outside its premises, waiting to nab him when he collected his review copies. Finding the front door repeatedly blocked by jostling bailiffs enquiring about Julian, the younger Mr Agnew —

who, with his father, owned a major stake in *Punch* — asked Tony Powell whether he might dispense with the services of their troublesome contributor. Out of loyalty to his friend, Tony negotiated a compromise. The deal entailed Julian being banned from their offices, but allowed him to carry on working for the magazine. Henceforth, each time he needed to collect a fresh batch of review copies, he'd phone Tony who would give him a list of books pending review. Tony would then deliver the chosen titles to a mutually agreed spot, often the half-lit bar of the vast Hotel Russell in Russell Square, its leather upholstered armchairs and chesterfields, its smartly attired waiters carrying drinks on gleaming trays, and its somnolent ambience akin to a gentlemen's club.

This brief spell of journalistic productivity and domestic harmony was already drawing to a close, heralded by Diana's increased drinking. The latest in their cycle of confrontations struck during mid-August, its ferocity compelling Julian to spend a "terrible night in Holland Park wandering about".[68] When he rang Diana in the morning, he couldn't repair the damage, her undiminished fury driving her into the clutches of another admirer.

Within about a week, though, Julian had won her back. By early September, he and Diana were sharing a flat in an enormously tall, once grand but now seedy Regency building at 27 Inverness Terrace, close to their old Queensborough Terrace digs. Not long after they had moved there, the BBC programmed two broadcasts of his play about Frank Harris, the repeat fee alone netting him £28. Intent on earning enough to reclaim the possessions still impounded in Oxford, he took on more commissions. For *The TLS*, he produced an essay on the wartime short story boom. And for *Time and Tide*, he wrote a long and fervent review of an anthology of modern French stories, edited by John Lehmann. Added to which, he made an appointment with Barbara Bray, the Script Editor at BBC Drama (Sound), to discuss the possibility of turning *Until the Day She Dies* into a radio serial. The appointment was scheduled for Monday 15 October. On the basis of his enthusiastic description of the projected series, Barbara Bray commissioned a 30-minute specimen instalment, together with a synopsis of the next five episodes. Later that day, equipped with the £15 he needed to pay off his debt to Mr Goodman, he went up to Oxford to recover his clothes and other possessions. He also used the visit to refresh his memory of the locations that would feature in his newly commissioned script. And he borrowed a music-box from the Davin sisters, the wistful tune from which he planned to incorporate into the eventual radio production.

Just when his life was starting to acquire some stability, he discovered that Diana had been making furtive phone-calls to his rival for her affections. On the Tuesday night after he got back from Oxford, she went out to meet her boyfriend while Julian flounced off to the Gargoyle. When they both converged on the flat afterwards, they had a row that concluded in them moving out.

The following afternoon Julian decided to stop off at the Caves before going on to the BBC to collect the advance payment for his script. He soon got talking to a girl named Sylvia, who loaned him the cost of his taxi-fare to Portland Place. There he visited the formidably efficient Miss Dean in the Copyright Department, who sanctioned an 18 guinea advance. Returning triumphantly to the Caves, he paid Sylvia back and spent the night with her in a hotel.

Despite their infidelities, Julian and Diana were back together by about the end of the week. They then rented a room or small flat from a German woman living in the north London suburb of Willesden, where Julian made a start on the script of *Until the Day She Dies*. A fortnight or so after they'd moved in, Diana — who had been to see her Mamma — came home drunk. Another altercation flared up the next day, climaxing in Diana's departure and her subsequent reappearance with her mother, who helped gather together her things.

Julian too, having fallen behind with the rent, had vacated their place in Willesden by around the start of November, just as the temperature was dropping. Not the best time to find himself destitute and alone. To keep warm, he rode round on the tube for several days, the nights passed in the waiting-rooms of various mainline railway stations, Marylebone being the preferred one. In an ironic twist, emphasising his family's declining fortunes, Marylebone was only a short distance away from the imposing St John's Wood home of his great-grandparents on his mother's side.

Probably by obtaining an advance from *Punch*, he raised enough money to escape from this miserable, vagrant existence, a room at the Imperial Hotel offering the perfect antidote. It was there that he was rejoined by Diana, who affectionately referred to him as "the Beetle",[69] presumably on account of his shiny black hair and tough carapace of cynicism. But they hadn't been back together for long before they parted again.

When he later spotted her kissing someone else, Julian was overwhelmed by the dispiriting impression that he'd "broken with her [...] utterly".[70] His sense of isolation becoming unbearable, he contacted Diana a few days after their latest split, and met her "in a

Coca Cola joint",[71] where they talked through the situation. Reunited, they found themselves a hotel in Clapham.

For the next week or so, Julian worked on both his script and a couple of reviews for the *London Magazine*, the contents of his wallet meanwhile thinning. His current attempt at cohabitation with Diana came to the usual sorry conclusion in about mid-November. They were having a drink in Berlemont's when hostilities broke out. Primed by a distressing trip to see her mother and daughter, Diana lost her temper with Julian and emptied her wine over him, the coup de grâce striking the next day when she got into an altercation with the hotelier, who asked them to leave.

Diana reacted by going back to George, her former boyfriend, whereas Julian found himself homeless again. On discovering his predicament, Terry Baysford, an eccentric drinking buddy, who didn't have anywhere to stay either, suggested they sleep in the Turkish baths under the Imperial Hotel. There you could get not only a bed but also some breakfast for less than a quid. Bereft of alternatives, desperation dispelling any qualms he might have had about the baths' reputation as a homosexual hang-out, Julian joined Terry on a late night post-pub expedition to Russell Square.

The entrance was reached via an arcade that ran through the central block of the hotel. Beyond a frosted glass door, there was a reception desk, where you took off your shoes before descending the double-staircase down to the lofty-ceilinged, ornately tiled baths. These were illuminated by two huge electric chandeliers, the light from them throwing into sharp relief the ornate stonework and the statuary inset into numerous niches. A narrow swimming-pool at the foot of the stairs was flanked by parallel rows of archways, one side leading to the various hot rooms, the other leading to curtained cubicles, arranged on two levels, each cubicle containing a couple of beds. Accompanied by the deep, steady breathing sounds that resonated round the baths, Terry made for his preferred spot on the balcony while an attendant escorted Julian to a cubicle on the lower level.

In the morning, he sampled the half-crown cooked breakfast, served in the foyer, where the other residents were busy exchanging racing tips. Once he'd shaved and retrieved his shoes, which had been polished overnight, he headed for the exit, ready for when the pubs opened.

Relishing the relaxed atmosphere of the baths, he returned there the following night. He was soon one of the regulars, getting onto first-name terms with the attendants, and investing in a nylon shirt, suitable for washing at night, then drying in the hot room. To finance his trips to the baths, not to mention his sessions in the pubs and clubs, he kept up his reviewing work for *Punch*, always meeting deadlines and seldom appearing drunk. Using his sporadic earnings, on Saturday 8 December he treated himself and a girl he'd met to a single night at the Newlands Hotel at 47 Bernard Street, off Russell Square. As an additional indulgence, he paid for breakfast to be brought up to their room.

One day towards the end of the second week of December, he was catapulted out of his lethargy by a fortuitous encounter with Alec C. Snowden in the Freelance Club. A Yorkshireman in his mid-fifties, who wore his greying hair slicked back to reveal a widow's peak, Snowden was an influential figure in the world of low budget British films. As well as running his own company, he held the post of General Production Manager at the Film Producers' Guild and sat on the Board of Directors of Merton Park Studios, among the many firms that operated under the Guild's banner. He and Julian ended up discussing British B-features. Instead of making inferior imitations of Hollywood movies, Julian felt they ought to be seeking inspiration in small-scale Continental pictures like *Quai des Brumes* and *I Vitelloni*. His forthright opinions impressed Snowden, who paid him £10 to write the synopsis of an original screenplay for a 60-minute feature. If Snowden liked it, the idea was that Julian would be commissioned to expand it into a full shooting script.

So he could concentrate on the project, Julian deserted the baths and booked a room for the weekend at the York Hotel at 31 Queensborough Terrace. That Sunday he completed the final draft of his synopsis for *The Key Man*, an ingeniously plotted crime story about an investigative reporter who becomes embroiled in a Soho gangster's attempts to track down the hidden proceeds of the robbery that landed him in gaol.

Elsewhere in London that day, a tragic real-life drama was being enacted. Julian's friend, Nina Hamnett, now living in Paddington, had — following her former benefactor Henry Yorke's refusal to give her any more money to ameliorate her grinding poverty — jumped from the window of her flat, fatally impaling herself on the railings below. Her suicide severed another link with Julian's wartime glory days.

Once he'd completed the synopsis, he tried to extend his stay at the York Hotel, but found that all the rooms had already been booked, so he went back to his old life at the baths. On Thursday 20 December, four days after he'd wrapped up his commission, Snowden announced that he wanted Julian to turn his synopsis into a screenplay, and that he was keen for him to work on a couple of other projects. In case Julian had any reservations about it, Snowden stressed that *The Key Man* wouldn't — unlike the majority of British B-movies which Julian so despised — be stuffed with American and Canadian actors, included merely "to curry favour with the US"[72] market.

For a fee of £185, Julian agreed to the offer. Flush with a £100 advance, he affected one of his periodic changes of costume, the familiar plum-coloured jacket and sponge-bag trousers replaced by a pale grey suit more in keeping with his new self-proclaimed role as a successful screenwriter. He also bought a bottle of perfume which he planned to leave at the Caves as a peace-offering for Diana. Arriving there not long after the club had opened, he found her sitting in the pokey basement with a friend. He and Diana then adjourned for a quiet chat upstairs, where they spent the afternoon together. Any lingering animosity she might have felt towards him banished by the gift of the perfume, she accepted his invitation to join him on a trip to the south coast, where he'd arranged to spend Christmas with the Jaegers. Reconciled to each other, he and Diana checked into a hotel in Kensington that night. Yet all the customary tensions revived in the morning. This time, though, these weren't allowed to precipitate a row.

En route to the station, from where they were due to travel to Bognor later in the day, Diana suddenly announced that she'd left something behind at the hotel. She said she had to go back and fetch it. She told Julian she'd meet him at the station, but she failed to turn up. Refusing to let her capricious behaviour spoil his plans, he took the train down to Bognor and registered at the small Sefton Lodge Hotel on Lyon Street, right in the centre of town. Several days running, he travelled from there to the Jaegers' house in Elmer Sands, where he enjoyed a restorative "Christmas binge".[73]

Such was his extravagance, by the first week of 1957, he'd spent the advance for his screenplay, which was still a long way off completion. Since the rest of his fee wasn't due until he'd delivered an acceptable shooting script, he was — as he admitted — in "a dreadful mess".[74] The only cause for New Year rejoicing was provided by the publication of *The Long and the Short and the Tall*, a brief army memoir salvaged from *They Can't Give You a Baby*. Juxtaposed with fittingly humorous Norman Thelwell illustrations, it featured in *Lilliput*. Yet even that didn't prevent him from feeling thoroughly disheartened by the phone-conversation he had with Alec C. Snowden on the evening of Sunday 6 January. Whereas Julian envisaged *The Key Man* as "a human-interest drama",[75] Snowden made it plain that he saw it as "primarily an action picture".[76] And, contrary to all his previous assurances, Snowden announced that the Canadian actor, Lee Patterson, had been cast in the lead role.

Julian was so annoyed that he wrote to Snowden next morning, detailing his concerns and resigning from the project. But Snowden talked him out of it, the prospect of another £85 offering an effective inducement for him to press ahead with the script. Far removed though the story was from his own experiences, he garnished it with plenty of autobiographical material, assigning the hero chronic debt problems and a girlfriend who bounces back and forth between him and her mother.

Shortly afterwards, Julian returned to London, where he resumed his relationship with Diana, who joined him at the York Hotel. Now virtually penniless, he subsidised the completion of his screenplay by obtaining an advance from *Punch*. By then, however, Diana — who was drinking heavily again — had gone back to her mother.

On Monday 14 January, Julian delivered the script to Snowden and collected £35, the rest of his fee payable when his work had been rubber-stamped. Though a couple of maladroit expository scenes betrayed the excessive haste with which it was written, Snowden approved the script. Two days later, he paid Julian the remaining £50. Pleased with the speed and fluency of his work, Snowden then hired him to polish the dialogue of a science-fiction thriller, due to be filmed at Merton Park Studios that spring. The screenplay — about an evil genius who plans to attain world domination through a revolutionary brainwashing technique — had been freely adapted by David McIlwain from *Escapement*, his own hamfisted novel, published under the pen-name of Charles Eric Maine. Julian must have enjoyed working on it since it harked back to the preposterous, cliff-hanging adventure stories he so loved as a boy.

Late one night, around then, he was at the bar of the Stag's Head when the relatively new landlord refused to serve him because he'd already had more than enough to drink. So tolerant of alcohol was his system, it required enormous quantities of it to make him drunk. When he *was* drunk, though, he tended to become stroppy and supercilious. His repeated demands for a nightcap having been snubbed, he threatened to call the police unless the landlord served him. But the man refused to budge, compelling Julian to march out of the Saloon Bar and down to the phone, from where he rang the police. Instead of backing him up, as he'd envisaged, the police arrested him for being drunk and disorderly. Mortified, Julian was taken to the nearby Saville Row police station, where he was held in the cells overnight, then released in the morning.

As a protest against his treatment by the landlord of the Head, Julian transferred his custom to the George, that other traditional haunt of BBC production staff, at the intersection of Great Portland and Mortimer Streets. Unlike the Head, it was not bisected into separate bars, the only division being a low wooden partition. Nor was it dominated by BBC staff. Its customers also included a high percentage of musicians, its popularity with whom led the conductor Sir Thomas Beecham to nickname it "the Gluepot" because they were so often stuck there.

In these new surroundings, amid Victorian acid-etched windows, dark woodwork, clattering slot machines, and a profusion of cut-glass mirrors, Julian carried on spending extended lunchtimes with Reggie Smith who, trailing a small retinue, split his allegiances between both pubs. But Julian's boycott resulted in him seeing much less of Raynor Heppenstall, whose devotion to the Head was unwavering.

Under the leadership of Laurence Gilliam, boss of the BBC's Radio Features Department, producers were encouraged to leave their desks and patronise either the George or the Head, where they'd meet scriptwriters, composers, and actors who might contribute to future productions. At one end of the George's long, brass-railed bar Louis MacNeice was usually to be seen, saying very little yet dominating his circle of London-Irish pals and photogenic actresses. Julian, who looked every bit as out of place in the George as he had in the Head, claimed the territory at the opposite end of the bar, where he was invariably to be seen clutching a glass of red wine, his sunglasses accentuating his deadpan expression. If he was in luck, one or other of his friends would be there: Tommy Waldron, Sir John Waller, Anthony Cronin, Tony Van den Burgh or, perhaps, Reggie Smith and Olivia Manning. To this roster of potential drinking partners, he made three significant additions. There was the hulking policeman-turned-producer, Bob Pocock, erstwhile friend of Dylan Thomas, unmistakable in a battered trilby with a bullethole in it. There was Jake Schwartz, a dealer in literary manuscripts. And there was the stooped, stocky Irish character-actor, Patrick Magee,[77] face topped by unkempt, prematurely silver hair. On days when none of them were around, Julian would conscript anyone nearby, even strangers like the sleek young poet Anthony Thwaite, into listening to his monologues. These often consisted of him recounting the entire plot of some old movie, at the end of which he'd tap his victim for a fiver.

It was hardly surprising, then, that Julian swiftly acquired a reputation as someone to be avoided. The moment he strode through the doors of the George, people would start to gravitate towards the exits, the majority of those who stayed behind shunning him. Since his friend Dan Davin, who continued to seek him out during occasional business trips to London, was also on good terms with Louis MacNeice and several other producers, none of them fans of Julian, Dan's visits to the George became tense and awkward. Their friendship further strained by countless irrecoverable loans, by the incessant attention Julian demanded, by Dan's waning interest in his work, they began to lose touch.

Well before the end of January, Diana had rejoined Julian at the York Hotel, yet they couldn't break out of what he saw as their pattern of "rows and reconciliations".[78] Alcohol again acting as the catalyst, on Thursday 24 January they had another spat, which led to Julian walking out on her. Unsure where he'd gone, a penitent Diana wrote to him care of the Mandrake, declaring that "All I want in life is to be with you, love and help you."[79]

That Saturday Julian checked into the impressive and pricey Great Eastern Hotel, next to Liverpool Street Station, where he remained for the next week, amassing a £41 bill, paid for with his earnings from his screenwriting. "[L]ost and alone without [him],"[80] Diana had, meanwhile, moved down to Brighton. From there, she wrote to the offices of *Punch*, appealing for him to contact her. "One beetle on its own is so lost. The feelers long to tangle with the others," she explained. "I love you so much darling and must put my arms round your neck soon."[81] But Julian, who had picked up another woman and taken a room with her at the Euston Hotel, didn't respond to Diana's appeal.

The Great Hall
at Euston Station, 1953

The Turkish Baths beneath
the Imperial Hotel, 1965
(© Crown Copyright,
reproduced by
permission of the National
Monuments Record)

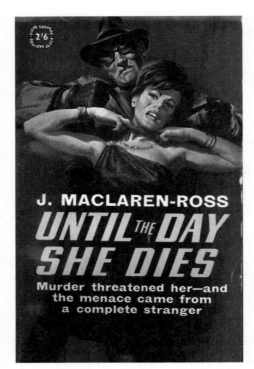

Cover of the paperback edition of
Until the Day She Dies, 1963
(© New English Library)

Eleanor Brill and John Gawsworth,
c. 1966
(© Jon Wynne-Tyson)

Night of
the Long Wives

It was less than two months since Julian, now living by himself at the Royal Court Hotel in Sloane Square, had completed the synopsis of *The Key Man*, yet the film was already in production by February 1957. Ignoring Julian's earlier protestations, Alec Snowden went ahead and hired the dark, high-cheekboned Canadian, Lee Patterson, for the starring role. Though Julian still didn't "see eye to eye [with Snowden] about the way [his script] should be handled",[1] he watched some of the filming during the final weeks of that month. Under the direction of Snowden's slightly younger collaborator, Montgomery Tully, a diminutive, balding, ex-public schoolboy known to most people as "Geoff", parts of the movie were shot on the streets of Soho. Perhaps making use of Julian's exhaustive knowledge of the area, they filmed a sequence featuring Newman Passage, a dog-legged alley off Rathbone Place which, he claimed, was often referred to "as Jekyll and Hyde Alley"[2] on account of its sinister ambience. In imitation of the equivalent American B-movies of the late Forties, Tully and his cameraman recreated what would come to be known as the film noir look, a pervasive sense of menace conveyed through acute camera angles and a proliferation of inky shadows.

Supporting himself by writing for *Punch*, Julian moved into the Tudor Court Hotel on the South Kensington stretch of Cromwell Road, where he registered as Mr Hyde. Miserable without Diana, his depression cranked up by the sense that his financial situation was going "from bad to worse",[3] he finally relented and arranged a reconciliation with her one evening towards the end of March. Things went well that night. Before long, though, he and Diana had got into another squabble. This resulted in them avoiding one another for about a week.

Over at Merton Park Studios, *Escapement* was, in the meantime, being filmed by two separate camera crews working concurrently. The leading roles were taken by the rugged Canadian, Rod Cameron; the German-born character actor, Peter Illing; and Mary Murphy who, only four years earlier, had appeared opposite the young Marlon Brando in *The Wild One*.

Unable to "bear it without [Diana] any longer",[4] and convinced that they were "hurting each other to no purpose",[5] Julian sent a conciliatory letter to the Soho hostel where she was living. "I will never give you up, darling," he wrote, "so it's no use trying to get away from me."[6] Besides pleading for her to meet him in the George at lunchtime next day, he asked her to lend him some money to keep him going until the following week when he expected to land an advance for a new novel. While she may well have met him in the pub that lunchtime, she certainly didn't have the spare cash to help him out.

Still living apart from her, still posing as Mr Hyde, on Tuesday 9 April Julian checked in to Knight's Hotel on Queensborough Terrace, where he remained only a couple of days. Then he settled his bill — presumably funded by his latest advance — and moved to the Belmont Hotel at 93 Highbury New Park, a lengthy road connecting Highbury with Stoke Newington.

Since Hamish Hamilton had no idea of his current whereabouts, Richard Brain, who was growing restive about his failure to deliver the novel they'd commissioned five-and-a-half years ago, wrote to him care of *Punch*, enquiring how the book was going. Julian reacted by phoning Brain and assuring him that he was making steady progress with *Business and Desire*. Whereas, in truth, work on it had, long before, juddered to a halt despite his best efforts to resuscitate it.

For almost a year now, Julian had dodged the consequences of the Judgement Summons issued against him. Disproving his frequent boast that "he'd been photographed so few times he could escape unnoticed if he was ever sought by the police",[7] they caught up with him on the afternoon of Friday 12 April when he was suddenly arrested, charged under the 1869 Debtors' Act, and gaoled on remand. The prison was "a dim-lit, high, hollow structure, where officers rattled bunches of keys and echoing steel flights twisted up towards tiered galleries with wire netting stretched below".[8] On arrival there, he was weighed, measured, bathed and, "having elected not to wear prison clothing",[9] escorted to a tiny cell which he shared with a garrulous West Indian. Had the weekend not intervened, he'd have been able to arrange bail. As it was, he had to wait until Monday morning.

That weekend was spent reading, chatting with the self-proclaimed crook in the adjoining cell, and trudging round the exercise yard with him, its "circular path worn slippery as a skating rink".[10] First thing the following week, he was bailed to appear at Bow Street Magistrates' Court on Wednesday. In preparation, he succeeded in recruiting both Tony Van den Burgh and the sober, well-spoken Tony Powell to speak on his behalf as character witnesses. The tactic worked, because he escaped with a light sentence, the magistrate placing him on probation and ordering him to settle his debt in instalments.

Oblivious to his recent travails, Diana — who had found herself a secretarial job — wrote to him saying she "now [had] money which [she] would like to share with [him]."[11] She told him she'd be in the Caves the following evening. Their reunion was so felicitous they ended up renting a room together at Knight's Hotel, where Julian insisted on them signing in as "Mr and Mrs Hyde". They remained there for just under a week, only parting because they could no longer afford to stay there. So Julian temporarily moved into a cheap cubicle in the Turkish baths under the Imperial Hotel.

To raise the money he needed to clear his debt to Karl Halle, he approached Tony Van den Burgh with a business proposition. Tony had just founded a paperback publishing firm called Four Square Books. Modelled on mass market American publishers, who decked the covers of their books with dramatic paintings, it aimed to sell so-called paperback originals — novels not previously released in hardback — through unconventional outlets like tobacconists' shops. When Julian requested an advance for a novel, the plot of which he sketched with undiminished verve and conviction, Tony took a gamble and paid him £200 for the book, though Tony had his doubts as to whether he was still capable of writing novels. Not that Julian could afford the time to bring the idea to fruition, just under half the money having been forwarded to the Magistrates' Court.

During the last few days of April, he resolved another untidy aspect of his life by putting his relationship with Diana on a more secure footing. Together they took a furnished flat in a giant, decrepit four-storey house at 39 Kensington Gardens Square, a side-street off the busy Pembridge Road in Bayswater, well away from the Soho scene whose grip on him had begun to slacken. He continued to patronise the pubs and clubs that flourished there, but he no longer found them the exhilarating places he once had. And he disliked the slow changes wrought on the area, in particular its colonisation by the sex industry, continental delicatessens, cafés, and restaurants making way for strip clubs, a trend even reflected by the Gargoyle Club, now staging a Dance of the Seven Veils. Above all, he viewed with undisguised horror the remorseless encroachment of the beatniks and brash late Fifties youth culture, old style bohemianism swept aside by a tide of brightly painted coffee bars and skiffle clubs, overflowing with duffle-coated students.

The rent on Julian and Diana's new flat was covered by a fresh screenwriting assignment he'd been handed by Alec C. Snowden, who employed him to work on an unusually lavish second feature. His task was to dramatise *Puzzle For Fiends*, one of a series of mediocre but popular English crime novels, all starring the debonair American detective Peter Duluth. Written by Hugh Callingham Wheeler and Richard Wilson Webb under the pseudonym of Patrick Quentin, it was an implausible yarn about a Machiavellian family who, taking advantage of the amnesia Duluth suffers after a purported car crash, enmesh him in their plot to claim a $2 million inheritance. Out of this gimmicky material, Julian endeavoured to create a lighthearted Hitchcockian romantic thriller. Other than altering the hero's surname and transplanting the action from Southern California to the south of France, an exotic backdrop which Merton Park Studios were well-versed in replicating, he remained fairly faithful to the novel. But the majority of the dialogue was his own, its periodic shifts in tone, from the wisecracking to the flirtatious, affording him the scope to demonstrate hitherto unseen versatility as a screenwriter.

His earnings from the assignment enabled him to hire a solicitor to draft the affidavit demanded by H.E. Bates's legal counsel, who was seeking a commitment from him not to republish the parody at the centre of the recent libel case. Due to the absurdly tight deadlines and the contempt with which quota-quickies like *Puzzle For Fiends* were treated by distributors, audiences, and critics alike, Julian was, however, growing as disenchanted with the film industry as he'd already become with the publishing business. Of course the situation wasn't helped when *Kinematograph Weekly*, gave *The Key Man*, which was earmarked for imminent release, a lukewarm write-up. This praised the concluding reels for being "purposeful and exciting",[12] yet quite rightly lambasted its performances. Sensing he had no future on the low-budget production-line, Julian was, by the summer, casting round for other ways of making a living.

In late June, Barbara Bray wrote to him about the script she'd commissioned eight months earlier. By informing him that the BBC hoped to broadcast it before the end of the year, she tried to exert some leverage on him. Yet he ignored her letter. Three weeks later, she contacted him again. At the second attempt, she adopted a more forthright approach which elicited no reply either.

Because he'd long since spent the advance she had authorised, he couldn't afford to sit down and write the specimen episode she wanted. He was, in any case, overburdened with other work now. Not only was he still receiving regular commissions from Tony Powell at *Punch*, but he may also have been busy with last minute revisions to his adaptation of *Puzzle For Fiends*.

Shooting started in the penultimate week of July. After a few days on location, the crew decamped to the set that had been constructed on one of the two far from spacious sound-stages at the north London home of Merton Park Studios. Julian, who was fascinated by the mechanics of movie-making, went there to watch the filming, directed by Geoff Tully. Courtesy of the relatively generous budget, Snowden had assembled a better than average cast, capable of delivering their lines with both conviction and style. Lex Barker, his stardom fading since his decision to relinquish the title role in the Tarzan movies, took the main part. The other principal roles were given to the Italian leading lady Lisa Gastoni, the glamorous Carole Matthews, and the veteran stage actress Nora Swinburne.

A hint of panic entered Barbara Bray's third letter to Julian in the space of just over a month. Another week drifted by before he made any effort to assuage her anxiety. Realising he couldn't string the BBC along indefinitely, he posted Reggie Smith a note suggesting they get together for a lunchtime drink, his undelivered script clearly top of the agenda. They met on Friday 16 August, most likely in the Saloon Bar of the George, where Reggie appears to have chivvied him about the missing script. In such situations, Julian "would invariably react with a look of outrage, as if Reggie had committed some unpardonable breech of etiquette."[13] Still, their meeting forced Julian to take the situation seriously: certainly a lot more seriously than he appears to have taken the letter that arrived from Elek Books, who wanted to know when he was going to deliver his overdue novel.

The day after his pow-wow with Reggie, Julian sent his friend a typically cheeky counter-proposal. Enclosing a copy of the screenplay of *The Key Man*, he suggested the BBC should broadcast this as an hour-long radio play, the fee from which would cover his expenses while he wrote *Until the Day She Dies*.

At the end of August he and Diana, who must have fallen behind with their rent once his screenwriting job had come to an end, vacated their flat in Bayswater. Rather than cart all their possessions round while they searched for somewhere else to live, Julian stored two suitcases full of inessentials in the Left Luggage office at Bayswater underground station. Initially, he and his girlfriend went back to Knight's Hotel. After only a few days, though, they moved to an alternative establishment in Kensington.

It was probably on one of Julian's trips to the George or the ML that Reggie Smith — who knew he created a lot of his own problems, yet persevered with him out of respect for his abilities — told him that the BBC had agreed to his proposed radio version of *The Key Man*. During the second week of September, by which time he and Diana had found themselves rented accommodation on the Porchester Road in Paddington, the film was released in London cinemas as a supporting feature. But it soon dropped out of sight, subsequently resurfacing on American television.

He and Diana had, by mid-September, left Paddington and moved to Kilburn. There they lived in a small flat in a ramshackle, two-storey greybrick house on the brow of a hill at 99 West End Lane, the residential section of a serpentine street, flanked for most of its length by shops. Instead of settling down in their new flat and resuming work on *Until the Day She Dies*, Julian took the rash step of embarking on a speculative radio adaptation of *The Reader Is Warned*, a John Dickson Carr thriller, written under the name of Carter Dickson. While he was doing that, he received another unwelcome letter — care of *Punch* — from Richard Brain at Hamish Hamilton. Increasingly embittered and negligent in his attitude towards publishers, Julian didn't bother responding to Brain's latest enquiry about his novel. He couldn't, however, ignore Tony Van den Burgh's comparable enquiries. Whenever Julian saw him, usually in the George, Tony would ask for sample chapters. And each time he'd make a different excuse, even claiming once that Diana had, in the course of a ferocious row, tossed the manuscript into the Regent's Park Canal.

Within about a week of their arrival in Kilburn, they were already in arrears with their rent. Desperate for money, he wrote to Reggie, announcing that he'd completed three episodes of a new radio thriller. Provided Reggie was prepared to advance him some cash, he offered to finish the rest of it by the end of the week. Always prepared to assist a friend in need, Reggie, who valued him "less as an adaptor than as an original writer who uses the book or story as a starting point for his very odd creations",[14] commissioned it as a six-part series for the Light Programme. Reggie even agreed to bend the normally inflexible BBC rule about not accepting scripts in manuscript form. All the same, it wasn't until the beginning of October that Julian received any payment for his adaptation, the title of which he'd changed to *The Listener Is Warned*. The generous 60 guinea advance must have cushioned the disappointment caused by the refusal of Anglo-Amalgamated, the film distribution company which owned the rights to

The Key Man, to allow the BBC to recycle his screenplay.

By Tuesday 8 October, he and Diana had transferred from Kilburn to Notting Hill Gate, where they had found a bedsit in a crowded rooming house at 37 Ladbroke Square. Over the next few weeks, he threw himself into a variety of projects. He tidied up the remaining three episodes of *The Listener Is Warned*. He tried to interest Alec C. Snowden in producing a film of *Until the Day She Dies*. He wrote another batch of reviews and an essay on American mystery magazines for *Punch*. He produced a vivid account of the night he'd spent sleeping in the waiting-room at Euston Station, which he tried unsuccessfully to sell to *The London Evening Standard* for their *Did It Happen?* series. And he turned his wartime story, *I Had To Go Sick*, into a short play, submitted to the BBC in early November.

He and his girlfriend had, by then, exchanged their room in Notting Hill for similarly cramped accommodation in Earl's Court, the £4-per-week rent probably covered by the fees he'd just received from the BBC for the final half of *The Listener Is Warned*. Their latest home was at 6 Courtfield Gardens, a huge four-storey house with marble steps and a handsome portico, its cracked white stucco façade facing an asymmetrical private park, only just visible through the bare branches of the trees that encircled it. In the name of "Mr and Mrs Maclaren-Ross", they rented a furnished room with a shared toilet and bathroom. They hadn't been living there for more than about a week before Diana announced she was pregnant. The news came as a shock to Julian who had, afraid that paternal responsibilities might undermine his literary career, made a deliberate decision not to become a parent. As someone troubled by bouts of impotence, maybe brought on by his drinking and drug-taking, he treated her repeated assurances that he was the father with hostile scepticism, amphetamine-induced paranoia stoking his doubts. These led to such "an "almighty row with Diana"[15] he stomped out of Courtfield Gardens on around Friday 15 November and retreated to the rooming house in Notting Hill Gate.

Encouraged by the 120 guineas he'd earned from *The Listener Is Warned*, he at last got down to his script of *Until the Day She Dies*. Under the influence of Hollywood crime movies like *The Locket*, in which the unravelling of the heroine's recurring nightmare acts as the central narrative thread, he designed his much-contemplated thriller. Progress was such that, by the final Thursday of November, he felt confident enough to contact Barbara Bray to let her know the first three episodes would be in her hands by the following week. Not that he managed to keep his promise. As things turned out, she had to wait until the second week of December before receiving his script and synopsis, along with a declaration that the rest of the six-part series would be ready "if not by Christmas at any rate by the New Year".[16] On receipt of these, the BBC released the remainder of what they were contracted to pay him.

Only a couple of days before Christmas, Julian patched up his differences with Diana. Now resigned to the idea of becoming a parent but still sceptical about whether he was the father, he collected one of his suitcases from Bayswater Station and moved back into the room in Earl's Court where Diana was still living.

Julian made a solid, if unspectacular start to 1958 with the publication in *Punch* of an amusing, lightly fictionalised piece about the Turkish baths where he had spent so many nights. Through January, he concentrated on finishing *Until the Day She Dies*. As soon as he tied up each episode, he'd take it round to Rothwell House. Leaving him to wait impatiently in her office, Barbara Bray would dash upstairs to the Copyright Department to arrange for Miss Dean to issue him with a chit authorising payment. He would then head for the BBC's bank on Upper Regent Street, where he'd exchange it for a cheque.

True to recent form, he missed his self-imposed target, only delivering the final episode at the beginning of February. His obligation to Barbara Bray belatedly satisfied, he sought to interest the BBC in a three-hour, six-part serial version of *The Girl in the Spotlight*.

As ever, Reggie contravened BBC regulations by returning his manuscript books once the script had been typed by the secretarial staff. Julian was then free to sell them to Jake Schwartz, who acted as an agent for American university libraries keen to acquire British literary memorabilia.

Despite the money his writing had recently been generating, he and Diana had fallen into rent-arrears, compelling their landlady to tell them to vacate their room and hand in their keys by midnight on Saturday 8 February. On the night of the deadline, they relocated to another bedsit in a turn-of-the-century house at 19 Canfield Gardens, a quiet residential street, mostly made up of tall blocks of mansion flats, close to Finchley Road tube station. They'd only been there a few days when Reggie Smith commissioned a specimen instalment of *The Girl in the Spotlight*, half of the fee for which was payable in advance. While Julian was toiling over this, the BBC's Light Programme broadcast the initial instalment of *The Listener Is Warned*, its title altered to the more catchy *You Have Been Warned*. The starring role was, to Julian's delight, taken by Patrick Magee, whose benign presence disguised an ability to portray malevolence.

Just before Julian put the finishing touches to his new radio script, *Escapement* — for which he received an "additional dialogue" credit — opened in London. Or, to be more specific, it opened in the less than august surroundings of the Regal, Brixton. Widespread but equivocal reviews in the trade press ensured only a brief tenure, though it did later earn a limited American release under the title, *The Electronic Monster*.

Before Reggie made up his mind whether to proceed with *The Girl in the Spotlight*, there was, for Julian, what must have been an anxious week's delay. This came to an end on Tuesday 19 March when Eric Ewens, the department's Assistant Script Editor, an affable and witty man who often used to join Julian in the George and the ML, told him that Reggie had decided to go ahead with it.

Work on *The Girl in the Spotlight* overlapped with the release of the other film he'd recently scripted — *Puzzle For Fiends*, by then re-named *The Strange Awakening*. Unlike any of its predecessors, it attracted favourable reviews in the trade press, the influential *Kinematograph Weekly* describing it as "a polished and workmanlike romantic crime melodrama"[17] which "tells an intriguing, if slightly far-fetched tale with commendable economy."[18] Backed by these, it opened in a major West End cinema: the enormous Dominion on Tottenham Court Road. But it lasted only a week there, then gravitated to the suburbs before enjoying a patchy release outside London.

In tandem with his scriptwriting, Julian kept up his reviewing for *Punch*, his endeavours punctuated by another change of address. During late March or early April, he and the heavily pregnant Diana returned to 6 Courtfield Gardens. While he still harboured misconceived doubts about the paternity of the child she was carrying, he had adjusted himself to the prospect of becoming a parent. He even made characteristically bibulous plans with Diana to celebrate the impending birth "with wine if it's a girl, champagne if it's a boy."[19]

Two days after handing in the third episode of his latest series, he had to take a break from his writing. Reggie Smith, who was producing *Until the Day She Dies* for the Light Programme, had succumbed to his frequent hints and hired him to play the role of the obsessive stranger, dubbed "the Waiting One". Just the type of role his limited thespian skills could accommodate. As he admitted to Tony Van den Burgh over a drink in the George, he had deliberately distributed the Waiting One's appearances across every episode in order to maximise his earnings. Each day from Friday 25 April until Saturday 3 May, he attended morning rehearsals for the six 30-minute episodes, some of them conducted at Broadcasting House, others at the Grafton Studios. Often these began at what must, to him, have seemed the dispiritingly early hour of 10.30am. His mood lifted by a lunchtime spent in the George, boozing away his actor's fee, he would go back to the studio with Reggie and the rest of the cast for late afternoon recording sessions, where he not only acted but also crooned a couple of verses from the romantic number *My Heart Has Wings*.

One evening around then, instead of going straight home and doing some shopping en route, as he'd promised Diana, he stopped off at the ML. No more than a few minutes after he'd downed his last drink and departed, a furious Diana burst through the door in search of him. Catching sight of her, Eric Ewens was heard to say, "Uh-oh, it looks like it's the Night of the Long Wives..."[20]

His stint as an actor out of the way, Julian switched his attention back to his writing. *The Girl in the Spotlight* was still unfinished, yet he approached the BBC with a proposal for a 60-minute drama called *The Contract*, which they commissioned for the *Thursday Night Play* slot on the Home Service. Funded by the 45 guinea advance they gave him, he started expanding his synopsis into a script. At the same time he tried to interest a film company in a screenplay he was planning, his hunger for ready-money neutralising his dissatisfaction with the movie business.

Sure of its appeal, the BBC featured *Until the Day She Dies* prominently in *The Radio Times*. To create an appropriate aura of mystery, Julian withdrew his name from the acting credits, choosing instead to be billed as "The Waiting One who prefers to remain anonymous".[21] Its opening instalment was broadcast on the evening of Monday 23 June.

Abandoning his newly commissioned play soon afterwards, Julian went back to working on *The Girl in the Spotlight*. He'd only just delivered the next episode to the BBC when Diana, who had been admitted to Queen Charlotte Hospital in Hammersmith, gave birth to a boy. In another of the strange coincidences that peppered Julian's life, the child shared his 7 July birthday.

The presence of a bawling baby in their already cramped quarters could so easily have had a disruptive effect on his work. Nonetheless, the ensuing weeks proved exceptionally productive. Alongside reviewing work for *Punch*, the job of delivering his copy and collecting his fee sometimes delegated to Diana, he penned a middle, commissioned by *The TLS*, on the supposed threat to the novel posed by movies. Through Donald McWhinnie, the tall, reticent Assistant Director of Drama

(Sound), he also obtained a commission for a sample episode from a projected thriller series. For once, he fulfilled his commission rapidly. But Donald opted not to proceed with it. Julian, however, redeemed the situation by persuading him to fund the composition of a 30-minute specimen episode of another mooted serial.

Like several of his previous radio scripts, *The Doomsday Book* had its origins in his own experience. Grafting his memories of G.S. Marlowe onto recollections of John Gawsworth's frenzied pursuit of the late M.P. Shiel's final missing manuscript, he conceived a tangled detective story about a writer searching for the last known work of a mysterious mittel-European novelist with whom he was once friendly. Yet again, Leo Marsh, the freelance writer and broadcaster at the heart of the story, was a transparent self-portrait, the context giving Julian the chance to project his notion of himself as someone who was tough, decisive, resourceful, cool under pressure, and unflinchingly brave.

For the sake of their child, he and Diana, to everyone's amazement, suddenly got married on Wednesday 13 August at Kensington Register Office, the ceremony witnessed by Julian's friend Patrick Magee. The following week Julian submitted the specimen episode of *The Doomsday Book* to the BBC, who lost no time in commissioning the rest of what, he now envisaged, would be an eight-part serial. He negotiated a 48 guineas-per-episode fee, offering a steady income with which to support his wife and putative son, whose birth they only got round to registering on the last Thursday of the month. They called him Alexander Vincent, his first-name an assertion of both the Scottish lineage Julian often spoke about, and a black, self-referential joke, Alexander being the name of the tall, stuttering, mother-fixated Waiting One in *Until the Day She Dies*.

Doubts about the baby's paternity persisted in Julian's mind, yet he treated the child with fondness and affection. Summoning hitherto untapped parental instincts, he even went to the trouble of going round the shops in search of a pram. But he couldn't afford any of them. During one of his regular forays to the BBC's Copyright Department, from whom "he was always trying to extract cash he wasn't entitled to",[22] Miss Dean advised him to look for a secondhand pram instead. His posture stiffening, he regarded her with an indignant expression.

Eventually he found a shop on Queensway which let him buy a new pram in instalments. Embracing his latest role with gusto, he was often to be seen wheeling Alex round Soho, together with Diana. To get round the ban on children entering pubs, he'd park the pram in front of Berlemont's, now the preserve of the more affluent bohemians. He would then fetch their drinks from the bar and carry the glasses back outside. During one of these expeditions, alone this time, his suit and mobster's mirror-shades adding to the incongruity, he bumped into Anthony Cronin. With the excitement of someone unveiling a significant discovery, he claimed that he was the model for the protagonist of the Iris Murdoch novel he'd been reading. "All these young women put me in their books," he said. "They think I'm wicked you see. Of course they put me in disguise, but that doesn't fool me. As you know, Cronin, I'm a master of disguise."[23]

Fatherhood bringing a new sense of urgency, he carried on reviewing for *Punch* and, that autumn, also pressed ahead with *The Doomsday Book*. In the second week of October, his routine was broken by what could easily have been a fatal accident. Diana was standing next to a heater which set fire to her nightdress. Living up to the heroic self-image propagated by his current script, Julian had the presence of mind to rip off the flaming nightdress. His wife appears to have emerged from the ordeal unscathed, but he scorched his writing hand and one of his legs. Because it made walking painful, he was temporarily unable to go out. Despite the discomfort, he carried on with his work, the household expenses covered by a £3 loan from his marginally less impoverished mother-in-law. But the loan was only obtained at a high emotional cost to Diana. As her mother pointed out, it contradicted Diana's assertion that she and Julian were in a secure enough financial position to provide a stable home for her daughter Sallie, now at secondary school. Much to Diana's distress, Sallie remained in the care of her guardian, who lived in rural Somerset.

A little over a week after Julian had saved Diana's life, he delivered the fifth episode of *The Doomsday Book*, though the fees from it must have been insufficient to defray his family's expenses, because he kept trying to drum up fresh commissions. He also pestered Eric Ewens to check whether Anglo-Amalgamated still held the copyright on *The Key Man*. And he paid a visit to the New Bond Street offices of Four Square Books in the hope Tony Van den Burgh would provide him with an advance for a new novel. Reminding Julian that he still hadn't delivered the last book, Tony refused. At which Julian parried with yet another excuse, ultimately resorting to his favourite put-down, accusing his friend of being "unbusinesslike".[24] Tony responded by offering him a fresh advance as soon as Julian gave him the manuscript that he owed Four Square Books.

All Julian's lobbying paid off in mid-November when he talked

Barbara Bray into commissioning a brief dramatisation of his wartime story, *I Had To Go Sick*. Four days later, on Tuesday 18 November, he wrote to her suggesting they produce his adaptation of *The Swag, The Spy and the Soldier* as a companion-piece. At the top of his letter, he left a blank space where his address would normally have gone, lest she leak his whereabouts to his pursuing creditors. The most persistent of these was his erstwhile landlady, Mrs Lyle, who had written to him several times at previous addresses without any reply. Even the company that had sold him Alex's pram was now pursuing him.

It was this fear of being tracked down by his creditors that seems to have been behind his partial falling out with Anthony Cronin. After a night's drinking with him and another friend, Cronin gave Julian a lift home. But they were stopped by the police, and Cronin was charged with drunken driving. When the case went to court, Julian refused to appear as a defence witness, probably because it would have meant divulging his address. He was subsequently peeved to discover that Cronin had, under cross-examination by the prosecuting counsel, gone on record as saying that "Maclaren-Ross never buys his round."[25]

Worn down by the strain of living together in a single room with a sixteen-month-old baby, the consequent tension precipitating angry exchanges between him and Diana, many of these at the bar of the Caves, Julian decided to look for somewhere larger. To cover the cost of this, he visited the Piccadilly offices of Ward Lock & Co, from whom he attempted to obtain an advance for a novelisation of *Until the Day She Dies*: an ingenious manouevre that would have enabled him to get paid twice for what was essentially the same piece of work. Though Ward Lock were keen to become his publisher, they informed him that it wasn't their policy to issue advances. He then reapproached Hamish Hamilton. In spite of his track-record, he persuaded Mr Hamilton to pay him a £250 advance for the planned book, as well as taking an option on his next two novels.

The money from Hamish Hamilton made the hunt for alternative accommodation feasible, yet he and Diana had difficulty finding a landlord willing to take on tenants with a baby. This paucity of choice forced them to consider a flat in suburban Cricklewood. Their prospective landlords, Leslie and Margaret Ashberry, were an elderly couple who wanted to rent out the upstairs rooms of their terraced house at 25 Anson Road. These consisted of a fully equipped kitchen with its own fridge; plus a bathroom, toilet, box-room, three bedrooms, and a combined dining-room and lounge, all carpeted and arrayed with knickknacks. The flat was even blessed with a phone. When Julian went round to view the place, the Ashberrys were so impressed by his talk of fees from the BBC, royalties from his publishers, and cash owed to him by German radio, they didn't bother to request any references. On Sunday 30 November, having paid the first week's rent, amounting to £10-10/-, Julian, Diana, and Alex settled into their large and comfortable new flat, bohemian interlopers in the world of neat, bay-windowed, privet-hedged respectability.

Since they now had the luxury of two spare bedrooms, one of which they must have earmarked for Alex when he got older, they were able to invite Diana's mother to stay with them. She took up the invitation early in December, the main purpose of the visit being to gloat over "the darling Frog",[26] as she'd dubbed her grandson. While she was there, Julian used the opportunity to ask whether she'd be prepared to allow his stepdaughter Sallie, whom he'd never met, to move in with them. But she told him it was out of the question because the court-order precluded Sallie from living with Diana.

Well aware of how deeply his wife felt about the enforced separation, Julian appears to have tried a different tactic by writing to Sallie's guardian. In the rough draft of his impassioned letter, he appealed to Philip Woolf to let Sallie stay with them either at Easter or "for a day or two after Christmas",[27] during which they'd "take her to various pantomimes etc before she returns to school."[28] Permission wasn't, however, forthcoming.

To safeguard his family's continued tenancy at Anson Road, Julian lavished as much effort on landing further commissions from the BBC as he put into scripting the sixth instalment of *The Doomsday Book*. Midway through December, he struck lucky with *The Forgotten Door*, a 60-minute murder mystery about a rising stage and screen star who finds himself reading a newspaper account of his own homicide. For this, Julian netted the usual 50-percent advance.

He'd already accumulated a daunting backlog of radio commissions to go with all the novels he owed various publishers, though his precarious financial situation led him to carry on soliciting advances from the BBC. In January 1959, having failed to interest them in his proposal to adapt a couple of suspense novels he'd sent them, he resumed work on *The Girl in the Spotlight*. When he delivered the next instalment, he explained that he was finding it impossible to cram everything into the original structure, so could they extend the series by one episode?

The BBC obligingly sanctioned his request, yielding a handy bonus.

Julian then reprised the ploy by seeking permission to expand two of his other previously commissioned scripts from 60 to 90 minutes. To speed up the process, Diana acted as a messenger. Again, the BBC gave him the thumbs up. Yet the extra money, supplemented by the fee from the now completed *Doomsday Book*, failed to extricate him from the financial mess in which he found himself.

His predicament can't have been helped by the vast taxi fares he must have run up, travelling all the way from north London to the George. Before long, he and his family had also built up large phone, milk, and laundry bills. In addition to which they'd slipped two weeks behind with the rent, prompting Mrs Ashberry to give them notice to quit. What's more, on successive visits to Rothwell House, Julian was handed a series of menacing letters. One of these was from Mrs Lyle, threatening legal action unless he paid off his debt to her. The other three were from the Inland Revenue who had, without him being aware of it, instigated High Court proceedings against him in a bid to extract £544 in unpaid income tax, dating back to the tax year 1953/54.

Now he had a wife and child, it was no longer so easy to sidestep his financial problems by doing a midnight flit. Though he ignored Mrs Lyle's threats, he wrote to the Inland Revenue offering to settle his arrears at a rate of £5-per-month. And when he and his family left Anson Road on Wednesday 18 March, he had to go through the charade of presenting Mr Ashberry with a written statement promising to settle the bulk of his £25 debt by the end of the month. Despite his lamentable record as a tenant, Julian had already found fresh accommodation at 235 Victoria Road, a terraced villa, midway along a copper-beech-lined road in similarly suburban Alexandra Park.

Following Malcolm Muggeridge's departure from the editorship of *Punch*, Tony Powell had been sacked from his job with the magazine. Deprived of regular work-related encounters, Julian's friendship with Tony waned.

Under the new regime, his contributions as a critic were supervised by the Assistant Editor, who changed the format, switching from a system where novels were reviewed individually to one where they were evaluated in groups. As a result, Julian — who had, meanwhile, made a start on his novelisation of *Until the Day She Dies* — was paid at a slightly lower rate per book, yet he was allocated more books. His work for *Punch* providing what seems to have been his only source of income, he was still hovering on the brink of financial implosion.

Lack of money wasn't his sole cause for concern. He was also worried about Alex, who was going through the excruciating pain of teething. What really disturbed him, though, was the knowledge that Alex was suffering from a serious eye complaint. Unlike Julian's financial woes, however, it soon cleared up.

At a rough guess, he reckoned their rent arrears would culminate in them being kicked out of their current accommodation by about the end of April. So he and his wife, who liked the idea of being within easy reach of the open-air swimming-pool in adjacent Wood Green, began looking for a flat there. By that stage the Ashberrys, infuriated by Julian's failure to make good his promise, had joined the ravening pack of creditors. To reduce the risk of them finding him, he used Broadcasting House as his mailing address: a stratagem that didn't endear him to the BBC administrators. Fortunately for him, Mr Ashberry's enquiries were rebuffed by Barbara Bray, who refused to disclose his address.

Against expectations, he managed to prolong their tenancy into May, assisted by two business deals struck with Tony Van den Burgh, whose company had rapidly established itself as a leading paperback publisher. When Four Square Books bought the paperback rights to *Of Love and Hunger*, a useful percentage of it going into Julian's leaky pockets, he approached Tony with a proposal for another novel. This, he hoped, might garner a convenient cash-payment. But his friend would only countenance it on condition Julian agreed to an offer that must be unique in publishing history. Tony stipulated that Julian should be locked in an upstairs room of the Northumberland Arms — at the junction between Goodge and Charlotte Streets — while he wrote the book for which he'd already been paid. Every hour, in exchange for a completed chapter, the landlord, who was a friend of Tony's, would reward him with a single large gin.

Julian reluctantly accepted the arrangement. Each morning, he would take a taxi from Alexandra Park to the Northumberland Arms. Two days into the novel, Tony stopped off to see how he was getting on. In place of the totally undisciplined scrawl Tony had expected, the manuscript blackened by incisions and amendments, Julian "presented him with a neat little exercise book containing three unblemished chapters."[29] After a further three days, Julian had completed the entire book, his exertions earning him a modest advance for another novel, which Tony regarded less as an investment than a charitable donation.

Penguin Books had, meanwhile, published his translation of *Maigret et la grande perche* in their famous green-striped paperback crime series. Its readability ensured such healthy sales it was soon reprinted.

In the face of all his accumulating problems, Julian remained surprisingly sanguine. Walking along Charing Cross Road early one afternoon that summer, he glanced through the window of Foyle's bookshop and spotted Mac browsing in the fiction section. He left Diana and the baby outside while he went in and positioned himself directly behind the shelf where Mac was standing. When his friend pulled out a book, Julian peered through the gap. It had been a long time since he'd last been in touch with Mac, yet he gave him a greeting of untempered bonhommie. "Come outside," he said, "and meet Alexander, my son. Or at least they *say* it's my son."

"Surely you must know whether it's your son or not," Mac replied.

"Oh, but I don't..."[30] Julian then led him out of the shop and introduced him to Diana and the baby. The three of them adjourned for a drink in a nearby pub, leaving Alex by the front door in his pram. From time to time, the doting Julian popped out to fill his bottle with lemonade and feed it to him. Back in the pub, Mac announced that Everest Pictures, now under the ownership of Herbert Wilcox and Anna Neagle, had bought the film rights to *The Man in the Top Hat*. They had, moreover, commissioned a screenplay, based on Mac's own treatment, and cast Kieron Moore in the role of Uncle Julian.

Milking all his contacts at the George, Julian tried to pick up some extra work from the BBC. Via Donald McWhinnie, he made an abortive attempt to interest "the Telly Boys"[31] in his screenplay of *Until the Day She Dies*. He had more luck, though, with Reggie Smith, who hired him to narrate his dramatisation of *I Had To Go Sick*. On Saturday 23 May, just under three weeks after he'd recorded it, he interrupted his normal hard-working, hard-drinking regime to attend the christening Diana had arranged for their son. They were joined at the ceremony by Diana's mother, her daughter Sallie, and presumably by their flamboyant friend Sir John Waller, who had agreed to become Alex's godfather. Marginal though the Davins had been in Julian's life lately, he persuaded Winnie to become godmother. Yet she seems to have been unable to attend the ceremony.

Around the end of that month, Julian completed his novelisation of *Until the Day She Dies*, his fractured sense of his own identity exposed by the way he projected himself into the characters of both the heroine's saviour and her nemesis. No further payments for the book were, however, scheduled by Hamish Hamilton until well after publication. Because his earnings hadn't been keeping pace with his expenditure, he was now in such "a desperate plight over money"[32] that he and Diana couldn't afford to replace Alex's threadbare baby clothes, their escalating rent arrears leading their landlady, Mrs Shead, to threaten eviction. The immediate future didn't look too encouraging either. Due to a printers' strike, the editorial staff at *Punch* were about to suspend production, cutting off Julian's reviewing work.

Under the strain of oppressive poverty and unremitting insecurity, Diana was feeling "dreadfully unwell and nervy".[33] Pushed to the point where she admitted that she "[couldn't] stand this worry anymore",[34] she planned to leave Julian and "get a living in job with Alex"[35] when he landed his next payment from the BBC, which she envisaged them dividing up. Though she made every effort to find someone willing to lend them the cash to avert the looming crisis, their position continued to deteriorate. By mid-June, they owed £37 on their rent, gas, and electricity.

Within a few days, their luck began to change. First, Julian scooped a cheque for the Dutch radio rights to one of his plays. Then he received a 24 guinea advance from the BBC. But Diana didn't go through with her plans, preferring to escape from their debilitating debt problems by hiring a letting agency to help them find fresh accommodation.

The advance Julian had just been paid by the BBC funded the composition of a sample episode of *The Midnight People*, an eight-part neo-Gothic mystery series he'd proposed, its plot inspired by the case of the Tichbourne claimant. His productivity accelerated by the lure of the remaining half of his fee, as well as by the fact that Alex wasn't waking up so often at night, he delivered the script only a week later. Early in July, the BBC gave him the verdict he wanted. They liked the first episode enough to commission the rest of the script, their interest untainted by his growing reputation for unreliability.

While he was working on it, the letting agency found them a fussily furnished one-bedroom flat in Finsbury Park, which he and his family moved into on Saturday 11 July. Their new flat, its four rooms made to appear even smaller than they were by its Regency striped curtains and the ornaments that dotted every available surface, was on the ground-floor of the annexe to a semi-detached Victorian house at 108a Tollington Park, a residential road that branched off the main shopping street. Most likely ensconced in one of the red moquette easy-chairs in the dining-room-cum-lounge, Julian applied himself with such vigour that he had, by the third week of August, already chalked up five more episodes of what he was now calling *The Midnight Men*. Each episode garnered a prompt payment from the BBC, yet within six weeks of moving to Finsbury Park, he was so far behind with the rent that the landlady asked them to leave. Safe in the knowledge they weren't legally obliged to move out until they'd received written notice, they refused to go.

Late on the afternoon of Wednesday 26 August, having spent lunchtime regaling Bob Pocock with the story of how he'd been reduced to sleeping in the waiting-room at Marylebone Station, Pocock engaged him as a last minute guest on a programme he was producing. The programme, written and narrated by René Cutforth, formed part of a radio series about London stations. For 5 guineas, Julian gave a brief talk about the waiting-room at Marylebone, highlighting its virtues as "the most comfortable mainline railway station in which to sleep."[36]

He was back in the studios the following Saturday when Reggie had arranged to start recording *The Doomsday Book*. Always on the lookout for ways of increasing his earnings, he had, with Reggie's connivance, once again created a minor but recurrent role for himself. From 10.30am until 6.00pm each day, he and the other performers rehearsed his script, ready for an hour-long evening recording session when they taped two episodes at a time. Besides acting, the versatile Julian sang extracts from *My Future Just Passed* and *Maybe You'll Be There*, the two plaintive numbers that featured in it.

These remunerative distractions behind him, at the beginning of September he went back to writing *The Midnight Men*. Not long afterwards, the Assistant Editor of *Punch* contacted him to ask if he wanted to resume work as a reviewer, the printers' strike having recently ended. But he turned down the opportunity, choosing instead to concentrate on scriptwriting.

Shortly before Diana and Alex went off to join her mother for a week's holiday in Bexhill-on-Sea, the Maclaren-Rosses received formal notice to vacate their flat by Saturday 3 October. With the place to himself, Julian completed three more episodes of *The Midnight Men*. In the thirteen days leading up to their eviction, he also approached a film producer with an idea for a screenplay, and attempted to obtain another commission from the BBC, this time for a 30-minute psychological thriller entitled *The Light Brown Hair*. Such was their belief in him, the BBC were prepared to overlook his past failings and stump up an advance for the play he'd outlined. His objective achieved, he knocked out another episode of *The Midnight Men*, now expanded to a whopping twelve parts.

Leaving behind an unpaid rates demand, a huge phone-bill and, in all likelihood, a hefty debt to their landlady, he and his family took a suite of rooms at the Royal Hotel. Positioned at the Russell Square end of Woburn Place, the Royal was a vast modern hotel with well over 700 rooms, a cavernous tiled entrance hall, a lavish winter garden, and a grand dining-room with a glazed ceiling. While he was there, Julian made a stab at satisfying one of his many outstanding commissions — for a play called *The Contract*, the drab title of which he amended to *Scorpio*. He also drafted a synopsis of *Double Analysis*, a new half-hour thriller about a psychoanalyst menaced by a disturbed patient. On Wednesday 14 October he sent this to Donald McWhinnie, who had no hesitation in commissioning it. Over the next fortnight Julian, keen to use his friendship with Donald to obtain much-needed work, submitted two more proposals for radio thrillers, the second of them bringing him a 45 guinea advance.

Possibly as a money-saving manouevre, at the end of the month the Maclaren-Rosses transferred from the Royal Hotel to the smaller, less grand Belgrave Hotel on Montague Street, parallel to the grey stone flank of the British Museum. By the second week of November they were, however, able to move back to the Royal, funded by his earnings from *Scorpio*, which he delivered to the BBC that Friday. He then polished off his latest commission: for *The Master of Suspense*, a thriller about a film director's obsession with his secretary. When he collected his payment for it from the BBC's bank, he bumped into the astringent Philip O'Connor, who was also picking up a cheque from the Corporation. On discovering that Julian's fee was larger than his, Philip "made harsh twanging noises in his throat" that "denoted wounded feelings and extreme annoyance",[37] yet Julian didn't gloat. During one of his occasional visits to the Wheatsheaf, now under new management, that evening he revealed his endearing, rarely seen streak of humility. Over a pint with Staggering Stephen in the Saloon Bar, where one of Nina Hamnett's portraits of the late Mrs Stewart hung above the old lady's favourite spot, Julian conceded that an injustice had been done, because Philip was "a more talented scriptwriter".[38]

The swift delivery of his latest piece redeemed Julian's reputation sufficiently for him to land another advance. Maintaining this sudden sense of punctiliousness, by mid-December he'd also delivered his script of *Dream Man*, formerly known as *Double Analysis*. In between working on it, he found time to pen the first quarter of a novel based on his stalled drama series, *The Girl in the Spotlight*. When he showed it to Hamish Hamilton, they decided to take up their option on it, triggering the payment of a £250 advance. With that and his earnings from *The Dancing Master*, a proposed detective story about a murdered Italian film star, which Donald McWhinnie had commissioned just before Christmas, he and his family checked out of the Royal Hotel and went down to the south coast, where they'd arranged to spend the holiday with the Jaegers. On Mac's recommendation, they booked a double-room in a converted sixteenth-century farmhouse, located down a tranquil country lane in Ancton, no more than a ten minute walk from the Jaegers' house.

He and Mac — who had recently heard that Everest's plans to film *The Man in the Top Hat* had been dashed by their inability to raise the necessary money — got on just as well as they always had, but their friendship was strained by Lydia's increasingly disparaging attitude towards Julian. For her at least, his foibles had lost whatever charm they once possessed. Though Christmas went well enough, she discouraged any further visits, ushering to a close a friendship that had sustained Julian through some of the most difficult periods of his life.

Scotch on the Rocks

On a superficial level, Julian had hardly changed between his wartime heyday and the end of the Fifties, which he'd come to regard as a decade he "could well have done without".[1] He still haunted London pubs and clubs. He still lived the same itinerant life. He still possessed an abundance of dense black hair, combed away from his forehead. He still favoured the same brand of sartorial flamboyance. He still looked the same indefinable age, neither young nor old. He still talked about books and films with the same unstoppable zest. He still scoured the secondhand bookshops on the Charing Cross Road, nowadays in search of rare, luridly jacketed American pulp fiction by the likes of David Goodis. Yet he was feeling ever more out of step with the times, his erstwhile ebullience and optimism inexorably vanishing. Now he exuded a palpable aura of disillusionment with the literary world which had failed to offer the material success he regarded as his due.

A mere two days into the new decade, the simmering hostility that characterised his dealings with publishers had already manifested itself. In advance of the imminent publication of *Until the Day She Dies*, he berated Mr Hamilton for advertising the novel in *The Bookseller* as a detective story when it was "specifically subtitled '*A Tale of Terror*'."[2]

Indeed, the first week of 1960 provided something of a microcosm of the problems that had dogged Julian for so long. Soon after he and his family had returned from their holiday, the management of the Royal Hotel, keen to pressurise them into settling their bill, notified him that they'd have to vacate their rooms by Wednesday 6 January. To avoid being kicked out, he quickly finished his script of *The Dancing Master*, its title now altered to *Mr Mephisto*. This earned him the outstanding half of his 90 guinea fee. Enough to settle the hotel bill.

His immediate accommodation worries receding, he got on with drafting the synopsis and opening scenes of *The Man in Aurora's Room*, a radio play about a private detective hired to re-examine an old murder case. As a means of saving money, he wrote it on hotel notepaper. He then sent it to Donald McWhinnie, who went ahead and commissioned it for the *Thirty Minute Theatre* slot. By the start of the next week, Julian had delivered the entire script, prompting his second cheque from the BBC within only a few days. Things took another turn for the better a couple of days later when Hamish Hamilton informed him that they'd sold the German translation rights to *Until the Day She Dies*.

Even so, he was still having trouble covering the cost of his family's suite at the Royal. Around the second weekend of January, they moved only a few hundred yards to the much smaller, less pricey White Hall Hotel on Montague Street, where they took a couple of rooms, one of these probably set aside for use as a study. Seeking to raise the money necessary to extend their stay, Julian visited the offices of Hamish Hamilton at 90 Great Russell Street, from where he emerged with a supplementary £25 advance for his novelisation of *The Girl in the Spotlight*. He also worked on a short radio adaptation of *They Put Me In Charge Of A Squad*, one of his army stories. And he tried to drum up some more screenwriting work. As well as offering to script a series of films, based on Edgar Wallace's work, for Merton Park Studios, he attempted to sell the concept of a screen version of *Until the Day She Dies* to BBC-TV, ATV, and Alec C. Snowden. Intrigued by the idea, Alec talked about casting Leslie Caron in the central role. But the potentially prohibitive cost of the sets and location-shooting seem to have stifled his interest.

While Julian's career as a writer was in the doldrums, his parallel career as a model for characters in other peoples' novels continued to prosper. The latest addition to the gallery of Maclaren-Ross alter egos appeared in Olivia Manning's new novel, *The Great Fortune*, which inaugurated what was to become her revered *Balkan Trilogy*.[3] Drawing on her knowledge of Julian, she bestowed many of his less prepossessing traits, not least his child-like egotism, on the key character of Prince Yakimov, an elegant but down-on-his-luck Anglo-Russian who swans around in a tatty fur coat, scrounging from his friends and addressing them as "dear boy".

In the final week of January, just before Julian and family were due to be kicked out of their hotel, where they were now squeezed into a single room, he completed his dramatisation of *They Put Me In Charge Of A Squad*. Despite the BBC's qualms about its supposedly coarse language, they accepted the script, the fee from it covering his family's mounting hotel bill and encouraging him to prepare an adaptation of another of his wartime stories.

At the start of the following week, he received more good news, this time from BBC-TV, who invited him to a meeting to discuss the proposed screenplay of *Until the Day She Dies*. But he was running short of cash again by Friday, compelling him to approach Hamish Hamilton with a request for an additional £50 advance, which they refused. Over the weekend, his mind was distracted from his predicament by Alex, in whom he was taking genuine fatherly pride, all his earlier doubts about the baby's paternity now banished.

That Tuesday the management of the White Hall Hotel issued them with the inevitable notice to quit. They were, however, "saved by the bell",[4] salvation coming in the shape of the BBC's decision to purchase his radio adaptation of *Y-List*. In the afternoon, he went round to the Copyright Department, where he signed the contract. Two hours after that, he drew a cheque for £58, the majority of it going towards paying off his debt to the hotel, who rescinded their notice to quit.

On Thursday that week, Hamish Hamilton published *Until the Day She Dies*. Walking past their offices, Julian stopped to admire the copies of the book displayed in the front window. He was particularly pleased with the design of its dustjacket, featuring a photo of the St Giles Fair in Oxford. But his delight had quickly metamorphosed into frustration, his subsequent meeting at BBC-TV yielding "a very disappointing reaction".[5]

As a mark of gratitude to Miss Dean and the other staff in the BBC's Copyright and Accounts departments, who always made sure he was paid with such alacrity, Julian distributed complementary copies of his latest novel. Another copy was despatched to Dan Davin's wife. In recognition of all the time she'd spent listening to him rabbit on about Sonia, he'd dedicated the book to Winnie. Unable to bring herself either to speak to him about it, or to write and thank him because she considered it "intolerably bad",[6] the dwindling friendship between he and the Davins expired. But her low opinion wasn't shared by the critics who, for the most part, liked it. *The TLS* even compared it to a Hitchcock movie, a comparison Julian, who had incorporated several allusions to the master, would have relished.

Only two days after the publication of his novel, he was again complaining of having "no money",[7] though that didn't deter him from spending the evening in Berlemont's with Reggie Smith, or from taking an extra room at the White Hall Hotel. For the second time within the past fortnight, he was rescued at the last moment. "Miracle No.2",[8] as he hailed it, consisted of a letter from the BBC announcing that *The Doomsday Book* had been approved for broadcast. More to the point, it meant he was now due the remainder of his fee — an invaluable £268. Late on the afternoon of Monday 15 February, he collected his cheque and paid off his family's £32 hotel bill. To celebrate his good fortune, he went to see Peter Cushing in *Flesh and the Fiends*, the new movie about a gang of nineteenth-century grave-robbers.

The financial pressure on him lifted for the moment at least, he appears to have striven to push forward two unresolved projects. These comprised both the radio script and the novel of *The Girl in the Spotlight*. But he was, during the final weekend of February, plunged back into penury when someone robbed his family's hotel suite. Stripped of most of his cash, he had to come up with a way of raising some quick money. So he set to work on a radio dramatisation of yet another of his Forties short stories, in this case *The Swag, the Spy and the Soldier*.

Again, destitution was averted as much by luck as design. Thanks to a previous contract to play the part of the narrator in Reggie Smith's production of *Y-List*, a role that he rehearsed and recorded on Wednesday 2 March, he earned a timely 15 guineas. Driven by the abiding fear of eviction, he worked straight through Thursday night, the aim being to deliver his latest script and get paid before the weekend. Next day he handed it in to Barbara Bray, who authorised the payment of the first half of a £94 fee, with which he chipped away at his two most pressing debts. Besides passing on £10 to the hotel management, guaranteeing that he and his family were now "safe until Tuesday morning",[9] he posted £4 to Mr and Mrs Ashberry in an effort to deter them from proceeding with their threatened legal action.

By Monday, his adaptation of *The Swag, the Spy and the Soldier* had received Barbara Bray's approval for use as a 60-minute play on the Home Service. That afternoon he was able to collect the rest of his fee, out of which he paid off an additional £35 from his hotel bill, ensuring their continued residence until Saturday. Just as one worry abated, though, another manifested itself. This took the form of a summons from Mr and Mrs Ashberry to appear in court in a little under a month from then.

To keep the hotel's management happy, he sold a couple of consignments of manuscripts to Jake Schwartz, who gave him £40, which paid for another six days there. Early the following week, Julian received just the boost he needed when Hamish Hamilton notified him that *Until the Day She Dies* was selling so well they'd ordered a reprint. Its popularity reinforcing his belief in the book's potential as a television drama, he made a start on the screenplay. But he soon had to abandon it in favour of something likely to generate more rapid remuneration.

On Thursday 17 March, the day before his next payment to the hotel was due, he persuaded the BBC to commission a 90-minute radio play based on *The Key Man*, permission to use his screenplay having at last been granted by Anglo-Amalgamated. With the initial instalment of his fee for it, he covered his family's hotel bill for the next few days, during which he rapidly expanded his script. The latest deadline set by the management of the White Hall Hotel was about to expire when he delivered the completed play and collected the other half of his money.

At that point, he took a break from writing in order to act in the BBC's production of *The Master of Suspense*. He and the other cast members spent most of Tuesday 29 March rehearsing it at the BBC's Maida Vale Studios. Then they recorded it that evening. Reggie Smith, who was producing it, afterwards congratulated Julian on his performance as Lester Reeve, an urbane former colleague of the film director at the heart of the story. Aside from gleaning Reggie's approbation, his performance earned him a £14 cheque, supplemented by the sale of the manuscript of *The Key Man* to Jake Schwartz, whom he most likely met in the George that night.

Concluding a successful week, he went on to obtain a commission for a 60-minute radio play called *The Christmas Box*. The subsequent £47 advance, which came through at the beginning of April, meant he was able to clear his entire debt to the White Hall Hotel. Sick of being hassled by its staff, he shifted his family to the Bedford Hotel, a larger establishment on nearby Southampton Row, backing on to its own gardens.

In that week's edition of *The Radio Times*, the BBC energetically plugged the first episode of *The Doomsday Book*, programmed for the evening of Monday 4 April, complete with a specially composed theme tune by Humphrey Searle, a former pupil of Webern. The BBC's efforts were repaid by a crop of positive reviews.

A couple of days after the opening broadcast, Julian polished off the script of *The Christmas Box*. And he also received a letter from Hamish Hamilton announcing that they'd sold the paperback rights to *Until the Day She Dies*. These had been bought by Ace Books for £200, 50-percent of which would be paid to Julian.

Things weren't all going his way, though. Mr and Mrs Ashberry's case against him was scheduled to be heard in court the following day. To placate the magistrate dealing with it, he wrote to the court, promising to "send a remittance after Easter."[10] Fearing they might not believe him, he promptly despatched 12 guineas. Otherwise he ignored the summons. Instead of appearing in court, he collected what he was owed for *The Christmas Box*, paid his family's hotel bill, and evaded any action that might be taken against him by transferring to the Bonington, another large hotel on Southampton Row. No sooner had he and his family arrived there than he wrote to Hamish Hamilton, requesting his share of the money from Ace Books. But he was told that the cheque hadn't appeared yet, so he'd have to wait.

For once he was unable to make good the shortfall by picking up scriptwriting work from the BBC. Their bill probably unpaid, the Maclaren-Rosses had left the Bonington Hotel by Thursday 14 April. They then returned to the White Hall Hotel. With the help of three convenient payments from the BBC, among them a 45 guinea advance for a dramatisation of *The Weeping and the Laughter*, he extended their stay until the evening of Friday 29 April.

When they moved out, they were unsure where to go next. In the end they decided to try their luck in the shabby area on the Bayswater edge of Kensington Gardens. They appear to have gone straight to the Queen's Hotel on Queensborough Terrace. So paranoid was Julian about disclosing their latest address in case someone tipped off his creditors, he even avoided revealing it to Hamish Hamilton, who were reduced to leaving letters and packages for him on reception at Broadcasting House.

Just under two weeks later, he restocked his wallet by persuading Reggie Smith to commission his proposed play about a private eye attempting to locate a girl who has eloped with an American serviceman. Only too aware of Julian's shaky finances, the considerate Reggie also found him work acting in a production of a double-bill of his short plays, recorded at the start of June.

Julian had, by the following week, transplanted his family to the New Court Hotel on Inverness Terrace. There he concentrated on writing the novelisation of *The Doomsday Book*, which Hamish Hamilton were taking as part of their three-book deal with him. They hoped to publish it in November, yet Julian had only completed the first six chapters by mid-June.

Unable to remain at the New Court Hotel, on Friday 24 June he and his family shifted from there to another hotel in the Queensway area. All his correspondence was, however, directed to the reception desk at the Imperial Hotel, where he'd cultivated a useful contact. His burgeoning sense of persecution, of being a marked man was lent credence by the discovery that Islington Town Council were pursuing him in an attempt to recover the rates he owed on the flat in Finsbury Park.

Paradoxically, while he was in hiding, he sustained his widely advertised career as a radio playwright and actor. During July, he not only landed another commission for a play, but also rehearsed and recorded performances in *The Swag, the Spy and the Soldier* and *The Key Man*, the latter affording him license to enact his fantasies about being an underworld figure. In the gaps between his acting engagements for the BBC, he wrapped up the remaining chapters of *The Doomsday Book* and delivered the manuscript to his publisher. He then turned his attention back to his uncompleted novelisation of *The Girl in the Spotlight*. But he knew he couldn't finish it without a fresh injection of cash.

Necessity inspired him to write an impudent letter to Hamish Hamilton in early August. His letter presented them with an ultimatum: either they double the size of their advance, £200 of which would be payable immediately, or else they release him from his existing contract. Refusing to be bullied by Julian, Mr Hamilton chose the second option, so Julian had to find another publisher, a task that proved far harder than he may have envisaged. Due in part to his reputation for being difficult to deal with and for failing to honour contracts, no hardback publisher would touch him. Devoid of any alternatives, he signed a deal with Frank Rudman at Four Square Books, now owned by Ace Books (whose take-over of the company had recently resulted in them shelving plans to publish the novel he'd written in the Northumberland Arms).[11] For a payment of £125, Julian sold them the worldwide paperback rights to *The Girl in the Spotlight*. Yet even that was insufficient to provide him with the time he needed.

By September, he'd returned to the scriptwriting treadmill, making frequent visits to the George. "He's an old has-been of course," one of his fellow regulars admitted to Anthony Cronin, "but if the rest of us could write like him we could be very proud of ourselves."[12] Their faith in his abilities unwavering, Reggie Smith and Donald McWhinnie granted him a string of commissions for new radio thrillers as well as adaptations of his prose work, interspersed by the occasional acting role.

Of the plays he wrote during that autumn and the early part of the winter, easily the most profitable was a domestic melodrama, commissioned at the end of September for *Thirty Minute Theatre*. Entitled *Threesome*, it was about a woman who becomes convinced that her husband is trying to kill her. A fraction over three weeks after Julian had received the 25 guinea down-payment on it, he handed in the completed script. The play was subsequently broadcast twice by the BBC and repeated a further four times on the Overseas Service before being sold to radio stations in Germany and East Africa. Its success led him to devote several days at the beginning of November to adapting it into an extended short story, narrated from the frightened wife's perspective.

That month, by which time he and his family were living at the

Sandringham Hotel at 3 Holford Road, on the fringe of Hampstead Heath, he was kept busy correcting the proofs of *The Doomsday Book* and scripting two brief dramatisations of old short stories of his, which the BBC had just commissioned. Though these realised initial fees of 50 guineas, he couldn't afford to settle his hotel bill. "Growing tired of the perpetual insecurity of life chez Julian",[13] Diana walked out on him in the first week of December, taking with their two-and-a-half-year-old son. This was the cue for Julian to sneak out of the Sandringham Hotel without paying their £69 bill.

Homeless again, his living expenses funded by loans from Tony Van den Burgh and other loyal friends, he was, as Reggie Smith put it, now "verging on the 'luny-bin' [sic]",[14] Diana's departure signalling his re-adoption of the pugnacious Mr Hyde persona. When, just over a fortnight later, he turned up at Broadcasting House where he was due to portray his father in an adaptation of one of his autobiographical short stories, "he kicked up a stink about how he wanted to be credited in *The Radio Times* as 'Edward Hyde'."[15]

One evening around then, having refused to go to the Caves with Anthony Cronin because he wanted to avoid "all those noisy Colquhouns and MacBrydes and people",[16] he took Cronin to a new upstairs drinking club on Old Compton Street. There, to his pride, the "customers and staff actually knew him as Mr Hyde and nothing else."[17]

Stricken by the mental anguish and turmoil brought about by the collapse of his marriage, he seems to have stopped writing for several weeks. He ended his silence in mid-January 1961 when he obtained a commission from the BBC for *The Intaglio*, a 60-minute radio play about a sleuth trying to retrieve a stolen amethyst brooch. For that, Julian was given a 50 guinea advance. He supplemented this with earnings from an acting role in *The High Priest of Buddha* — the second of two short plays he'd written late the previous year — and from the sale of the manuscript of *The Dark Diceman*. Its sale marked his acknowledgement that the book would "never be completed."[18]

At the start of February, he delivered the finished script of *The Intaglio*. And, not long after that, he acquired a commission from the BBC to dramatise the poignant true story of a poor, elderly New Yorker who started forging dollar bills to buy food for his dog. Kept going by an unexpected repeat fee for another play, Julian pushed on with *Old Eighty-Eight, the Counterfeitor*, which was recorded for the Home Service in April, starring Cyril Cusack as the small-time forger who foiled the FBI for over a decade.

As it happens, Julian was proving every bit as elusive to *his* creditors. By concealing the addresses of the various Knightsbridge hotels where he was living, any letters to him being forwarded via Reggie Smith or the barman at the George, he dodged even the determined efforts of the Post Office, who were trying to reclaim the money he owed them for his Finsbury Park phone-bill.

Furtive though his existence was, Julian kept his name in circulation through regular broadcasts of his plays, not to mention the publication of *The Doomsday Book* that June. Despite his rift with Hamish Hamilton, the company did their best to publicise the book. But it attracted scant attention, a rare exception being a hostile thumbnail review it received in *The TLS*. Sales were, in consequence, so low it struggled to recover even the advance Julian had been paid.

Officially he was no longer part of the stable of Hamish Hamilton authors, yet that didn't deter the by now slightly dishevelled Julian from paying occasional visits to their offices. Claiming to be one of their writers, he would buttonhole the company's employees and try to borrow money, ostensibly for his bus fare. Short of cash as he was, he made a point of sending what little he could afford to Diana to help provide for Alex, who was living with her in a hotel in South Kensington.

He appears to have spent July revising and expanding the radio version of *The Girl in the Spotlight*, the overdue script of which filled seven large notebooks. He also set aside the time to go for a drink in the ML with Eric Phillips, a fan of his writing who had, for several years, been pestering him to grant an interview about his work. Referring to Phillips as "my dear boy", Julian fielded a sequence of general questions with a mixture of candour, guile, and arrogance. The interview covered his "natural ear"[19] for dialogue, honed by standing "in pubs, boarding houses and hotels [and] listening to the way people talked"[20]; his dissatisfaction with the lack of influence accorded screenwriters by film producers; his relish for writing radio drama; his method of constructing a novel; his scorn for most of the current crop of novelists; and his admiration for the up-and-coming playwright Harold Pinter. Though Julian had been courteous and cooperative, he was evidently relieved to escape from his interviewer, who sold the piece to *The Writer*, a magazine for literary aspirants.

Either because he wanted to give his creditors the slip, or maybe because he was wearying of the pleasures of metropolitan life, Julian toyed with the idea of leaving London but ended up staying put. By then, he was based at 74 Little Albany Street, on the Regent's Park side of Euston Station. Not all that far from where Tony Powell and his wife used to live.

His sole income during the first two weeks of August consisted of a fee for appearing, alongside Tony Van den Burgh, in a recording of *The Man With A Background in Flames*, a thriller he'd adapted almost a year earlier. Being "in a very difficult position financially",[21] he became extremely excited when he heard that Ivan Obolensky Inc, a small New York publisher, had bought the American rights to *The Doomsday Book*. On Sunday 13 August, he wrote to Roger Machell at Hamish Hamilton asking for an advance on his share of the deal. But his excitement was dampened by Machell's response, which revealed that there was likely to be a delay, since Obolensky was in the middle of being taken over. The disappointment was compounded by the news that the novel's paltry sales had dissuaded Four Square Books from releasing a paperback edition.

Consolation of sorts was provided by Reggie Smith, who had made plans to proceed with a recording of *The Girl in the Spotlight*, in readiness for which Reggie paid Julian 12 guineas to spend part of that Tuesday morning at the BBC's Piccadilly Studios. There he sat at the piano and played the tune Stanley Hume had, almost exactly six years before, composed in honour of Sonia Orwell. Over it, Julian sang the plangent lyrics he'd written to go with it, lyrics that would serve as a refrain through the play. Listening to his performance was a specialist capable of transcribing and arranging the tune, so that Julian's singing could later be recorded and accompanied by a group of professional musicians.

Towards the end of the month, hounded by the Post Office, who had obtained his address from Hamish Hamilton, Julian left Little Albany Street and found accommodation on Baker Street. Lest the same thing happen, he avoided divulging his new address, even to close friends like Reggie, who continued to do everything he could to help reinvigorate Julian's career. Besides hiring him to appear in another of his one-off plays, Reggie also contracted him to act in six of the nine half-hour episodes of *The Girl in the Spotlight*. These were due to be recorded at both the Grafton and Piccadilly Studios over a period of fourteen days, commencing on Friday 15 September. From 10.00am until 5.00pm each day, the cast rehearsed Julian's script, ready for an hour of it to be taped afterwards. Julian, for whom working with a talented cast and producer were "a fine experience",[22] was assigned the part of the effete magazine-editor Mark Rumbold. In place of Emlyn Williams, who had originally been offered the pivotal role of Mr Hyde, Reggie recruited the ageing stage-actor Ralph Truman, best known for his appearances in films such as *Henry V* and *Oliver Twist*. Another familiar performer, the dark-haired, toothy Nicolette Bernard, took the part of Luna Morell.

Once that day's rehearsals and the ensuing recording session were out of the way, Julian — attired in a battered tweed suit and scuffed suede shoes — would go with Reggie, his secretary, and the rest of the cast to the George. Usually they were joined there by Diana, who had just got back together with him. She'd match him drink for drink, their boozy reputation inspiring the cast, unknown to Julian, to compose alternative, satirical lyrics about them, sung to *The Girl in the Spotlight*'s lilting signature tune.

About halfway through the show's production schedule, the Home Service broadcast *The Man With A Background in Flames*. It earned a rapturous review in *The Listener* which proclaimed Julian "radio's Alfred Hitchcock".[23] His fame as a writer of thrillers meant that the critics treated *The Girl in the Spotlight* — the first instalment of which was broadcast in the final week of September — as a crime drama rather than the dark romance he intended. Yet it attracted a large following, its popularity made all the sweeter by the arrival of the first £120 instalment of what Julian was owed by Ivan Obolensky Inc, who were publishing *The Doomsday Book* in November. The money from America seems to have bought him the time he needed to restart his much-interrupted novelisation of *The Girl in the Spotlight*. Not that he viewed it as simply a novelisation. By expanding and re-shaping it, he felt that he was creating an entirely separate work.

His relationship with Diana re-established despite the weekly reminders of his former Sonia-fixation, offered by the radio serialisation of *The Girl in the Spotlight*, they resumed their old itinerant existence. Over the next few weeks he earned only a £26 repeat fee from the BBC, probably augmented by the odd £2 or £3 payment from Jake Schwartz who, convinced of his claim to literary greatness, persisted in buying up his manuscripts.

On Sunday 15 October Julian rented a room for himself and his family at the Winterbourne Hotel in Pembridge Gardens, just off Notting Hill Gate. Three days after that, they were back on the road. With 25,000 words of his new novel completed, he endeavoured to drag himself out of the financial quicksand by cheekily tendering the book to Roger Machell at Hamish Hamilton. If they'd give him an immediate advance of £100, he promised to deliver the manuscript within one month. Along with his letter to Machell, he enclosed his contract with Four Square Books which, he felt, could easily be renegotiated. Disinclined to let Hamish Hamilton have his address, especially after their treacherous collaboration with the Post Office, he informed Machell that he'd ring him the following afternoon to get his decision.

As arranged, he phoned Machell on Friday 10 November, only to be told that "(a) in view of past experience [they] had decided against going on publishing him, (b) no publisher in his senses would take on a book without paperback rights and (c) he'd probably killed all chance of an American hardcover sale by selling world paperback rights."[24] Together with Diana, playing the role of the "nice pathetic wife",[25] Julian went round to Hamish Hamilton's offices to pick up the Four Square contract from reception. They were confronted by Machell who, with the full backing of Mr Hamilton, left him in no doubt as to their unflattering opinion of him.

Money being tight, another repeat fee providing their only apparent income, he and his family continued moving from address to address, "one jump ahead of the duns and the police [...], angry hoteliers impound[ing] his correspondence when they [could not] impound his possessions."[26] By mid-November the Maclaren-Rosses were living at the large White Park Hotel at 9 Lancaster Gate, where Julian maintained his time-honoured habit of not setting foot outside until about midday. From there, they moved to one of numerous bedsits at 24 York Street, a narrow townhouse close to Gloucester Place, somewhere replete with memories of the courtship of his first wife.

Hearing that his mother-in-law was seriously ill, he made arrangements to move down to Brighton so Diana could be near her, though it must have been a wrench for them both, given their love of big city life. On Saturday 16 December they quit York Street and headed for Hove, where they'd already secured accommodation. For 9 guineas-a-week, plus the electricity, gas, and phone bills, they rented a flat at 24 Brunswick Terrace, part of a row of decaying stucco-fronted Regency houses. These had an unobstructed view of both the sea and, looking towards Brighton, the ornate West Pier, its associations with Patrick Hamilton (who had used the pier as the backdrop to the first of his Gorse novels) enhancing the spectacular location.

Settled in their new home, where they rapidly fell into debt with Mrs Tanchan, their landlady, Julian resumed work on his novel and also went back to writing radio scripts. At the top of his itinerary were two adaptations of Edgar Wallace novels. He'd finished these by late January 1962. But it had become hard for him to place his scripts with the BBC now that two of his influential allies, Barbara Bray and Donald

McWhinnie, had left the Corporation, and now that he no longer saw Reggie Smith on a daily basis. All the same, Reggie was still an invaluable sponsor who, at Julian's behest, went to the trouble of submitting his script of *Threesome* for consideration by BBC-TV.

His financial problems unabated, the anticipated second instalment of his payment from America having not yet come through, he nonetheless pressed on with his novel, embellishing it with barely disguised portraits of Cyril Connolly and Dylan Thomas. As he was writing the book, which now had the alternative title of *My Name Is Love*, the resentment he'd formerly felt towards George Orwell dispersed. In its place, he was left with a sense of kinship, borne out of their shared attraction to Sonia, as well as their overlapping realist aesthetic, underpinned by what he saw as their "crypto-romantic"[27] sensibilities.

He finally finished his novel on Saturday 10 February. He then commenced the hunt for a publisher, submitting it to William Heinemann, Hodder & Stoughton, and Anthony Blond, all of whom turned it down on the grounds that the paperback rights had already been sold. The run of bad tidings continued when the impending soft-cover publication of *Until the Day She Dies*, which would have triggered a cheque for £50, was held up by New English Library's acquisition of Ace Books. A decision on whether Penguin would go ahead with a mooted softback edition of *The Weeping and the Laughter* was also delayed.[28]

Four days later, some of which he devoted to the opening passage of a lengthy new novel he'd been mulling over, Julian resorted to asking the Royal Literary Fund for an application form. While awaiting a reply, he sent Michael Bakewell, Barbara Bray's successor at the BBC, the uncommissioned 40-minute play he'd just finished. His covering letter, which solicited sympathy by stating that he faced imminent eviction and needed the money to finance the completion of his latest novel, requested rapid payment.

Accompanying the application form from the Royal Literary Fund, there was a friendly note from Captain Broadbent. It invited Julian to visit their offices to discuss his problems. But he had to decline the invitation, because he was so broke he couldn't spare the money for the fare to London. With the end of February approaching, he filled out the form in his usual meticulous handwriting. To boost its chances of success, he enclosed copies of his two most recent novels and a lengthy supporting statement that set out the reasons for his present plight. As with each of his previous applications, he mustered a couple of impressive testimonials to support it, one of them from Sir John Waller, the other from Reggie Smith and Olivia Manning who, in a jointly signed letter, acclaimed him as someone possessing "a talent of a rare and original kind."[29]

A decision on his application was scheduled to be made by mid-March. In the fortnight before that, Julian and his family's financial position deteriorated steadily, their morale sapped still further by the distressing condition of Diana's mother, who was now comatose in hospital. Though there was the possibility of him getting a lift up to London to see Captain Broadbent, Julian didn't take up the offer because he felt that his wife needed him with her.

Instead of announcing their decision, the eagerly awaited letter from the Royal Literary Fund informed him that the next meeting of the committee, due to consider his application, had been postponed until Wednesday 11 April. Naturally, it came as a "great blow"[30] to him, yet he persevered with his writing, spending the next few days drafting a television adaptation of his most recent play.

The bad luck that had beset he and his family was mitigated the following week by the news of his mother-in-law's tentative recovery. By Wednesday, she'd emerged from her coma and rallied sufficiently to be transferred from hospital to a nursing home. But this represented no more than the briefest of respites for Julian and family.

Nearly a month had gone by since he'd written to Michael Bakewell. The delay must have prepared him for the worst. On Thursday or Friday of that week, he at last received a response from Bakewell, who not only rejected his latest script, but also refused to pay him any additional advances until he'd worked through the list of five previous unfulfilled commissions, dating back three-and-a-half years.

Tenacious as ever, he sought to haggle with Bakewell even though there was no scope for negotiation. His swift riposte took the form of a four-point proposal, its misguidedly unapologetic and truculent tenor more appropriate to someone bargaining from a position of strength. In another move sure to antagonise Bakewell, he gave him until only the following Thursday to make up his mind. The days slipping past without the hoped for phone-call, he decided to resume his quest to raise some cash by finding a publisher for *My Name Is Love*. First, though, he had to contact Frank Rudman at Ace Books and ask him to relinquish the paperback rights. Rudman said he'd only cancel the contract if Julian repaid the money they'd already advanced him, effectively ruling out that option.

Julian's room for manouevre was further curtailed by a predictably tart note from Bakewell, who explained that the BBC weren't prepared to accept his terms. Exasperated by the way Julian "tended to regard the BBC as a philanthropic organisation",[31] Bakewell also threatened to write off all his outstanding plays unless they were delivered soon.

Bypassing Bakewell, Julian went straight to Reggie Smith. All his earlier conditions abandoned in favour of a more straightforward approach, he tried to get Reggie to commission an adaptation of *The Bamboo Girl*, a melodramatic pulp novel about a married man who gets blackmailed when he falls for a nightclub singer. But Reggie, who had come to realise that his friend was "frozen in a vicious circle",[32] supported his colleague by refusing to give Julian any more commissions until the backlog had been cleared.

Two stills from
Julian Maclaren-Ross's appearance
on the television documentary,
In The Shadow of Cain, 1964
(© BBC Photo Library)

C.K. Jaeger
holding one of
Julian Maclaren-Ross's
canes, 1997
(© Roger Dobson)

Closing Time

The situation was fast becoming "completely desperate",[1] his debt to Mrs Tanchan having risen to insurmountable heights. If he didn't pay up, his landlady warned him that she'd instigate legal action. But her threats made no difference because he simply couldn't lay his hands on the £214 she wanted. No longer willing to listen to his excuses for his failure to pay up, she gave the Maclaren-Rosses notice to leave by noon on Wednesday 8 April 1962. As eviction day loomed, Julian — his funds so depleted he was unable to rustle up the cash for a deposit on another flat — arranged to have all his correspondence sent via Jake Schwartz's Brighton address.

On vacating their sea-front flat, Julian and family registered at the large, seedy Hotel Brunswick, situated at 69 Brunswick Place, right on the crest of the short hill leading up from where they'd been living. From their new base, he wrote to Roger Machell to find out whether his American publisher had forwarded the £119 they owed him. Without it, he knew he wouldn't be able to cover his family's hotel bill beyond the end of that week. Machell wrote back to say there was no sign of the money, but sent £10 to help him get through the impending Easter break.

Around the beginning of the holiday period, Diana — who had been having an affair with a Scottish theatre director named of John Maxwell — left Julian. She took their three-and-a-half-year-old son with her, the abrupt separation causing her husband "considerable anguish".[2] It appears that Diana and Alex moved straight into Maxwell's flat, elsewhere in Hove. Freed from the obligation to remain in Sussex, Julian had gone back to London by Easter Monday. Yet his return to the capital heralded no immediate improvement in his woeful circumstances. Initially, he was so broke he couldn't afford anywhere to stay. Until he found someone prepared to put him up, he had little alternative but to sleep in station waiting-rooms. Desperate for cash, he wrote to Machell again and asked for "another £25 — or even £15 — as an advance on the Obolensky money."[3]

Late on either Tuesday or Wednesday afternoon, he phoned Machell for a verdict. Outraged by Machell's refusal to stump up the money he so urgently required, Julian composed a disgruntled letter insisting it was Hamish Hamilton's duty to settle the debt incurred by their

American counterparts. He told Machell he'd ring at midday on Friday to find out when it would be convenient for him to collect his money — in cash, of course.

When he called Hamish Hamilton, they said that Machell — who hadn't yet received the letter — was in a meeting. Julian's unstamped missive eventually reached Hamish Hamilton's offices on Monday. Machell then wrote to him to say that a cable was being sent to Ivan Obolensky Inc, requesting immediate payment. Not that it did any good.

In spite of his empty wallet, Julian reclaimed his position at the bar of the George, where he cadged drinks and borrowed whatever money he could, his mood veering from the "expansively benign"[4] to the "violently persecuted".[5] Still "between flats",[6] as he liked to put it, he used the pub as a mailing address.

His lack of cash didn't stop him from asking a young actress, who was a member of the BBC Repertory Company, out to dinner. After four hungry hours spent in various pubs, he took her to the Mandrake, where they were sitting when Anthony Cronin appeared. Cronin's presence encouraged her to complain bitterly about Julian's failure to buy her the promised dinner. With straightfaced solemnity, Julian pointed at the inedible sandwich that accompanied her drink and said, "There is your dinner..."[7]

For the time-being at least, he was resigned to doing no more script-writing for Reggie Smith's department, so he concentrated on trying to find work with radio producers from other sections of the BBC. It was in the Saloon Bar of the George that he probably encountered Teresa McGonagle and David Geary from the Talks Department, who hired him to appear in a series they were producing for the Home Service in the south-east. Billed as offering both urban and rural "comment, controversy and character",[8] the series was called *Town and Country*. They paid Julian to perform four brief scripted anecdotes from his repertoire. These were recorded on Thursday 10 May.

Over drinks in the George not long afterwards, he put forward a bizarre programme proposal to "the rather aloof and superior"[9] Douglas Cleverdon, a producer in the BBC's Features Department. His idea was for a musical version of *The Picture of Dorian Gray*, for which he planned to write the lyrics. Without even bothering to consult the red-faced, slightly stammering composer Humphrey Searle, who was now part of his clique in the George, he announced that Searle would be composing the score.

Cleverdon's interest in his proposal spurred Julian to spend some of that weekend drafting a synopsis of the story, which he submitted to the

BBC. Should the project be commissioned, he assured Cleverdon that the lyrics would be completed within a fortnight, ready for when Searle came back from a short trip to the Continent. Cleverdon remained positive about the idea, yet understandably reluctant to make any commitments until it had been discussed with Searle.

The consequent hold-up led Julian to look for another escape-route from poverty and homelessness. Perhaps hoping that Graham Greene might help to find a publisher for *My Name Is Love*, Julian sent him the manuscript. But Graham appears not to have been able to assist. Julian also asked Reggie Smith, whom he continued to see in the George, to pass on the script of *Threesome* to ABC Television. His old friend obliged, though Reggie's famously plentiful reserves of sympathy and forbearance were beginning to run dry, exhausted by Julian's incessant demands, by his sudden shifts in mood, by his insistence on playing "the grand author",[10] and, above all, by what Reggie viewed as his "demented"[11] behaviour.

Julian could have registered as unemployed, but he seems to have steadfastly refused. To do so would have been both an admission of defeat and an unwelcome reminder that his career had come full circle. Instead, he survived by borrowing from Tony Van den Burgh among others, his borrowings supplemented by the small fee he received when the Tuesday 12 June edition of the BBC's popular *Pick of the Week* radio show featured his contribution to *Town and Country*.

At lunchtime in the George three weeks later, Reggie broke the disappointing news that ABC Television had rejected his script. All Julian's hopes were now invested in his Dorian Gray project, his conception of which was growing ever more inflated. Keen though the BBC remained on the idea, Douglas Cleverdon had become concerned that it might prove too costly to produce.

Penniless and resentful about the dispiriting course his life had taken, by mid-July Julian was, for want of any better alternatives, willing to enslave himself to the journalistic grind from which he'd escaped only the summer before last. Through Arthur Crook, who had taken over the editorship of *The TLS*, he earned £25 for writing a middle celebrating the storytelling skills of C.S. Forrester. And, in the George, he cornered Anthony Thwaite, now Literary Editor of *The Listener*. Onerous as Thwaite found his monologues and his habit of always trying to borrow money, he succumbed to Julian's all too accurate hard-luck stories and commissioned a short review of William Saroyan's latest book. With a characteristic lack of self-awareness,

Julian's piece marvelled at Saroyan's spendthrift tendencies, at his ability to fritter away money on drink and gambling. In a piquant coda, he noted that "at present Saroyan lives in an ice-cold flat in Paris, where he hopes to earn enough to pay the tax collector if he can hold on to the money long enough when earned; a situation which may be familiar to his colleagues in other parts of the world."[12]

Julian delivered the handwritten, punctually completed review to *The Listener*'s offices on Marylebone High Street where, contrary to the magazine's normal procedure, he expected to be paid immediately in cash. By "sheer cheek and persistence",[13] his long-term prospects sacrificed on the altar of short-term needs, he got his way, in the process souring what might have been a remunerative relationship.

To recoup the debts Julian had accumulated while he was living in Hove, Mrs Tanchan took out a writ against him on Friday 10 August. Julian was, by that time, lodging at 51 Blenheim Crescent, a huge house near the junction with Ladbroke Grove — not the most salubrious of neighbourhoods. Since his former landlady didn't know his current address, the summons was served in the Saloon Bar of the George.

But he had other more pressing uses for his money. The following Wednesday he went round to his solicitor's offices on Hammersmith Broadway and gave them a £25 deposit on the divorce proceedings he'd decided to initiate. As a prelude to legal action, his solicitor arranged for two private detectives to visit the flat in Hove where his wife and son were still ensconced with John Maxwell. While he was waiting to hear from his solicitor, who was taken aback by his refusal to disclose his address, Julian received a letter from Douglas Cleverdon, care of the George. It notified him that the Third Programme would not be pursuing his Dorian Gray proposal.

A couple of opportune developments helped to allay the inevitable disappointment. For a start, there was the discovery that the New English Library had rescheduled the paperback edition of *Until the Day She Dies* for April 1963. Then there was the exhilarating upturn in his love life. By the beginning of September he'd embarked on an affair with a Dublin-based poet and friend of Brendan Behan. Such was his conviction that he and Claire, his latest girlfriend, could be happy together, he was, within only a fortnight, contemplating going back to Dublin with her. It all went wrong, however, on the evening of Wednesday 12 September when she made a tactless remark which deeply offended him. That Friday she wrote to him to apologise, but he found what she'd said so inexcusable he appears to have broken off the affair with a regretful postcard, quoting one of her poems: "The dream, like a perfect crime, must remain in the head."[14]

Only a few days after their romance had ended in such anti-climax, he rebounded into a liaison with a wealthy married woman by the name of Inez. Surreptitiously escorting her back to the Bayswater tube one afternoon towards the end of September, he almost collided with Elizabeth Smart, who told him that her great friend Robert Colquhoun had died.

His adulterous relationship having swiftly lost its transgressive frisson, he met Eleanor Brill, the slim, dark-haired, dark-eyed Northern Irishwoman who lived in the flat above Donald McWhinnie and his wife Pauline. Drawn to her warm, understanding manner and conspicuous intelligence, Julian became romantically entangled with Eleanor, who had previously been married to a musician, by whom she had a daughter, Caroline, now nine-years-old and away at boarding school. By about October Julian had left the Regent Palace Hotel on Piccadilly Circus, where he'd been staying, and joined Eleanor and her cat, Gogo, in her first-floor flat at 16 Chepstow Place: a tall, plain-looking, stucco-fronted Georgian terraced house in Notting Hill. Because he was still being hunted by creditors, he retained his uneasiness about revealing his new address to anyone, even friends, his few confidants being sworn to secrecy.

In moving to Chepstow Place, he was bowing to a trend that had seen west London usurp Soho's role as the heartland of literary bohemia. Breaking the habit of thirty years, he virtually abandoned his old haunts and took to spending most lunchtimes and evenings, Saturdays aside, in the Catherine Wheel, a warm, homely pub at the far end of Kensington Church Street. Formerly the playground of Dylan Thomas and Roy Campbell, whose drunken antics continued to provide material for anecdotes, it had become a fashionable venue. Still handsome and deceptively fit-looking, Julian vied for the title of "Resident Rudeman",[15] the asperity of his remarks ensuring that he soon established himself as a lonely figure amid the youngish crowd that thronged the bar, his isolation alleviated by occasional visits from long-standing friends like John Davenport and Tony Van den Burgh, whose wife Ursula was normally in tow.

On Saturdays, however, Julian deserted the Catherine Wheel in favour of the Alma, a much larger pub on Westbourne Grove, only a short stroll from Chepstow Place. Despite its proximity to the flat he shared with Eleanor, she rarely went with him. Except on days when some cash had come his way, he tended not to drink much. His main purpose in going there was, instead, to chat with Charles Wrey Gardiner and John Gawsworth, the booze-sodden King of Redonda, whose perpetual presence at the centre table in the Saloon Bar led a waggish friend to call it "Almadonda".[16]

Defiantly debonair, a carnation in his buttonhole, his eyes screened by the green-tinted, aviator-style sunglasses that had replaced his reflective ones, he took a taxi to the offices of the *London Magazine* sometime around the beginning of November. In the six-year gap since his last appearance in its pages, it had changed editors, John Lehmann having sold it to Alan Ross. It was now based upstairs at 22 Charing Cross Road, the ascent leaving Julian winded. When he'd got his breath back, he talked his way into becoming a contributor to the magazine. As an admirer of his writing, Alan was happy to commission one of the articles he suggested: a reappraisal of the work of the popular novelist A.E.W. Mason. Yet Alan was sufficiently familiar with Julian's reputation not to fall for his pleas for advance payment, arranging instead to pay him "cash-on-the-nail".[17] Alan also did him a good turn by offering to pass on the manuscript of *My Name Is Love* to a contact at Collins & Co.

During November, Julian worked on his essay in parallel with a long story which he also envisaged publishing in the *London Magazine*. Well within the deadline, he sent Alan the finished essay, his covering letter appealing for quick cash payment because he was "damnably short of the ready".[18]

He had hoped to get 1963 off to a good start by selling *My Name Is Love*, but a rejection letter from Collins arrived just after the New Year. By the end of January, though, things were looking up. As well as being offered £17 for the Dutch radio rights to *Threesome*, he received a handy £10 repeat fee from the New Zealand Broadcasting Corporation. And he was given some more work by Arthur Crook at *The TLS*, who commissioned him to review several novels and produce two middles, one devoted to spy fiction, the other to the work of William Sansom, wittily titled *Sansom and Delilah*. But he soon seems to have been broke again.

In the final week of February, he wrote to Roger Machell, asking when he was due to receive both the long-awaited payment from America and his share of the paperback rights to *Until the Day She Dies*. Machell conceded that there was no hope of recovering the debt from Julian's American publisher. He was, however, able to supervise the payment of the £50 fee from the New English Library. This came through in late March, coinciding with the earlier than expected paperback release of *Until the Day She Dies*, its cover emblazoned by a florid painting of a murderous figure in a hat and dark glasses. The book's soft-cover publication prompted Julian to attempt to make some cash by offering the New English Library the rights to a paperback original of *My Name Is Love*. He asked for an immediate payment of £100, but they weren't interested. His hopes of publishing what he regarded as his finest work once again dashed, he was left to ponder the "big novel"[19] he yearned to write.

It wasn't until the end of the month that his divorce petition was at last scheduled. On Wednesday 27 March, he met his solicitor, Ralph Myers, outside the Law Courts on the Strand, where the case was about to be heard. Using the evidence gathered the previous summer, Myers presented proof of adultery. The judge then granted his divorce. And John Maxwell agreed to pay his legal costs.

About two weeks later, Julian obtained his second commission from Alan Ross, who gave him the go-ahead to write an article about the novels of M.P. Shiel. The piece was ready by the first weekend of May. Before handing it over to Alan, he showed it to John Gawsworth, who was delighted with it. In his capacity as Redondan monarch, Gawsworth announced his intention to elevate Julian to the Grand Dukedom of Ragusa, news of the promotion proudly inserted into the article before it went to press. The title, Gawsworth said, would be conferred at a formal ceremony on Julian's birthday.

Early that month Julian was trawling through *The Writers' and Artists' Yearbook* in search of untapped markets for his work when he spotted a reference to the Sexton Blake Library. Astonished that it was still in existence, he started looking for examples of its current output. His search came to an end at the bookstall on Paddington station, where he found one "hidden in among copies of the *Schoolgirl Picture Library*, *Thrilling War Pictures* and something entitled simply *Bombs Down!*"[20] It inspired him to approach Alan Ross with an idea for a study of the great detective's seventy-year career. With Alan's blessing, he penned a lengthy and amusing dissection of this overlooked aspect of popular culture, focusing on the ways in which the character of Sexton Blake had evolved to suit contemporary social and literary fashion. He completed it in the second week of May, just in time to register the impending demise of the series.

Always eager to write about people whose work he admired, towards the end of the month he began a long essay on Raymond Chandler.

"Because it's impossible to write about one without the other",[21] he soon expanded it to encompass Dashiell Hammett. Besides placing his essay with the *London Magazine*, which had relocated to the top-floor of 30 Thurloe Place in South Kensington, he raised a 30 shilling bonus by selling the manuscript to Jake Schwartz.

To mark his fifty-first birthday on Sunday 7 July, he arranged a small lunchtime get-together at the Alma, where John Gawsworth went through the elaborate ritual of ennobling him, the ceremony validated by specially printed, elaborately decorated state papers from the Realm of Redonda. After the pub closed, he dashed into town to catch a train down to the south coast, so he could be present at his five-year-old son's birthday party, which Diana was keen for him to attend.

Worried that Alex wasn't being properly cared for, parental scruples maybe meshing with animosity towards his ex-wife, Julian contacted his solicitor when he got back to London. In response to his disquiet, an inspection by the Court Welfare Officer was fixed up. Julian meanwhile got on with a review he'd been commissioned to write for *The TLS*, plus an article for the *London Magazine* on the pulp novelist Robert Bloch, best-known as the author of the book on which Hitchcock's *Psycho* was based.

Near the end of July, Julian received a letter from Ralph Myers, informing him that the Court Welfare Officer had filed a report. Its findings resulted in Diana being summoned to London to appear in court on the morning of Wednesday 31 July. Together with Myers, Julian attended the hearing, which seems to have allayed his concerns. But he now started fretting over the possibility that Diana might, tiring of his interference, take Alex out of the country. Regardless of the fact that his only income over the past couple of weeks appears to have been the £5 he'd earned by doing some reviewing for *The TLS*, he incurred yet more legal costs when he asked Myers to write to the Passport Office, requesting that they prevent his son from going abroad without his permission.

Through Alan Ross, he went on to land three more commissions from the *London Magazine*. The first of these was for a piece on the neglected comic novels of Douglas Hayes. His own books having passed into comparable obscurity, Julian must have empathised with their author. A feeling of injustice, borne out of just such neglect, coloured his next assignment: an appreciation of the work of Mary McCarthy. Momentarily wavering in his stance of critical impersonality, he applauded what he saw as her unerring depiction of a world in which "the shoddy and the untalented, the pushers and the thrusters [...] make their way to the 'top'."[22] As if to demonstrate the eclecticism of his tastes, he also produced an erudite yet entertaining essay on Sheridan Le Fanu.

By that summer, he'd staked his place as a valued and reliable contributor to the *London Magazine*. Nevertheless, he remained unable to shake off the financial crisis which had been stalking him for years. In a move smacking of desperation, he switched agents, his gap-toothed drinking buddy, James Graham-Murray, taking the place of the kindly Edmund Hughes, with whom he remained on friendly terms. Though the paperback rights to *My Name Is Love* were still the property of the New English Library, Julian instructed James to offer the novel for £250 to Anthony Gibbs, who now ran Panther, the paperback publishing house. But Gibbs was annoyingly tardy. For all his apparent interest, he still hadn't committed himself by the second week of October, so Julian and James concentrated on attempting to sell the film rights to *The Doomsday Book*. These, Julian optimistically imagined as he scraped by on reviewing work for *The TLS*, might bring in as much as £3000. More than enough to rescue him from his present penury. Yet no millionaire film producer stepped forward. By the beginning of November, there hadn't been any word from Gibbs either. Temporary salvation came in the form of commissions from Alan Ross for a review of Raymond Chandler's *Killer in the Rain*, and from *The TLS*, who paid him £25 for a middle on Raynor Heppenstall.

His patience with Gibbs waning, he made one last phone-call to Panther's offices. Gibbs wasn't there, so Julian left the phone number of the ML and asked him to call back that afternoon. He hung round for a couple of hours, only the call never came, at which he gave up on Panther and requested they return his manuscript.

The news that the paperback edition of *Until the Day She Dies* had gone into a second edition bracing his faith in the commercial potential of his writing, he drew up plans for a long, episodic roman-à-clef. Spanning the period from his first meeting with "the Tall Girl"[23] to their eventual divorce, he envisaged it depicting both the tangled love life and the equally complicated working life of his alter ego, Quentin Murdoch, author of *They Can't Give You A Baby*. Into its detailed chapter-plan, he slotted at least two previously written pieces — about sleeping in both the Turkish baths and the waiting-room at Euston Station. To increase its chances of being published, he came up with the ingenious trick of passing it off as *Business and Desire*, the absurdly overdue novel he owed Hamish Hamilton. But the new book proved no easier to write than its namesake, his ample preparatory work, which even extended to designing its dustjacket, yielding only another series of frustrating false-starts.

Meanwhile, James Graham-Murray carried on trying to find a publisher for *My Name Is Love: A Romance*, the subtitle appended as a corrective to anyone anticipating another crime drama. In about the third week of November, James submitted the manuscript to the Times Press, an ambitious new firm, based in Douglas on the Isle of Man. One afternoon around then, Julian and Eleanor went drinking with him in the ML. At about 4.30pm, Julian took a taxi into the West End, leaving James and Eleanor to continue talking. Much later on, presumably after Julian had got home, he heard that Eleanor had ended up in hospital, where she needed stitches for a deep head-wound. Yet she couldn't remember anything about how she'd acquired it. Piecing together the evidence with all the relish of a literary gumshoe, Julian deduced that she'd either fallen "or more probably was coshed on the back of the head"[24] and then robbed as she left the bar that evening.

After only a brief delay, the Times Press — undaunted by the earlier sale of the book's worldwide paperback rights — made an offer for *My Name Is Love*. With James acting as an intermediary, Julian negotiated an acceptable contract. This gave his new publisher an option on his next thriller, provisionally titled *My Father's Ghost*, which he planned to deliver by the following summer at the latest. So pleased were they to have Julian as one of their authors, they even agreed to follow his proposed design for the book's cover, featuring a boldly stylised two-colour print of a languid and seductive woman.

On Friday 6 December he received their cheque for £200, his pleasure tempered by the fact that this was £50 less than he'd been expecting. Next day he wrote them a tetchy letter demanding the outstanding money. But they stood their ground, citing the contract he'd signed, which specified precisely the figure they'd paid him.

Once he'd cashed their cheque, he sent the price of a few Yuletide drinks to Bert Barton, a struggling journalist friend from the George, who had recently decamped to Birmingham. Instead of using his earnings to fund the "new long novel"[25] he'd been contemplating, Julian took the opportunity to have another crack at television scriptwriting. His initial project was *It's Different In July*, a play adapted from a Hitchcock-like conspiracy thriller he'd reviewed for *The Listener* nearly ten years earlier.

Furious with the Times Press for their failure to pay what he thought they'd promised him, he threatened them with litigation. His relationship with them now on an adversarial footing, the firm posted him the proofs of his novel just before Christmas, accompanied by "a rather peremptory note [...] saying that if they didn't arrive corrected by the 27th the work would go on regardless."[26] Julian obediently went through the proofs that same day and sent them straight back.

Because the Times Press still hadn't capitulated to his demands, he proceeded with his threat. In the second week of January 1964, he asked his solicitor to take out an injunction against them, preventing them from launching his book the following Thursday. Just as his spat with the Times Press was intensifying, he reached an amicable resolution to another of the legal disputes in which he'd been embroiled. His fears for Alex having ebbed, he agreed to let Diana include their son on her passport.

Though he was beginning to run short of cash, Julian persevered with his screenwriting and also took the time to write a foreword to an edition of his selected stories which he hoped to publish. Only two weeks into February, setting aside *It's Different In July*, he started to turn *The Midnight Men* — his unfinished neo-Gothic radio thriller — into a television series. Yet before he could even contemplate placing *The Midnight Men*, now simply called *Midnight*, with a television company, he first had to obtain permission from the BBC's Drama (Sound) department, which still owned the copyright on the original scripts. Since they'd already advanced £400 for them, he offered to reimburse the department if he succeeded in selling the series. While they were considering his offer, he fulfilled a commission from *The TLS*, who gave him the latest novel by H.E. Bates to review. Refusing to stoop to the commonplace practice of exacting revenge through the medium of literary criticism, he lavished fulsome praise on Bates's talents.

With permission from Reggie Smith's department, Julian submitted a specimen episode of *Midnight* to a producer at BBC-TV. Encouraged by Reggie, whose friendship with him had revived, he went on to make a brief return to radio scriptwriting by adapting *The Shoestring Budget*, his droll account of working for Roger and Nigel Proudfoot, originally published in *Punch*. But the BBC turned it down, his problems multiplying when their counterparts in television reached the same decision about *Midnight*.

Two fortuitous payments during the first half of March averted his impending cash crisis. Besides being paid by Avon, the American paperback publisher, for the right to reprint his memoir of Frank Harris in an anthology of recent British writing, he garnered a "finder's fee" from Jake Schwartz for introducing him to John Lehmann, from whom

Jake purchased what appears to have been a substantial cache of manuscripts.

Despite his bitter legal wrangle with the Times Press, he insisted on attending the launch party they'd organised for *My Name Is Love*. This was held in the Art Gallery at Foyle's on Wednesday 18 March. When he got there at 6.30pm, he was appalled to discover that they had, without notifying him, rescheduled it for an hour-and-a-half earlier. By then, "the whole thing was over and people were being turned away at the door".[27]

As a gesture of gratitude to John Lehmann for all his assistance over the years, Julian had dedicated *My Name Is Love* to him. Yet John considered it "a pathetically botched job, quite unworthy of the author of *The Swag, the Spy and the Soldier*."[28] His opinion was echoed by John Willett who, reviewing it in *The TLS*, lamented its failure to match the laconic style and dark comedy of his previous books. It was otherwise largely ignored, an exception being the terse and withering write-up it received in *Punch*.

Never someone who let himself be deterred by the sneering comments of critics, Julian went ahead and adapted *My Name Is Love* into a television play. Even though his screenwriting wasn't bringing in any money, he splashed out on an Easter egg and a toy torch for Alex. Shortly afterwards, he submitted *It's Different In July* to an independent television company. But they still hadn't made up their mind about it by mid-April, at which point he was so short of cash Edmund Hughes felt obliged to give him £5. And, more as an act of charity than a business transaction, Jake Schwartz purchased the manuscript of one of the middles he'd written for *The TLS*.

Having failed to earn anything from his television scripts, Julian went back to supplying essays for the *London Magazine*. Under the pretext of the publication of a new collection of the work of Mikhail Zoshchenko, sometime in May he persuaded Alan Ross to commission a piece celebrating Zoshchenko, whose slide from wartime popularity to post-war neglect mirrored the trajectory of his own career. Alan also agreed to him reviewing *A Moveable Feast*, Ernest Hemingway's posthumously published memoir of Twenties Paris.

Much as Julian still revered his erstwhile hero's achievements, he was irked by the book's romanticisation of the bohemian poverty and hunger he himself had endured all too often. Reading Hemingway's nostalgic memoirs, their pages strewn with appearances by the legendary artistic figures of the day, must have fired Julian's imagination, because he promptly started planning a similar book about his own experiences in Forties London — to be called *Memoirs of the Forties*.

"Things [were] still tough"[29] for Julian: so tough he doesn't appear to have been able to afford a mooted trip down to Brighton to visit Alex. Yet his projected memoirs gave him cause for optimism. He envisaged writing the book in self-contained sections, the most obviously marketable of these being the short, evocative reminiscence he planned to write about his time working with the late Dylan Thomas. Hoping someone might pay him an advance for it, he circulated the proposal round several magazines, none of which seized the bait.

In the second week of June, he completed his review of *A Moveable Feast* and headed for South Kensington to collect his fee. Not that it made much difference to the straitened circumstances in which he, Eleanor, and Caroline were living. When Edmund Hughes went round to lunch with them that weekend, their lack of money was so glaring Hughes included another £5 gift with his subsequent, diplomatically phrased thank-you note.

Julian's confidence in his latest scheme undented by the discouraging response to his Dylan Thomas proposal, he drew up a plan for his memoirs, his recent court appearances leading him to retitle them *Everything That Has Been Taken In Evidence*. On Thursday 2 July, only a few days shy of his fifty-second birthday, he wrote to Hamish Hamilton from the flat in Chepstow Place, offering the book — which he anticipated finishing by September or October — for "an immediate part-advance payment of £150".[30]

But his previous dealings with the company had rendered them impervious to his overtures. For Mr Hamilton, "the mere thought of re-opening negotiations [was enough to make] the blood run cold."[31] The very next day, he wrote back to Julian, politely declining his offer.

Compelled to look elsewhere, Julian discussed his plans with Alan Ross who, anxious to retain him as a contributor, agreed to serialise his memoirs in the *London Magazine*. Their publication now assured, he set to work on the opening episode, describing his mid-Thirties visit to the offices of Jonathan Cape. The piece had been completed by Tuesday 11 August when he began the second instalment, devoted to his earliest encounter with Graham Greene. So as to make it neater and more self-sufficient, he avoided any reference to their long friendship or their inglorious professional dealings, portraying their meeting as a single, never-to-be-repeated episode.

Probably that week, he went over to drop off the pristine manuscripts, written not with the Hooded Terror (which must have been lost, sold, or pawned), but with a cheap, fine-tipped biro. No sooner had he arrived than he complained about how he was being followed by someone. Hugo Williams, the magazine's boyish Advertising Manager was, meanwhile, despatched downstairs to pay for his taxi.

Whenever Julian made these periodic visits, Alan would whisk him only four doors down the road to the Hoop and Toy, a cosy, low-ceilinged pub, generally packed with students and lecturers from the nearby Royal College of Art. After an hour or so of being plied with drinks and retelling his favourite monologues, Julian would find himself decanted into a taxi.

A little later that month, he, Eleanor, and Caroline (to whom he doesn't seem to have developed any particular attachment) left Chepstow Place and moved into another flat, positioned on an intersecting street. Their new home was on the top-floor of 4 Dawson Place, a four-storey end-terrace townhouse, the rear windows looking out across a row of small gardens. They hadn't been living there long when Julian was contacted by one of the staff from the BBC's *Writers' World* television series. He was asked to appear on a programme about British literature in the Second World War. Welcome as the invitation was, it must have reinforced his sense of being more part of the literary past than the present.

During the final week of August, he received a contract from the BBC, confirming their arrangement to pay him a 35 guinea fee for a five or six minute scripted reminiscence, scheduled to be filmed the following month. Within a day of receiving it, he'd drafted a witty and irreverent piece about wartime Soho and his failure to become an army officer, already the subject of not only a short story but also an oft-repeated anecdote.

Attired in a descendant of his famous teddy-bear coat, worn over a subfusc tweed jacket and a gangsterish combination of a dark shirt and pale tie, his twitchy eyes just about visible through his usual sunglasses, on the morning of Thursday 24 September he travelled to the BBC's Riverside Studios, where he made a favourable impression on the programme's producer, the young Melvyn Bragg. At midday in Studio 2, he joined John Betjeman, Cyril Connolly, and John Lehmann, who were all due to rehearse their contributions to the programme, hosted by their contemporary, the novelist Jocelyn Brooke. John was struck by how "oddly ghost-like"[32] Julian appeared. That apart, he was "not noticably older",[33] merely a bit plumper than he had been in the days when he was encamped in the Wheatsheaf.

Under the direction of Anthony Powell's elder son, Tristram, now in his early twenties, Julian sat in front of a wartime propaganda poster proclaiming that "Careless Talk Costs Lives", from where he rehearsed his script. The preamble over, he sloped off, only returning in time for the recording of the programme which began at 3.00pm. When the camera turned on him, he flatly refused to remove his dark glasses. With all the aplomb of a veteran performer, he delivered his lines in a deadpan, lugubrious style, heavy with the disillusionment he'd long been radiating, his monologue punctuated by leisurely puffs on the fat cigar he'd lit up, just to enhance the underworld look.

A couple of weeks after that, the programme — portentiously entitled *In the Shadow of Cain* — was transmitted on BBC-2. It provoked an enthusiastic reaction from Anthony Burgess in *The Listener*, purring over both Julian's performance and the way he evoked the era he was describing.

In the five months since he'd commenced his memoirs, their sequence had been revised and their scope expanded. To accommodate the changes, on Friday 9 October he drew up a fresh chapter-plan, the book reverting to its original title. As he envisaged it, a Thirties prologue and an epilogue set in the present-day would frame the main body of the book. The central section would cover his army service, his breakthrough as a published writer, his time with the Strand Film Company, and his relationships with people such as André Deutsch, John Lehmann, Alan Ross, Tony Powell, Nina Hamnett, and John Gawsworth. The sizeable supporting cast would include vignettes and sketches of Malcolm Muggeridge, Sonia Orwell, and Leonard Russell, alongside acquaintances like Mulk Raj Anand and Count Potocki. He even planned to write about Alfred Hitchcock, with whom he'd had a single phone conversation, backed up by many enjoyable hours in the cinema. But there was to be no mention of Northfield Military Hospital, Julian's failure to live up to his chosen self-image providing an enduring source of shame. Nor was there any reference to Nelson Scott or *The Naked Heart*, a mixture of professional pride and fear of another libel suit, in all likelihood, dictating its omission.

The first published extract from the book, consisting of the chapter about working with Dylan Thomas, featured in the November edition of the *London Magazine*.[34] Julian had, by the end of October, written thirteen more of the projected thirty-eight chapters, covering among other things the Fitzrovian pubs, as well as his friendships with Peter Brooke and Tambimuttu. On completing the latest instalment, depicting a party at which he and his pseudonymous former girlfriend, Barbara (who appears as "Adair"), briefly chatted with Pablo Picasso, he took a taxi over to South Kensington to claim his fee. When he boarded the cab outside his flat that afternoon, the driver thought he'd asked for "Soho Square",[35] not "Thurloe Square".[36] Engrossed in his newspaper, oblivious to the misunderstanding, he found himself in the West End, miles away from his destination. A startlingly large fare was displayed on the meter by the time the taxi pulled up near Thurloe Place. Tremulous with rage, Julian clambered out and refused to pay. He then marched up to Alan Ross's office, the speed of his ascent leaving him even more out of breath than normal, his flushed face slick with sweat. At first Alan thought he was on the verge of a heart-attack. As soon as he'd recovered sufficiently, he explained what had happened, adding, "I'm not going to pay the fucker."[37]

Reluctant to see him arrested, Alan went down and paid off the cabbie, who was still parked outside.

The heart-attack which had seemed imminent struck only a few days later. In the early hours of Tuesday 3 November, while he was downing some brandy to celebrate the windfall of a repeat fee from the BBC, he complained to Eleanor that he had a pain in his chest. But neither of them took the symptoms seriously. To anaesthetise himself against the discomfort, Julian drained what remained of the bottle of brandy. It wasn't until daybreak that Eleanor, belatedly alarmed by his persistent chest pains, rushed him to St Charles Hospital in Ladbroke Grove, no more than about half-a-mile away. The moment they got there, Julian suffered a heart-attack, its severity the product of years of fatty food, lack of exercise, stress, drinking, smoking, and amphetamine use. Had he been brought in earlier, the doctors told Eleanor that they might have been able to save him. But it was already too late. Before his heart stopped beating, he only had time to gulp "Graham Greene"[38] and "I love you",[39] death finally stemming the compulsive torrent of words that had poured out of him for so long.

Left to make the funeral arrangements, Eleanor placed an announcement in that Friday's edition of *The Times*, the entire front page of which was, in those days, dedicated to a drab inventory of births, deaths, and marriages. Her announcement gave details of the funeral service and the undertakers where bouquets should be sent. A few pages further on, there was an obituary, headlined "Mr Julian Maclaren-Ross: Dedicated Writer of High Talent".[40] The ensuing half-column offered a balanced assessment of his erratic career, comparing *The Weeping and the*

Laughter, Of Love and Hunger ("his best and profoundest book"[41]), and his first three volumes of short stories with his disappointing output as a thriller writer. At the same time it conceded that "anything he wrote has a certain distinction".[42] A subsequent obituary in *The Spectator* reiterated this verdict, mourning his failure "to produce the great novel about the Forties which many people confidently expected him to write."[43] The prevailing sentiment was shared by Roy Fuller, one of the few people who seem to have spotted Eleanor's advert in *The Times*. Saddened by the news, he sent flowers accompanied by a carefully considered message that read "With admiration and regret":[44] regret at his death, regret that he hadn't properly expressed this admiration before Julian's death, and regret elicited by the sense that Julian, for all his achievements, had never fulfilled his even greater potential.

Deprived of even Julian's sparse income, Eleanor couldn't afford more than a rudimentary funeral, dispensing with even the luxury of a headstone to mark his grave. The service was scheduled for Monday 9 November. Earlier in the day a heavy mist had hung over London, enhancing the melancholy of the occasion. But it was quickly burnt off by a spell of unexpectedly warm sunshine. The undertaker's broad-fronted, modern premises, midway down Westbourne Grove, provided the starting point for the funeral cortège. Several wreathes, including a large one paid for by the staff and customers of the Alma, were waiting to be loaded into the hearse when Charles Wrey Gardiner arrived. He was joined by an atypically spruce John Gawsworth, clad in a borrowed suit. Eleanor, smartly got up but emotionally ruffled, was the last to appear. Mute with grief, the three of them made the long, slow drive to the cemetery in the back of the limousine that tailed the hearse, Julian's flower-strewn coffin visible through the rear window.

Just before 2.00pm, the procession cruised through the narrow streets of suburban Mill Hill and up the gentle slope leading to the sprawling, well-maintained grounds of the misleadingly named Paddington Cemetery. Despite the built-up setting, the densely planted shrubberies and flowerbeds lent it a bucolic ambience, the surrounding houses almost concealed behind the trees that skirted it, their thinning, autumnal foliage glowing in the sunshine. The cortège made its way through to the new section of the cemetery, where it pulled up next to the grave which had been dug in a plot of unconsecrated ground, its muddy rim fringed by duckboards for the mourners to stand on.

Unaware of Julian's death, many of his oldest friends and business associates, such as Alan Ross, Mac Jaeger, and Tony Van den Burgh, were absent. So too was his poverty-stricken sister, Carol, now divorced from her second husband, but still living in New Zealand. Nonetheless, a small crowd of mourners were present, among them Reggie Smith, the former Diana Maclaren-Ross, and Sir John Waller. Fresh from his recent European tour, John turned up in a caravan, together with Diana and a gaggle of his boyfriends. They parked about twenty yards away in the cemetery's Central Avenue.

Julian hadn't been a regular church-goer since his teens, yet Eleanor had opted for a Catholic ceremony. While John and his retinue hovered by his caravan and watched the service from there, Diana — dyed-blonde hair capped by an elegant black turban — stood a few yards behind the main graveside group, mourning the death of the man whom she thought of as "the love of her life".[45] The white-cassocked priest sped through the protracted liturgy like a horse-racing commentator, pausing only to sprinkle holy water onto the coffin from a small tin, his voice rising above the faint rumble of distant traffic, his practised haste rendering the Latin phrases indistinguishable. In a show of diplomacy, he concluded the service by bringing "Eleanor and Diana together with a paternal gesture":[46] a gesture that did nothing to heal their mutual hostility.

At the wake, held in the Alma that evening, the two women met again, their encounter witnessed by Charles Wrey Gardiner and John Maxwell, Diana's current husband. Still "very much in love with [Julian]",[47] not to mention "deeply upset and hysterical",[48] she blamed Eleanor for his death, saying that Eleanor should have got him to hospital sooner than she did. Eleanor retaliated by accusing Diana of not feeding him properly. It was an unseemly row that culminated in Eleanor storming out of the pub, leaving the others to continue drinking to Julian's memory.

The funeral appeared to provide the anti-climactic denouement to a wayward and unpredictable life, which Julian had lived as if he was the star of a continuous movie being screened inside his head. In fact, the story still held a few more surprises in the closing reel.

Between December 1964 and March 1965, Alan Ross carried on serialising *Memoirs of the Forties* in the *London Magazine*. Though Julian had lived to complete less than half of it, Alan decided to publish the unfinished manuscript in hard-cover form under his own recently launched imprint. To bring it up to a conventional length, he bolstered it with Julian's already published piece about Alun Lewis, a representative sample of his short stories, and a selection of photographs, including shots of his preparatory notes and chapter-plan.

With its publication that autumn, Julian scored a major critical hit, obtaining more widespread coverage than he'd ever received during his lifetime. In addition to being the subject of an enthusiastic V.S. Pritchett essay in *The New Statesman and Nation*, it attracted praise from, among others, *The TLS*, *The Times*, and *The Spectator* which applauded it for providing "an unrivalled picture of those almost mythical Forties".[49]

Regretful as they were at Julian's failure to fill in the huge canvas he'd sketched out, friends such as Dan Davin and John Lehmann expressed relief that "the negative of what his photographic eye had registered of [them] was never to be developed",[50] enabling them to escape "what would have been a painful exposure."[51] Others weren't so fortunate. Not that there was anything malicious about his verbal portraiture. Even so, many of Julian's former friends and acquaintances who appeared in the book were irritated by the way he'd depicted them, by the way he'd perpetuated apocryphal Saloon Bar anecdotes about them — anecdotes like the one about Staggering Steven keeping Gerald Wilde locked in a room until Wilde had finished a painting. Or the one about Mac hurling his landlord's son down a flight of stairs. Enraged by Julian's sharp and, by all accounts, accurate portrait of him, Tambi condemned *Memoirs of the Forties* as "a highly coloured book of misrepresentations and fairy-tales."[52] Years later, still smarting from it, Tambi forced Derek Stanford, who drew on Julian's description for *Inside the Forties*, his own account of the period, to insert a printed retraction-slip into the book.

Most of the people Julian had upset were, however, ready to admit he'd conveyed the flavour of the period with poignancy and unerring precision. *Memoirs of the Forties* represented a triumphant, if overdue return to the scintillating form that had seen his short stories and *Of Love and Hunger* installed as "small classics of [their] time".[53] As someone captivated by dramatic reversals of fortune, it offered an apt conclusion to his literary career. "To some extent at least," Anthony Cronin wrote, "the big spender had recouped his losses, the maestro had surprised those who thought he was finished, the rightful heir had frightened the interlopers, the Jacobite exile had had a last revenge."[54]

From an early age, Julian put as much effort into propagating his personal myth as perfecting his prose style. It's scarcely surprising, then, that he should feature in so many of his friends' memoirs, in Gavin Ewart's autobiographical poem, *The Last Days of Old Poets*, and in books about wartime Soho, the potent allure of which he was responsible for defining. Since his death, he has also enjoyed a uniquely productive afterlife as the inspiration for at least two more vibrant characters in other people's novels. There's the eponymous Soho-ite in *Robinson*, Christopher Petit's debut novel, its title alluding to a sequence of enigmatic poems by Weldon Kees, whose mysterious disappearance would have intrigued Julian. And, most famously of all, there's the cane-carrying dandy and bohemian writer X. Trapnel who, next to the unxious Widmerpool, must be the most memorable character in Anthony Powell's *A Dance To The Music of Time*.

For a writer as industrious and gifted as Julian, it's ironic that his sporadically brilliant work should, even now, nearly four decades after his death, be overshadowed by the brash and indolent persona he so effectively projected. Yet, beneath that carefully assembled disguise, peeled off for the benefit of only a few intimates, there was a vulnerable and troubled man who, with the self-destructive obduracy of a true romantic, pursued his literary dreams right to the very end.

Epilogue & Acknowledgements

Soon after I'd made up my mind to write this book, I spent several wearisome hours thumbing through a complete set of British phone directories in search of Maclaren-Ross's son, Alex. Or anyone else who shared their surname. Not for the first time, luck was on my side. Whenever I opened another of the daunting row of battered directories, I found myself praying that Alex hadn't emigrated or chosen to remove his name from the listings. Just as I was beginning to wonder whether my efforts would prove worthwhile, I came up with an entry under "Maclaren-Ross, A". Like a footballer netting the winning goal, I felt so elated I wanted to hug someone. Since the nearest person was a pungent tramp, muttering over *The Financial Times*, I restrained myself.

The sensible thing would have been to write to Alex straightaway, instead of which I put off contacting him for almost a year. Part of the reason was that I was apprehensive about how he'd react to the news that someone was unearthing potentially unsavoury facts about his father. I was also terrified that he'd refuse to cooperate with me on the grounds of my lack of credentials as a biographer. Either way, I knew he could have expressed his disapproval by denying me the opportunity to quote from his father's writing. Not just his fiction, but even his letters and notebook jottings. Lurking at the back of my mind, there was the supplementary fear that he might already be collaborating with some well-known writer. I even caught myself drawing paranoid conclusions about a request for *The Funny Bone*, made from a branch library near to where an established biographer was living.

To compound all these anxieties, the elderly poet, John Heath-Stubbs, who remembered meeting Maclaren-Ross junior at Diana's funeral, suddenly revealed that Alex had become a Born Again Christian. From what I knew about Alex's unsettled childhood, I could well imagine him taking refuge in the gleaming certainties of fundamentalist religion. Now I had to contend with the probability that Alex would find his father's antics — and, by extension, *my* book — morally repugnant.

When I eventually mustered the courage to approach him, I tried to anticipate this by informing him that I had "no wish to condone his father's way of life", or some such insincere phrase, borne out of desperation. My letter provoked a friendly and unexpectedly enthusiastic phone-call. Because he'd been so young when his father died, Alex admitted that he couldn't even remember what Julian looked like. Stranger still, he had never seen any pictures of him.

A few weeks later, armed with a clutch of rare photos and a videotape of his father's composed performance on *Writers' World*, I met him for the first time. Aside from his height and colouring, I could discern no particular resemblance between them. Propped on a shelf in the hallway, however, there was a framed photo of his elder son who, even though he wasn't yet in his teens, looked like a scaled-down version of Julian, stripped of his characteristic accessories.

All my previous fears were, in the course of two, maybe three hours of conversation, proved groundless. Indeed, Alex could hardly have been more encouraging and helpful, his own palpable excitement about the project driven by a desire to add to his meagre stockpile of knowledge about his father. As I got ready to leave, a fretful expression crossed his hitherto sanguine features. This was the signal for him to quiz me about whether his father had some dreadful secret. "Julian wasn't a child-molester, was he...?" Alex asked, my earlier letter having inadvertently primed him for a revelation of that sort.

Little did I realise when I began the project that I'd become an intermediary between Alex and the father he scarcely knew, the father whom, he always feared, might not have harboured any paternal feelings for him. I hope that I've been able both to correct this damaging misapprehension and to enable him to understand his father.

Through my research, Alex has also been reunited with his long-lost half-sister, Sallie, whose very existence he'd begun to question. My book has, in other words, had altogether unforeseen ramifications. However tactfully I handled the situation, I realised that my meddling might have a catastrophic impact on other people's lives, Alex's in particular. Yet, once again, luck was on my side. Far from providing the catalyst for anguish and conflict, I found myself thrust into the role of a reluctant but ultimately successful social worker.

I can't take the credit, though, for the other welcome addition to Alex's extended family. While I was labouring over the second draft of my book, Judith Bourne, a delightful New Zealander, now living in Australia, entered the picture. On behalf of her deceased father, an adopted child who had conducted an obsessive but fruitless hunt for his biological mother, she was determined to complete the quest. Her previously anonymous grandmother turned out to be none other than Julian Maclaren-Ross's sister. A hectic exchange of information about the two sides of the family ensued. I am, of course, extremely grateful to Judith for all her assistance, which continued right until the brink of publication.

In researching my subject's chaotic life, a process reliant on such tiny, apparently insignificant clues it sometimes felt as if I was conducting a police investigation, I'm also indebted to the following people and institutions:

Dr Dannie Abse; the late Dr Mulk Raj Anand; Diana Athill; Sallie Baker; Michael Bakewell; Professor Charles Barr; Gavin Beattie, Senior Cataloguer, B.F.I. Collections; the late Bruce Bernard; Oliver Bernard; Michael Billington; the staff in the Reference Section of the Bognor Regis Library; Jennifer Booth, Archivist at the Tate Gallery, London; Michael Bott, Keeper of Archives and Manuscripts at the University of Reading; Mrs Katharine Spackman of the Reference and Local Studies Section of Bournemouth Reference Library; Lord Melvyn Bragg; Barbara Bray; Neville Braybrooke; Alan Brownjohn; the B.T. Archive; Milissa Burkart of the McFarlin Library, Department of Special Collections at the University of Tulsa; Miss K.M.J. Caine, Archives Assistant at the Devon Record Office; Charles Causley; the staff of the Periodicals and Rare Books Rooms at Cambridge University Library; the staff in the Reference Section of the Chichester Library; Companies House; Peter J. Conradi; Christine Corner of the Local Studies Library of Croydon Library; Fay Crofts; Arthur Crook; Paul Cummins; Anthony Curtis; Anna Davin; Brigid Davin; Delia Davin; Heather Dean; Judy Dennison, Archivist at Birmingham Central Library; the late André Deutsch, CBE; Roger Dobson; Lord Dunboyne; Shirley Edrich of I.D. Edrich First Editions and Periodicals; Margaret L. Evans, Historian of the Royal Canadian Mounted Police; Dr Craig Fees, Archivist of the Planned Environment Therapy Trust; Lynn Finn of the Centre for Kentish Studies; Charles Fisher of the Royal Bank of Canada Europe Ltd; Bryan Forbes; Stephen Fothergill; John Franklin; Ann Fridd of the Reference Section of Norwich Library; Michelle Froissard, the Archivist in Antibes; Ms K.A. Garvey, Archivist at the Oxfordshire Archives; the late David Gascoyne; Peter Gearing; Eileen Gunn of The Royal Literary Fund; Lesley Hall, Archivist at the Wellcome Library; Michael Hamburger; Lady Hart-Davis; the late Sir Rupert Hart-Davis; John Heath-Stubbs, OBE; Victoria Hesford, Reference Assistant at the Robert W. Woodruff Library, Emory University, Atlanta, Georgia; Mark Holloway; Peter B. Howard of Serendipity Books, San Francisico; John Huntley; Zara Hutchings; C.K.Jaeger; Nick Jaeger; Alan Kibble; Scott Krafft, Bibliographer/Reference Librarian at the Charles Deering McCormick Library of Special Collections at Northwestern University, Illinois; Peter Krämer; Shanon Lawson; Cressida Lindsay; Ms Hannah

Lowery, Archivist, Special Collections at the University of Bristol, which holds the Hamish Hamilton Archive; my agent, Andrew Lownie; Sandrine Malotaux, Head Librarian at the Institut Français in London; Mireille Massot, the Chief Archivist of the Municipal Archives in Nice; Derwent May; Nicholas R. Mays of the News International Archive Department; Mrs Bronia McDonald (formerly Kennedy); Brian McFarlane; the Records Section of the Ministry of Defence; George Melly; Guy Myhill; Conan Nicholas; Ann Nicholls; Caroline Oulton of The City of Westminster Archives Centre; Keith Ovenden; Andrea Paci, Archivist for the Hudson Bay Company's Archives in the Provincial Archives of Manitoba, Canada; Janetta Parlade' (formerly Woolley); Rowland Parsons of cyber-lex.com; John Pikoulis; Dorothy Carr Porter, Research Assistant in the Manuscripts Department of the University of North Carolina at Chapel Hill; the late Anthony Powell; Tristram Powell; the late Lady Violet Powell; Kara Quinn, Archivist of the Provincial Archives of Manitoba, Canada; Rita Read, the Local History Officer at Haringey Museum and Archive Service; Andrew Rosenheim, Managing Director of Penguin Press; the late Alan Ross; Brigid Sandford Smith; Vernon Scannell; Dr Sara Serpell; Christine Slattery, Television Archivist at the BBC Information and Archives; Neil Somerville, Senior Document Assistant at the BBC Written Archives Centre; Dame Muriel Spark; Derek Stanford; Mrs Peta Steele; Kevin L. Stewart of the Manuscripts and Archives Section of the Andrew Turnbull Library, Wellington, New Zealand; D.J. Taylor; Gwyn Thomas of the Suffolk Record Office; the late David Sylvester; Matt Thomas; Tim Thomas and Penny Rowland of the Oriental and India Office Collections at the British Library; Beth Thomson of the Reference, Information and Local Studies Section of Margate Library; Anthony Thwaite; the TNL Archive for providing access to the records of *The Times Literary Supplement*; Professor A.T. Tolley; Jess Tunstall; the late Tony Van den Burgh; Peter Vansittart; Anne Valery; Tara Wenger, the Research Librarian at the Harry Ransom Research Centre at the University of Texas; Hugo Williams; Val Wilmer; Joan Wyndham; Jon Wynne-Tyson; and Jo Willingham.

More general assistance was provided by Ann and Stuart Bayley, Sandy Brownjohn, Sally Fiber, Kirk Laws, Rachel Lumsden, Matthew Noel-Tod, Kirstie Maclaren-Ross, Hamish Maclaren-Ross, Chris Petit, John Smith, Lee Westrop, David Willetts, Neil Wylie and Branka Viker-Young.

Notes

It's appropriate, given Maclaren-Ross's own enthusiasm for most things American, be it Hemingway or Hollywood, that the bulk of his surviving manuscripts have crossed the Atlantic — a journey their author never made. Listed below are the various archives and libraries whose collections contain material which has helped in the preparation of this book. Next to each institution, there's an abbreviation, used to denote the location of manuscripts to which I've referred.

In the case of books quoted in the main text, their publication details are only included in the notes if they don't feature in the Selected Bibliography.

Collections of Manuscripts: Key to Abbreviations

HR	The Harry Ransom Research Center at the University of Texas in Austin, Texas, USA
RLF	The Royal Literary Fund, London, England
BBC	The BBC Written Archive, Caversham, England
NU	Northwestern University, Illinois, USA
UT	University of Tulsa, Oklahoma, USA
JC	The Jonathan Cape Archive at the University of Reading, England
HH	The Hamish Hamilton Archive at Bristol University, England
DD	The Dan Davin Archive at the Andrew Turnbull Library, Wellington, New Zealand
CA	Collection of the author
—	Emory University, Atlanta, Georgia, USA
SU	Stanford University, California, USA
—	The University of North Carolina at Chapel Hill, USA

Epigraph

Cyril Connolly, *The Enemies of Promise*, Penguin 1961, p.121.

Introduction

1. Anthony Powell, *Temporary Kings*, p.32.
2. J.Maclaren-Ross, *Punch*, Wednesday 11 December 1957, p.69.

A Wandering Disposition

1. J.Maclaren-Ross, *My Father Was Born In Havana*, included in *The Nine Men of Soho*, p.141.
2. Fitzwilliam Thomas Pollok's baptismal certificate, held in the Oriental and India Office in the British Library.
3. Fitzwilliam Thomas Pollok, *Sport in British Burmah, Assam and the Cassyiah and Jyntiah Hills*, Vol. 1, p.23.
4. J.Maclaren-Ross, *The Weeping and the Laughter*, p.23.
5. J.Maclaren-Ross, *The Weeping and the Laughter*, p.23.
6. J.Maclaren-Ross, *The Weeping and the Laughter*, p.51.
7. J.Maclaren-Ross, *The Days of the Comet, Winter Pie*, November 1946, p.58.
8. J.Maclaren-Ross, *The Weeping and the Laughter*, p.80.
9. *The Bournemouth Daily Echo*, Monday 7 January 1918, p.1.
10. J.Maclaren-Ross, *The Weeping and the Laughter*, p.72.
11. *The Bournemouth Daily Echo*, Monday 11 November 1918, p.1.
12. J.Maclaren-Ross, *The Weeping and the Laughter*, p.146.
13. J.Maclaren-Ross, *The Weeping and the Laughter*, p.141.
14. J.Maclaren-Ross, *The Weeping and the Laughter*, p.145.

The Boy Most Likely To Exceed

1. J.Maclaren-Ross, *The Weeping and the Laughter*, p.196.
2. J.Maclaren-Ross, *The Weeping and the Laughter*, p.197.
3. J.Maclaren-Ross, *The Weeping and the Laughter*, p.197-198.
4. J.Maclaren-Ross, *The Weeping and the Laughter*, p.200.
5. J.Maclaren-Ross, *The Boy Who Might With Luck Have Been Chess Champion of the World*, included in *Better Than A Kick In The Pants*, p.77.
6. J.Maclaren-Ross, *Monsieur L'Abbé, Encounter*, December 1953, p.36.
7. For reasons that remain obscure, May's second child, Montague Lambden Miller — her choice of middle name, endorsing their reconciliation — was brought up by foster parents, who renamed him. Around the same time, his brother, Logan, died of meningitis.
8. J.Maclaren-Ross, *Monsieur L'Abbé, Encounter*, December 1953, p.37.
9. J.Maclaren-Ross, *Monsieur L'Abbé, Encounter*, December 1953, p.36.
10. J.Maclaren-Ross, *Monsieur L'Abbé, Encounter*, December 1953, p.40.
11. John Heath-Stubbs in conversation with the author.
12. J.Maclaren-Ross, *Monsieur L'Abbé, Encounter*, December 1953, p.36.
13. J.Maclaren-Ross, *Monsieur L'Abbé, Encounter*, December 1953, p.39.
14. J.Maclaren-Ross, *The Far West*, included in *The Nine Men of Soho*, p.52.
15. Anthony Carson, *A Rose By Any Other Name*, p.49.
16. *The Monte Carlo and Menton News*, Saturday 11 January 1930, p.3.
17. J.Maclaren-Ross, *A Visit To The Villa Edouard Sept, London Magazine*, June 1955, p.55.
18. J.Maclaren-Ross, *A Visit To The Villa Edouard Sept, London Magazine*, June 1955, p.55.
19. J.Maclaren-Ross, *A Visit To The Villa Edouard Sept, London Magazine*, June 1955, p.55.
20. J.Maclaren-Ross, *A Visit To The Villa Edouard Sept, London Magazine*, June 1955, p.56.
21. J.Maclaren-Ross, *A Visit To The Villa Edouard Sept, London Magazine*, June 1955, p.56.
22. J.Maclaren-Ross, *A Visit To The Villa Edouard Sept, London Magazine*, June 1955, p.56.

23. J.Maclaren-Ross, *A Visit To The Villa Edouard Sept: An Autobiographical Memoir of Frank Harris*, dramatised for the BBC Third Programme, broadcast on Tuesday 4 September 1956.
24. Dan Davin, *Closing Times*, p.8.
25. Letter from J.Maclaren-Ross to John Lehmann, Saturday 17 July 1954 (HR).
26. J.Maclaren-Ross, *A Visit To The Villa Edouard Sept*, *London Magazine*, June 1955, p.64.
27. Anthony Carson, *Carson Was Here*, p.8.
28. Anthony Carson, *Carson Was Here*, p.8.
29. J.Maclaren-Ross, *Memoirs of the Forties*, p.165.
30. *The Monte Carlo and Menton News*, Saturday 19 December 1931, p.11.

Immodest Proposals

1. *The Monte Carlo and Menton News*, Saturday 12 March 1932, p.12.
2. J.Maclaren-Ross, *Quoth The Raven, Winter Pie*, October 1947, p.59.
3. C.K. Jaeger, *The Man in the Top Hat*, p.182.
4. J.Maclaren-Ross, *The Weeping and the Laughter*, p.229.
5. J.Maclaren-Ross, fragment of unpublished manuscript of *House of Cards* (CA).
6. J.Maclaren-Ross, unpublished foreword to *Selected Stories*, Sunday 4 February 1964 (NU).
7. J.Maclaren-Ross, unpublished foreword to *Selected Stories*, Sunday 4 February 1964 (NU).
8. She landed the starring role in a play called *Unnatural Scene*, performed at the Grafton Theatre on 12 November 1933. She also appeared on Sunday 3 June 1934 in a supporting role in a single performance of another forgotten play entitled *Sicilian Christmas*, the cast of which included Bernard Lee later to find fame in *The Third Man* and numerous James Bond movies.
9. C.K. Jaeger in conversation with the author.
10. Letter from J.Maclaren-Ross to the BBC Drama Department, Thursday 7 April 1938 (BBC).
11. Letter from J.Maclaren-Ross to the BBC Drama Department, Thursday 7 April 1938 (BBC).
12. *The Bognor Regis Observer*, Wednesday 10 February 1937, p.1.
13. C.K. Jaeger in conversation with the author.
14. *The Bognor Regis Observer*, Wednesday 10 February 1937, p.6.
15. *The Bognor Regis Observer*, Wednesday 10 February 1937, p.1.
16. C.K. Jaeger in conversation with the author.
17. C.K. Jaeger in conversation with the author.
18. C.K. Jaeger in conversation with the author.
19. C.K. Jaeger in conversation with the author.
20. J.Maclaren-Ross, unpublished manuscript of *The Dark Diceman*, p.1 (HR).
21. J.Maclaren-Ross, unpublished manuscript of *The Dark Diceman*, p.2 (HR).
22. C.K. Jaeger in conversation with the author.
23. Martin Jordan, *Maclaren-Ross at the Mower*, *London Magazine*, December 1971/January 1972, p.117.
24. Martin Jordan, *Lancashire Life*, May 1980, p.35.
25. Martin Jordan, *Maclaren-Ross at the Mower*, *London Magazine*, December 1971/January 1972, p.117.
26. Martin Jordan, *Maclaren-Ross at the Mower*, *London Magazine*, December 1971/January 1972, p.117.
27. J.Maclaren-Ross, unpublished foreword to *Selected Stories*, Sunday 2 February 1964 (NU).

Don't Forget To Smile

1. *The Bognor Regis Observer*, Wednesday 12 January 1938, p.6.
2. *The Bognor Regis Observer*, Wednesday 12 January 1938, p.6.
3. *The Bognor Regis Observer*, Wednesday 2 February 1938, p.4.
4. *The Bognor Regis Post*, Saturday 5 February 1938, p.6.
5. C.K. Jaeger in conversation with the author.
6. C.K. Jaeger in conversation with the author.
7. C.K. Jaeger in conversation with the author.
8. C.K. Jaeger in conversation with the author.
9. C.K. Jaeger, *The Man in the Top Hat*, p.28.
10. C.K. Jaeger, *The Man in the Top Hat*, p.28.
11. C.K. Jaeger in conversation with the author.

12. C.K. Jaeger in conversation with the author.
13. C.K. Jaeger in conversation with the author.
14. C.K. Jaeger in conversation with the author.
15. C.K. Jaeger in conversation with the author.
16. No trace of this appears to have survived.
17. J.Maclaren-Ross, *The Weeping and the Laughter*, p.218.
18. C.K. Jaeger in conversation with the author.
19. C.K. Jaeger in conversation with the author.
20. Letter from J.Maclaren-Ross to "The Editor", *New Writing*, Saturday 12 March 1938 (HR).
21. J.Maclaren-Ross, *Memoirs of the Forties*, p.29.
22. J.Maclaren-Ross, *Memoirs of the Forties*, p.29.
23. C.K. Jaeger in conversation with the author.
24 Letter from J.Maclaren-Ross to Moray McLaren, 25 April 1938 (BBC).
25. Letter from Moray McLaren to J.Maclaren-Ross, 8 June 1938 (BBC).
26. Letter from Moray McLaren to J.Maclaren-Ross, 17 June 1938 (BBC).
27. Letter from J.Maclaren-Ross to Val Gielgud, 25 June 1938 (BBC).
28. "The Paramount film version, retitled *This Gun For Hire*, scripted by W.R. Burnett and set in America, starring Alan Ladd as Raven and Veronica Lake and Laird Cregar, was shown over here in 1942 and contained nothing from my version," Julian wrote. (Julian Maclaren-Ross, *Memoirs of the Forties*, p.2.)
29. J.Maclaren-Ross, *Memoirs of the Forties*, p.15.
30. J.Maclaren-Ross, *Memoirs of the Forties*, p.15.
31. J.Maclaren-Ross, *Memoirs of the Forties*, p.19.
32. J.Maclaren-Ross, *Memoirs of the Forties*, p.19.
33. J.Maclaren-Ross, *Memoirs of the Forties*, p.19-20.
34. J.Maclaren-Ross, *Memoirs of the Forties*, p.20.
35. Letter from J.Maclaren-Ross to Moray McLaren, Monday 8 August 1938 (BBC).
36. C.K. Jaeger in conversation with the author.
37. C.K. Jaeger in conversation with the author.
38. John Lehmann, *I Am My Brother*, p.204.
39. Letter from J.Maclaren-Ross to Moray McLaren, Monday 8 August 1938 (BBC).

The Man in the Teddy-Bear Coat

1. J.Maclaren-Ross, *Of Love and Hunger*, p.180.
2. C.K. Jaeger in conversation with the author.
3. C.K. Jaeger in conversation with the author.
4. Letter from J.Maclaren-Ross to Val Gielgud, Sunday 30 October 1938 (BBC).
5. C.K. Jaeger in conversation with the author. The scene where the monstrous brother finally confronts his normal-looking sibling occurs on p.65-66 of G.S. Marlowe's *I Am Your Brother*, Collins, 1935.
6. C.K. Jaeger in conversation with the author.
7 C.K. Jaeger in conversation with the author.
8. C.K. Jaeger in conversation with the author.
9. Letter from Val Gielgud to J.Maclaren-Ross, Tuesday 21 February 1939 (BBC).
10. C.K. Jaeger in conversation with the author.
11. C.K. Jaeger, *The Man in the Top Hat*, p.12.
12. C.K. Jaeger in conversation with the author.
13. C.K. Jaeger, *Angels on Horseback*, p.6.
14. J.Maclaren-Ross, *Mr Hamilton and Mr Gorse*, *London Magazine*, January 1956, p.58.
15. Letter from Moray McLaren to J.Maclaren-Ross, Wednesday 15 March 1939 (BBC).
16. Letter from Moray McLaren to J.Maclaren-Ross, Thursday 3 August 1939 (BBC).
17. J.Maclaren-Ross, *The Swag, the Spy and the Soldier*, included in *The Nine Men of Soho*, p.117.
18. J.Maclaren-Ross, *The Swag, the Spy and the Soldier*, included in *The Nine Men of Soho*, p.117.
19. J.Maclaren-Ross, *The Swag, the Spy and the Soldier*, included in *The Nine Men of Soho*, p.117.
20. J.Maclaren-Ross, *The Swag, the Spy and the Soldier*, included in *The Nine Men of Soho*, p.117.

21. C.K. Jaeger in conversation with the author.
22. J.Maclaren-Ross, unpublished manuscript of *Accused Soldier* (CA).
23. J.Maclaren-Ross, *The Weeping and the Laughter*, p.149.
24. Martin Jordan, *Maclaren-Ross at the Mower*, *London Magazine*, Dec. 1971/Jan. 1972, p.116.
25. J.Maclaren-Ross, *Memoirs of the Forties*, p.59.
26. Letter from Janetta Parlade' (formerly Woolley) to the author, Tuesday 18 June 2002.
27. J.Maclaren-Ross, *Memoirs of the Forties*, p.61-62.
28. C.K. Jaeger in conversation with the author.
29. In February 1940, she was brought in to provide secretarial help for John Lehmann's *Penguin New Writing*.
30. Letter from J.Maclaren-Ross to John Lehmann, Sunday 14 August 1955 (HR).
31. J.Maclaren-Ross, *Punch*, September 23 1959, p.219.
32. J.Maclaren-Ross, unpublished foreword to *Selected Stories*, Sunday 2 February 1964 (NU).
33. J.Maclaren-Ross, unpublished foreword to *Selected Stories*, Sunday 2 February 1964 (NU).
34. Letter from J.Maclaren-Ross to the BBC, Friday 3 May 1940 (BBC).
35. V.S. Pritchett, *The New Statesman and Nation*, Friday 24 September 1965, p.446.

Soldier of Misfortune

1. J.Maclaren-Ross, *Memoirs of the Forties*, p.81.
2. J.Maclaren-Ross, *The Long and the Short and the Tall*, *Lilliput*, January 1957, p.34.
3. J.Maclaren-Ross, *The Long and the Short and the Tall*, *Lilliput*, January 1957, p.34.
4. J.Maclaren-Ross, *The Long and the Short and the Tall*, *Lilliput*, January 1957, p.34.
5. J.Maclaren-Ross, *The Long and the Short and the Tall*, *Lilliput*, January 1957, p.34-35.
6. J.Maclaren-Ross, *The Long and the Short and the Tall*, *Lilliput*, January 1957, p.35.
7. J.Maclaren-Ross, *Monsieur L'Abbé*, *Encounter*, p.39.
8. J.Maclaren-Ross, review of T.E. Lawrence's *The Mint*, *London Magazine*, July 1955, p.72.
9. Letter from C.K. Jaeger to J.Maclaren-Ross, Monday 29 July 1940 (HR).
10. Letter from Eileen Cooke to J.Maclaren-Ross, Monday 12 August 1940 (HR).
11. J.Maclaren-Ross, *The Long and the Short and the Tall*, *Lilliput*, January 1957, p.36.
12. J.Maclaren-Ross, *The Long and the Short and the Tall*, *Lilliput*,January 1957, p.36.
13. Letter from Eileen Cooke to J.Maclaren-Ross, Monday 12 August 1940 (HR).
14. J.Maclaren-Ross, quoted in a letter to him from Eileen Cooke, Tuesday 20 August 1940 (HR).
15. J.Maclaren-Ross, quoted in a letter to him from Eileen Cooke, c. Wednesday 14 August 1940 (HR).
16. *The News of the World*, Sunday 25 August 1940, p.2.
17. *The News of the World*, Sunday 25 August 1940, p.2.
18. *The News of the World*, Sunday 25 August 1940, p.2.
19. J.Maclaren-Ross, *The Swag, the Spy and the Soldier*, included in *The Nine Men of Soho*, p.136.
20. J.Maclaren-Ross, *The Swag, the Spy and the Soldier*, included in *The Nine Men of Soho*, p.136.
21. J.Maclaren-Ross, *The Swag, the Spy and the Soldier*, included in *The Nine Men of Soho*, p.136.
22. J.Maclaren-Ross, *The Swag, the Spy and the Soldier*, included in *The Nine Men of Soho*, p.136-137.
23. C.K. Jaeger in conversation with the author.
24. C.K. Jaeger, *Angels on Horseback*, frontispiece.
25. J.Maclaren-Ross, *I Had To Go Absent*, Tuesday 2 February 1943 (UT).
26. J.Maclaren-Ross, *I Had To Go Absent*, Tuesday 2 February 1943 (UT).
27. Letter from Eileen Cooke to J.Maclaren-Ross, Monday 9 September 1940 (HR).
28. Letter from Eileen Cooke to J.Maclaren-Ross, Monday 9 September 1940 (HR).
29. Letter from Eileen Cooke to J.Maclaren-Ross, Thursday 3 October 1940 (HR).
30. Letter from Eileen Cooke to J.Maclaren-Ross, Thursday 3 October 1940 (HR).
31. J.Maclaren-Ross, *I Had To Go Absent*, Tuesday 2 February 1943 (UT).
32. J.Maclaren-Ross, *I Had To Go Absent*, Tuesday 2 February 1943 (UT).
33. J.Maclaren-Ross, *Memoirs of the Forties*, p.88.
34. Letter from J.Maclaren-Ross to John Lehmann, Saturday 11 July 1942 (HR).
35. Letter from J.Maclaren-Ross to John Lehmann, Saturday 11 July 1942 (HR).
36. J.Maclaren-Ross, *I Had To Go Absent*, Monday 2 February 1943.
37. J.Maclaren-Ross, *I Had To Go Absent*, Monday 2 February 1943.

38. J.Maclaren-Ross, *I Had To Go Absent*, Monday 2 February 1943.
39. J.Maclaren-Ross, *Seven Days of Heaven*, included in *The Stuff To Give The Troops*, p.153.
40. J.Maclaren-Ross, *Seven Days of Heaven*, included in *The Stuff To Give The Troops*, p.157.
41. Letter from J.Maclaren-Ross to Rupert Hart-Davis, Monday 3 March 1941 (UT).
42. Letter from J.Maclaren-Ross to Rupert Hart-Davis, Monday 3 March 1941 (UT).
43. Letter from J.Maclaren-Ross to Rupert Hart-Davis, Monday 3 March 1941 (UT).
44. Letter from J.Maclaren-Ross to Rupert Hart-Davis, Monday 3 March 1941 (UT).
45. Letter from J.Maclaren-Ross to Rupert Hart-Davis, Monday 3 March 1941 (UT).
46. J.Maclaren-Ross, *I Had To Go Absent*, Monday 2 February 1943.
47. *The Suffolk Regimental Gazette*, September-October 1941, p.239.
48. Letter from J.Maclaren-Ross to John Lehmann, Thursday 30 July 1942 (HR).

Military Manouevres

1. Letter from J.Maclaren-Ross to Rupert Hart-Davis, Thursday 27 August 1942 (UT).
2. Letter from J.Maclaren-Ross to John Lehmann, Saturday 11 July 1942 (HR).
3. Letter from J.Maclaren-Ross to John Lehmann, Saturday 11 July 1942 (HR).
4. Letter from J.Maclaren-Ross to John Lehmann, Wednesday 5 August 1942 (HR).
5. Letter from J.Maclaren-Ross to John Lehmann, Wednesday 5 August 1942 (HR).
6. Letter from J.Maclaren-Ross to Rupert Hart-Davis, Thursday 27 August 1942 (UT).
7 Letter from J.Maclaren-Ross to Rupert Hart-Davis, Tuesday 6 July 1943 (UT).
8. J.Maclaren-Ross, unpublished foreword to *Selected Stories*, Sunday 2 February 1964 (NU).
9. Letter from J.Maclaren-Ross to Rupert Hart-Davis, Saturday 10 April 1943 (UT).
10. J.Maclaren-Ross, *I Had To Go Absent*, Monday 2 February 1943.
11. Letter from J.Maclaren-Ross to John Lehmann, Thursday 30 July 1942 (HR).
12 Letter from J.Maclaren-Ross to John Lehmann, Thursday 30 July 1942 (HR).
13. Letter from Evelyn Waugh to the Royal Literary Fund, Tuesday 4 July 1950 (RLF).
14. J.Maclaren-Ross, *Memoirs of the Forties*, p.146.
15. John Lehmann, *I Am My Brother*, p.204.
16. John Lehmann, *The Listener*, Wednesday 7 October 1965, p.539.
17. Letter from J.Maclaren-Ross to John Lehmann, Wednesday 5 August 1942 (HR).
18. Letter from J.Maclaren-Ross to John Lehmann, Wednesday 12 August 1942 (HR).
19. Letter from J.Maclaren-Ross to John Lehmann, Wednesday 12 August 1942 (HR).
20. Rupert Hart-Davis, *The Power of Chance*, p.153.
21. Letter from J.Maclaren-Ross to Rupert Hart-Davis, Thursday 3 September 1942 (UT).
22. J.Maclaren-Ross, *I Had To Go Absent*, Tuesday 2 February 1943 (UT).
23. Letter from J.Maclaren-Ross to Rupert Hart-Davis, Monday 15 November 1942 (UT).
24. Letter from J.Maclaren-Ross to Rupert Hart-Davis, Thursday 3 September 1942 (UT).
25. Letter from J.Maclaren-Ross to Rupert Hart-Davis, Tuesday 15 September 1942 (UT).
26. Letter from J.Maclaren-Ross to Rupert Hart-Davis, Thursday 3 September 1942 (UT).
27. Letter from J.Maclaren-Ross to John Lehmann, Tuesday 27 October 1942 (HR).
28. Letter from J.Maclaren-Ross to The Officer Commanding, Saturday 3 October 1942 (HR).
29. J.Maclaren-Ross, *I Had To Go Absent*, Tuesday 2 February 1943 (UT).
30. J.Maclaren-Ross, *I Had To Go Absent*, Tuesday 2 February 1943 (UT).
31. Letter from J.Maclaren-Ross to Rupert Hart-Davis, Tuesday 10 November 1942 (UT).
32. Letter from J.Maclaren-Ross to Rupert Hart-Davis, Tuesday 10 November 1942 (UT).
33. Letter from John Lehmann to J.Maclaren-Ross, Thursday 22 October 1942 (HR).
34. John Lehmann, *The Armoured Writer, New Writing and Daylight*, August 1942, p.158.
35. Letter from J.Maclaren-Ross to Rupert Hart-Davis, Monday 15 November 1942 (UT).
36. Letter from J.Maclaren-Ross to Rupert Hart-Davis, Tuesday 2 February 1943 (UT).
37. Letter from J.Maclaren-Ross to Rupert Hart-Davis, Tuesday 2 February 1943 (UT).
38. Anthony Cronin, *Dead As Doornails*, p.145.
39. Anthony Cronin, *Dead As Doornails*, p.145.
40. Anthony Cronin, *Dead As Doornails*, p.145.
41. J.Maclaren-Ross, *I Had To Go Absent*, Tuesday 2 February 1943 (UT).
42. Letter from J.Maclaren-Ross to Rupert Hart-Davis, Sunday 7 February 1943 (UT).

43. Letter from J.Maclaren-Ross to Rupert Hart-Davis, Sunday 7 February 1943 (UT).
44. Letter from J.Maclaren-Ross to Rupert Hart-Davis, Sunday 7 February 1943 (UT).
45. J.Maclaren-Ross, *I Had To Go Absent*, Tuesday 2 February 1943 (UT).
46. J.Maclaren-Ross, *I Had To Go Absent*, Tuesday 2 February 1943 (UT).
47. J.Maclaren-Ross, *I Had To Go Absent*, Tuesday 2 February 1943 (UT).
48. Letter from J.Maclaren-Ross to Rupert Hart-Davis, Wednesday 31 March 1943 (UT).
49. J.Maclaren-Ross, *I Had To Go Absent*, Tuesday 2 February 1943 (UT).
50. J.Maclaren-Ross, *I Had To Go Absent*, Tuesday 2 February 1943 (UT).
51. Letter from J.Maclaren-Ross to Rupert Hart-Davis, Sunday 7 February 1943 (UT).
52. Letter from J.Maclaren-Ross to Rupert Hart-Davis, Monday [8 February 1943] (UT).
53. Rupert Hart-Davis, *The Power of Chance*, p.153.
54. Letter from J.Maclaren-Ross to Rupert Hart-Davis, Tuesday 16 February 1943 (UT).
55. Letter from J.Maclaren-Ross to Rupert Hart-Davis, Tuesday 16 February 1943 (UT).
56. Raynor Heppenstall, *The Lesser Infortune*, p.130.
57. Raynor Heppenstall, *The Lesser Infortune*, p.130.

Hospital Blues

1. Letter from J.Maclaren-Ross to Rupert Hart-Davis, Wednesday 17 February 1943 (UT).
2. Letter from Major Charles M. Ross to Rupert Hart-Davis, Monday 8 March 1943 (UT).
3. Letter from J.Maclaren-Ross to Rupert Hart-Davis, Wednesday 17 March 1943 (UT).
4. Letter from J.Maclaren-Ross to Mishka,Wednesday 10 March 1943 (HR).
5. Letter from J.Maclaren-Ross to Rupert Hart-Davis, Monday 22 February 1943 (UT).
6. Letter from J.Maclaren-Ross to Rupert Hart-Davis, Wednesday 17 March 1943 (UT).
7. Letter from J.Maclaren-Ross to Rupert Hart-Davis, Wednesday 17 March 1943 (UT).
8. Letter from J.Maclaren-Ross to Rupert Hart-Davis, Monday 1 March 1943 (UT).
9. Letter from J.Maclaren-Ross to Rupert Hart-Davis, Wednesday 24 March 1943 (UT).
10. Letter from J.Maclaren-Ross to Rupert Hart-Davis, Wednesday 24 March 1943 (UT).
11. Letter from J.Maclaren-Ross to Rupert Hart-Davis, Tuesday 31 March 1943 (UT).
12. Letter from J.Maclaren-Ross to Rupert Hart-Davis, Tuesday 31 March 1943 (UT).
13. Letter from J.Maclaren-Ross to Rupert Hart-Davis, Tuesday 31 March 1943 (UT).
14. Letter from J.Maclaren-Ross to Rupert Hart-Davis, Saturday 3 April 1943 (UT).
15. Letter from J.Maclaren-Ross to Rupert Hart-Davis, Thursday 8 April 1943 (UT).
16. Letter from J.Maclaren-Ross to Rupert Hart-Davis, Thursday 8 April 1943 (UT).
17. Letter from J.Maclaren-Ross to Rupert Hart-Davis, Thursday 8 April 1943 (UT).
18. Letter from J.Maclaren-Ross to Rupert Hart-Davis, Saturday 10 April 1943 (UT).
19. Letter from J.Maclaren-Ross to Rupert Hart-Davis, Saturday 10 April 1943 (UT).
20. Letter from J.Maclaren-Ross to Rupert Hart-Davis, Saturday 10 April 1943 (UT).
21. Rupert Hart-Davis, *The Power of Chance*, p.153-154.
22. Letter from J.Maclaren-Ross to Rupert Hart-Davis, Saturday 10 April 1943 (UT).
23. Letter from J.Maclaren-Ross to Rupert Hart-Davis, Saturday 10 April 1943 (UT).
24. Letter from J.Maclaren-Ross to Rupert Hart-Davis, Tuesday 14 April 1943 (UT).
25. Letter from J.Maclaren-Ross to Rupert Hart-Davis, Tuesday 14 April 1943 (UT).
26. Letter from J.Maclaren-Ross to Rupert Hart-Davis, Friday 23 April 1943 (UT).
27. Letter from Scylla Yates to Rupert Hart-Davis, Saturday 1 May 1943 (UT).
28. Letter from Scylla Yates to Rupert Hart-Davis, Saturday 1 May 1943 (UT).
29. Raynor Heppenstall, *The Lesser Infortune*, p.110.
30. Raynor Heppenstall, *The Lesser Infortune*, p.110.
31. The dialogue comes from Raynor Heppenstall, *The Lesser Infortune*, p.113-114.
32. Rayner Heppenstall, *The Lesser Infortune*, p.116.
33. Rayner Heppenstall, *The Lesser Infortune*, p.120.
34. Walter Allen, *As I Walked Down New Grubb Street*, p.153.
35. Letter from J.Maclaren-Ross to Rupert Hart-Davis, Friday 30 April 1943 (UT).
36. Letter from Scylla Yates to Rupert Hart-Davis, Sunday 16 May 1943 (UT).
37. Letter from J.Maclaren-Ross to Rupert Hart-Davis, Friday 14 May 1943 (UT).
38. Letter from J.Maclaren-Ross to Rupert Hart-Davis, Saturday 15 May 1943 (UT).

39. Letter from J.Maclaren-Ross to Rupert Hart-Davis, Thursday 20 May 1943 (UT).
40. Letter from J.Maclaren-Ross to Rupert Hart-Davis, Saturday 5 June 1943 (UT).
41. J.Maclaren-Ross, The *London Magazine*, July 1955, p.73.
42. Anthony Powell, *To Keep The Ball Rolling*, p.328.
43. Synopsis to *The Hunted Man: A Melodrama* (UT).
44. Letter from J.Maclaren-Ross to John Lehmann, Sunday 13 June 1943 (HR).
45. Joan Wyndham, *Love Is Blue*, p.118.
46. Army record, held by the Ministry of Defence.
47. Letter from J.Maclaren-Ross to Rupert Hart-Davis, Friday 25 June 1943 (UT).
48. Letter from J.Maclaren-Ross to John Lehmann, Sunday 13 June 1943 (HR).

London Calling

1. Letter from J.Maclaren-Ross to John Lehmann, Sunday 13 June 1943 (HR).
2.. J.Maclaren-Ross, notebook, c.1952 (NU).
3. J.Maclaren-Ross, notebook, c.1952 (NU).
4. Stephen Fothergill in conversation with the author.
5. Stephen Fothergill in conversation with the author.
6. J. Maclaren-Ross, *Memoirs of the Forties*, p.138.
7. J. Maclaren-Ross, *Memoirs of the Forties*, p.138.
8. C.K. Jaeger in conversation with the author.
9. J. Maclaren-Ross, *Memoirs of the Forties*, p.186.
10. J.Maclaren-Ross, *Memoirs of the Forties*, p.186.
11. Alan Ross, *Blindfold Games*, p.248.
12. C.K. Jaeger, *The Man in the Top Hat*, p.19.
13. Derek Stanford in correspondence with the author, Thursday 11 November 1999.
14. Derek Stanford, *Inside the Forties*, p.67.
15. Derek Stanford, *Inside the Forties*, p.67.
16. J.Maclaren-Ross, *Memoirs of the Forties*, p.154.
17. J.Maclaren-Ross, *Memoirs of the Forties*, p.201.
18. Derek Stanford, *Inside the Forties*, p.133.
19. Anne Valery, *The Edge of a Smile*, p.148.
20. Anne Valery, *The Edge of a Smile*, p.148.
21. J.Maclaren-Ross, *Memoirs of the Forties*, p.161.
22. J.Maclaren-Ross, *Memoirs of the Forties*, p.112.
23. J.Maclaren-Ross, *Memoirs of the Forties*, p.112.
24. Charles Wrey Gardiner, *The Dark Thorn*, p.42.
25. Julian Symons, *London Magazine*, April/May 1979, p.64.
26. John Davenport, *The Spectator*, Thursday 1 October 1964, p.630.
27. John Davenport, *The Spectator*, Thursday 1 October 1964, p.630.
28. Ruthven Todd, *Fitzrovia and the Road To The York Minster*, no page numbers.
29. Letter from J.Maclaren-Ross to John Lehmann, Sunday 14 August 1955.
30. Alan Ross, *Blindfold Games*, p.249.
31. J.Maclaren-Ross, *Memoirs of the Forties*, p.131.
32. J.Maclaren-Ross, *Memoirs of the Forties*, p.131.
33. J.Maclaren-Ross, *Memoirs of the Forties*, p.131.
34. Letter from J.Maclaren-Ross to John Lehmann, Sunday 14 August 1955 (HR).
35. C.K. Jaeger in conversation with the author.
36. Letter from J.Maclaren-Ross to John Lehmann, Sunday 14 August 1955 (HR).
37. J.Maclaren-Ross, notebook, c.1952 (NU).
38. Letter from Leonard Russell to the Royal Literary Fund, Tuesday 23 January 1945 (RLF).
39. J.Maclaren-Ross, Personal Note to *The Funny Bone*, p.12.
40. Dan Davin, Closing Times, p.3-5. This is also the source of all the ensuing dialogue.
41. C.K. Jaeger in conversation with the author.
42. J.Maclaren-Ross, *Memoirs of the Forties*, p.106.

43. Robert Westerby and P.J. Bruce, Foreword to *The First Eighteen: Stories By Writers In Uniform*, edited by Robert Westerby and P.J. Bruce, Nicolson and Watson, 1943.
44. Leonard Russell, Foreword to Christmas Pie, Hutchinson, December 1943.

Doodlebugs and Green Bombs

1. Letter from J.Maclaren-Ross to Rupert Hart-Davis, Friday 9 June 1943 (UT).
2. Letter from J.Maclaren-Ross to Rupert Hart-Davis, Saturday 12 February 1943 (UT).
3. This and the subsequent dialogue comes from Anthony Carson, *Carson Was Here*, p.7-10.
4. Anthony Carson, *Carson Was Here*, p.9.
5. J.Maclaren-Ross, Author's Note to *Bitten By The Tarantula*.
6. Charles Wrey Gardiner, *The Dark Thorn*, p.82.
7. J.Maclaren-Ross, Author's Note to *Bitten By The Tarantula*.
8. Letter from J.Maclaren-Ross to Rupert Hart-Davis, Friday 9 June 1944 (UT).
9. Letter from J.Maclaren-Ross to Cyril Connolly, Thursday 15 June 1944 (UT).
10. Letter from Peter Vansittart to the author, December 2000.
11. Anthony Burgess, *Little Wilson and Big God*, p.289.
12. Anthony Burgess, *Little Wilson and Big God*, p.289.
13. Stephen Fothergill in conversation with the author.
14. Peter Vansittart, *Paths From A White Horse*, p.216.
15 Bruce Bernard in conversation with the author.
16. Walter Allen, *As I Walked Down New Grubb Street*, p.153.
17. Anthony Powell, *The Daily Telegraph and Morning Post*, Friday 22 November, 1946, p.6.
18. John Lehmann, *I Am My Brother*, p.204.
19. John Lehmann, *I Am My Brother*, p.204.
20. *John O'London's Weekly*, Friday 8 September 1944, p.222.
21. *The Times Literary Supplement*, Saturday 12 August 1944, p.389.
22. Philip Toynbee, *The New Statesman and Nation*, Saturday 19 August 1944, p.125.
23. J.Maclaren-Ross, *The Oxford Manner*, included in *Better Than A Kick In The Pants*, p.130.
24. J.Maclaren-Ross, *The Episcopal Seal*, *The Strand Magazine*, November 1948, p.75.
25. C.K. Jaeger, *The Man in the Top Hat*, p.34.
26. Dan Davin, *Closing Times*, p.7.
27. C.K. Jaeger, *The Man in the Top Hat*, p.34.
28. Bronia McDonald (formerly Kennedy) in conversation with the author.
29. Walter Allen, *As I Walked Down New Grubb Street*, p.156.
30. Walter Allen, *As I Walked Down New Grubb Street*, p.156.
31. Letter from J.Maclaren-Ross to Dan Davin, Sunday 21 November 1954 (DD).
32. Letter from J.Maclaren-Ross to Dan Davin, Sunday 21 November 1954 (DD).
33. Dan Davin, *Closing Times*, p.18.
34. Letter from J.Maclaren-Ross to Dan Davin, Sunday 21 November 1954 (DD).
35. Dan Davin, *Closing Times*, p.8.
36. Dan Davin, *Closing Times*, p.16.
37. Dan Davin, *Closing Times*, p.16.
38. Alan Pryce-Jones, *The Observer*, Sunday 24 September 1944, p.3.
39. *John Bull*, Thursday 11 November 1944, p.10.
40. Anne Valery, *The Edge of a Smile*, p.148.
41. Anne Valery in conversation with the author.
42. Anne Valery, *The Edge of a Smile*, p.150.
43 Anne Valery, *The Edge of a Smile*, p.150.
44. Anne Valery, *The Edge of a Smile*, p.177.
45. Anne Valery, *The Edge of a Smile*, p.163, and Anne Valery in conversation with the author.
46. Letter from J.Maclaren-Ross to the Royal Literary Fund, Wednesday 30 January 1945 (RLF).
47. Letter from Leonard Russell to the Royal Literary Fund, Tuesday 23 January 1945 (RLF).
48. Letter from Leonard Russell to the Royal Literary Fund, Tuesday 23 January 1945 (RLF).
49. Letter from John Lehmann to the Royal Literary Fund, Wednesday 30 January 1945 (RLF).
50. André Deutsch in conversation with the author.

51. André Deutsch in conversation with the author.
52. Walter Allen, *As I Walked Down New Grubb Street*, p.153.
53. J.Maclaren-Ross, *Memoirs of the Forties*, p.153.
54. André Deutsch in conversation with the author.
55. Dan Davin, *Closing Times*, p.7.
56. John Lehmann, *The Listener*, Wednesday 7 October 1965, p.539.

How to be Bohemian

1. Anthony Carson, *Carson Was Here*, p.15.
2. John Lehmann, *I Am My Brother*, p.204.
3. Letter from J.Maclaren-Ross to John Lehmann, c. August 1945 (HR).
4. Letter from J.Maclaren-Ross to John Lehmann, c. August 1945 (HR).
5. John Heath-Stubbs in conversation with the author.
6. Letter from John Lehmann's secretary to J.Maclaren-Ross, Wednesday 19 September 1945 (HR).
7. Letter from J.Maclaren-Ross to John Lehmann, Saturday 22 September 1945 (HR).
8. Anthony Carson, *Carson Was Here*, p.13.
9. Stephen Fothergill, *The Last Lamplighter*, p.104.
10. Stephen Fothergill, *The Last Lamplighter*, p.104.
11. Stephen Fothergill, *The Last Lamplighter*, p.104.
12. Anthony Carson, *Carson Was Here*, p.13.
13. Anthony Carson, *Carson Was Here*, p.15.
14. Anthony Carson, *Carson Was Here*, p.15.
15. Dan Davin, *Closing Times*, p.20.
16. Dan Davin, *Closing Times*, p.20.
17. Letter from J.Maclaren-Ross to John Lehmann, Sunday 16 February 1947 (HR).
18. Letter from J.Maclaren-Ross to John Lehmann, Sunday 16 February 1947 (HR).
19. Dan Davin, *Closing Times*, p.9.
20. Dan Davin, *Closing Times*, p.9.
21. Henry Reed, *The New Statesman and Nation*, Saturday 5 January 1946, p.12.
22. Henry Reed, *The New Statesman and Nation*, Saturday 5 January 1946, p.12.
23. Raynor Heppenstall, *London Magazine*, November 1966, p.64.
24. C.K. Jaeger in conversation with the author.
25. C.K. Jaeger in conversation with the author.
26. C.K. Jaeger in conversation with the author.
27. C.K. Jaeger in conversation with the author.
28. Anthony Carson, *Carson Was Here*, p.13.
29. R.D. Smith, BBC Memo, Friday 23 January 1959 (BBC).
30. Letter from J.Maclaren-Ross to the BBC, Saturday 19 January 1946 (BBC).
31. Henry Reed, *The New Statesman and Nation*, Saturday 2 March 1946.
32. Ralph Strauss, *The Sunday Times*, Sunday 3 February 1946, p.3.
33. Questionnaire: *The Cost of Letters*, *Horizon*, September 1946, p.155.
34. Questionnaire: *The Cost of Letters*, *Horizon*, September 1946, p.156.
35. John Heath-Stubbs in conversation with the author.
36. John Heath-Stubbs in conversation with the author.
37. Questionnaire: *The Cost of Letters*, *Horizon*, September 1946, p.155.
38. Questionnaire: *The Cost of Letters*, *Horizon*, September 1946, p.157.
39. Anthony Curtis in conversation with the author.
40. Anthony Powell, *The Daily Telegraph and Morning Post*, Friday 22 November, 1946, p.6.
41. Elizabeth Bowen, *The Tatler and Bystander*, Wednesday 25 December 1946, p.437.
42. J.Maclaren-Ross, *The Days of the Comet*, *Winter Pie*, November 1946, p.59.
43. Letter from J.Maclaren-Ross to John Lehmann, Sunday 18 May 1947 (HR).
44. Letter from J.Maclaren-Ross to John Lehmann, Sunday 16 February 1947 (HR).
45. Anthony Powell, *To Keep The Ball Rolling*, p.330.
46. Anthony Powell, *To Keep The Ball Rolling*, p.330.

Into the Red

1. Letter from J.Maclaren-Ross to Captain Broadbent, Friday 7 February 1947 (RLF).
2. J.Maclaren-Ross, Notebook, c.1952 (NU).
3. Letter from J.Maclaren-Ross to Captain Broadbent, Friday 7 February 1947 (RLF).
4. Letter from J.Maclaren-Ross to Captain Broadbent, Friday 7 February 1947 (RLF).
5. Letter from Anthony Powell to the Royal Literary Fund, Sunday 5 January 1947 (RLF).
6. Letter from Frank Swinnerton to the Royal Literary Fund, Friday 7 March 1947 (RLF).
7. Letter from John Lehmann to the Royal Literary Fund, Wednesday 12 February 1947 (RLF).
8. Letter from J.Maclaren-Ross to John Lehmann, Sunday 18 May 1947 (HR).
9. John Heath-Stubbs, *Hindsights*, p.141.
10. Letter from J.Maclaren-Ross to John Lehmann, Sunday 18 May 1947 (HR).
11. Letter from J.Maclaren-Ross to John Lehmann, Sunday 18 May 1947 (HR).
12. Noel Sircar, *News From The Lesser Burrows*, p.47.
13. Noel Sircar, *News From The Lesser Burrows*, p.26.
14. Noel Sircar, *News From The Lesser Burrows*, p.26.
15. C.K. Jaeger, *The Man In The Top Hat*, p.48.
16. C.K. Jaeger, *The Man In The Top Hat*, p.179.
17. C.K. Jaeger, *The Man In The Top Hat*, p.224-225.
18. J.Maclaren-Ross, *Memoirs of the Forties*, p.185.
19. John Davenport, *The Spectator*, Thursday 1 October 1964, p.414.
20. John Davenport, *The Spectator*, Thursday 1 October 1964, p.414.
21. John Davenport, *The Spectator*, Thursday 1 October 1964, p.414.
22. John Davenport, *The Spectator*, Thursday 1 October 1964, p.414.
23. J.Maclaren-Ross, *Lit. Slug: Books Four*, included in *The Funny Bone*, p.139-140.
24. Letter from J.Maclaren-Ross to C.K. Jaeger, Tuesday 2 August 1955.
25. Arthur Crook in conversation with the author.
26. Arthur Crook in conversation with the author.
27. Walter Allen, *As I Walked Down New Grubb Street*, p.155.
28. Tony Van den Burgh in conversation with the author.
29. Letter from Anthony Bevir to Captain Broadbent, Tuesday 17 February 1948 (RLF).
30. Letter from J.Maclaren-Ross to Captain Broadbent, Monday 26 June 1950 (RLF).
31. Letter from J.Maclaren-Ross to Charles Wrey Gardiner, Friday 14 May 1948 (HR).
32. Letter from J.Maclaren-Ross to Captain Broadbent, Monday 26 June 1950 (RLF).
33. J.Maclaren-Ross, *The Episcopal Seal, The Strand Magazine*, November 1948, p.73.
34. Letter from "Monica Maclaren-Ross" to Captain Broadbent, Monday 13 December 1948 (RLF).
35. Letter from J.Maclaren-Ross to Captain Broadbent, Monday 26 June 1950 (RLF).
36. Arthur Crook in conversation with the author.
37. Letter from J.Maclaren-Ross to Captain Broadbent, Sunday 4 September 1949 (RLF).
38. C.K. Jaeger in conversation with the author.
39. John Heath-Stubbs in conversation with the author.
40. J.Maclaren-Ross, *Bop*, included in *The Funny Bone*, p.170.
41. J.Maclaren-Ross, *Bop*, included in *The Funny Bone*, p.170.
42. J.Maclaren-Ross, *Bop*, included in *The Funny Bone*, p.170.
43. J.Maclaren-Ross, *Bop*, included in *The Funny Bone*, p.170.
44. J.Maclaren-Ross, *Bop*, included in *The Funny Bone*, p.172.
45. Letter from J.Maclaren-Ross to Captain Broadbent, Sunday 4 September 1949 (RLF).
46. Letter from J.Maclaren-Ross to Captain Broadbent, Sunday 9 October 1949 (RLF).
47. Anthony Carson, *I Return to 'The Load of Hay'*, The Leader Magazine,
    Saturday 29 October 1949, p.26.
48. Anthony Carson, *I Return to 'The Load of Hay'*, *The Leader Magazine*,
    Saturday 29 October 1949, p.26.
49. Anthony Carson, *I Return to 'The Load of Hay'*, *The Leader Magazine*,
    Saturday 29 October 1949, p.27.
50. Anthony Carson, *I Return to 'The Load of Hay'*, *The Leader Magazine*,
    Saturday 29 October 1949, p.27.

51. Anthony Carson, *I Return to 'The Load of Hay'*, The Leader Magazine, Saturday 29 October 1949, p.27.
52. Anthony Carson, *I Return to 'The Load of Hay'*, The Leader Magazine, Saturday 29 October 1949, p.27.
53. Anthony Carson, *I Return to 'The Load of Hay'*, The Leader Magazine, Saturday 29 October 1949, p.27.
54. Anthony Carson, *I Return to 'The Load of Hay'*, The Leader Magazine, Saturday 29 October 1949, p.27.
55. Peter Brooke, using that very pseudonym, went on to achieve fame as a columnist and humorous travel writer.

Cash-on-Delivery

1. Dan Davin, *Closing Times*, p.13.
2. Letter from J.Maclaren-Ross to Dan Davin, Sunday 21 November 1954 (DD).
3. Letter from J.Maclaren-Ross to Dan Davin, Sunday 21 November 1954 (DD).
4. Daniel Farson, *Soho in the Fifties*, p.95.
5. Letter from J.Maclaren-Ross to John Lehmann, Monday 26 September 1955 (HR).
6. Anthony Carson, *I Return to 'The Load of Hay'*, The Leader Magazine, Saturday 29 October 1949, p.26.
7. Roland Camberton, *Scamp*, p.23-24.
8. Peter Vansittart, *In The Fifties*, p.81.
9. Peter Vansittart, *In The Fifties*, p.81.
10. Peter Vansittart, *In The Fifties*, p.81.
11. Anthony Carson, *Carson Was Here*, p.14.
12. Walter Allen, *As I Walked Down New Grubb Street*, p.157.
13. J.Maclaren-Ross, *The Shoestring Budget*, included in *The Funny Bone*, p.90.
14. J.Maclaren-Ross, *The Shoestring Budget*, included in *The Funny Bone*, p.92.
15. J.Maclaren-Ross, *The Shoestring Budget*, included in *The Funny Bone*, p.92.
16. Letter from J.Maclaren-Ross to Captain Broadbent, Monday 26 June 1950 (RLF).
17. Letter from John Betjeman to the Royal Literary Fund, Friday 30 June 1950 (RLF).
18. Letter from Evelyn Waugh to the Royal Literary Fund, Tuesday 4 July 1950 (RLF).
19. John Guillermin later took charge of 1970s big budget spectaculars such as *The Towering Inferno*.
20. J.Maclaren-Ross, *The Shoestring Budget*, included in *The Funny Bone*, p.92.
21. *The Times Literary Supplement*, Friday 27 October 1950, p.673.
22. J.Maclaren-Ross, *Memoirs of the Forties*, p.154.
23. Roland Camberton, *Scamp*, p.19.
24. Roland Camberton, *Scamp*, p.21.
25. Roland Camberton, *Scamp*, p.179.
26. Roland Camberton, *Scamp*, p.179.
27. Letter from J.Maclaren-Ross to C.K. Jaeger, March 1951 (CA).
28. Letter from J.Maclaren-Ross to C.K. Jaeger, March 1951 (CA).
29. Letter from J.Maclaren-Ross to C.K. Jaeger, March 1951 (CA).
30. Letter from J.Maclaren-Ross to C.K. Jaeger, March 1951 (CA).
31. Letter from J.Maclaren-Ross to C.K. Jaeger, March 1951 (CA).
32. C.K. Jaeger in conversation with the author.
33. *Kinematograph Weekly*, Thursday 30 November 1950, p.22.
34. C.K. Jaeger in conversation with the author.
35. Walter Allen, *As I Walked Down New Grubb Street*, 155-156.
36. Walter Allen, *As I Walked Down New Grubb Street*, p.155-156.
37. Walter Allen, *As I Walked Down New Grubb Street*, p.156.
38. J.Maclaren-Ross, notebook, c.1952 (NU).
39. Letter from J.Maclaren-Ross to Mr. Hamilton, Wednesday 28 November 1951 (HH).
40. *Kinematograph Weekly*, Thursday 6 September 1951, p.18.
41. J.Maclaren-Ross, *The Shoestring Budget*, included in *The Funny Bone*, p.94.
42. Anthony Powell, *To Keep The Ball Rolling*, p.327.

43. J.Maclaren-Ross, notebook, c.1952 (NU).
44. J.Maclaren-Ross, notebook, c.1952 (NU).
45. J.Maclaren-Ross, notebook, c.1952 (NU).
46. Conan Nicholas in conversation with the author.
47. Conan Nicholas in conversation with the author.
48. Diana Athill in conversation with the author.
49. J.Maclaren-Ross, notebook, c.1952 (NU).
50. J.Maclaren-Ross, notebook, c.1952 (NU).
51. J.Maclaren-Ross, notebook, c.1952 (NU).
52. J.Maclaren-Ross, notebook, c.1952 (NU).
53. J.Maclaren-Ross, notebook, c.1952 (NU).
54 J.Maclaren-Ross, notebook, c.1952 (NU).
55. J.Maclaren-Ross, notebook, c.1952 (NU).
56. J.Maclaren-Ross, notebook, c.1952 (NU).

Balancing the Books

1. Letter from J.Maclaren-Ross to Rupert Hart-Davis, Thursday 25 September 1952 (UT).
2. Letter from J.Maclaren-Ross to Dan Davin, Thursday 28 September 1952 (DD).
3. Dan Davin, *Closing Times*, p.12.
4. Letter from J.Maclaren-Ross to Rupert Hart-Davis, Saturday 25 October 1952 (UT).
5. Letter from J.Maclaren-Ross to Dan Davin, Sunday 18 January 1953 (DD).
6. Letter from J.Maclaren-Ross to Rupert Hart-Davis, Saturday 28 February 1953 (UT).
7. Letter from J.Maclaren-Ross to Dan Davin, Sunday 18 January 1953 (DD).
8. Letter from J.Maclaren-Ross to Rupert Hart-Davis, Friday 3 September 1953 (UT).
9. Letter from J.Maclaren-Ross to Rupert Hart-Davis, Saturday 28 February 1953 (UT).
10. Letter from J.Maclaren-Ross to Dan Davin, Sunday 15 March 1953 (DD).
11. J.Maclaren-Ross, Author's Note at the beginning of *The Weeping and the Laughter*.
12. Letter from J.Maclaren-Ross to Rupert Hart-Davis, Saturday 16 May 1953 (UT).
13. Letter from J.Maclaren-Ross to Rupert Hart-Davis, Saturday 16 May 1953 (UT).
14. Arthur Marshall, *The New Statesman and Nation*, Saturday 4 April 1953, p.405.
15. *The Times*, Wednesday 1 April 1953, p.6.
16. *The Times*, Wednesday 1 April 1953, p.6.
17. Letter from John Betjeman to J.Maclaren-Ross, Thursday 2 April 1953 (RLF).
18. Certificate from Dr D.V. Merritt of 4 Norfolk Place, Paddington (RLF).
19. Certificate from Dr D.V. Merritt of 4 Norfolk Place, Paddington (RLF).
20. Anthony Powell, *To Keep The Ball Rolling*, p.354.
21. Letter from J.Maclaren-Ross to Dan Davin, Tuesday 14 July 1953 (DD).
22. J.Maclaren-Ross, *Lansdowne and Grosvenor*, *Punch*, Wednesday 24 June 1953.
23. Letter from Mrs Lyle to the Royal Literary Fund, Thursday 25 June 1953 (RLF).
24. Letter from J.Maclaren-Ross to Dan Davin, Saturday 27 June 1953 (RLF).
25. Dan Davin, *Closing Times*, p.12.
26. Letter from John Betjeman to J.Maclaren-Ross, Thursday 2 April 1953 (RLF).
27. Raynor Heppenstall, *Portrait of the Artist As A Professional Man*, p.65.
28. Raynor Heppenstall, *Portrait of the Artist As A Professional Man*, p.65.
29. Letter from J.Maclaren-Ross to Dan Davin, Tuesday 14 July 1953 (DD).
30. J.Maclaren-Ross, letter published in *The New Statesman and Nation*, Saturday 11 July 1953, p.49.
31. J.Maclaren-Ross, letter published in *The New Statesman and Nation*, Saturday 11 July 1953, p.49.
32. J.Maclaren-Ross, letter published in *The New Statesman and Nation*, Saturday 11 July 1953, p.49.
33. J.Maclaren-Ross, *Monsieur L'Abbé*, *Encounter*, December 1953, p.40.
34. Letter from J.Maclaren-Ross to Dan Davin, Sunday 29 November 1953 (DD).
35. J.Maclaren-Ross, unpublished fragment of *Business and Desire*, c.November 1963 (NU).
36. J.Maclaren-Ross, unpublished fragment of *Business and Desire*, c. November 1963 (NU).
37. J.Maclaren-Ross, unpublished fragment of *Business and Desire*, c. November 1963 (NU).

Maigret and the Writer's Widow

1. Letter from Mrs Lyle to the BBC, Friday 16 January 1959 (BBC).
2. Letter from J.Maclaren-Ross to Dan Davin, Sunday 29 November 1953 (DD).
3. Letter from J.Maclaren-Ross to John Lehmann, Friday 27 August 1954 (HR).
4. Letter from J.Maclaren-Ross to Dan Davin, Sunday 21 November 1954 (DD).
5. Gordon Craig, quoted by Keith Ovenden, *A Fighting Withdrawal*, p.254.
6. Keith Ovenden, *A Fighting Withdrawal*, p.267.
7. Dan Davin, *Closing Times*, p.15.
8. Dan Davin, *Closing Times*, p.15.
9. J.Maclaren-Ross, rough draft of *Astrid*, p.2 (HR).
10. Stephen Fothergill, *The Last Lamplighter*, p.104.
11. J. Maclaren-Ross, *Punch*, reviewing *Not Honour More*, Wednesday 13 April 1955, p.479.
12. Letter from J.Maclaren-Ross to Hamish Hamilton Ltd, Sunday 24 October 1954 (HH).
13. Letter from J.Maclaren-Ross to Hamish Hamilton Ltd, Sunday 24 October 1954 (HH).
14. Letter from J.Maclaren-Ross to Hamish Hamilton Ltd, Thursday 3 November 1954 (HH).
15. Letter from J.Maclaren-Ross to Hamish Hamilton, Friday 11 November 1954 (HH).
16. Letter from J.Maclaren-Ross to Hamish Hamilton, Friday 18 November 1954 (HH).
17. Letter from J.Maclaren-Ross to Rupert Hart-Davis, Monday 19 September 1955 (UT).
18. Letter from J.Maclaren-Ross to Richard Brain, Sunday 20 November 1954 (HH).
19. Letter from J.Maclaren-Ross to Richard Brain, Sunday 20 November 1954 (HH).
20. Letter from J.Maclaren-Ross to Dan and Winnie Davin, Sunday 21 November 1954 (DD).
21. Letter from J.Maclaren-Ross to Dan and Winnie Davin, Sunday 21 November 1954 (DD).
22. Letter from J.Maclaren-Ross to Dan and Winnie Davin, Sunday 21 November 1954 (DD).
23. Letter from J.Maclaren-Ross to Dan and Winnie Davin, Sunday 21 November 1954 (DD).
24. Letter from J.Maclaren-Ross to Dan and Winnie Davin, Sunday 21 November 1954 (DD).
25. Letter from J.Maclaren-Ross to Dan and Winnie Davin, Sunday 21 November 1954 (DD).
26. Letter from J.Maclaren-Ross to Dan and Winnie Davin, Sunday 21 November 1954 (DD).
27. Letter from J.Maclaren-Ross to Dan and Winnie Davin, Sunday 21 November 1954 (DD).
28. Letter from J.Maclaren-Ross to Dan and Winnie Davin, Sunday 21 November 1954 (DD).
29. Dan Davin, *Closing Times*, p.19.
30. Letter from J.Maclaren-Ross to Richard Brain, Thursday 24 November 1954 (HH).
31. Letter from Richard Brain to J.Maclaren-Ross, Wednesday 30 November 1954 (HH).
32. Quoted in a letter from Richard Brain to J.Maclaren-Ross, Tuesday 5 January 1955 (HH).
33. J.Maclaren-Ross, *My Name Is Love*, p.14.
34. Letter from J.Maclaren-Ross to John Lehmann, Sunday 14 August 1955 (HR).
35. Dialogue from a letter J.Maclaren-Ross wrote to John Lehmann, Sunday 14 August 1955 (HR).
36. Letter from J.Maclaren-Ross to John Lehmann, Sunday 14 August 1955 (HR).
37. Letter from J.Maclaren-Ross to John Lehmann, Sunday 14 August 1955 (HR).
38. Letter from J.Maclaren-Ross to John Lehmann, Sunday 21 August 1955 (HR).
39. Letter from J.Maclaren-Ross to John Lehmann, Sunday 21 August 1955 (HR).
40. J.Maclaren-Ross, *My Name Is Love*, p.10.
41. J.Maclaren-Ross, *My Name Is Love*, p.10.
42. Letter from J.Maclaren-Ross to Dan Davin, Friday 10 December 1954 (DD).
43. Tony Van den Burgh in conversation with the author.
44. Letter from J.Maclaren-Ross to Dan Davin, Sunday 12 December 1954 (DD).
45. Letter from J.Maclaren-Ross to Dan Davin, Sunday 12 December 1954 (DD).
46. Letter from J.Maclaren-Ross to Dan Davin, Sunday 12 December 1954 (DD).
47. Letter from J.Maclaren-Ross to Dan Davin, Tuesday 8 November 1955 (DD).
48. Letter from J.Maclaren-Ross to Richard Brain, Thursday 6 January 1955 (HH).
49. Dan Davin, *Closing Times*, p.12.
50. Dan Davin, *Closing Times*, p16.
51. Letter from J.Maclaren-Ross to Dan Davin, Monday 7 February 1955 (DD).
52. Letter from J.Maclaren-Ross to John Lehmann, Sunday 21 August 1955 (HR).
53. Letter from J.Maclaren-Ross to John Lehmann, Sunday 14 August 1955 (HR).
54. Letter from J.Maclaren-Ross to Winnie Davin, Saturday 4 February 1956 (DD).

55. Letter from J.Maclaren-Ross to C.K. Jaeger, Monday 8 August 1955 (HR).
56. J.Maclaren-Ross, *The Man From Madagascar*, *Punch*, Wednesday 25 May 1955.
57. Letter from J.Maclaren-Ross to John Lehmann, Monday 15 May 1955 (HR).
58. Letter from J.Maclaren-Ross to Dan Davin, c.late May/early June 1955 (DD).
59. Letter from J.Maclaren-Ross to Dan Davin, c.late May/early June 1955 (DD).

A Face in the Dark

1. Letter from J.Maclaren-Ross to John Lehmann, Sunday 21 August 1955 (HR).
2. Letter from J.Maclaren-Ross to John Lehmann, Sunday 21 August 1955 (HR).
3. Letter from J.Maclaren-Ross to John Lehmann, Sunday 21 August 1955 (HR).
4. Letter from J.Maclaren-Ross to John Lehmann, Sunday 21 August 1955 (HR).
5. Letter from J.Maclaren-Ross to John Lehmann, Sunday 21 August 1955 (HR).
6. Letter from J.Maclaren-Ross to John Lehmann, Sunday 21 August 1955 (HR).
7. Letter from J.Maclaren-Ross to John Lehmann, Sunday 21 August 1955 (HR).
8. Letter from J.Maclaren-Ross to John Lehmann, Sunday 21 August 1955 (HR).
9. Letter from J.Maclaren-Ross to C.K. Jaeger, Friday 18 November 1955 (CA).
10. Letter from J.Maclaren-Ross to John Lehmann, Sunday 21 August 1955 (HR).
11. Letter from J.Maclaren-Ross to John Lehmann, Sunday 21 August 1955 (HR).
12. Letter from J.Maclaren-Ross to John Lehmann, Sunday 21 August 1955 (HR).
13. Letter from J.Maclaren-Ross to John Lehmann, Sunday 14 August 1955 (HR).
14. Letter from J.Maclaren-Ross to John Lehmann, Sunday 14 August 1955 (HR).
15. Letter from J.Maclaren-Ross to John Lehmann, Sunday 21 August 1955 (HR).
16. Letter from J.Maclaren-Ross to John Lehmann, Sunday 21 August 1955 (HR).
17. Letter from J.Maclaren-Ross to John Lehmann, Sunday 21 August 1955 (HR).
18. Letter from J.Maclaren-Ross to John Lehmann, Sunday 21 August 1955 (HR).
19. Letter from J.Maclaren-Ross to John Lehmann, Sunday 21 August 1955 (HR).
20. Letter from J.Maclaren-Ross to John Lehmann, Sunday 21 August 1955 (HR).
21. Letter from J.Maclaren-Ross to C.K. Jaeger, Friday 18 November 1955 (CA).
22. Synopsis of *My Name Is Love*. Enclosed with a letter from J.Maclaren-Ross to the BBC, Saturday 17 March 1956 (BBC).
23. Letter from J.Maclaren-Ross to John Lehmann, Sunday 21 August 1955 (HR).
24. Letter from J.Maclaren-Ross to John Lehmann, Sunday 21 August 1955 (HR).
25. Letter from J.Maclaren-Ross to C.K. Jaeger, Friday 18 November 1955 (CA).
26. Letter from J.Maclaren-Ross to John Lehmann, Sunday 21 August 1955 (HR).
27. Letter from J.Maclaren-Ross to John Lehmann, Sunday 21 August 1955 (HR).
28. Letter from J.Maclaren-Ross to John Lehmann, Sunday 21 August 1955 (HR).
29. Letter from J.Maclaren-Ross to John Lehmann, Sunday 21 August 1955 (HR).
30. Letter from J.Maclaren-Ross to John Lehmann, Sunday 14 August 1955 (HR).
31. Synopsis of *My Name Is Love*. Enclosed with a letter from J.Maclaren-Ross to the BBC, Saturday 17 March 1956 (BBC).
32. Letter from J.Maclaren-Ross to John Lehmann, Sunday 21 August 1955 (HR).
33. Letter from J.Maclaren-Ross to John Lehmann, Sunday 14 August 1955 (HR).
34. Letter from J.Maclaren-Ross to John Lehmann, Sunday 14 August 1955 (HR).
35. Letter from J.Maclaren-Ross to John Lehmann, Sunday 14 August 1955 (HR).
36. Letter from J.Maclaren-Ross to John Lehmann, Sunday 14 August 1955 (HR).
37. Letter from J.Maclaren-Ross to Winnie Davin, Saturday 27 August 1955 (DD).
38. Letter from J.Maclaren-Ross to Winnie Davin, Saturday 27 August 1955 (DD).
39. Letter from J.Maclaren-Ross to C.K. Jaeger, Monday 8 August 1955 (CA).
40. Letter from J.Maclaren-Ross to John Lehmann, Sunday 14 August 1955 (HR).
41. Tony Van den Burgh in conversation with the author.
42. Charles Causley, *Collected Poems*, Macmillan, 1992, p.81.
43. J.Maclaren-Ross, *Memoirs of the Forties*, p.185.
44. Letter from J.Maclaren-Ross to C.K. Jaeger, Friday 18 November 1955 (CA).
45. Letter from J.Maclaren-Ross to John Lehmann, Sunday 14 August 1955 (HR).
46. Letter from J.Maclaren-Ross to John Lehmann, Sunday 14 August 1955 (HR).

47. Letter from J.Maclaren-Ross to John Lehmann, Sunday 21 August 1955 (HR).
48. Letter from J.Maclaren-Ross to C.K. Jaeger, Monday 8 August 1955 (CA).
49. Letter from J.Maclaren-Ross to John Lehmann, Sunday 14 August 1955 (HR).
50. Letter from J.Maclaren-Ross to C.K. Jaeger, Monday 8 August 1955 (CA).
51. Letter from J.Maclaren-Ross to C.K. Jaeger, Monday 8 August 1955 (CA).
52. Letter from J.Maclaren-Ross to C.K. Jaeger, Monday 8 August 1955 (CA).
53. Letter from J.Maclaren-Ross to John Lehmann, Sunday 14 August 1955 (HR).
54. Letter from J.Maclaren-Ross to John Lehmann, Sunday 14 August 1955 (HR).
55. Letter from J.Maclaren-Ross to John Lehmann, Sunday 14 August 1955 (HR).
56. Letter from J.Maclaren-Ross to John Lehmann, Sunday 14 August 1955 (HR).
57. Letter from J.Maclaren-Ross to Winnie Davin, Saturday 27 August 1955 (DD).
58. Letter from J.Maclaren-Ross to Winnie Davin, Saturday 27 August 1955 (DD).
59. Letter from J.Maclaren-Ross to Winnie Davin, Saturday 27 August 1955 (DD).
60. J.Maclaren-Ross, *The Gem*, included in *The Funny Bone*, p.116.
61. Tony Van den Burgh in conversation with the author.
62. Letter from J.Maclaren-Ross to Dan Davin, c. September 1955 (DD).
63. Letter from J.Maclaren-Ross to Winnie Davin, c. September 1955 (DD).
64. Letter from J.Maclaren-Ross to John Lehmann, Sunday 16 October 1955 (HR).
65. The testimonial — mentioned in J.Maclaren-Ross's letter to Mr Hamilton, dated Sunday 25 September 1955 — was quoted on the dustjacket of *The Funny Bone*.
66. Letter from J.Maclaren-Ross to John Lehmann, Sunday 16 October 1955 (HR).
67. Letter from J.Maclaren-Ross to John Lehmann, Sunday 16 October 1955 (HR).
68. Letter from J.Maclaren-Ross to John Lehmann, Wednesday 26 October 1955 (HR).
69. Letter from J.Maclaren-Ross to John Lehmann, Wednesday 26 October 1955 (HR).
70. Letter from J.Maclaren-Ross to John Lehmann, Wednesday 26 October 1955 (HR).
71. Letter from J.Maclaren-Ross to C.K. Jaeger, Friday 18 November 1955 (CA).
72. Dan Davin, *Closing Times*, p.18-19.
73. Letter from J.Maclaren-Ross to Dan Davin, Tuesday 8 November 1955 (DD).
74. Letter from J.Maclaren-Ross to C.K. Jaeger, Friday 18 November 1955 (CA).
75. Letter from J.Maclaren-Ross to Dan Davin, Tuesday 8 November 1955 (DD).
76. Letter from J.Maclaren-Ross to C.K. Jaeger, Friday 18 November 1955 (CA).
77. Letter from J.Maclaren-Ross to C.K. Jaeger, Friday 18 November 1955 (CA).
78. Letter from J.Maclaren-Ross to C.K. Jaeger, Friday 18 November 1955 (CA).
79. Synopsis of *My Name Is Love*, p.1. Enclosed with a letter from J.Maclaren-Ross to the BBC, Saturday 17 March 1956 (BBC).
80. Synopsis of *My Name Is Love*, p.1. Enclosed with a letter from J.Maclaren-Ross to the BBC, Saturday 17 March 1956. (BBC)
81. Letter from J.Maclaren-Ross to Richard Brain, Friday 2 December 1955 (HH).
82. Letter from J.Maclaren-Ross to Richard Brain, Friday 2 December 1955 (HH).
83. Letter from J.Maclaren-Ross to John Lehmann, Saturday 10 December 1955 (HR).
84. Letter from J.Maclaren-Ross to John Lehmann, Saturday 10 December 1955 (HR).
85. J.Maclaren-Ross, notes (DD).
86. J.Maclaren-Ross, notes (DD).
87. Roy Fuller, *Spanner and Pen*, p.170.
88. Roy Fuller, *Spanner and Pen*, p.170.
89. Roy Fuller, *Spanner and Pen*, p.170.
90. Letter from J.Maclaren-Ross to C.K. Jaeger, Friday 18 November 1955 (CA).
91. Letter from J.Maclaren-Ross to John Lehmann, Thursday 29 December 1955 (HR).
92. Letter from J.Maclaren-Ross to Winnie Davin, Wednesday 11 January 1956 (DD).
93. J.Maclaren-Ross, lyrics enclosed with letter to Winnie Davin, Wednesday 11 January 1956 (DD).
94. Letter from J.Maclaren-Ross to Winnie Davin, Wednesday 11 January 1956 (DD).
95. Letter from J.Maclaren-Ross to Winnie Davin, Wednesday 11 January 1956 (DD).
96. Letter from J.Maclaren-Ross to John Lehmann, Thursday 29 December 1955 (HR).

Hyde and Seek

1. Letter from J.Maclaren-Ross to Rupert Hart-Davis, Saturday 20 December 1952 (UT).
2. Letter from J.Maclaren-Ross to Winnie Davin, Saturday 4 February 1956 (DD).
3. Letter from J.Maclaren-Ross to Winnie Davin, Saturday 11 February 1956 (DD).
4. Letter from J.Maclaren-Ross to Winnie Davin, Saturday 11 February 1956 (DD).
5. Letter from J.Maclaren-Ross to Winnie Davin, Saturday 4 February 1956 (DD).
6. Letter from J.Maclaren-Ross to Winnie Davin, Saturday 4 February 1956 (DD).
7. Letter from J.Maclaren-Ross to Winnie Davin, Saturday 4 February 1956 (DD).
8. Letter from J.Maclaren-Ross to Winnie Davin, Saturday 4 February 1956 (DD).
9. Letter from J.Maclaren-Ross to Winnie Davin, Saturday 4 February 1956 (DD).
10. Letter from J.Maclaren-Ross to Winnie Davin, Saturday 4 February 1956 (DD).
11. Letter from J.Maclaren-Ross to Winnie Davin, Saturday 11 February 1956 (DD).
12. Letter from J.Maclaren-Ross to Winnie Davin, Saturday 11 February 1956 (DD).
13. Letter from J.Maclaren-Ross to Winnie Davin, Saturday 11 February 1956 (DD).
14. Letter from J.Maclaren-Ross to Winnie Davin, Saturday 11 February 1956 (DD).
15. Letter from J.Maclaren-Ross to Winnie Davin, Saturday 11 February 1956 (DD).
16. Letter from J.Maclaren-Ross to Winnie Davin, Saturday 11 February 1956 (DD).
17. Dan Davin, *Closing Times*, p.19.
18. Bruce Bernard in conversation with the author.
19. Bruce Bernard in conversation with the author.
20. Anthony Cronin, *Dead As Doornails*, p.145.
21. Anthony Cronin, *Dead As Doornails*, p.145.
22. Anthony Cronin, *Dead As Doornails*, p.145.
23. Anthony Cronin, *Dead As Doornails*, p.146.
24. Anthony Cronin, *Dead As Doornails*, p.147.
25. J.Maclaren-Ross, *Time and Tide*, Saturday 21 April 1956, p.455.
26. Anthony Cronin, *Dead As Doornails*, p.147.
27. Anthony Cronin, *Dead As Doornails*, p.147.
28. Anthony Cronin, *Dead As Doornails*, p.148.
29. Quoted by J.Maclaren-Ross as the epigraph to *My Name Is Love*.
30. Anthony Cronin, *Dead As Doornails*, p.150.
31. Anthony Cronin, *Dead As Doornails*, p.150.
32. Anthony Cronin, *Dead As Doornails*, p.150.
33. Anthony Cronin, *Dead As Doornails*, p.150.
34. Anthony Cronin, *Dead As Doornails*, p.150.
35. Anthony Cronin, *Dead As Doornails*, p.150.
36. Anthony Cronin, *Dead As Doornails*, p.154.
37. Anthony Cronin, *Dead As Doornails*, p.152.
38. Anthony Cronin, *Dead As Doornails*, p.152.
39. Anthony Cronin, *Dead As Doornails*, p.152.
40. Anthony Cronin, *Dead As Doornails*, p.152.
41. Anthony Cronin, *Dead As Doornails*, p.153.
42. Anthony Cronin, *Dead As Doornails*, p.153-54.
43. Anthony Cronin, *Dead As Doornails*, p.154.
44. Anthony Cronin, *Dead As Doornails*, p.154.
45. J.Maclaren-Ross, unpublished fragment from *Business and Desire*, c.November 1963 (NU).
46. J.Maclaren-Ross, unpublished fragment from *Business and Desire*, c.November 1963 (NU).
47. J.Maclaren-Ross, unpublished fragment from *Business and Desire*, c.November 1963 (NU).
48. J.Maclaren-Ross, notes for *Business and Desire*, c.November 1963 (NU).
49. Letter from J.Maclaren-Ross to Winnie Davin, Sunday 29 April 1956 (DD).
50. Letter from J.Maclaren-Ross to Winnie Davin, Sunday 29 April 1956 (DD).
51. J.Maclaren-Ross, *The Times Literary Supplement*, Friday 18 May 1956, p.296.
52. J.Maclaren-Ross, *The Times Literary Supplement*, Friday 18 May 1956, p.296.
53. J.Maclaren-Ross, notes for *Business and Desire*, c.November 1963 (NU).
54. Bronia McDonald (formerly Kennedy) in conversation with the author.

55. J.Maclaren-Ross, notes for *Business and Desire*, c. November 1963 (NU).
56. J.Maclaren-Ross, notes for *Business and Desire*, c. November 1963 (NU).
57. J.Maclaren-Ross, notes for *Business and Desire*, c. November 1963 (NU).
58. Anthony Cronin, *Dead As Doornails*, p.155.
59. Anthony Cronin, *Dead As Doornails*, p.155.
60. J.Maclaren-Ross, notes for *Business and Desire*, c. November 1963 (NU).
61. J.Maclaren-Ross, *Some Time I Shall Sleep Out*, unpublished memoir, p.1 (HR).
62. J.Maclaren-Ross, *Some Time I Shall Sleep Out*, unpublished memoir, p.1 (HR).
63. J.Maclaren-Ross, *Some Time I Shall Sleep Out*, unpublished memoir, p.3 (HR).
64. J.Maclaren-Ross, notes for *Business and Desire*, p.2, c. November 1963 (NU).
65. *The Times*, Wednesday 25 July 1956, p.12.
66. *The Times*, Wednesday 25 July 1956, p.11.
67. Godfrey Smith, *The Sunday Times*, Sunday 19 August 1956, p.5.
68. J.Maclaren-Ross, notes for *Business and Desire*, p.2, c. November 1963 (NU).
69. Letter from Diane Bromley to J.Maclaren-Ross, Friday 25 January 1957 (HR).
70. J.Maclaren-Ross, notes for *Business and Desire*, p.3, c. November 1963 (NU).
71. J.Maclaren-Ross, notes for *Business and Desire*, p.3, c. November 1963 (NU).
72. Letter from J.Maclaren-Ross to Alec C. Snowden, Monday 7 January 1957 (HR).
73. J.Maclaren-Ross, notes for *Business and Desire*, p.4, c. November 1963 (NU).
74. Letter from J.Maclaren-Ross to Alec C. Snowden, Monday 7 January 1957 (HR).
75. Letter from J.Maclaren-Ross to Alec C. Snowden, Monday 7 January 1957 (HR).
76. Letter from J.Maclaren-Ross to Alec C. Snowden, Monday 7 January 1957 (HR).
77. Patrick Magee was destined to find fame as one of the stars of *A Clockwork Orange*.
78. J.Maclaren-Ross, notes for *Business and Desire*, p.1, c.November 1963 (NU).
79. Letter from Diane Bromley to J.Maclaren-Ross, Friday 25 January 1957 (HR).
80. Letter from Diane Bromley to J.Maclaren-Ross, Friday 25 January 1957 (HR).
81. Letter from Diane Bromley to J.Maclaren-Ross, Sunday 17 February 1957 (HR).

Night of the Long Wives

1. Letter from J.Maclaren-Ross to Alec C. Snowden, Monday 7 January 1957 (HR).
2. J.Maclaren-Ross, *Memoirs of the Forties*, p.154.
3. Rough draft of a letter from J.Maclaren-Ross to "Child", undated, c. early April 1957 (HR).
4. Rough draft of a letter from J.Maclaren-Ross to "Child", undated, c. early April 1957 (HR).
5. Rough draft of a letter from J.Maclaren-Ross to "Child", undated, c. early April 1957 (HR).
6. Rough draft of a letter from J.Maclaren-Ross to "Child", undated, c. early April 1957 (HR).
7. Tony Van den Burgh in conversation with the author.
8. J.Maclaren-Ross, *Inside Story, Punch*, Wednesday 9 July 1958, p.51.
9. J.Maclaren-Ross, *Inside Story, Punch*, Wednesday 9 July 1958, p.50.
10. J.Maclaren-Ross, *Inside Story, Punch*, Wednesday 9 July 1958, p.52.
11. Letter from Diane Bromley to J.Maclaren-Ross, Wednesday 17 April 1957 (HR).
12. *Kinematograph Weekly*, Wednesday 27 June 1957, p.23.
13. Tony Van den Burgh in conversation with the author.
14. R.D. Smith, BBC memo, Monday 26 January 1959 (BBC).
15. Tony Van den Burgh in conversation with the author.
16. Letter from J.Maclaren-Ross to Barbara Bray, Thursday 12 December 1957 (BBC).
17. *Kinematograph Weekly*, Wednesday 20 March 1958, p.21.
18. *Kinematograph Weekly*, Wednesday 20 March 1958, p.21.
19. Alex Maclaren-Ross in conversation with the author.
20. Vernon Scannell in conversation with the author.
21. *The Radio Times*, Friday 20 June 1958, p.27.
22. Heather Dean in conversation with the author.
23. Anthony Cronin, *Dead As Doornails*, p.156.
24. Tony Van den Burgh in conversation with the author.
25. Anthony Cronin, *Dead As Doornails*, p.156.
26. Letter from Mrs Brailsford to Diane Bromley, Saturday 20 December 1958 (HR).

27. Draft of letter from J.Maclaren-Ross to Philip Woolf, mid-December 1958 (HR).
28. Draft of letter from J.Maclaren-Ross to Philip Woolf, mid-December 1958 (HR).
29. Tony Van den Burgh in conversation with the author.
30. C.K. Jaeger in conversation with the author.
31. J.Maclaren-Ross, *My Name Is Love*, p.37.
32. Letter from Diane Maclaren-Ross to Mrs Brailsford, Saturday 6 June 1959 (HR).
33. Letter from Diane Maclaren-Ross to Mrs Brailsford, Saturday 6 June 1959 (HR).
34. Letter from Diane Maclaren-Ross to Mrs Brailsford, Saturday 6 June 1959 (HR).
35 Letter from Diane Maclaren-Ross to Mrs Brailsford, Saturday 6 June 1959 (HR).
36. John Heath-Stubbs in conversation with the author.
37. Stephen Fothergill, *The Last Lamplighter*, p.105.
38. Stephen Fothergill in conversation with the author.

Scotch on the Rocks

1. J.Maclaren-Ross, Author's Note to *Memoirs of the Forties*, p.xv.
2. Letter from J.Maclaren-Ross to Mr Hamilton, Saturday 2 January 1960 (HH).
3. The character of Prince Yakimov also appeared in *The Spoilt City*, the second novel in the trilogy, published in 1962.
4. J.Maclaren-Ross, diary, Tuesday 9 February 1960. (NU).
5. J.Maclaren-Ross, diary, Thursday 11 February 1960 (NU).
6. Dan Davin, *Closing Times*, p.21.
7. J.Maclaren-Ross, diary, Saturday 13 February 1960 (NU).
8. J.Maclaren-Ross, diary, Saturday 13 February 1960 (NU).
9. J.Maclaren-Ross, diary, Friday 4 March 1960 (NU).
10. J.Maclaren-Ross, diary, Wednesday 6 April (NU).
11. Nothing appears to have survived of the book, not even its title.
12. Anthony Cronin, *Dead As Doornails*, p.156.
13. Tony Van den Burgh in conversation with the author.
14. BBC Memo, R.D. Smith, Wednesday 12 February 1964 (BBC).
15. Tony Van den Burgh in conversation with the author.
16. Anthony Cronin, *Dead As Doornails*, p.157.
17. Anthony Cronin, *Dead As Doornails*, p.157.
18. J.Maclaren-Ross, note added to title-page of *The Dark Diceman*, Thursday 26 January 1961 (HR).
19. *J. Maclaren-Ross Talks To Eric Phillips*, *The Writer*, September 1961, p.4.
20. *J. Maclaren-Ross Talks To Eric Phillips*, *The Writer*, September 1961, p.5.
21. Letter from J.Maclaren-Ross to Mr R.V. Machell, Sunday 13 August 1961 (HH).
22. *J. Maclaren-Ross Talks To Eric Phillips*, *The Writer*, September 1961, p.4.
23. *The Listener*, Thursday 5 October 1961, p.534.
24. Memo from Roger Machell to Jamie Hamilton, Friday 10 November 1961 (HH).
25. Memo from Roger Machell to Jamie Hamilton, Friday 10 November 1961 (HH).
26. BBC Memo, R.D. Smith, Wednesday 23 May 1962 (BBC).
27. J.Maclaren-Ross, *My Name Is Love*, p.110.
28. Penguin ultimately decided not to proceed with it.
29. Letter from R.D. Smith and Olivia Manning to Royal Literary Fund, Monday 5 March 1962 (RLF).
30. Letter from J.Maclaren-Ross to Captain Broadbent, Wednesday 21 March 1962 (RLF).
31. Michael Bakewell in conversation with the author.
32. BBC BBC Memo, R.D. Smith, Tuesday 16 April 1962 (BBC).

Closing Time

1. Letter from J.Maclaren-Ross to Captain Broadbent, Sunday 8 April 1962 (RLF).
2 Tony Van den Burgh in conversation with the author.
3. Letter from J.Maclaren-Ross to Roger Machell, Monday 22 April 1962 (HH).
4. BBC Memo, R.D. Smith, Wednesday 23 May 1962 (BBC).
5. BBC Memo, R.D. Smith, Wednesday 23 May 1962 (BBC).

6. Letter from J.Maclaren-Ross to Douglas Cleverdon, Sunday 13 May 1962 (BBC).
7. Anthony Cronin, *Dead As Doornails*, p.157.
8. *The Radio Times*, Thursday 10 May 1962, p.32.
9. Tony Van den Burgh in conversation with the author.
10. BBC Memo, R.D. Smith, Wednesday 23 May 1962 (BBC).
11. BBC Memo, R.D. Smith, Wednesday 23 May 1962 (BBC).
12. J.Maclaren-Ross, *The Listener*, Thursday 2 August 1962, p.185.
13. Letter from Anthony Thwaite to the author, Monday 8 November 1999.
14. Draft of a postcard from J.Maclaren-Ross to Claire, Sunday 16 September 1962 (HR).
15. Letter from Bert Barton to J.Maclaren-Ross, Thursday 4 April 1963 (HR).
16. Jon Wynn-Tyson in conversation with the author.
17. Alan Ross in conversation with the author.
18. Letter from J.Maclaren-Ross to Alan Ross, Monday 26 November 1962 (HR).
19. Letter from Jake Schwartz to J.Maclaren-Ross, Sunday 10 March 1963 (HR).
20. J.Maclaren-Ross, *Seventy Years of Sexton Blake*, *London Magazine*, November 1963, p.51.
21. Letter from J.Maclaren-Ross to Alan Ross, Monday 3 June 1963 (HR).
22. J.Maclaren-Ross, *Mary McCarthy and the Class of '33*, *London Magazine*, January 1964, p.101.
23. J.Maclaren-Ross, notes on *Business and Desire*, Saturday 23 November 1963 (NU)
24. Letter from J.Maclaren-Ross to James Graham-Murray, late November 1963 (HR).
25. Letter from J.Maclaren-Ross to Jake Schwartz, Monday 7 December 1963 (HR).
26. Letter from J.Maclaren-Ross to James Graham-Murray, Friday 27 December 1963 (HR).
27. Letter from J.Maclaren-Ross to Alan Ross, Friday 27 March 1964 (HR).
28. John Lehmann, *The Listener*, Wednesday 7 October 1965, p.539.
29. Letter from J.Maclaren-Ross to Alan Ross, Monday 1 June 1964 (HR).
30. Letter from J.Maclaren-Ross to Mr Hamilton, Thursday 2 July 1964 (HH).
31. Memo from Mr Hamilton, Friday 3 July 1964 (HH).
32. John Lehmann, *The Listener*, Wednesday 7 October 1965, p.539.
33. Anthony Burgess, *The Listener*, Wednesday 15 October, p.603.
34. A short section about the relationship after Strand Film Company folded was included in the original *London Magazine* piece, but dropped from that chapter of the posthumously published *Memoirs of the Forties*.
35. Alan Ross in conversation with the author.
36. Alan Ross in conversation with the author.
37. Alan Ross in conversation with the author.
38. Charles Wrey Gardiner, *The Octopus of Love*, Vol. 2, p.149-150, unpublished manuscript (SU).
39. Charles Wrey Gardiner, *The Octopus of Love*, Vol. 2, p.149-150, unpublished manuscript (SU).
40. *The Times*, Friday 6 November 1964, p.16.
41. *The Times*, Friday 6 November 1964, p.16.
42. *The Times*, Friday 6 November 1964, p.16.
43. *The Spectator*, Friday 13 November 1964, p.630.
44. Roy Fuller, *Spanner and Pen*, p.171.
45. Diana quoted by Alex Maclaren-Ross in conversation with the author.
46. Charles Wrey Gardiner, *The Octopus of Love*, Vol. 2, p.149-150, unpublished manuscript (SU).
47. Charles Wrey Gardiner, *The Octopus of Love*, Vol. 2, p.149-150, unpublished manuscript (SU).
48. Charles Wrey Gardiner, *The Octopus of Love*, Vol. 2, p.149-150, unpublished manuscript (SU).
49. John Davenport, *The Spectator*, Thursday 1 October 1964, p.414.
50. Dan Davin, *Closing Times*, p.22.
51. Dan Davin, *Closing Times*, p.22.
52. J.M. Tambimuttu, *Tambimuttu: Bridge Between Two Worlds*, p.223.
53. *The Times*, Thursday 23 September 1965, p.15.
54. Anthony Cronin, *Dead As Doornails*, p.197.

Selected Bibliography

All books published in London unless otherwise stated.

Allen, Walter: *As I Walked Down New Grub Street*, Heinemann, 1981.

Amos, William: *The Originals: Who's Really Who In Fiction*, Jonathan Cape, 1985.

Athill, Diana, *Stet*, Granta, 2000.

Bailey, Nick: *Fitzrovia*, Historical Publications in association with Camden History Society, 1981.

Bakewell, Michael: *Fitzrovia: London's Bohemia*, National Gallery Publications, 1999.

Bishop, Alan: *Gentleman Rider: A Life of Joyce Cary*, Michael Joseph, 1988.

Burgess, Anthony, *Little Wilson and Big God: Being the First Part of the Confessions of Anthony Burgess*, William Heinemann, 1987.

Camberton, Roland: *Scamp*, John Lehmann Ltd, 1950.

Carson, Anthony: *A Rose By Any Other Name*, Methuen, 1960.

— *Carson Was Here*, Methuen, 1962.

Connolly, Cyril: *The Golden Horizon*, Weidenfeld and Nicolson, 1953.

Crisp, Quentin: *The Naked Civil Servant*, Jonathan Cape, 1968.

Crofts, Fay: *History of Hollymoor Hospital*, Brewin Books, 1998.

Cronin, Anthony: *Dead as Doornails*: A Memoir, The Dolmen Press, 1976.

Davin, Dan: *Closing Times*, Oxford University Press, 1975.

Farson, Daniel: *Soho in the Fifties*, Michael Joseph, 1987.

— *Never A Normal Man*, HarperCollins, 1997

Ferris, Paul: *Dylan Thomas*, Hodder and Stoughton, 1977.

Fiber, Sally (as told to Clive Powell-Williams): *The Fitzroy: The Autobiography of a London Tavern*, Temple House Books, 1995.

Fisher, Clive: *Cyril Connolly: A Nostalgic Life*, MacMillan, 1995.

Fitzgibbon, Constantine: *The Life of Dylan Thomas*, J.M. Dent and Sons, 1965.

Foster, Malcolm: *Joyce Cary: A Biography*, Michael Joseph, 1969.

Fothergill, Stephen: *The Last Lamplighter*: A Soho Education, London Magazine Editions, 2000.

Fraser, GS: *A Stranger and Afraid*, Carcanet New Press, 1983.

Fuller, Roy: *Spanner and Pen: Post-War Memoirs*, Sinclair-Stevenson, 1991.

Gardiner, Charles Wrey: *The Dark Thorn*, The Grey Walls Press, 1946.

— *The Flowering Moment*, The Grey Walls Press, 1949.

— *The Octopus of Love*, Volume 2, unpublished manuscript, held by Stanford University, USA.

Hamburger, Michael: *A Mug's Game: Intermittent Memoirs, 1924-54*, Carcanet Press, 1973.

Harrison, Tom: *Bion, Rickman, Foulkes and the Northfield Experiments*, Jessica Kingsley Publishers, 2000.

Hart-Davis, Rupert: *The Power of Chance: A Table of Memory*, Sinclair-Stevenson, 1991.

— *Halfway to Heaven: Concluding Memoirs of a Literary Life*, Sutton Publishing, 1998.

Heath-Stubbs, John: *Hindsights: An Autobiography*, Hodder and Stoughton, 1993.

Hémon, Louis: *Maria Chapdelaine: A Story of French Canada* (translated by W.H. Blake), The MacMillan Company of Canada, 1923.

Heppenstall, Raynor: *The Lesser Infortune*, Jonathan Cape, 1953.

— *Four Absentees*, Barrie and Rockliff, 1960

— *Portrait of a Professional Man*, Peter Owen, 1969.

— *The Intellectual Part*, Barrie and Rockliff, 1963.

Hewison, Robert: *Under Siege: Literary Life in London, 1939-45*, Weidenfeld and Nicolson, 1979.

Hoffe, Monkton: *Four Days: A Play*, English Theatre Guild, 1947.

Hooker, Denise: *Nina Hamnett: Queen of Bohemia*, Constable, 1986.

Horwitz, Julius: *Can I Get There By Candlelight*, André Deutsch, 1964.

Howarth, Patrick: *When the Riviera Was Ours*, Routledge and Kegan Paul, 1977.

Hutchings, Roger: *Maverick Bohemian: Growing Up In London and Paris In The 1930s*, The Book Guild, 2001.

Jaeger, C.K.: *Angels on Horseback*, George Routledge & Sons, 1940.

— *The Man in a Top Hat*, The Grey Walls Press, 1949.

Lehmann, John: *Introduction to The Penguin New Writing*, Penguin 1985.

— *I Am My Brother*, Longman, 1960.

— *The Ample Proposition*, Eyre and Spottiswoode, 1966.

Lewis, Jeremy: *Cyril Connolly: A Life*, Jonathan Cape, 1997.

Lexton, Maria (edited by): *The Time Out Book of London Short Stories*, Penguin, 1993.

Luke, Michael: *David Tennant and the Gargoyle Years*, Weidenfeld and Nicolson, 1991.

Maclaren-Ross, Julian: *The Stuff to Give the Troops*, Jonathan Cape, 1944.

— *Better than a Kick in the Pants*, Lawson & Dunn, jointly with the Hyperion Press, 1945.

— *Bitten By The Tarantula*, Allan Wingate, 1946.

— *The Nine Men of Soho*, Allan Wingate, 1946.

— *Of Love and Hunger*, Allan Wingate, 1947.

— *The Weeping and the Laughter*, Rupert Hart-Davis, 1953.

— *The Funny Bone*, Elek Books, 1956.

— *Until the Day She Dies*, Hamish Hamilton, 1960.

— *The Doomsday Book*, Hamish Hamilton, 1961.

— *My Name Is Love*, the Times Press, 1964.

— *Memoirs of the Forties*, Alan Ross, 1965.

Maine, Charles Eric: *Escapement*, Hodder and Stoughton, 1956.

Ovendon, Keith: *A Fighting Withdrawal: The Life of Dan Davin, Writer, Soldier, Publisher*, Oxford University Press, 1996.

Pollok, Fitzwilliam Thomas: *Sport in British Burmah, Assam and the Cassyah and Jyntiah Hills*, 2 volumes, Chapman and Hall, 1879.

— *Incidents of Foreign Sport and Travel*, Chapman and Hall, 1894.

— *Fifty Years' Reminiscences of India: A Retrospect of Travel, Adventure and Shikar*, Edward Arnold, 1896.

— and William Sinclair Thorn, *Wild Sports of Burma and Assam*, Hurst and Blackett, 1900.

Powell, Anthony: *To Keep the Ball Rolling: The Memoirs of Anthony Powell*, Penguin, 1983.

— *Books Do Furnish a Room*, William Heinemann, 1971.

— *Temporary Kings*, William Heinemann, 1973.

— *Hearing Secret Harmonies*, William Heinemann, 1975.

Pryce-Jones, Alan: *The Bonus of Laughter*, Hamish Hamilton, 1987.

Pullar, Phillippa: *Frank Harris*, Hamish Hamilton, 1975.

Queneau, Raymond: *Pierrot* (translated by J.Maclaren-Ross), John Lehmann, 1950.

Quentin, Patrick: *Puzzle For Fiends: A Peter Duluth Mystery*, Victor Gollancz, 1947.

Ross, Alan: *Blindfold Games*, Collins Harvill, 1986.

Shelden, Michael: *Friends of Promise: Cyril Connolly and the World of Horizon*, Hamish Hamilton, 1989.

— Graham Greene: *The Man Within*, William Heinemann, 1994.

Sherry, Norman: *The Life of Graham Greene*, volume one, 1904-1939, Jonathan Cape, 1989.

Simenon, Georges: *Maigret et la grand perche* (translated as *Maigret and the Burglar's Wife* by J.Maclaren-Ross), published by Hamish Hamilton, 1955.

Sircar, Noel: *News From The Lesser Burrows*, Hollis and Carter, 1947.

Stanford, Derek: *Inside the Forties: Literary Memoirs, 1937-57*, Sidgwick and Jackson, 1977.

Stevenson, Robert Louis: *The Strange Case of Dr Jekyll and Mr Hyde*, Penguin Popular Classics, 1994.

Thwaite, Anthony: *Anthony Thwaite in Conversation With Peter Dale and Ian Hamilton*, Between the Lines, 1999.

Tolley, A.T. (edited by): *John Lehmann: A Tribute*, Carleton University Press, Ottawa, Canada, 1987.

Todd, Ruthven: *Fitzrovia and the Road To The York Minster: An Exhibition At The Michael Parkin Gallery*, Michael Parkin Fine Art, 1973.

Valery, Anne: *The Edge of a Smile*, Peter Owen, 1977.

Vansittart, Peter: *Paths From A White Horse: A Writer's Memoir*, Quartet, 1985.

— *In The Fifties*, John Murray, 1995.

Wyndham, Joan: *Love Is Blue: A Wartime Diary*, William Heinemann, 1986.

Wright, Adrian: *John Lehmann: a Pagan Adventure*, Duckworth, 1998.

Wyatt, Woodrow: *Confessions of an Optimist*, Collins, 1985.

The author and publisher are grateful to the following authors, literary estates, publications and companies for granting permission to quote from their published and unpublished work: the BBC; John Betjeman letters reprinted by kind permission of the Random House Group Ltd; *The Bognor Regis Observer*; Anthony Burgess (© The Estate of Anthony Burgess); Charles Causley; Daniel Farson (© The Estate of Daniel Farson); David Higham Associates Ltd for John Lehmann (© The Estate of John Lehmann), Olivia Manning (© The Estate of Olivia Manning), Anthony Powell (© The Estate of Anthony Powell) and Walter Allen (© The Estate of Walter Allen); Stephen Fothergill; John Fuller for the Estate of Roy Fuller (© The Estate of Roy Fuller); the Harry Ransom Humanities Research Center, the University of Texas at Austin; letters and memos from the Hamish Hamilton Archive reproduced by permission of Penguin Books Ltd; C.K. Jaeger; John Heath Stubbs; Lady Hart-Davis for Sir Rupert Hart-Davis (© The Estate of Rupert Hart-Davis); Deirdre Levi for Cyril Connolly (© The Estate of Cyril Connolly); Keith Ovenden; PFD for Evelyn Waugh (letter from Evelyn Waugh of 4 July 1950 to the Royal Literary Fund reproduced by permission of PFD on behalf of the Estate of Laura Waugh); Alex Maclaren-Ross for J.Maclaren-Ross (© The Estate of J.Maclaren-Ross); Alex Maclaren-Ross for Diane Maclaren-Ross; the McCormick Library of Special Collections, Northwestern University Library; News International plc for *The Times*, *The Sunday Times*, and *The Times Literary Supplement*; *The Observer* (© *The Observer*); *The New Statesman*; Jane Ross for the *London Magazine* and Alan Ross (© The Estate of Alan Ross); *The Spectator*; Brigid Sandford Smith for Dan Davin (© The Estate of Dan Davin); Olivia Swinnerton for Frank Swinnerton (© The Estate of Frank Swinnerton); the Suffolk Regiment; Anthony Thwaite; the University of Tulsa; Anne Valery; Peter Vansittart; and Joan Wyndham. Every effort has been made to contact all copyright holders. The author and publisher apologise for any inadvertent omissions.

INDEX

Paul Willetts is a freelance writer whose
journalism has appeared in publications such as
The Times Literary Supplement, *The Spectator*,
and *The London Magazine*. This is his first book.